T0413693

New Lives in an Old Land

Brill's Specials in Modern History

Series Editor

Aristotle Kallis (*Keele University*)

VOLUME 4

The titles published in this series are listed at *brill.com/smh*

Tony, Sue and Bronwyn, 1948

New Lives in an Old Land

*Re-turning to the Colonisation
of New South Wales through
Stories of My Parents and Their Ancestors*

By

Bronwyn Davies

BRILL

LEIDEN | BOSTON

Cover illustration: Tony, Bronwyn and Sue with toy koala in front of the abelia. Photo, 1948.

The Library of Congress Cataloging-in-Publication Data is available online at http://catalog.loc.gov
LC record available at http://lccn.loc.gov/2021001652

Previously published at Ornithorhynchus Paradoxus Books, Sydney (2019).
Typeface for the Latin, Greek, and Cyrillic scripts: "Brill". See and download: brill.com/brill-typeface.

ISSN 2468-578X
ISBN 978-90-04-44670-0 (hardback)
ISBN 978-90-04-44671-7 (e-book)

[Memory] is written into the fabric of the world. The world 'holds' the memory of all traces; or rather, the world is its memory ...

BARAD, 2014: 182

• • •

Responding—being responsible/response-able—to the thick tangles of spacetimematterings that are threaded through us, the places and times from which we came but never arrived and never leave, is perhaps what re-turning is about.

BARAD, 2014: 184

• •
•

Contents

Foreword

New Lives in an Old Land is an extraordinary book of narrative scholarship in relation to the great global colonisation of the world in the eighteenth century. It traces the origins of the settler colonial establishment of Australia through the major historic events of the time, such as the Irish uprising, the American revolution and the fierce wars for land and culture in Scotland, that led to extreme poverty and displacement of large numbers of people. Through a delicately narrated family history Bronwyn Davies teases out the threads of complex networks of entanglement that produced the numerous lives through which she interprets the coming of settlers to the Australian colony. Not shying away from the horrendous impact on the Aboriginal custodians who had cared for the land for tens of thousands of years, or the brutal treatment of convicts on whose labour the settlement was built, the book looks unstintingly at the complex characters involved in this entanglement. In its forward-looking possibilities, it is essential reading for all Australians who struggle to comprehend the ethical, social and environmental challenges of this land.

> *Margaret Somerville*
> Professor, Western Sydney University

Bronwyn Davies' *New Lives in an Old Land* has ambitious, glorious, scope. The book spans centuries; it traces and re-traces its protagonists' arduous, sometimes violent, journeys across the oceans; and it addresses the micro- and macro-politics that infuse, shape, and are shaped by, actions and actors. The book, however, is also a work of profound intimacy, in which the author takes the reader into hers and her ancestors' worlds, "re-imagin[ing] the vital specificity of their lives". Compelling, provocative, and scholarly, Davies' book is joyously impossible to categorise, a historico-literary-theoretical portrayal of family, social and political life.

> *Jonathan Wyatt*
> Professor, University of Edinburgh

New Lives in an Old Land is a deep journey into the colonisation of New South Wales through the lives of Bronwyn Davies' ancestors. Davies re-turns to historical events that most Australians would be familiar with, events that are re-animated in surprising ways in this book. Drawing on family lore, personal documents, photographs and following every possible trail of evidence, Davies moves beyond the silences and myths that are passed down, to confront the realities of colonisation and the part her forebears played in it. This book reveals the webs of connection across generations, unexpected continuities across time, even where people made strenuous efforts to make breaks. The people in this book come to life in ways that evoke compassion and empathy, refusing the judgement that slips so easily into historical work. Recognising the threads that bind past and present, Davies shows how we risk becoming ignorant of ourselves, and of what is to come when we forget our ancestors, the lives they lived and the passions that drove them. This book weaves a gripping and deeply moving account of migration, generation, of love and power, of aspiration and struggle, of 'what it was to be' her ancestors, each in the context of their time and place as they built new lives in this old land.

Johanna Wyn
Redmond Barry Distinguished Emeritus Professor, The University of Melbourne

New Lives in an Old Land is a gift to readers. There are astonishing insights about ancestors whose lives are intertwined with people today. But, more than this, Bronwyn Davies has used the much-lauded writing skills she has developed over a lifetime to create a ground-breaking shift in the way history can be written. These subtle and audacious moves offer new ways to grapple with old contradictions within Australian history. While writing this book, Bronwyn discovered that her family emerged from a tangled romantic conjunction of convicts exiled to 'terra nullius' and affluent entrepreneurs from England, Wales, Denmark and beyond. These people of different social origins, who might never have met in their countries of origin, were thrown together in this land that claimed to be 'new' while failing to acknowledge the ubiquitous presence of the indigenous peoples already in place. The book brings these ancestors to life with their own words (evidence that writing talent goes back a long way in this family) supplemented by a haunting archive of photographs. These diverse stories give the reader poignant insights into the doubts and angst early colonists experienced as they carried out sometimes horrendous acts of appropriation and even murder, acts that had direct resonance with earlier experiences in countries such as Ireland. This alternative history rattles the comfort of long-held clichés about the founding and flowering of European life in this 'great southern land'. These ancestors often knew what they were doing and, as we come to grips with this insight, we have to wonder how our descendants will view us.

Lise Claiborne
Professor at Waikato University, New Zealand

The joys of this work for me are many. At a time/place when I am examining my 'ancestry' this work opens up exhilarating new possibilities. Bronwyn writes of family. It is not my family, yet it is. Through the tracing of the colonisation of NSW and the different ways her family members became part of this wide, brown land I am excited to examine the traces of my family differently – to look at the stories of my family differently. Indeed, to do history differently. At the same time, this book inspires new possibilities of thinking our ways into the interconnectedness of lives, both human and more than human, and into the inter-connectedness of time, of place and of what is being made to matter. It is the ways of thinking and teasing out the entanglements that I find most exciting for my own writing, teaching and research. Just as Bronwyn's work on the past lives of her relatives is entangled in the present and the future, I have joyfully and gratefully become more entangled in who I have become and go on becoming.

Dr Cath Laws
Australian Catholic University

Acknowledgements

So many wonderfully generous people have helped me with this project. My first break in getting underway with the research for this project came from my cousin Andrew Barton who had put his ancestry website on line. Dee Read helped me at the beginning in building my own ancestry website, which I needed to do as a way of taming the complexity of a project with so many people in it—worse by far than any Russian novel.[1] She also went with me to the 220-year celebration of the building of William Cox's road.

Through my ancestry site I met Helen Boyd, who had grown up among my Perth cousins. Helen has been a wonderful guide and supporter of this work throughout, finding details of births, deaths and marriages for me, and helping me to crack open the intricate puzzles associated with sorting out my various family trees. Helen has read every chapter, in multiple drafts as I have worked my way through the writing of this book, and she has persisted with her love of it even when the courage to continue was failing me. She even went so far as to persuade her son Roger and his wife to take us on trips to places relevant to my project, such as Cunningham Plains Station, Nant Gwylan, and Denham Court. Roger led our searches in each of these places and made beautiful photographic records of them. Helen, further, introduced me to my cousins in Perth, Dorothy Parkinson and Madeline Few, who have been researching the Davies family for decades and who were extraordinarily generous in sharing their findings. Dorothy, like Helen, read every chapter of this book more than once and gave me wonderful feedback and encouragement. She was also very helpful in helping me to identify the photos from my old family album.

Through Dorothy I found another cousin, Venetia McMahon in Victoria, who has the most extraordinary collection of Campbell and Davies memorabilia. Venetia, too, generously gave me access to her collection. Another cousin, who I had known when we were children, Sandy Blomfield, re-connected with me after meeting my son Dan and hearing from him that I had got the family history bug. Sandy has the most wonderful collection of Blomfield material which he very generously shared with me. My collection of material further rapidly multiplied when I visited Clarendon in Tasmania. Jennie Staal, the events coordinator at Clarendon and the volunteer workers there, were unbelievably helpful, opening up for me one of the richest seams of material in the entire project, which until then had been entirely hidden from view. My sister Susanne has been a wonderful ally, reading every chapter with great interest,

---

1 See my family ancestry pages at https://www.ancestry.com.au/family-tree/tree/
55726527/family.

and answering endless questions about her memories of our shared childhood. My brother John has also read many of the chapters and found himself moved by them. A distant cousin, Vicki Fisher, tracked me down from our shared DNA, and was enormously helpful in unpicking the silence about my grandmother that I had until then simply failed to break through. Other cousins who have generously shared their documentation and their insights are Joan Davis, Alex Campbell, Meg Buchanan, Helen Bathgate, Jillian Oppenheimer and Carl Kallenbach. I am indebted to you all.

Friends who have read my chapters along the way include Lise Claiborne, Cath Laws, Peter Bansel, Jonathan Wyatt, Margaret Somerville and Maria Kecksmetti. Robert Baker helped me identify the cars in two old photos. Johanna Wyn offered me her usual generous hospitality in Melbourne, photographed the portraits at the Victorian National Art Gallery, and listened to my thoughts over all these years as I struggled to get my head around what I was trying to do, knowing it didn't fit inside anyone else's schema. Two others who took me completely by surprise, hunting me down through a photo of me in their grandmother's album, are Robert Taylor and Wendy Davis, who have helped me gain a different angle on my childhood.

I have saved for last my wonderful research assistant and now friend Jody Thomson, who stepped in and carried out research for me in all the places I was blocked, searching out archival material, finding and even creating new portraits, transcribing, Photoshopping, and researching material that I did not have easy access to. She also read every chapter as I wrote it, giving me valuable feedback and encouragement.

The institutions that were helpful included the archives at the Universities of New England and Newcastle, the New South Wales State Library, New South Wales State Archives and the National Gallery of Victoria. Thanks to Margaret McCredie for permission to use the engraving of Denham Court on page 309. I am deeply grateful for the permissions to use the material people have given me access to. And I should not forget the people at *Douce France*, my local coffee shop, who provided the haven in which much of this writing was done.

Thank you all!

Illustrations

Figures

Maps

Prologue

Our landscape is overwritten by its history. Its scarification is only visible
if one looks hard, listens closely and is prepared not to look away.

WILLIAMS, 2018

∶∶

The Australian Government has repeatedly failed to recognise the indigenous
people as the original custodians of the land. In 2017 the original custodians
met with each other to find a way past that failure. *The Uluru statement from
the heart* came out of that meeting. It is a generous document that searches
for a way through the impasse created by 230 years of non- and mis-recognition:

> We seek constitutional reforms to empower our people and take *a
> rightful place* in our own country. When we have power over our destiny
> our children will flourish. They will walk in two worlds and their culture
> will be a gift to their country.
>
> We call for the establishment of a First Nations Voice enshrined in the
> Constitution ...
>
> We invite you to walk with us in a movement of the Australian people for a
> better future. (Referendum Council, 2017)

When this was presented to the government, Prime Minister Turnbull rejected
it out of hand: "The Government does not believe such a radical change to our
constitution's representative institutions has any realistic prospect of being
supported by a majority of Australians in a majority of states," he said (Gordon,
2017). Two hundred and thirty years of non-recognition, and ignorance, was
to continue. This book enters into that space of ignorance that makes such a
refusal possible.

The mistreatment of indigenous people, the seizing of their land and the
destruction of language and culture, took place hot on the heels of the brutal colonisation of Ireland. The treatment of the convicts, many of them Irish,
was, if anything, more brutal than the treatment of the original custodians of
the land. The current treatment of refugees, and of indigenous people suggests

we have not moved past our own history—in part perhaps because we are so ignorant of it.

My own ancestors migrated from Britain to New South Wales, by boat, between 1788 and 1870. In this book I tell the stories of their lives, drawing on the fragments and traces they have left of themselves—in letters, diaries, portraits, legal documents, locks of hair, jewellery, houses, loved landscapes—and memory. The task I have set myself is to re-imagine the vital specificity of their lives, and to explore the ways that life in the colony made sense to them—not to justify the act of colonisation, or to judge it, but to make sense of it.

I thought of my project at first in literary terms as an act of remembering—a way of honouring my ancestors. I hoped I would not bump into those scarifications that Williams speaks of, though I surely knew they were there. But I was prepared to look hard, to listen intently, and not look away. By looking through my own ancestors' eyes I would not be able to dismiss the harm done to the original custodians of the land as having nothing to do with me. Rather, I would enter into the space of colonisation through my portraits of them and of events they were caught up in, drawn with words and images, and so come to the process of colonisation from inside itself.

To begin with I had some stories from my parents to work with, some genealogical work some of my cousins had engaged in, and bit by bit, access to documents kept by my cousins and by state and national libraries. Ancestral stories, and the webs of relationships they are embedded in, are strange things to work with. They involve pulling memories out of your own body, making links with other bodies, others' memories, and with new and unexpected documentation. It is work that is always in process, always unfolding something new, a struggle to create a workable whole that at the end of the day, like a spider's web, might catch some new delectable morsel, or partially break; or collapse entirely.

In the beginning my project was intimate and personal, and I had little information to work with. I felt my work to be like that of the orb weaver spider, who begins with a fine thread that drifts on the faintest breeze across a gap. When the thread sticks to a surface, she feels this by a change in the vibrations; she reels it in and tightens it, carefully walking along it and strengthening it with a second thread. She repeats this process until the thread is strong enough to support the rest of the web. All of this out of her own body and inextricably in relation to other bodies—trees, fences, grass .... She makes a Y-shaped netting that will form the first three radials. Adding more radials, she makes sure that the distance between each radial and the next is small enough to cross. The number of radials in her web is determined by the relations between her own size, and the size of the gaps. After the radials are completed, she strengthens the centre of the web with five or more circular threads. Working from the inside out, she makes a spiral of smooth, widely spaced threads to enable her to move around her web during construction. Then, from the outside in, she replaces this spiral with a spiral of closely spaced sticky threads. She uses the initial radiating lines as well as the non-sticky spirals as guidelines, and also as the means of moving about her own web without getting caught in it. Then, amidst her smooth and sticky always-emergent web (which she may start again tomorrow) she waits. Drops of dew sparkle on her lines; something walks or flies right through, breaking some of her lines; sometimes a morsel lands, caught on the sticky threads. She wraps it up with more threads from her own body.

I discovered it takes both stillness and perseverance, and many breaks, to be a weaver of entangled family webs. It's to do with the matter and mattering of your own body, your own life, as it is penetrated by, and emergent within the lives of others. The landscapes my ancestors lived in, the historical trajectories that formed the waves of thought and action they rode on, the class structures and religious formations that shaped them, and their individual bodies—all of these impacted on the way the specificity of their lives could be lived:

> The world around us folds into our bodies; shaping not only our movements, postures, emotions and subjectivity, but also the very matter of which we are composed. We are folded by our genes, the food we consume and the air we breathe; by sound, texture, light and taste; by our relationship with others, and our interaction with the spaces around us. At the same time, bodies continually fold out into the world: shaping—and transforming—the spaces and places around them. (Malins, 2007: 157–8)

Who anyone is, is not a simple matter of mapping past facts, nor a matter of creating a web made once and for all. Any beginning, Barad (2010: 244) says, like my spider's web, "is always already threaded through with anticipation of where it is going" but unlike the spider's, a family web is searching for a destination it "will never simply reach" and is searching for "a past that has yet to come" (Barad, 2010: 244). Telling tales of ancestral lives is never a simple matter of discovering what has already been. It is an act of love and of responsibility, but it is also, sometimes, a coming apart and a tearing open—an entanglement in a past that has yet to come: "a repetition, another layer, the return of the same, a catching on something else, an imperceptible difference, a coming apart and ineluctable tearing open" (Deleuze, 1995: 84).

The telling of the entangled tales of my ancestors, entanglements of bodies, and places, and times, and beliefs, is part of an ongoing process that can never be ended—the stories repeat, invent, rupture, and reinvent; they are open to the vicissitudes of the other—of the breeze, the tremor, the break. The writing of these lives is entangled in my rural childhood, in the rural landscape I grew up in, and in my current life in inner city Sydney. For seven years I have been caught in this search—a search that is inevitably multiple, mobile and multi-directional.

This book became, then, not just a construction of past family connections. It is also a fragile, permeable storying of the present that feeds directly into the challenge of recognition. Working with letters, journals, photos, portraits, newspaper clippings and official records, I sought to understand how their lives made sense to them. As I read into the history of the times, my documents took on a new complexion and intensity. My search shifted to one of coming to understand the spacetimemattering in which the lives I was exploring made sense. How had migration on dangerous seven-month journeys come to make sense to them? How had they made sense of the land they came to, of the people whose land they were moving onto and of the brutality that went with it? And what sense had historians made of them, and how, when I focussed on the traces of their lives that they had left behind, did my interpretation differ from those historical analyses?

Sometimes I felt weighed down by the clichés and certainties of many of the historians, by their repetitive language, which installed the truth of the matter without much need for further thought. I had so much information to gather from them; and such a hard struggle at the same time to disentangle my thinking and my language from their certainties. My task became as much a process of erasing clichés and taken-for-granted knowledges as it was a process of making something new. As Deleuze and Guattari (1994: 204) say:

> The painter does not paint on an empty canvas, and neither does the writer write on a blank page; but the page or canvas is already so covered with pre-existing, pre-established clichés that it is first necessary to erase, to clean, to flatten, even to shred, so as to let in a breath of air from the chaos that brings us the vision.

In erasing those 'pre-existing, pre-established clichés' I had to find a new language, a new means of opening up thought about migration and colonisation. I didn't want to produce another objective, authoritative document whose methodic practices guaranteed some kind of Truth. I wanted something that opened up new possibilities of thinking our way into the inter-connectedness of lives, both human and more than human, and into the interconnectedness of time, of place and of what is being made to matter. I had to write my way into something I did not yet know how to think:

> *Listening to Thought* is not the spending of time in the production of the
> autonomous subject (even an oppositional one) or of an autonomous
> body of knowledge. Rather, to listen to Thought, to think beside each
> other and beside ourselves, is to explore an open network of obligations
> that keeps the question of meaning open as a locus of debate. Doing
> justice to Thought, listening to our interlocutors, means trying to hear
> that which cannot be said but which tries to make itself heard. (Readings,
> 1996: 165)

The fragments of memory, of writing, and of images that I draw on here work
like single notes of a composition, or brush strokes in a work of art. In bringing
the fragments together, I explore how we singly and collectively fold ourselves
out into the world, with all our passionate intensities, our similarities to the
families we are born into, and our profound differences. It is not an attempt
to speak for the people whose lives I write about, "but trying to trace a trans-
versal, diagonal line running from [them] to me (there's no other option) and
saying something about what [they were] trying to do ..." and what they were
up against (Deleuze, 1995: 88). This is not a book of separate autonomous lives,
but of connection and dispersion.

There's a sculpture garden between Macquarie St and the Botanic Gardens
in Sydney called *Memory is creation without end*. From a distance, it looks like
a graveyard, but up close it's a scattering of beautiful old pieces of crumbling
sandstone that were once parts of the buildings in early Sydney—stone that
has absorbed the breath of past lives through its porous surface.

The stones hold an older memory, too, of when the sandstone lay quietly
beneath the very ground the sculpture garden sits on, a ground that prior to
1788 had been made, by its own people—the custodians of the land—into a
rich parkland (Gammage, 2011).

Lachlan Macquarie, Governor of the colony of New South Wales from 1810
to 1821, had a vision of Sydney as a place that would be more beautiful than any
European city of the time. He set about transforming it from the degraded and
degrading penal colony it had become in the first two decades of British occupation, into a place that was built of golden sandstone and brick—designed
and built by the convicts who had been cast out from their British home-lands.
That vision and that labour gave birth to the city I now live in. These fragments
of stone lie here, apart and together, torn apart from the buildings they were
once part of, creating something new, now, out of their submerged memories.
Collectively they evoke a nostalgia for that past, when such visions as Macquarie's could be realised; a past when people could come here, from lives that
were not viable elsewhere, and make new lives in an old land—at incredible
cost to those whose land they occupied.

FIGURE 1   *Memory is creation without end.* Kimio Tsuchiya
PHOTO AUTHOR, 2016

The stones are silent. This book seeks to enter the space of that silence, inviting the stones to speak.

My project of focussing on the individual lives of my family and their ancestors, is like looking at each of these stone fragments up close, of listening for their stories, and also standing back to see what sense I can make of them as a composition. The carved stones are crumbling back into the earth in this graveyard of layered and incongruous memories, improbably scattered here, provoking the viewer to see, perhaps, that all our works crumble eventually. Yet, even in that crumbling, lies the possibility of new connections, new encounters—new compositions.

The fragments of memory, and the material fragments I draw on to write these entangled tales, are fragments scattered together/apart, like the sculpture *Memory is creation without end.*

I begin in Part One, with my own birthplace in rural New South Wales, and with my parents' and grandparents' lives there. The portraits here come very much from my own memories, thus threading me into the ancestral lives that come in Parts Two and Three. In Part Two I tell the stories of my father's ancestors, who came from Wales, Denmark (via India), Ireland and England. In Part Three I trace the lives of my mother's family, who came from England and

Scotland. In both Two and Three I begin with ancestral lives before migration, and then I turn to the migrations to the colony that took place between 1788 and 1870, and to the new lives lived out in this old land. By telling these stories so personally, and linking them to my own life, I create my own history, and through that history a window onto the colonisation of New South Wales.

MAP 1   'The Colony of New South Wales', based on a map by Sidney Hall originally published
by Longman, Rees, Orme, Brown and Green, of London, in 1828

The Colony of
NEW SOUTH WALES
Based on a map by Sidney Hall, published London 1828

Hardwick's Range

Camden Valley

Fine open country

Irregular range of high rocky hills

Tryal Bay

High broken country

Smoky Cape

BRIDGE

Mountains dividing Eastern Western waters

Sea View Hill

PORT MACQUAIRIE

AYR

Liverpool Plains

Hastings R.

Camdens Haven

Impassable rocky mountains

Manning R.

Gloucester Vale

Browns Range

C. Hawke Wallis

Innis

Turin Plains

DURHAM

Karuah R.

Mt Burchell

Hunters R.

ROXBURGH

Blue Mountains

Port Stephens, or Yacaaba

Mt Warren

Port Hunter

NORTHUMBERLAND

L. Macquarie

Hawkesbury R.

BATHURST

Mt Blaxland

CUMBERLAND

outh Hills

Cox's R.

BROKEN BAY

Blue Mountains

PORT JACKSON

WESTMORELAND

Sydney

CAMDEN

BOTANY BAY

Port Hacking or Deeban

P A C I F I C   O C E A N

ARGYLE

Shoal Haven

Shoalhaven R.

Ellendon

Jervis Bay

PART 1

Picking at the Skin of Silence:
Stories of My Parents and Grandparents

∵

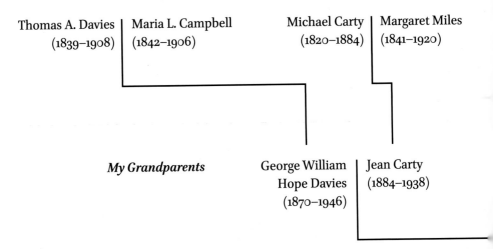

My Great Grandparents

Thomas A. Davies | Maria L. Campbell Michael Carty | Margaret Miles
(1839–1908) | (1842–1906) (1820–1884) | (1841–1920)

My Grandparents George William | Jean Carty
Hope Davies | (1884–1938)
(1870–1946)

FIGURE 2   Family tree of Bronwyn Davies

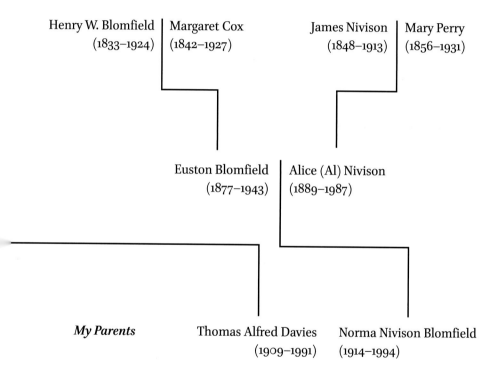

Henry W. Blomfield (1833–1924) | Margaret Cox (1842–1927)

James Nivison (1848–1913) | Mary Perry (1856–1931)

Euston Blomfield (1877–1943) | Alice (Al) Nivison (1889–1987)

My Parents

Thomas Alfred Davies (1909–1991)

Norma Nivison Blomfield (1914–1994)

Growing Up at 98 Upper Street

Any family story such as this is necessarily an act of imagination, imagination that puts life into the cold 'facts' of births, deaths and marriages, and of property ownership. How can I tell the complexity of life in my childhood home? How can I make that particular *placetimemattering* come to life in its specificity? The dialogue between the 'facts' and the literary act of bringing them to life on the page is hard to trace. It takes place in sudden leaps and in moments of complete stillness. It is writing from the body in Cixous's sense, and at the same time it depends on a vast amount of reading and thinking and fact-finding. I have sought all the facts I can, to enable me to write the chapters of this first part of the book. At the same time, I have struggled not to be weighed down with them as ends in themselves.

An objective fact is static, a kind of repetition in which something is known in such a way that it loses its virtuality—its liveliness, its capacity to respond and to change. But the universe "is made up of modifications, disturbances, changes of tension and of energy, and nothing else" (Deleuze, 1991: 76). There is a kind of weighty stickiness to objective facts, which comes with their repeatability.

In animating memories of childhood, much more than clichés and facts are involved. The writing comes from the body, from images in photos, from the entanglement of bodies and images and things, and memories that surface as I trace the lines of my web, or as startled realisations click into place when pieces are brought together in a new way—like the pieces of glass in a kaleidoscope making a new pattern out of the same material. Those pieces—remembered words, old photos, old letters—are themselves alive; they affect things:

> Words more than signify; they affect and effect. Whether read or heard, they complexly pulse through bodies (live or dead) rendering their effects in feeling and active response. They are a first level of animation, one in which we deeply linguistic creatures attached to our own language are caught, but not the last. Indeed language is but one discourse among many in a cacophony of anti-, re-, and mis-coordinations between objects, things and beings. (Chen, 2012: 54)

I begin again, then, with the place my siblings and I grew up in: 98 Upper Street, Tamworth. The first, smaller house Tom and Norma had lived in was called 'Nant Gwylan', named after Dad's Welsh ancestral home, and his grandfather's farm at Murrumburrah in mid New South Wales. The first photo I have of me is at Nant Gwylan. When Mum brought me home from hospital, a photo was planned of Mum and her three children. Tony, then two and a half, saw her with one arm around me and the other around Sue, and ran away crying. Mum only had two arms and they were taken, he sobbed, when she caught up with him. He was holding on to her tight, and tearful still, when the photo was taken.

When we moved to 98 Upper Street, Norma would not agree to it, too, being called Nant Gwylan. Something had changed for her in between those two houses, and our new home was simply referred to as 'Ninety-eight'.

Tamworth is a small city on the Liverpool Plains west of the Great Dividing Range with the Peel River winding its way through the centre of the city. It was small enough that by the time I was six or seven I could make my own way about town on my bicycle. My sister taught me to ride on her little 24-inch bicycle. Once that bike was passed on to me, I experienced the same freedom and autonomy that my parents and grandparents had grown up with. I could ride to school and to the swimming pool or to my friends' places. The other girls at my school depended on buses, or on their parents driving them about. The autonomy my parents granted me was, for my classmates, unthinkable.

The Liverpool Plains are part of the now famous Murray-Darling Basin, where farmers and environmentalists fiercely contest the way the precious, limited water is used. The Peel River teeters on the brink of death (Watson, 2016). It runs through the middle of the town, parallel to the main street, Peel Street. One hot summer, Sue and Tony built a canoe out of an old sheet of corrugated iron they found under one of the rambling hedges in the back garden. They lashed its two ends together with wire and filled the gaps with hot melting bitumen off the road. We carried it all the way to the river and it sank within seconds, but we were all strong swimmers, so it didn't matter.

Sometimes the river turned into a raging brown torrent, spreading out over the flood plains, drowning the houses and paddocks, spreading itself through the shopping centre, and flooding all the shops along the main street. Our house was above the flood-line, tucked under the hills of the Liverpool Range. From our living room window, we could see the river spread out over the flood plain with the rooftop of one small farm-house just visible above the water.

Mum loved the excitement of the floods. She took me once to walk the main street through the brown flood-waters, which lapped above our knees. The torrent had ripped huge chunks of cement out of the footpath, which I particularly remember, as a helpful local, also presumably revelling in the excitement of the flood, advised us to veer left away from a hole in the pavement hidden

FIGURE 3   Sue, Norma with baby Bronwyn and Tony, 1945

by the water. I followed his advice and fell into the deep gutter, scraping my leg on the jagged cement on my way down into the murky swirling waters. I might have been sucked into the drain and drowned, an observer remarked, after I had managed to climb back out onto the unreliable, invisible pavement.

As kids, one of our weekend adventures would be to go 'up the hills'. At the edge of the town there was a farmer's paddock we had to cross. I don't remember whether there was a NO TRESPASSING sign, but at the fence we would stop and discuss whether the farmer was likely to shoot us if we put a foot on his land. After waiting a while, and seeing no farmer and his gun appear, we would focus on the big old bull. Sue would check whether anyone was wearing red. If we were, we had to take it off. She put fear into Tony's heart by pointing out the red stitching in his khaki shorts. Tony was an especially fast runner, so he would run first, and if he survived without being charged by the bull, we, who were wearing no red, would climb through the barbed-wire fence and follow him. The bull always stood still gazing at us, or else ignored us completely. But who knew when the red stitching might drive him into a stampeding frenzy? Once across the farmer's paddock, we came to the wilderness of the eucalypt forest that covered the hills. There was lots of long dry grass, with large granite outcrops, and, occasionally, a cool shady track under the trees with a clear trickle of water and delicate maiden-hair ferns. There we must be especially careful of the stinging nettles, as they too loved the water. And there were poisonous snakes, though I don't remember that we worried about them much. Our attention was on the climb itself, and how far we could go before we had to

FIGURE 4   98 Upper Street, Tamworth

sit down and rest, calf-muscles stinging from the exertion, skin hot and sweaty, legs scratched by the dry grass, and a stone or two to tip out of our shoes. We had to calculate when half our energy was used up, as then we would have to turn back. Tony once went alone and climbed over seven hills, he said, before he came to a farm. I thought at the time he told us that, that he might be learning the art of tall stories from Dad.

Our house was a large rambling double-brick house built in 1930. Our life there was deeply affected by Tony contracting polio when he was seven. He was a bright, cheeky boy before that brush with death, looking very much like Dad would have looked at that age. He is now, in his seventies, the image of his father.

The polio paralysed half of his soft palate and he temporarily lost the capacity to speak in such a way that anyone could understand him. When no-one could decipher what he was trying to say, his rages were vast and uncontrollable. There was no help for him during those terrible years and his rages affected almost everything we did as a family.

The house itself, despite the ever-present danger for me of a big brother given to violent tantrums, was a place I loved. On the eastern wall of the kitchen there was a cupboard that had both a door into the kitchen and a door to the outside. At night, the empty milk jugs would be put in the cupboard, and early in the morning the milkman with his horse-drawn vat of milk would fetch the

FIGURE 5
Tony, Sue and Bronwyn, 1948

jugs and fill them with creamy milk. Alongside the milk-jugs, would be a loaf of sweet- smelling freshly-baked bread from Mr Fowler the baker. During the morning Mr Moore the greengrocer would come to the kitchen door with a basket full of veggies for Mum to choose from.

Inside the lounge room I especially remember the cold winter nights warming our backs by the open fire with the brass firedogs glowing and the light flickering on the wood-panelled walls. Sometimes there would be a loud crack when a burning piece of pine wood exploded, sending sparks out onto the hearth rug, followed by the pungent smell of wool burning. Mum taught us to quickly pick up the burning coal with our bare fingers and throw it back into the fire.

It was hard to leave that open fire and go to bed on cold winter nights, to run down the hall and jump into the ice-cold sheets, teeth chattering from the cold. With luck Uncle Llewellyn would be there, and he would chase us laughing into bed. Putting the palms of both his hands flat on our shivering chests, he would bounce us rapidly up and down until we were warm—with laughter and with love.

Later there were peaceful times in that lounge room, curled up with a book on the sofa, or listening to the serials on the radio. I remember one evening, lying on the carpet watching the fading light and wondering what it meant to say twilight was 'gathering'. I stared intently at the fading light and saw the particles of darkness quivering and gathering against the light of the west facing window. I stared until there were no light particles left, only the thick velvet blackness.

One game we sometimes played, when we were small, was to run in a large circle through the hallway and dining room and lounge room at great speed, jumping up onto and over the big comfy green arm chairs and sofa, out into the lobby and back into the hallways, and round again many times. When Sue and Tony first invented that game, Mum protested at the damage we might do to the lounge suite. Dad promised her that if she would tolerate this exuberance while we were kids he would buy her a brand-new lounge suite when we were grown.

Mostly, though, we were sent outside to play.

Our garden was a magic place for me, at least when there were no fights happening—always two against one, it seemed, with the fourth being lucky enough to have stayed inside. In Spring there were sweet-smelling freesias making a cream carpet around the spiky red-blossomed japonicas; under the jacaranda a carpet of blossoms heavy with bees, radiating violet light; pale plum blossoms with their exquisite brown calyxes and stems; and the glorious wisteria winding its way over the wooden trellis and up through the gum tree, creating a magical space where we sat together as a family, or with guests. Dad built a barbecue there, and we spent nights gazing at the stars and learning the constellations.

In one secluded garden outside my parents' bedroom windows was a fishpond with lion's head fountain that spurted water from its mouth. The water weed, when you pulled a frond of it under the water, held bubbles of air that looked like jewels. It was into that pond that cousin Alexander Blomfield threw the book *Alexander's Beetle* in a fit of outrage that a book should have his name on its cover.

For a time, while I was small, the garden seemed like the whole world to me, and I had no wish to go outside it.

One tumultuous morning Sue had an argument with Mum and she decided that she and I were running away from home. I was given the job of finding a straight stick on which to tie the scarf with our possessions in it. I was also given the job of finding a big enough scarf. The branches that had fallen from the eucalypts were all bent, and not fit for her purpose. As I searched in vain for a straight one, I looked through the fence and worried about how far away we would have to go. There was a telegraph pole on the footpath, and I hoped we could make our camp beside it, so we would still be able to see the flowering peach in the back corner of the garden. Luckily Sue and Mum made up, and I was called in to lunch. To my enormous relief, running away wasn't mentioned again.

Our 'maid', Shirley, came to live with us when she was 14, the year before I was born. She lived in the small room out the back near the kitchen, never eating with the family, never even sharing a cup of tea with my Mum. She cleaned the large rambling house when Mum was out playing golf, or bridge, because she couldn't see who else would do it. At night she heated her tin of beans on a little gas burner, and she washed in the small hand basin in her room. She went home to her mother on Saturdays.

FIGURE 6   Bronwyn by the fishpond, 1947

It came as a shock to me to realise, when Shirley's nephew contacted me, in search of the 'unknown flower girl' in his grandmother's album, how deeply embedded we had been in a world that made Shirley's life in that small room unremarkable. She made our privileged lives possible, and she accepted, without question, her own spare existence. She married Reggie the year I went to school, and indeed I was her flower-girl.

In this photo I am standing in the back yard of our house at 98 Upper Street. The clothes line is in the background, and the back corner of the house, along with the jacaranda tree, not yet in bloom. You can see behind it the hill at the back of the town. In my hands I hold a glorious bunch of Spring flowers from our garden. I am wearing the pretty white dress that Mum had made for me. I am trying hard not to cry; my lips are sucked in tight, so they don't tremble, and my eyes are dark with unshed tears. My right foot is twisted outward, my leg muscles held tight. I am concentrating on maintaining control of myself. I had asked Mum:

Are you coming to the wedding?
No
What do I have to do?
You'll work it out.
I don't know what flower girls have to do. Can't you please come?

FIGURE 7   Unknown flower girl 1950
          PHOTO FROM ROBERT TAYLOR, FROM HIS GRANDMOTHER'S COLLECTION

But it was no good. I would be alone at the wedding, and no-one would tell me what to do. Panic was pressing on my breastbone. Every muscle in my body was held tight against the treacherous tears that threatened to spurt out of the fizzing space behind my eyes. Dad had no tolerance for children who cried.

In these photos, I recognise myself, more than in any others, as my father's daughter. Self-mastery, for him, was paramount. Overcoming fear was an ever-present struggle. Being able to figure out what to do in strange situations was essential. One must rise to the challenge, and one must succeed, no matter how difficult it may seem to be.

For the wedding photo I stood to attention, feet together and knees locked in place. The bridal party stood behind me, Shirley and Reggie and the brides-maid and best man. Reggie was smiling at Shirley. I still held the bouquet of

FIGURE 8   Shirley and Reggie's wedding
            PHOTO FROM ROBERT TAYLOR, FROM HIS GRANDMOTHER'S COLLECTION

flowers, and my eyes were dark, still, from unshed tears. I looked straight at the camera. At least for the photo I knew what was expected of me. Shirley's white gloved hand was touching my back to reassure me.

Decades later, when I was working on this project, Shirley's daughter, Wendy, told me Shirley had named her first child Bronwyn. Her baby hadn't lived long. Wendy, too, named her baby Bronwyn, in memory of her sister, and that baby died too.

When Shirley left to marry Reggie, she worried about leaving us. Who would take care of us, she wondered. After Shirley left we had other maids who stayed briefly, and then young women who came on Monday morning to clean the house. But they were often unreliable, causing my Mum sleepless nights fretting about whether they would turn up. In the 1950s, the conditions my parents offered were no longer appealing.

When I was just turned four, and Shirley was about to marry Reggie, the decision was taken that I would go to school a year early. Sue showed me the way to school, and for a few years I would walk the eight blocks to school, and then home, until Sue taught me to ride her small bike and she got a bigger one. Riding to school was wonderful.

Dad's siblings came to stay at Ninety-eight the year after I was born. Colin and Llewellyn were back from the war. Here four of them are together out in the secluded little back lawn with the wisteria in full bloom cascading over the trellis behind them. Llewellyn had come home weighing six stone after four horrendous years in a Japanese prisoner of war camp. He was by now revelling in the return of his healthy fit body. Colin is missing—perhaps he is the one taking the photo.

Sev and Doc both lived in Sydney, and Colin in Queensland. Llewellyn had come to live in Tamworth. He slept at the Men's Club and came to us for dinner

FIGURE 9   Sue and Bronwyn off to school, 1949

FIGURE 10   Sev, Tom, Doc and Llewellyn under the wisteria, 1946

and at the weekend. He was always playing the clown, and his big belly laugh was contagious.

The day it snowed would have been, I think, around August 1951. I was six and a half years old. None of us had ever seen snow. Tony was eight, and still struggling after his polio. Sue was eleven and my little brother John was three. In what follows I tell the story from my six year-old point of view, and then from Llewellyn's. In telling the story in this way I have teased open some of the multi-layered complexity 'in my blood', and in my family's blood:

THE DAY IT SNOWED

We woke up to snow. We couldn't believe our eyes! We ran out into the garden, arms stretching out toward the white sky. Each flake is different, someone said, each with a magic pattern of its own never to be repeated. I wanted to catch one, to see its pattern before it was gone.

Each flake melted as soon as it landed, drifting down through the cold air, then gone. Tony was crying because he wanted to make a snowman and the snow wouldn't settle on the ground.

Up on the hills the snow was settling. Dad decided to drive us to the top of the Lookout where we would gather some snow and bring it home to build a snowman.

We must go quickly before the snow melts on the hilltop.

I ran very fast to the toilet, as I knew my father could not be kept waiting. I ran down to the driveway moments later, only to see my father's car driving off down the road without me.

I ran out onto the road and waved to my father. He could surely see me in the rear vision mirror, but he didn't stop. Slowly the car pulled away and on up to the Lookout. Tony was probably bouncing with joy that I had been left behind. There would be more snow for him.

I ran back inside, wailing, disbelieving that my father could leave me behind. Then Llewellyn arrived. He talked quietly to my mum, and together in the murmur of their talk the idea came that he would take me to the Lookout in his beautiful new car. But I may not put the snow inside the car, just on the running boards. It might fall off on the way home, but it is a risk we must take.

On the hill-top my brother laughs loudly at us. He and my sister are putting snow into my father's boot. He taunts me that I will have no snow when I arrive home whereas they will have a lot. They will have a much better snowman than me.

Uncle Llewellyn and I drive slowly down the hill, and some of my snow falls off, but not all of it. Llewellyn helps me carry my snow into the garden. My brother yells in disbelief. It is not fair. I have more snow than he does. There are two of them so they need twice as much. My father orders me to give them some of my snow.

I make a very small snowman. I find small thin sticks for his arms and brown leaves for eyes. I give him a red smiling mouth with cotoneaster berries. My brother is in a state of rage because his snowman must have buttons on his coat and must smoke a pipe and have a broom and a scarf.

My sister has long since gone.

I abandon my tiny sweet snowman and go back inside to the peace and quiet of my bedroom to read a book.

LLEWELLYN'S STORY: THE DAY IT SNOWED RE-TOLD

I wake in my small cold room in my narrow bed at The Club, white sheets and grey blankets drawn up around my chin. I lie there, gazing at the white ceiling, and dirty white walls. A strip of white morning light shines through the edge of the blind. It's Saturday. I can hear the buzz of early morning traffic on its busy way down town. Road sounds wet. Tom will be at home, but soon on his way to the office. I'll mow the lawn, that'll cheer him up. I can show Normie the car, maybe even persuade her to come out for a spin with little John Llewellyn. Better give it the once over with the chamois first.

Let's take a peek at it through the blind. Jings! It's snowing! Feet out of bed onto the cold lino floor. Have a quick shave, use that aftershave Normie loves, god you're a handsome dog, pull on warm pants and boots, singlet, shirt, pullover, jacket, slick my hair with some Brylcreem. Blue scarf. Will that do? No time to eat. Could do with the hair of the dog. Keys, wallet, lock door, and out into the swirling white air. And there is my beautiful car.

Tom says I can't afford it, which is true. I'm not making enough with this insurance gig to keep body and soul. But you can't sell insurance without a car. We just keep going over the same old ground. If I make some sales I can pay my debts.

The car glides up White Street, its low motor purring, the flakes of snow swirling over and around its elegant lines. Around the corner into Upper Street. Heart thumps once as I turn the corner. Little Norma. Little bird.

At Ninety-eight Tom's garage is empty. I park behind Normie's little Austin A40 and run up the stairs into the kitchen. Bronny's face is a picture, her mouth turned down, her eyes looking up at me, wide with disbelief, and Normie is furious. He's taken the others to the Lookout to get some snow and left Bronny behind. No, no good reason, she hadn't been naughty. They'll share their snow when they get back, I suggest. Whoever heard of bringing snow home in the car? In my beautiful new car? Oh no no no. But apparently it's yes. OK but only on the running boards, and no muddy snow allowed. It will fly off on the way home I say, but no, Normie says, pack it on tight. So off we go, joy-riding with a six-year-old, through the frozen air and the occasional flurries of snow. Every now and then a sob comes up out of her little chest.

On top of the lookout Tom is supervising the packing of snow into his boot. It's half full already. We'd better get cracking. When we start to pack the snow onto my running boards, Tom loses half his team. Tony can't resist prancing over and laughing at Bronny telling her she won't have as much as they have, because they will have a whole boot full. Poor kid. He can't talk clearly since he had his polio. We wind down the windows and shut the car doors so we can pile the snow high. We plan to get back in through the windows. I've covered my seats in newspaper. We work away steadily, ignoring the prattling, prancing, boastful boy. Susannie works away steadily throwing me the odd baleful look, and Tom looks on, quietly smoking his pipe. Bronny and I pretend we've got pipes too and we laugh, blowing out plumes of white mist as we work.

When we arrive back down at the house, we climb out the car windows and carry the snow into the back garden. I feel a brief moment of victory as it becomes obvious we have the most snow. But the boy yells unfair, and Tom orders Bronny to give him enough snow to keep him happy. I go up into the kitchen for a morning cup of tea. Norm is still cross. Tom is on his way to work. I figure the lawn-mower won't start in this cold. Tony is howling about something, and Bronny and Susannie have disappeared. I'll go out to see if I can calm the boy down. He gets on Normie's nerves. I'll get him to help me clean the car.

Until this memory arose I had totally forgotten Tony's rage if things were 'not right', but it was a perpetual cry. He wanted things done just so and no other way. His tantrums would rise very quickly to the surface if things were not right. And he always wanted to be the best. We had never seen snow before and never built a snowman, but he had decided what would count as right and would try to make it so—not by cleverly finding a pipe or a scarf or buttons but by crying loudly. I can hardly bear to remember it, the painfulness of it, the frustration I felt that he could not play happily and make a snowman with whatever we might find. It was the same if he couldn't do his schoolwork. If Mum tried to help him he would yell "That's not right! That's not how you do it". Even when Mum went to his school to find out from his teacher the right way, it was not right.

We could so rarely relax as a family. The kids were usually choofed outside away from the adults. My older sister and brother became co-conspirators and got up to all sorts of mischief; somehow, she could pull him along into her adventures, pushing his boundaries quite a long way. Once she persuaded him to dress up as a girl and wear yellow plaits made out of corn-silk from the vegetable garden. We walked two whole blocks away from home, when a kind old woman asked the new little girl's name, and he said 'Tony Davies'. Realising at once he'd blown his cover, he took fright and ran very fast all the way home.

In the entangled becomings in the day of the snow are me, my brother, my mother and uncle, the snow, the cars, and Tony's terrible anxiety since the polio. The three-year-old, little John Llewellyn, is also an invisible animating force; and my father's anger.

The year of the snow Tony was eight years old and desperately trying to make the world work for him. Each day at school he got the cane for not doing his homework, but he said it was easier to get the cane. He took great pride in being tough. He wouldn't wear shoes to school even when it was cold. He was proud of his tough feet that could walk over stones and thorns and frost. If Mum bought him new school shoes he'd throw them down the deep drain under the road.

Once he told Mum he knew what he would do if he had a kid who was as naughty as he was—he would put him to bed without any dinner. Next time he was naughty she did just that. When Dad got home he refused to accept this as a solution, and took him his dinner to eat in bed. He felt a bond with this diffi-cult son of his—not least because he had been the one who had visited him in hospital when he was in the isolation ward and at risk of dying, while Mum had been taken up with caring for the new baby—John Llewellyn.

The relationship between my mother and uncle is also animated in the story of the snow. The fact that he might have been my little brother's father was something Mum didn't tell me, or anyone else, until after Dad died in 1991, 40 years later.

The fact that Llewellyn had been in a Japanese prisoner of war camp for four years, made my father's attitude to him impossibly ambivalent. Dad had not been to the war. He stayed home, got his business established, got his fam-ily started, bought a beautiful house. He was a respected lawyer and member of the Citizen Military Forces. How could he throw Llewellyn out, who had almost died for his country, had been through unspeakable horror, and who now had absolutely nothing except his new car? Llewellyn, who Mum adored. Llewellyn, who I adored. Llewellyn who had been Dad's best man at his wed-ding. Llewellyn who laughed big belly laughs and had time to play with us. Llewellyn who would chase us laughing up the hallway to bed on freezing cold nights. Llewellyn who would be there on Saturday mornings, silent and mow-ing the lawn, atoning for something that we didn't understand. Dad silent and in a fury. Llewellyn who my sister saw kissing my mum late one night by the living room fire.

The family gathered again in 1952.

In the photo (*on page 21*), no-one but Mum smiles. Even now, at this gath-ering, she is the bright-eyed laughing girl. Dad has his hand possessively on John's shoulder. Llewellyn is almost out of the photo.

In 1952 he was banished—from our home, our town, and our lives.What is animated for me in unfolding the layers of the story of the day it snowed, is, once more, my father's rage. I can feel it clamping me down hard as if it is my rage too. I feel buttoned down into the rage, as if I simultaneously want to harm someone and embrace someone and be embraced by them. It is a needy rage, a despairing rage, a tight inexpressible rage—like two sides of a chasm and a scream that wants to break loose.

Mum said, when she finally told me the story of her love for Llewellyn, that Dad hadn't known about their affair. He banished Llewellyn from our house and from our town, not because of the affair but for 'running up bad debts', embarrassing Dad in his legal practice. She could only tell me about it after

FIGURE 11   Sev, Tom, Doc, Colin, Llewellyn 1952

Dad died. I asked her why she hadn't chosen Llewellyn. He couldn't have supported her, she said, and because Dad would not have let her keep the children. His fancy new car had of course created one of those 'bad debts'. If I contemplate the way our life shaped up after 1952, I think it highly improbable that he didn't know. But it was never spoken about. And nor was Llewellyn.

Llewellyn went to Sydney and got a job as a records control officer. He never married. He lived at 38 Caldwell St in Paddington, quite near Doc, who lived in Elizabeth Bay Road, very near to where I live now. Fourteen years later, on 13 May 1966, he was struck by a car when he was drunk and died on that same day. At the time Mum and Dad were driving home from a holiday. Mum got Dad to stop the car, and she got out and threw up. When they got home the phone was ringing with the news of Llewellyn's death.

Ninety-eight Upper Street functioned as an illusory puzzle of different spaces, with complex functions in relation to each other. It was Dad's illusory castle, the place he could be proud of, the place where a roof was placed firmly over his children's heads. It was the place where he could arrive home at lunchtime, sit in his armchair and read the paper, chortle at the day's comic strips, and read any letters from the kids away at boarding school. He and Mum would have lunch together—cold cuts from the lamb roast, slices of tomato fresh out of the garden, lettuce, beetroot in jelly, home-made mayonnaise and fresh bread and butter. No other space was so real, or so perfect in his eyes.

It was also a family home, each of the four children made it their own place in their own way—the place they could have an illusion of safety and of

FIGURE 12   Norma, Sev, Tom, Doc, Llewellyn with John in front, 1952

normality and predictability—it will always be like this—Mum and Dad and the four kids. This included the illusion that Dad's upright character and status in the town would override any wish or tendency that his family might have to do wrong. Sue and Tony were always getting up to mischief. Sue told me years later that she always knew Dad could put it right, so she could do whatever she wanted. I interpreted our autonomy quite differently—it came with an unquestionable obligation to be responsible—to *be* that person of character that Dad would respect—though I lost whatever respect I had gained when I came home pregnant.

Ninety-eight Upper Street was Mum and Llewellyn's place when we were at school and when Dad was at work. This was the most romantic of the illusions—that somehow they would not come undone—that their love was possible, and that laughter and light-heartedness could reign, and that all the horror of the prisoner-of-war camp could be banished.

The illusion of belonging to, and being part of, Britain was also a significant element of the story. We knew 'real' winters from Christmas cards, and that's how we knew what snowmen looked like. Our Christmas cards that we sent to each other in the broiling December heat, and that we hung over the mantle piece, always had pictures of a real, northern hemisphere Christmas that none of us had ever experienced. We sprayed Santa snow on the windows so we could imagine them covered in snow while we sweltered in the December heat. On the morning when it snowed in Tamworth, it was August. This one snowy morning, the only time it ever snowed in our entire childhood, was as close as we would get to a real Christmas. In this sense, the whole thing was a gigantic illusion. Except that it was also intensely real. Each one of us intensely alive, each one mattering in his or her specificity.

In animating my stories in this way, throughout this first part of the book, I have pulled them out of any lodging they might have had in a linear, causal or moral storyline. There is no judgement of anyone, but nor is anyone airbrushed. In searching for words—poetic *and* philosophical—with which to animate the complex intersecting emplacements of family members through multiple historical moments, I have sought to make them live in all their incompatibilities, their openings and closings, their illusions and constraints.

Alice (Al) Nivison and Euston Blomfield

A photograph does not simply preserve the likeness of its subject; it retains a trace of the light that once illuminated (and bounced off) the subject itself... [Photographs] trace impressions that hold onto their subjects like an echo.

PHILIP, 2016: 22 & 25

• • •

Memory stories, too, bounce off their subject; the reverberating light and sound defy linear conceptions of time that separate the present from the past.

∴

FIGURE 13 James and Mary Maude Nivison with the first ten of their children in 1897. *Back row:* Frank (Towser) (13), Maude (10), Jim (12), Abe (15), Norman (19). *Front row:* Kathleen (Snow) (5) James Nivison (55) holding Poss (3), Selina (Girl) (17), Mary Nivison (41) holding Norma (1), Alice (Al) (8)
PHOTO FROM JILLIAN OPPENHEIMER'S COLLECTION

© BRONWYN DAVIES, 2021 | DOI:10.1163/9789004446717_002

My Gran, Alice Nivison, stands at the far right of this photo. She was born in 1889, the seventh child of James and Mary Nivison. Al grew up on Ohio station on the New England Tablelands, in rural New South Wales. Her paternal grandparents, Abraham and Mary Nivison, had been Scottish tenant farmers who came to the colony in 1839. After some years of searching for the land they wanted, they leased Ohio station, next to the tiny township of Walcha, and they later bought it, and built the Ohio homestead in the mid 1840s. Al's father, James, was Abraham and Mary's seventh child, born in 1848. After Abraham died in 1895 James bought the Ohio home block and homestead from his siblings, and that is where Al grew up.

Al's mother, Mary Maude Perry, was born in 1856, and like James had grown up on the New England Tablelands; her parents, Thomas Augustus Perry and Selina Rose Marlay, had taken up nearby Bendemeer Station in 1857. Her grandfather, Samuel Augustus Perry, had come to New South Wales as the Deputy Surveyor General in 1829.

I have vivid memories of Al. When I was a child, every school holidays, my mother and I drove up the mountains to visit her. We would drive from Tamworth over the rattling planks of the wooden bridge that straddled the sluggish brown Peel River, over the flat Liverpool Plains, toward the distant blue-grey mountains. We would pass the turn-off to the farm at Limbri, where Mum had lived from the age of 11, driving past that turn-off with barely a comment, on up the winding road of the Moonbi Ranges, and onto the New England Tablelands. Just before Bendemeer and the bridge over the MacDonald River named after Thomas Augustus Perry, and just before the turn-off to Walcha, and Ohio, we would turn left to Birallee.

The house at Birallee was a rambling weatherboard farmhouse with wide shady verandas, and a glorious garden, surrounded by gently rolling hills, soft green in spring turning to spiky pale gold in late summer and winter. The paddocks, where sheep and cattle grazed, had small stands of grey–green eucalypts and smooth round clusters of enormous granite rocks. When we arrived, we would sit in my grandmother's living room, my mother, my Gran and I, sipping cups of black tea. I would curl up quietly in a corner of the comfortable sofa and let their talk of family, and family connections, flow over me.

My grandfather, Euston Barrington Blomfield (1877–1943), had died before I was born, and in 1945 Gran had married his younger brother Henry (known as Harry or Nipper, or to me, Uncle Nipper). That was the year I was born. I always thought it was a curious thing to have been present at my grandmother's wedding. So it was always Gran and Uncle Nipper that we visited. Nipper was always out, seeing to the work on the Station.

FIGURE 14   Birallee

It is a bizarre feature of the Blomfield family history that the name Barrington is so often associated with an untimely death. The earliest Barrington Blomfield I have found was an exception, living for 73 years, from 1689 to 1762, and Rev Barrington Blomfield another, dying at the age of 97 in 1852. But then there was a Barrington Blomfield who lived to 23, from 1784 to 1807, and a Barrington Wingfield Blomfield who lived only five years from 1830 to 1835, and a Barrington Blomfield who lived only four months in 1754. And then there was my Uncle Barry, who accidentally shot himself at the age of 53 in 1954. And my grandfather, Alice's first husband, Euston Barrington Blomfield, who died in a terrible accident at the age of 64.

OBITUARY: MR. EUSTON BARRINGTON BLOMFIELD
WALCHA.—The death occurred at Walcha District hospital of a well-known resident, Mr. Euston Barrington ("Dick") Blomfield as a result of an accident on his property "Binowee," Aberbaldie Road. He was riding on a load of hay with his son, Max (AIF, home on leave) leading the horse, when the load shifted and he was thrown to the ground on his face. Deceased had a pipe in his mouth, and when picked up by his son, he was bleeding from the nose and mouth and lapsed into unconsciousness. Dr Morgan was summoned and on arrival ordered him to hospital, where he died a few hours later from cerebral lacerations, without regaining consciousness. The deceased who was the son of the late Mr. and Mrs. Henry

Blomfield was born at Carcoar 64 years ago. He was in his early days looked upon as one of the finest amateur horsemen in the state. For some years after his marriage to Miss Alice Nivison, daughter of the late Mr. and Mrs. J. A. Nivison, of "Ohio" Walcha, he was engaged by McDougall and Co., stock and station agents, of Warwick. He later secured a grazing area in the Northern State, which he disposed of, securing a property at Limbri, NSW, which he controlled until he came to reside at "Binowee." He is survived by his wife and daughters Sister Nancye Blomfield (AIF), Mrs. J. Bull (Walcha), Mrs. J. Buchanan (Mount Victoria),[1] and sons Barry and Max (both of the AIF), together with his sisters, Miss Isla Blomfield (Sydney), Mrs. Holdship (Sydney), Mrs. Willan (Sydney) and brother Harry of "Eurella" station, Mitchell (Qld.). The interment took place at the Church of England cemetery, after service at St. Andrew's Church, Rev. J. S. H. Cawte officiating.

It was an indelible feature of my childhood—the fear of falling with a stick in my mouth. I still become intensely anxious if I see children oblivious to that danger.

Gran and Uncle Nipper used to visit us when they came down to Tamworth for the day to do their shopping. My father was critical of Al. He would comment sardonically, after they had visited, that she 'wore the pants' in her marriage. He blamed her for the qualities he least liked in my mother. Years later when my own marriage was falling apart, he accused me of having those same qualities. Al, Norma, Bronwyn, all the same, he said, not willing enough wives in bed. He and Nipper had commiserated with each other over their difficulties in asserting their conjugal rights. Given the family story that I was like my mother, then it followed, in my father's eyes, that if my violent marriage was failing, I must have inherited my mother's and my grandmother's (alleged) frigidity. In post-war Australia women were supposed to be home-makers and men were still legally entitled to assert their conjugal rights with 'more than usual force'.[2]

My parents agreed, in those conversations about Al, that strong, dominant women were unacceptable. My mother deferred to my father in all her decision-making—even after his death her decisions were informed by what she believed he would have wanted.

---

1   The obituary lists his surviving children but inadvertently leaves out my mother, Norma, Mrs T. A. Davies.

2   These were words used by a judge in the 1970s in Australia, when defining in what ways it was acceptable for men to demand sex from their wives.

FIGURE 15   Euston Blomfield, *c.* 1940
             PHOTO FROM MEG BUCHANAN'S COLLECTION

The 'problem' of strong women, and the ambivalence toward them, dated back at least as far as Alice's childhood in the late 1800s. Looking at her in the photo in her white cotton dress and black stockings, puts me in mind of my favourite childhood novel, *Seven Little Australians*, which was first published in 1894 when Alice was five years old. The central protagonist was a strong, much-loved girl called Judy, who rebelled against the tyrannical power of her father. The author, Ethel Turner, was required by the publishers to rewrite the ending. The publishers deemed it unacceptable to allow such a strong, rebellious girl to survive (Davies et al, 2006).

I will never forget my own first reading of Judy's death. I couldn't believe what I was reading. I thought I must have misread it. Turning back the pages, I read it again, and was even more shocked. There could be no mistaking the meaning of the words on the page. Judy was dead. She had died saving the

FIGURE 16
Alice Blomfield: 'from me to you',
c. 1909

life of her little brother. That someone as brave and as good as Judy could be imagined, was still a miracle for me, even 60 years after the book's publication. And the lesson of what happens to rebellious girls was just as devastating for me as I imagine it had been for Al, and then for my mother, reading that story when they were girls.

That ambivalence toward strong women haunted me and haunted my mother and grandmother. We each found different ways of moving in between the romantic ideal of pliable subservience, and the strength to make a claim on our lives.

The beautiful portrait of Al above, inscribed for Euston 'from me to you' is perfect in its evocation of the romantic ideal, with the pearl earrings, the rose in her white hat, the black velvet ribbon,[3] and her understated expression of longing.

Norma (*above right*) loved that romantic image of her mother. She loved even more the softness of her father, Euston, and wanted to be more like him. She was a shiny-eyed, light-hearted, romantic girl, full of laughter. Not for her the assertiveness my father derided in Al.

---

3   In the sub-tropical Queensland climate the velvet ribbon took the place of the hot high collars that were fashionable then.

FIGURE 17   Norma, *c.* 1935   FIGURE 18   Alice Blomfield, *c.* 1935

In plumping for softness and romanticism as her ideal, Norma needed not only a husband who would support her and keep her safe, but a prince in shining armour to fulfil her dreams of happiness. But the subservience that went with the romantic ideal came at a terrible price. When she wanted to disagree with my father she did it with stony silence, or with sarcastic muttering, as if the ruling out of her own power had forced her power underground where it would squirt out in tiny twisted bursts.

She held on to her unfulfilled romantic longing until the day she died.

My favourite photo of Al (*above right*) reveals another image entirely from the earlier romantic photo. Here she is a strong woman secure in her own presence, gazing off, enigmatically, into the distance. She is not so much the object of the gaze, but the one who looks out on the world with wry amusement. She looks as though she could fly a plane solo around the world.

In contrast, a photo of Euston suggests a man gently, intimately connected with the viewer. He seems softer than Al—not effeminate or weak—but connected with the imagined other at whom he gazes.

When I first saw this photo of my grandfather, I felt a shock of recognition, perhaps because he was looking directly at me, and perhaps, too, because he looks so like my mother; I felt as though I was connected to him, and as if I had always known him, and loved him—loved the gentleness of him.

I include my favourite photo of my mother opposite—little Norma—a photo she kept hidden because she thought she looked unacceptably fat. Euston's and Norma's smiles are identical as is the softness and directness of their gaze.

FIGURE 19   Euston (Dick)
Blomfield, *c.* 1935

As Euston's obituary observed, he was known as the finest amateur horse-man in the state. He and his younger brother Henry (Uncle Nipper) vied for first place in horse-races in Queensland and New South Wales. They also did a good trade, at the beginning of the 1900s, taking horses across country to Perth to be shipped across the Indian Ocean to the Boer War.

Al was also a fine horse-woman. She and her sisters played polo against their brothers at home on the farm. Although the girls couldn't play polo in pub-lic, they formed an excellent team for their brothers to practice against. The ambivalence about what women could and couldn't do ran, thus, through the entire fabric of rural life at the turn of the century.

As I've searched through old family photograph albums of the Blomfield families, I've found almost as many pictures of horses as of people.

Another of my favourite novels was *Robbery Under Arms,* written by Eus-ton's uncle and first published in 1888. The author, Thomas Alexander Browne[4] (whose pseudonym was Rolf Boldrewood), married into the Blomfield family

---

4   Thomas Browne was married to Margaret Marie Riley, who was Euston's aunty and also cousin-once-removed. Margaret Riley was the daughter of Honoria Rose Brooks and had been adopted by Honoria's sister, Christiana. Christiana and her husband Thomas Valentine Blomfield adopted and raised Honoria's three children when she was unable to care for them herself after her husband died.

FIGURE 20
Norma Nivison Blomfield, c. 1924

in 1861. He was a pastoralist, a police magistrate and a gold fields commissioner, and he had a deep insight into, and sympathy for, the young men whose lives cast them up on the other side of the law. The central character, Dick Marston, was one such man, whose love of horses had led him astray:

> My word, Australia[5] is a horsey country, and no mistake. With the excep-
> tion of Arabia, perhaps, as they tell us about, I can't think as there's a

---

5   It is interesting that Browne refers to 'Australia' rather than the colony of New South Wales as it was then. The name Australia was derived from the Latin term for south. *Terra australis* was the name for the imagined great south land, so named before it was actually explored and mapped by European explorers. The separate colonies, including New South Wales, were not officially joined together into a country called Australia until 1900 though in 1824 the British Admiralty agreed that the continent should be known officially as Australia. When the

FIGURE 21   Al on Laddie, 1923
PHOTO FROM MEG BUCHANAN'S COLLECTION

country on the face of the earth where the people's fonder of horses. From the time they're able to walk, boys and girls, they're able to ride, and ride well. See the girls jump on bare-backed, with nothing but a gunnybag under 'em, and ride over logs and stones, through scrub and forest, down gullies, or along the side of a mountain. And a horse race, don't they love it? Wouldn't they give their souls almost—and they do often enough—for a real flyer, a thoroughbred, able to run away from everything in a country race. The horse is a fatal animal to us natives,[6] and many a man's ruin starts from a bit of horse-flesh not honestly come by. (Boldrewood, 1990 [1888]: 358–9)

Constitution of Australia came into force, on 1 January 1901, the colonies collectively became states of the Commonwealth of Australia. Browne's choice of words reveals that the idea of Australia as a country had already taken hold before the Commonwealth was established.
6   By which he means people born in Australia.

I remember Al telling Mum a story they both found hilarious of horses being ridden into the pub by two young men, who ordered and drank their beers while still seated on their horses. Her story didn't ever explain why it might be that members of my otherwise conservative family might find this moment so amusing. Now, 100 years later, during the centenary celebrations of Gallipoli, I imagine the horse riders as young men home from Gallipoli. The Australian men at Gallipolli have often been called madmen, because they would ride their horses where others dared not go.

Perhaps the two men in the pub were Gran's brothers, Towser and Poss. Towser enlisted when he was 29 years old, served at Gallipoli, and was awarded the Military Cross. His younger brother Poss, enlisted five months later:

> Poss Nivison had his 22nd birthday on board the troopship and landed with his brigade at Marseilles on 24 March 1916. … Poss and his 'second cousin' Tom Fenwicke were in the same battery, the 14th, in action at Fleurbaix from 15 April. On 27 April, during a lull in the barrage, Tom decided to go back to the English horse lines to see if he could find some better horses to pull their gun. He was fortunate to escape the renewed fighting when a shell exploded on their position, killing horses and two men. Poss was seriously wounded with a large piece of shrapnel in his back, close to his heart and just below his left shoulder blade. For the rest of his life he had a deep hole in his back. (Oppenheimer and Mitchell, 1989a: 92)

The thought of Poss and Towser riding their horses, victorious, miraculously alive, back home in Walcha, into the pub, and the thought of the older men there raising their glasses to them, brings me up short, with tears in my eyes. Gran and Mum talked about such stories with dry humour, without any of the liquid emotion that I find myself bringing to it now, all these years later.

Another of Al's stories was of herself, as a young woman, hitching up a horse and riding into town to demand her inheritance from the family solicitors; that story was woven in with another story about the solicitors mis-investing the money left by her father, James, who had died in 1913, causing her to lose most of it. Her stories, at least the ones I remember, were of audacious rule-breaking, against a backdrop of the incompetence and unreasonableness of men in authority (whether British Generals, or doctors, or the family law firm). And Al survived, where Judy in *Seven Little Australians* had not.

Heroic self-mastery was also an enduring thread in Al's stories. One of them was of a woman she knew who had a stroke and had been told by the doctor she'd never walk again. She had defied the doctors and each day took one more step, until finally she was walking around the block. She had kept up this disciplined regime until she could run around the block, thus making nonsense of the authoritative medical pronouncements about her invalid status. It was clear, in my hearing of these stories, that this was the kind of determination women should aspire to—and the kind of scepticism one should have toward men with their specialised knowledges. No wonder, my Dad, who was a lawyer, was confronted by Al.

The heroism in Al's stories also had its foolish limits. In 1936 her older brother, Abe, had been in obvious pain at the local Walcha Show, a big event in the rural calendar and in Nivison family life. Abe was as white as a sheet, the story went, but refused to give in to the pain. Everyone told him he looked terrible, but he just carried on until it was too late. He died of a burst appendix. Jillian, his grand-daughter, tells Abe's story thus:

> Abe Nivison was still the 'popular president' of the P and A society, Towser was in charge of the ring events, Poss organised the sheep pavilion, and 'Snow' Ewing was in charge of the women's section—the jams, handicrafts and numerous female works. With little warning Abe suffered a ruptured appendix and was rushed into the local hospital. As he could not be moved, one of Sydney's best surgeons, Dr Hugh Poate, was flown to Walcha—a rare event at that time. But despite his two flights to the hospital, there was little that could be done for peritonitis in the days before antibiotics, and the death of Abe Nivison on the opening day of the show cast an atmosphere of gloom over the whole community. He was fifty-three years old and as head of the Nivison family was greatly missed by everyone. (Oppenheimer and Mitchell, 1989a: 108)

Stoic endurance and intolerance of weakness was what my mother took out of those stories. She showed no sympathy if her children were sick, confining them to bed and giving them none of the attention that might make them want to stay there. Once, when I was seven years old, I told her my knee hurt really badly. Without so much as looking at it, she told me to stop whingeing and to go outside. I hung in there telling her again and again that it hurt. At some point she must have relented, as the next thing I remember I was in hospital with a chloroform bag coming down toward my face and the doctor telling me it wouldn't hurt. Liar! I struggled hard against that hateful black bag, and later woke with tubes coming out of my knee to drain out the poison from the potentially lethal spider bite. I still have the scars on my knee, and no memory of my mother visiting me in hospital. Early training, you might say, in the development of character.

On the visits to Gran in the 1950s I learned very early to stay quiet, and my bonus was that I got to listen to stories. The murmur of story back and forth between Gran and Mum created an intimate geography of family and place; the tone of voice soft, familiar, full of dry amusement, ravelled me into the web of extended family, creating a longing and belonging—a childhood grounded in that safe place on my grandmother's sofa. My mother drank Gran's stories in, as if they were her life's vital knowledge—stories to be told and re-told. She added her own stories into the mix. They told who belonged and they left out those who didn't belong—or no longer belonged—like Euston's cousin, Geoffrey Blomfield, who I met for the first time many years later. I didn't know Geoffrey existed until I heard him give a lecture at the University of New England on the indigenous massacres. He told me he had been rejected by the family after writing his book, *Baal Belbora. The end of the dancing* (1981).

The sound of their voices provided my first poetry, embedding me in that country around Walcha, a small country town perched on the edge of the New England Tablelands:

> *Ohio, Poss, Mirani,*
> *Waroo, Babe, Petali,*
> *Maudie, Bub, Babe,*
> *Bet, Buri, Abe*
> *Towser, Girl, Margie ...*

The sound of the names was soothing, and is soothing still.

In 1989, seven years after Al died, I visited Ohio with Mum for a family reunion hosted by Jillian Oppenheimer and her partner Bruce Mitchell. Jillian and Bruce had renovated the homestead and written their books about the Nivison family (Oppenheimer and Mitchell, 1989a & b).

When Mum and I arrived at the reunion, and Mum parked her car, I gave her a gift of my latest book about preschool children and gender (Davies, 1989). My feminist friends were certain she would love to read my work, and despite my misgivings, I had brought her a copy. Barely looking at it, she thrust it far into the back of the boot of her car underneath whatever was already there. She was embarrassed and affronted that I had become a writer, an academic, and perhaps even worse, a feminist. I had entered a world that was not her world. I had broken the thread of the family story that said I was like her, and that I should become the wife of a landed gentleman, as her mother and grandmothers had done before her. I had already blotted my copybook by making the wrong sort of marriage, and blotting it further when I refused to re-marry after my husband died. Writing my books caused her a complicated kind of shame, particularly at a Nivison family re-union, where her daughter was self-evidently an outsider.

She told me years later that she wanted to be able to chat about her children with her bridge friends, and my incomprehensible life in the university, and as a single woman with three children, couldn't be made to make sense in those conversations. My choices had silenced her, deprived her of the things she would have liked to talk about. It seemed especially that to the extent that I had given up on the romantic storyline she could feel no bond with me.

In those earlier, more innocent days, in the 1950s, Gran's stories wove and mended knotted webs of family that I imagined would always be there, always making a place where I could sit and listen, and where I could drift off into worlds of my own imagining. I didn't know then those webs could be broken, their tensile threads snapped like the threads of a spider's web.

In the corner shadows of Gran's living room there was a round brass vase that glowed softly, full of deep blue hydrangeas, an extraordinary blue that only my Gran knew how to create, a mystic blue, a deeply meditative blue. If my soul has a colour it is the deep blue of Al's hydrangeas and the soft gold of the vase they sat in.

A highlight of each of our visits to Gran at Birallee, was the tour around the flower garden. Mum and Gran were both passionate gardeners, as I was also to become. On one visit, a flock of Indian Runner ducks, ran in a gaggle to greet us. They had long necks and were very excitable. They were great egg layers, Gran explained, and specialised in eating snails rather than her vegetables, as the last lot of ducks (now deceased) had done. And there was the large cage full of budgerigars of brilliant blues, greens and yellows that Gran was breeding. In one enormous ancient leafy shade tree hung a coolamon, the breeze keeping the food cool, blowing through the wet hessian that hung on each side of it. Superior to a fridge, Gran said, while Mum quietly scoffed her disagreement.

When, as a child, I began to write stories, they were not set there, on the New England Tablelands, or in the country town I was growing up in. The *written* word, I had learned at school, belonged elsewhere. It was not just that it was mostly British literature we studied. My imagination had also taken root in the lands of my ancestors, lands I'd never set foot in, though I had an intense, romanticised yearning for them, particularly for Scotland. I remember in sixth grade receiving an award in a national poetry competition, for a poem about an old Miss Emma Brown who lived in London; another award was for a story about a convict escaped from Dartmoor Prison. I didn't know the name, then, of Australian prisons. Britain was still called 'home', though none of the family I knew had ever been there, except for the young men who had gone to war.

In this book I am travelling back to that sofa, to those blue hydrangeas, and to the family stories that I cut myself apart from, in almost every life choice I ever made. I go "back home" to the places my ancestors came from, and to the places they settled in when they came here.

Why now? In part because I have a sense of potential loss for my children and their children if I don't record what I remember—in effect a kind of staving-off of the end of my own life—insofar as memories are life. But in greater part, as this project has unfolded, I realise that through the lives of my family it is possible to open up significant questions about the colonisation of this country. These two agendas are not easily woven together. My descendants would, most likely, want only positive stories, and preferably heroic stories of success against the odds; but the history of this country is a harsh one, and the colonial past can make for very hard reading. In a way a genealogy of family weaves back up the web of family, mending the breaks and cuts, or at least making sense of them. And if you stay with it long enough, and listen carefully enough, it risks substantial new cuts.

Mum made her own significant cuts from Gran's life. She didn't marry a landed gentleman; she married my father and became a modern town housewife, going out each day to play bridge or tennis or golf while the live-in maid, Shirley, took care of the children. Dad's status required that she not work in paid work, which was no problem, as paid work was not ever what she wanted. Her desire, like the best of Jane Austen's characters, was for a man who both supported her and loved her. Even at the end of her life she was still, in many ways, the bright-eyed laughing girl, longing for her prince to come, and at the same time bitterly disappointed that Dad had not been that prince. She had resolved that deep ambivalence toward strong women by opting for romance, and by giving up on her own strength; so her story, as she told it to me, became one of regret and longing. At her funeral, her sisters surprised me when they rejected that story. She was still for them, that bright-eyed laughing girl, and the one who had caught the best husband. The story of sadness and missed opportunities had not ever been one for their ears.

Being strong and having character were not the same thing. You could forego strength, but not character. Gran mentioned, on one of our visits, that it was her job to interview the men who applied for jobs on the Station. Uncle Nipper thought she was better at selecting workmen than he was. One of her rules was that if they had dirty fingernails she wouldn't bother to interview them. Mum scoffed at that, exclaiming 'what do dirty fingernails matter in a dirty job!' But for Gran, dirty fingernails at an interview revealed poor character.

'Character', as I understood it, through her stories, was more important than anything else. Money was important, but that was not something you should talk about. Boldrewood's outlaw hero, from a much poorer background, observed that money and character were equally important:

> ...money can do a lot. It aint everything in this world. But there's precious little it won't get you, and things must be very bad it won't mend. A man must have very little sense if he don't see as he gets older that character and money are the two things he's got to be carefullest of in this world. If he's not particular to a shade about either or both of 'em, he'll find his mistake. (Boldrewood, 1990/1888: 395–6)

I still find myself horrified by dirty fingernails and toenails—not a willed or rational moral judgement, but a horror that wells up unexpectedly and takes me over. But I did refuse to go to the elite boarding school I had been booked into since the day I was born, which is where, my father explained, I would get my character. All my mistakes followed, he believed, from that decision to let me stay at home.

Family stories lodge themselves materially and emotionally, and they have a habit of leaping up and taking you by surprise.

Once, when I stayed with Gran in the school holidays I discovered she was a passionate reader of fiction. She gave me novels to read, and I spent all day curled up on the sofa, reading. One, called *White Ears* I think, was about a dingo that killed many sheep, not just for food, but for the sheer pleasure of the hunt. The killings were told in terrible and bloody detail. But the author also took me deep inside White Ears' mind—giving me my first vivid experience of seeing the world sympathetically from an entirely different point of view—from the life-world of a differently embodied being, a hunted outlaw. *Robbery Under Arms* had a similar storyline running through it, though the outlaws this time were bushrangers. Another novel she chose for me, was about a girl called Possum who had grown up on a farm in Gippsland in Victoria. Possum was shy, like I was, and didn't say much, but she was extraordinarily competent at her work on the farm—she could out-ride any of the men. Gran worried that I must be bored reading novels all day, but actually I was in heaven.

And now to Norma, my mother, the shiny-eyed romantic girl, sometimes called Pud and sometimes called Pete. She has already appeared here as Al's daughter, and as my mother. In the next chapter I try to tease her apart a little from those stories and tell her life more from her own point of view.

CHAPTER 3

Norma Nivison Blomfield

FIGURE 22
Mother and child: Al and Norma (Pud),
1914

I begin again with Norma as a baby with her face as round and as delectable as a delicious pudding. The photographer has clearly loved his subject, adding touches of pink to mother's and baby's cheeks and giving Norma red–gold curls to match her bangle, and a pretty blue ribbon threaded through her white dress. Both Al and Norma look intently at the photographer, who captures the baby's attention long enough for the baby to stay perfectly still. Al's embrace is probably more about holding little Pud (short for Pudding) still for the camera than it is her habitual mode of mothering.

Norma's first ten years were spent in Queensland, where Euston was a stock and station agent. Each Christmas they travelled back to 'Ohio' to spend the holidays with Al's parents. In 1924 they moved back for good to take up a life among the rural Nivison clan who lived on the New England Tablelands. They bought a farm at Limbri, down off the Tablelands on the edge of the Liverpool Plains.

Pud's oldest sister, Tim, took a photo of that journey when they stopped to cool the engine and have a picnic lunch.

© BRONWYN DAVIES, 2021 | DOI:10.1163/9789004446717_003

FIGURE 23 Warwick to Ohio in the Hupmobile, 1924. Al is smoking in the background. Euston is looking in the boot. Leaning against the car are Barry (13), Norma (10), and Max (8). Seated on ground are Nan (12), Betty (7). Standing in the foreground is Joan (known as Bub, 3)
PHOTO FROM HELEN BATHGATE'S COLLECTION

If Norma had written a diary at that time it might have read like this:

Excerpts from the diary of Norma Nivison Blomfield (b. 1914) written between the ages of 11 and 16

Name: Norma (Pete) Nivison Blomfield
Address: Ohio, Walcha, New South Wales, Australia, The World, The Universe

14 February 1925.
Today is Saint Valentine's day, and it's my birthday. I am 11 years old. Boo hoo I didn't get a Valentine's card or any flowers.

Nobody loves me,
everybody hates me,
I'll have to go and eat worms!

Except for my cousins I don't know anyone here in Walcha. Tim is extra grumpy. She is 15 years old and she left her boyfriend behind in Goondiwindi. That's a secret. She has been crying all day and won't talk to anyone. Mum and Dad are going to buy a farm at Limbri and we are never going back to Queensland. We lived our whole lives in Queensland. We lived at Charleville, at Chiverton near to the Darling Downs, and at Warwick, at Kircher's vineyard, and at Goondiwindi. At Goondiwindi we used to write plays and dress up and act them out in the garden.

It was good living at Goondiwindi. I had the best teacher. When I finished my work early I could teach the little kids to read. It was funny. I had to teach Maybelle Urquhart how to spell. I would tell her h is for hat and she would say 'haitch is for 'at'. I told her 'no aitch is for hhhhat'. She couldn't get the h to go in the right place.

Ohio is where I was born. The year before I was born my Granpa James got sick and Mum came down to see him. He died two days before Christmas, so Mum and the kids didn't go back to Queensland. She stayed here to help Granny, and I was born on February 14th 1914. Everyone was still sad then because Granpa James was such a lovely man. Granny Nivison is still wearing black even though it's ten years since Granpa James died.

Granny Nivison is beautiful and funny; she always makes me laugh. Granpa James really loved her.

My cousin Mollie is the same age as me, but she hasn't turned 11 yet, so I'm the oldest.

Max is happy as a lark because they have let him go out mustering with the men, and he's only 8. Barry's gone mustering too. He's nearly 14 so he's one of the men.

Bub doesn't know anything. She's only 3. She blows bubbles with her spit. We call her Bubbles.

Nan is 2 years older than me. She is so bossy. I'm sick of her.

Bet is not much use. She's only 7 and Mum says "leave her alone, poor skinny little thing. Let her read her book". She never has to do anything!

Granny Nivison says to buck up. There's going to be a cake with candles, and some lemon delicious pudding.

There are so many Norms in my family, Uncle Norman and Aunty Norma, and Great Uncle Norman. It gets confusing when anyone calls me Norma, so now my name is Pete. I got a silver serviette ring for my birthday and it has 'Pete' written on it. I'm glad it's not Pud.

Bet is Skin and I am Pud because I'm fat. Granny took us in to have our photos taken and I hate mine because I look like a pudding.

Dear Diary

Today I learned how to skin a rabbit. We catch them in traps and if they're not dead yet you have to flick them quick and break their necks. Your pocket-knife has to be really sharp so you might need to sharpen it on a grinding stone. Barry showed me, if you cut in exactly the right places, phfft! You can pull the whole skin off in one go. You get money for the skins from the rabbito, so you peg them out to dry. The meat is not fit for humans but it's good tucker for the dogs.

In China they eat cats. You have to be careful if you go out to a restaurant, my Uncle Towser says, and make sure it's not cat they serve you, an old stray cat out of a back alley somewhere.

Uncle Towser is married to Aunty Nell and they have a baby the same age as Bub. Towser is a superb horseman, same as my Dad.

Uncle Poss went to England during the war and met Lord Glendyne and his family. They are genuine upper crust. Uncle Poss made everyone laugh. He was so embarrassed in case the other soldiers saw him being driven back to the barracks in a coach driven by footmen all dressed up in velvet. At dinner those footmen in their fancy livery would stand behind your chair, which made it even worse if you didn't know what to do with all the knives and forks and got your banana tangled up in the paper doily.

Lord Glendyne was descended from a cousin of Great Granpa Abraham Nivison. Lady Glendyne, his wife, was Great Granny Nivison's niece. That means that these lords are our double cousins. Great Granny was called Mary Wightman before she married Abraham Nivison. She was born in Scotland in 1812, 102 years before I was born.

• • •

Dear Diary

We are moving to Limbri, which is 20 miles north east of Tamworth. It's a tiny village on Swamp Oak Creek, and 5 miles southeast of Moonbi. There is a small school there that we'll go to. We'll ride our horses to school. It's a one-teacher school. Looks like I might get practice at being a teacher again.

The house is not finished yet. We all have to pitch in and help. The worst job is putting brown shoe polish on all the floorboards and then shining them.

• • •

Dear Diary

We have been to Ashton's Circus. The best was the man on the high wire who was pretending to be drunk. It was really scary. Also a man who leapt over 20 horses at once. There were 2 trapeze artists in spangly outfits who flew on the trapeze, holding on by their teeth! The acrobats did somersaults on horseback while the horses trotted around the ring. The clowns were very funny. They could do anything—their bodies were like elastic. There was a band with a man playing the cornet, and lions and a lion-tamer cracking his whip, and elephants.

When we got home we practiced and practiced at being clowns and acrobats. I can bend over backwards and come up into a handstand, do cartwheels, and I've just about got the knack of somersaults in the air. We've got an old mattress we can fall on, so we don't break our necks.

• • •

Dear Diary

Today we went to Mirani to see Uncle Poss and his family and all our cousins. We rode to a pool on the creek, with our swimmers and towels in our saddle bags. We swam in the creek all day. The temperature was over 100 degrees. The rocks were hot, but the water was icy cold. When we got too cold and started shivering, and our mouths were turning blue, we lay on the smooth rocks and shivered until we warmed up in the sun.

• • •

Dear Diary,

It is 1928. I am going to Wenona in Sydney. We have to choose between finishing school here at the local school, where we can do the Leaving, or one year at boarding school. So this will be my last year of school. People always ask 'what school did you go to?' They would laugh you to scorn if you said Limbri one-teacher school, or Walcha Public. I will do my Inter at Wenona...[1]

• • •

---

[1] The Inter, or Intermediate Certificate was awarded on the basis of a public exam at the end of the 3rd year of secondary school. The Leaving, or Leaving Certificate, was awarded on the basis of a second public exam at the end of the 5th year, through which you could matriculate and gain university entrance.

Dear Diary

My best friend at school is Nerida Capp. She is called Ned. She is beautiful and funny and she makes me laugh. She is a good runner like me, and good at her school work. We do everything together. We are learning tennis and golf and I am in the A grade tennis team. Next week we go to the Regatta to see the boys rowing.

1929 The market has crashed, and there is no money. At home, men come to our door and ask for work and some food. We get them to do odd jobs and give them a good meal. They are really polite. Some of them have left their families behind in the city while they go on the road to find work. They are dressed in suits, but they are dusty from living on the road. Some of them are doctors and lawyers but now they chop wood and do odd jobs to stay alive. They need money for their wives and children, but we haven't got any money, so we just feed them and let them sleep in the hay shed.

Nan wants to be a nurse but she has to buy her own uniform. Dad can't afford it. Uncle Poss has given her the money. She is really excited. I don't want to be a nurse. Tim is going to Barraba to work on Bereen Station, doing dress-making.

Mum says I have to earn some money too. She has arranged with the Capps that I will live with them and be their dress-maker. I am so ashamed. What will Ned think?

The End[2]

The place Norma had sought to secure for herself in society, by choosing to go to Wenona rather than complete her schooling, was lost during the Depression. To be regarded as a suitable wife or husband for the children of the landed gentry, attendance at an elite boarding school was essential. It is fascinating, in that regard, that Al and Euston gave their children the choice between completing the Leaving Certificate and attending boarding school. In effect it was a choice between marrying into the rural elite or getting an education. Whenever Norma told me this story she was scathing about the alternative offered— two further years at the local public school. What were her parents thinking of? You would be a social outcast. When I refused to go to boarding school, and then wanted to study at university, Norma was deeply opposed to my choices. Although she didn't say so in so many words, I was supposed to be making my way into the rural elite marriage market.

---

2 This diary is primarily based on my memories of what Norma told me about her childhood, but also includes some memories of her cousin, Jillian Oppenheimer.

After her year at Wenona Norma discovered that the Depression meant she had to work in her best friend's household. She was filled with shame—but fees still had to be found to send Max and Bet and Bub to boarding school, so the older children must now go out to work. Norma worked for the Capp family throughout the years of the Great Depression and though they were very kind to her, taking her on her very first trip to the beach, being forced through poverty into servitude filled her with an abiding horror of being poor. She had grown up as the poor cousin of her wealthier relations on Ohio Station and on the adjoining properties of her uncles. She loved the wealthier, more comfortable life at 'Ohio' and she loved the stories of how her grandfather James had adored his wife Mary Maude, who was so beautiful and full of life.

After the years on the Capp's property, my story of Norma becomes quite sketchy. I knew she broke her engagement to a man with red hair because Al had rejected him after he quizzed her about the family tree. Tim, Norma's favourite sister, had died in childbirth. She hoped Tim's husband, Kim, would ask her to marry him, to take Tim's place. She had been deeply disappointed when he did not. Kim was one of a panoply of romantic heroes that she yearned for, including the man with the red hair who was too curious about our family history.

While I was writing about that sketchy knowledge of those years of Norma's life, I had an inexplicable compulsion to explore the deep drawer of photos that I hadn't touched for years. As I pulled out the unsorted photos in their hundreds, and sorted them out in piles on desk and floor, I kept telling myself it was a silly thing to be doing. I didn't have time or any need to tidy that drawer. Quite the reverse—I needed to be tidying up and vacuuming and getting ready for the first visit from Jody, my new research assistant. But I kept on going, sorting the photos, with no way of making sense of what I was doing.

After several days, and many interruptions, I got to the bottom of the drawer. There I found a small plastic bag with a brown envelope inside. In the brown envelope were three letters addressed to Norma, one from Tim, her beloved sister, and two from Kim, Tim's husband. I had no memory of having seen these letters. Could it be that in some inaccessible part of my brain the memory of them was stored, a memory that had been activated by this project? Or were the letters demanding that I find them? That is certainly how I felt when I saw the brown envelope—as if it had been calling to me. Either way, the letters and I had finally found each other.

The first letter was from Tim written in 1933. She was working as a dressmaker, in the house of a wealthy relation, and she offered her little sister, Norma, advice about finding a husband (she must only marry someone she loves). She wrote about what life was like then, during the Depression in the early 1930s, for both of them. Their working conditions were, on the one hand, quite arduous, and on the other, they were included in the social life of the people they worked for—partying among the sons and daughters of the landed gentry. Tim's letter, written to Norma when she was 19, mentions Norma's new boyfriend (the one Gran took an objection to because of his quizzing her on the family tree) and discusses her own boyfriend, Kim, who is an amateur horseman. The sharing out of duty to their mother, Al, is also a consideration.

c/- Mrs Ewing
Koorool
Walcha
7 June [1933]

Norma Dearest,
This is just a note to you as Mum tells me that you have another job. Good luck to you and I hope you like it. Write and tell me all about it and any other news.

How is the new boyfriend and what is he like, tell big sister everything. I was talking to Mum last night and she said that he was enquiring about the family tree. She also said that she was feeling better and Nancye was at home to help her.

I had a great time at Moree didn't get to bed till after six o'clock the second night and had plenty of cocktails. The dance ended about four then we went to the hotel and fooled around for a bit and eventually got into a room at the back where several of the boys were sleeping and there we had sandwiches and fruit salts of all things. I saw Murray and Red Crossing and met Struan. She seems very nice but I only talked to her dancing round the floor.

Didn't do very much while I was at Wea [Kim's property]. Kim was busy so I only went for two rides with him but one of those was thirty-seven miles. Kim rode one winner at the races and several seconds.

I have only done the front of my gray and blue jumper but I have nearly finished the other skirt.

Went skating for the first time last Wednesday and couldn't stand up. I now have a blister on my finger from hanging onto the ropes also some skin off the back of my hand. Went to a dance on Monday night and it was packed. I enjoyed it in a way.

It is very cold up here and I nearly freeze when I am sewing so don't know how I will see the winter out.

I suppose either you or I will have to go home when Nan goes to [ ] at the end of August. But there is plenty of time to decide who it will be. If you like your job and want to stay I will gladly go home but it's only necessary for one of us to go.

Don't say anything about it but I think Kim and I will be married early next year but it's not definite yet so I haven't told Mum or anyone else, in case we don't.

I must go and get some chips for the heater now so will finish this later.

Excuse the writing but I am sitting almost in the fire to keep warm.

Go for your life kid and get yourself a husband while you are away remember what I told you that night at Bereen. You may not get another chance once you come home again, only don't take anyone you don't love.

Write to me soon Norm, I haven't seen any of your letters since you went away. Mum told me last night that she had one from you which was to read and burn so it must have been interesting, so tell me something too

Lots of love
from your loving sister
Tim

The read and burn letter was most likely a response to Al's rejection of Norma's fiancé. What did he know, or hint at, when he quizzed Al on the Nivison/Blomfield family tree? What was the secret that could lead to the breakup of an engagement? (I'm sorry Al, but some of those secrets will emerge here in Part 3).

Tim and Kim did indeed get married in May of the following year, on 4 May 1934. A month later Kim, Tim's husband, wrote to Norma while he and Tim were still on their honeymoon, to thank her for all the work she had done in organising the wedding. His letter is charming and flattering, chatty and a little risqué, alluding to his time in bed with Tim. He uses Norma's childhood nickname, Pete. He adores his wife, but still has enough room in his heart to write to her little sister while on their honeymoon, praising her sweetness and her competence, and jokingly hinting at what else he might be refraining from saying since he doesn't want her to get a swollen head. The flattery, and the friendly chat of the letter, about the things they had seen on their honeymoon warmed Norma's heart. He hadn't forgotten her, even on his honeymoon:

Grafton
8 June 34

Dear Pete,
Just a line Pete from your new Brother-in-law to let you know how he
appreciated everything you did for Tim and I. It was very sweet of you and
I think you ran it wonderfully. I had better not give you any more kid you
might be wanting a new hat.

We had a very good trip to Armidale getting there at 8.30. both a bit
tired after the day.

Came on down here yesterday through Glen Innes, it's a wonderful
drive from Glen Innes here especially down the Big hill the growth of
timber and stuff was wonderful and the views were just as wonderful got
here about 5 o'clock, we are at a bosker Hotel one of the nicest I have seen
in the country so we are having a day's spell and a look around, spent
most of the morning on the bridge and were luckie enough to see them
lift the centre span to let a boat through, I never saw such a place for
flowers. I think people must just stick them in and they grow, but they are
really wonderful and such colours.

Don't forget to answer this and tell us all about the party after we left,
so Pete write to [ ] Hotel and it will sure find us. And I won't forget the
floor polish either.

Tim has managed to catch a cold and of course blames me, says I didn't
keep her warm enough, but I don't know.

We are going on to Porte tomorrow, don't know yet what day we will be
in Sydney. Just at present we are going where the mood takes, and enjoy-
ing every minute of it.

Some nice ladies filled one of Tim's suitcases with confetti but lucky
we noticed some at Armidale so were very careful, so we unpacked it on
the road yesterday and so got rid of the mess. Am afraid the maid at Armidale will find quite a lot of confetti under the wardrobe if she looks there.
We had the room that you and Tim had at Picnic Race time.

Well Pete I think we will go and have some lunch, and afterwards for a
drive round. So for the present Cheerio, and the best of luck.

Love from us both
Kim

The third letter that she had kept for the rest of her life, also from Kim, was
written to her from their home at 'Wea', in Barraba. Kim refers to Tim, his new,

and by then, very pregnant wife, as 'the Boss' in the way Euston might have done of Al. In this letter he congratulates Norma on her engagement—this time to Tom.

Once again Kim's letter was charming and extraordinarily flattering. Norma dreamed that he actually loved her, a complicated dream, since she firmly believed that true love was exclusive. If you found yourself loving two people, then you could know you were not 'in love' she later told me when I was a teenager. Was she therefore not 'really in love' with Tom, the man she was engaged to? And was Kim not 'really in love' with Tim? Tim was, moreover, her favourite sister. The letter tells her he is coming to visit, and Tim is coming too. His letter can be read as a very clear acceptance that Norma has committed herself to Tom, yet it remains deeply ambiguous, given how loving it is. This time he uses the other of her nicknames, one that only her inner family circle still used— and she is now 'dearest', rather than just plain 'dear'.

Wea
Barraba
Thursday 1935

Pud Dearest
Just got your letter little sister and was most thrilled. Warmest congrats old girl and I hope you will be most happy and have plenty of luck. I don't know the Boy Friend, but if he is half as good as his little wife to be well you will be a very luckie woman, it doesn't matter now how much I think of you does it sister well I think that B.F. of yours is the luckiest chap I know and I only hope he realises still, as you are one girl in a thousand.

Well Dear this letter is only short as I am off to the [ ] and won't be home till tomorrow night, am still hard at work but [ ] well I will be in Tamworth on Monday to see the Rhodeo so hope to see you and the family there. I am taking the Boss down. Well sister I must be off. The best of luck in the future

love
Kim

Tim died in childbirth on 9 March 1935, not very long after Kim's letter was written. The incompetent young doctor was afraid of doing a cæsarian, and both the baby and Tim died. The outrage at that doctor's incompetence was a story told and retold in those conversations in Birallee so many years later.

FIGURE 24
Thomas Alfred Davies, *c.* 1940

Norma and Tom didn't marry until 1939. It was a long engagement. Tom's law firm was doing well. He was handsome and charming, and in those early days there was a great deal of laughter and fun—playing tennis and golf, and swimming, and partying; the promise of laughter and wealth. He promised, as well, international travel, a car of her own at a time when only one in ten families owned a car. He would employ a maid to do the housework and to take care of the children. She need never work again. Was she marrying for love as Tim had advised? Quite possibly not. The wife he believed was frigid quite simply didn't love him.

A frock of white lace was worn by Miss Norma Nivison Blomfield, daughter of Mr. and Mrs. E.B. Blomfield, of Binowee, Walcha, at her marriage with Mr. Thomas Davies, eldest son of Mr. George Davies and the late Mrs Davies, of Orange, which took place at St Andrew's Church, Walcha. She added a halo hat of white felt, and carried a bouqet of frangipani. Misses Nerida Capp (Quirindi) and Nancye Blomfield, who were bridesmaids, wore gowns of aqua-blue lace, with Dolly Varden hats, and their

FIGURE 25   The bride in a halo hat: Norma Nivison Blomfield, 21 February 1939

flowers were pink tiger-lilies and red roses. Mr. Llewellyn Davies was best
man, and Mr. Geoff Stephens (Walcha) groomsman. The Rev. J.S.H. Cawte
officiated. Afterwards, at the Apsley Tennis Club, the bride's mother
was assisted by the bridegroom's aunt, Mrs. A.T. Fenwicke, in receiving
a number of guests, including Mr. and Mrs. A.B. Nivison, Mr. and Mrs.
Geoff. Blomfield, Mr. and Mrs. F. W. Nivison, Mr. and Mrs. Norman Turton, Mr. and Mrs. Frank Ewing, Mr. and Mrs. George Taylor (Gunnedah),
Mesdames Digby (Tenterfield), Clifford Minter (Sydney), and Mrs Geoff
Stephens, Misses Betty and Joan Blomfield, Mary, Meg and Judy Ewing,
and Peggie Turton. (*Sydney Morning Herald*, 22 March 1939)

The wedding took place seven months before the outbeak of the Second World
War. In a photo of the wedding party (*overleaf*), Llewellyn, Tom's younger
brother, is far left. He was later to enlist, only to find himself in the Fall of Singapore and a Japanese prisoner of war for the duration of the war. Nancye,
next to Llewellyn, was later to nurse the troops. Her boyfriend was killed at

FIGURE 26   The wedding party: Llewellyn Davies, Nancye Blomfield, Tom Davies, Norma,
              Geoff Stephens, Nerida (Ned) Capp, 1939

war, and she never married. After the war she worked as a nurse in Aden and
every two years travelled the world and came home to visit. Tom, in the centre,
not dressed as elegantly as his younger brother, seems to have his arms around
both Norma and Nancye. He looks as though he has had quite a lot to drink.
Geoff Stephens, in the back row, was Dad's favourite cousin. Geoff was the son
of Tom's Aunt Alice, who lived in Walcha. She had married the GP Sam Stephens. And Norma's friendship with Ned (*far right*) had, apparently, survived
her servitude in Ned's family. The photo of Ned in her fairy princess wedding
gown had pride of place on Mum's wardrobe throughout my childhood.

CHAPTER 4

Jean Carty and George William Hope Davies

My father's father was George William Hope Davies (1870–1946). He died the year after I was born. I have no memories of him of my own, but his is the name I heard most often from my father. George was the son of Maria Louisa Campbell, a Dane who grew up in India, and Thomas Alfred Davies, a Welsh soldier serving in the British army, who grew up on the island of Jersey. George was born at sea in 1870 when Maria Louisa, Alfred and their first two children were on their way to make a new life for themselves in the colony of New South Wales. The colony, originally called New South Wales, stretched along the entire east coast of the Australian continent, including Van Diemen's Land, now called Tasmania. It was later divided into separate colonies, Queensland to the north and Victoria and Tasmania to the south. George was named after Maria Louisa's cousins, George and William Salting, and Hope, after the Cape of Good Hope, which they were sailing around when he was born.

George spent the first ten years of his life living on a farm on the Cunningham Plains, called 'Nant Gwylan', named after Alfred's ancestral home in Wales. Life on the properties out on the plains in the 1870s offered a magical freedom to the children of the gentlemen landholders. While the children of the farm-workers, usually ex-convicts, grew up in a strict disciplinary regime, the children of the graziers, in Banjo Patterson's words, were more like wild horses:

> They had their own dignity, these 'old hands', the dignity of men who had suffered. They had been disciplined in their day and they felt that it was only right that their sons should know discipline. Not like the sons of the free settlers who were brought up anyhow, like wild horses. I knew several of these old hands in the early days and, whatever their failings might have been, they always kept order in their families. (Paterson, 1983: 15)

Banjo Paterson grew up 20 miles away from Nant Gwylan, and the families sometimes visited each other. Some of the gentlemen graziers were ex-soldiers, like Alfred, who believed in some of that same tough discipline.

Banjo describes the farms in the 1870s as quite isolated from each other, before sealed roads and motorised vehicles. The landholders travelled by horse and horse-drawn carriages to visit each other, while the poor, often evading unjust laws, travelled by foot, looking for shelter and food and work:

© BRONWYN DAVIES, 2021 | DOI:10.1163/9789004446717_004

NEW SOUTH WALES, C. 1830–1840

SCALE 1: 20,000,000

MAP 2   New South Wales, *c.* 1830-1840

... such strangers as came along were just as likely to be bad characters, dodging the police. I remember my mother loading a gun (muzzle-loader) in the sitting-room one evening when all the men were away and a particularly villainous-looking stranger had cast up. Putting the hammer down, she let it slip and the gun went off with a frightful bang, bringing down a shower of whitewash from the calico ceiling and scaring the life out of a family of possums who lived up among the beams and were just preparing to go out for the night. I suppose the stranger must have heard the shot down in the travellers' hut, for he was very civil when he came along in the morning to draw his meat, tea and sugar. 'And if you could spare a bit of bread, lady, I'd be glad of it. I ain't much hand at makin' damper.' (Paterson, 1983: 15)

In return, the travellers were expected to cut a certain amount of firewood [since] ... a little work was expected of every traveller in return for his dole. (Paterson, 1983: 15)

Children, like Banjo and George, might occasionally join in the work of the farm when they weren't at their lessons or out climbing trees and playing down at the creek. Banjo tells of climbing trees to bring down wild silk-worm nests, and of watching the shearers who looked like big kangaroos when they squatted on the ground to take their tea. He and his sister raised orphaned lambs, cared for sick horses, and played in the woods and down at the creek. They observed the details of the lives of every kind of bird, hunted with their dog for water-rats, and watched the teaming life of the creek:

... the creeks were chains of big waterholes in which the inhabitants splashed and dabbled and swam and dived: wild ducks which spent a lot of their time lazing on the banks; energetic little dabchicks perpetually diving and working hard, though there could not really have been much need for it. Old Man Platypus ... swam up the creek against the current without leaving a ripple, or he drifted down it, silently as a brown streak of water-weed. Sometimes, but very rarely, Mr Platypus would come ashore and comb his fur or lie on a patch of warm sand like an old gentleman sunning himself on the verandah of his club. He hated the pushing noisy rabble, and he was about the only creature in the bush who never attracted the attention of the soldier birds, which meant a lot, for the soldier birds missed very little. (Paterson, 1983: 44–5)

The freedom that children like Banjo and George had growing up in the bush was also a freedom Maria Louisa, George's mother, had experienced growing up in a Danish colony in India in the mid 1800s. In New South Wales in the 1870s, the children's freedom was interrupted by lessons from tutors, or parents, and then by schooling in small one-teacher schools that sprang up in remote areas, and later by being sent to boarding school with its strict disciplinary regimes. That freedom to run wild, combined with authoritarian discipline, was still being extended to me and to my siblings growing up on the edge of the rural town of Tamworth in the mid 1900s. We had a great deal more freedom than our class-mates, and with that, a great deal more responsibility.

The successive generations of children, George, then Tom, then me, were blissfully unaware of the price of their freedom to roam wild in the bush, in forests and waterways. We grew up in an intimate relationship with the countryside around us, unaware that we were trespassing, and unaware that the traditional custodians of the land had been displaced, enslaved, and massacred. And we were no more aware of our debt to the enslaved convicts, who our ancestors had depended on to build the colony.

Our savage history had been neatly tucked away, leaving no visible trace in my memory as a child, except perhaps for a lingering fear of trespassing. I had a mortal dread of placing my foot on land where it did not belong.

By the time George and his family were living on Nant Gwylan there were almost no Wiradjuri people living in the district. Wiradjuri land had stretched between Gilgandra to the north, Wagga Wagga to the south, Darlington to the west and the Blue Mountains to the east. Martial law had been declared in the 1820s, and the Wiradjuri wars—squatters and troopers against the local indigenous people—were fought, with devastating effect. Banjo Paterson tells a story of only one Wiradjuri family remaining in the district in the 1870s. His account of them reveals a humiliating dependence on handouts and a distinct animosity toward them, on the part of the neighbouring landholders.

The old Wiradjuri man of Banjo's memoir wore a brass name-plate saying Billy Budgeree, King of Lachlan: "It gave us a thrill to think that we were meeting royalty face to face, begging cold mutton for him from the cook, and hinting to father (who in our eyes was the usurper of Billy's throne) that he might spare a fig of tobacco from the store for Billy's insatiable pipe" (Paterson, 1983: 25). King Billy was an admirable spear thrower and could be persuaded to show off his skill to visitors in return for tobacco or blankets. On one remarkable occasion, during a terrible drought, Billy Budgeree brought rain to Illalong, and with it an incantation, in which he accused Banjo's Dad of refusing to give him the goods he had come to depend on:

> It rained three inches that night. The creek came down a banker, and in the morning the frogs started to croak, the birds to sing, the wild duck

and wild turkeys came in from all surrounding districts and the water rats displayed their black and gold coats in the exuberance of spring fashions. Not only had the station got rain, but the downfall seemed to have missed all other places.

Marching up to the boss, King Billy said, 'No got him tobacco, no got him sugar bag, what about it nobbler?' This was enough to take anyone's breath away.

My father said, 'S'pose I gibbit nobbler, you beat 'um gin, you beat 'um piccaninny, policeman kill you deadfellow. Me gibbit you three figs tobacco, plenty flour, plenty sugar, plenty tea. What happened that other Government blanket you got from policeman?'

'Me bin loss him,' whined Sally.

'You bin let puppy dog tear him up, mine thinkit. Missus go look out old feller blanket for you.'

Thus was an honourable peace concluded, and King Billy's fame spread far and wide. Truth to tell, Billy had been looked upon as a cadging old nuisance at the neighbouring stations, and his dogs were in even less favour than himself. Now, he was told that he could come along and bring his dogs any time that he liked. They could not afford to overlook a rainmaker of his class. (Paterson, 1983: 27)

The chilling subtext in this childhood story is the history of massacre. Mr Paterson reminds King Billy that if he steps out of line "policeman kill you deadfellow". Billy Budgeree and his small family must speak to the man who now owns their land in pidgin English. They must demonstrate their spear throwing like circus animals, and call down rain in a drought, in return for food, tobacco and a blanket—and perhaps, if they were in luck, a glass of whiskey.

The only fragment of Billy Budgeree's language remaining in my childhood in the 1940s, was our 'dilly bag', in which we carried all the bits and pieces we needed when we went as a family to the town baths. It was not anything like the fine bag made of twisted grass in which Sally had "carried anything from the remains of their last meal to a clutch of wild duck eggs" (Paterson, 1983: 27), but an old khaki canvas bag passed down from George—its name and purpose providing the flimsiest of threads connecting us to the traditional owners of the land—traditional owners who were, throughout my childhood, denied entry to those same baths.

It is hard to continue with this story in the face of that devastating history. How can I write about the privileged lives of my ancestors when the story of massacre is a much larger story, still reverberating in the lives of the descendants of the original custodians of the land? How can I proceed without a

moral judgement that presses me into silence? Yet I must go on; reconciliation can only be accomplished when we all know what we are coming from.
The new and unexpected emerges in a dynamic interplay with old, habituated
structures and practices. So, I continue ...

The Move to Kempsey

In 1881 the family left Nant Gwylan, and Alfred took up a full-time paid appointment as Police Magistrate in Kempsey. George was then 11 years old and Llewellyn was 6. Each holiday the two boys travelled home to Kempsey from their
boarding school, All Saints College in Bathurst, by train and by horse-drawn
coach. Llewellyn's daughter, Dorothy, remembers Llewellyn's stories of those
train trips: "they liked to have the carriage to themselves, so Uncle George
would put on this mentally deranged act, very convincingly, so no one entered.
Dad thought it was hilarious. I think Dad always looked up to Uncle George
as being the daring & funny one in the family" (Dorothy Parkinson, personal
communication). Another tale from Great Uncle Llewellyn was of George and
Llewellyn going through Alfred's legal files to discover the gossip and scandals
about the locals in Kempsey.

In my childhood home, my father's legal files, each in their manila folders
tied with pink tapes, were stored under the house on long shelves in the dirt-
floored cellar. The entrance to the cellar was through a heavy wooden door—
for us, a castle door into the dungeon. Behind the door hung a light-bulb on
a long lead. The lead would take us as not to the files as we hadn't discovered
how interesting they were, but to the hole in the far brick wall. Through that
hole were our very own unlit catacombs—a myriad of small rooms that bore
no apparent relation to the floor plan above. The roof grew lower and lower as
we moved deeper into the dungeon. Susanne would lead our expeditions into
the depths with a box of matches to light our way. She was four and a half years
older than me, and two years older than Tony. She had a great deal of authority
over us, and over the neighbourhood children. She was often left in charge of
us, while our parents had their afternoon 'nap'. Sometimes we dropped leaves
behind us to ensure that we could find our way back to the hole in the wall, to
the light bulb at the end of the lead, the heavy wooden door, and safety. One
day we came to leaves leading off in two directions. I was tearfully sure we must
follow the left-hand trail, but Sue insisted on the right. I guess she was teasing,
because we did eventually turn to the left, and we did find our way out, certainly
not lingering to explore the shelves of legal files—not realising, as George had
done with his father's files, what fascinating stories they might contain.

FIGURE 27
George William Hope Davies,
c. 1890

At boarding-school George had done well at boxing. My father told, with amusement, the story of when he was a small boy, going out walking with George. They were confronted by a group of hoodlums spoiling for a fight. "Stand aside son" said George to my father, raising his fists. He polished them off as my father stood and watched in amazement. I never quite got why that story amused my father so much, but it was central to his decision that both of his sons, John and Tony, would take boxing lessons when they went to boarding school—whether they liked it or not.

My first glimpse of George was on Andrew Barton's family tree website,[1] which enabled me to recognise him in this photo in the old family album that Dad had inherited. The photo is actually signed by him, though the ink is so faded it took me a long time to decipher it.

The love of George's life was Jean Carty (1885–1938). His family disapproved of her. She had grown up in East Orange and had been the first generation in her family to learn to read and write. *And* they were Roman Catholic. George's family with its romantic history of Welsh and Danish princes and its staunch Anglicanism (the religion, then, of the elite) could not imagine one of their own marrying into the Carty family. George was compelled to break off his

---

1   Andrew Barton is the son of Lynette Hibble, daughter of Tom's sister Severin.

FIGURE 28   Jean and George in the Talbot with Tom, sister Severin and Nanny, 1911 Kempsey.
             This photo was the gift of my cousin Helen Bathgate, daughter of Colin, Tom's
             brother

engagement. Jean went to Bourke to stay with her aunt and uncle—who was
the local blacksmith—and George followed her there in 1906 where he worked
in the court-house as Clerk of Petty Sessions. Bourke, known as the back of
beyond, was a place of red dust and sweltering heat.

Even though Alfred's stroke had left him speechless for the last decade of
his life, it was not until after he died, on 31 May 1908, that Jean and George
were free to marry. Jean was 23 and George was 38. They were wed on 4 July,
in the Church of England church in Bourke, five weeks after Alfred died, and
five weeks after their first baby, my father, to be named Thomas Alfred after his
grandfather, was conceived. He was born on 28 February 1909.

On the day of their wedding, George sent a telegram to each of his siblings:
"married Jean today". His brother, Llewellyn, was highly amused, knowing the
history of the broken engagement. He read the telegram as George having the
last laugh.

In 1909, after my father was born, George and Jean moved to Kempsey. Not
nearly as hot as Bourke, nor so dry and dusty, Kempsey was on the eastern sea-
board, 20 miles from the beach. The work of Clerks of Petty Sessions was highly
mobile, and each move, generally every 4 years, brought with it a raise in pay.
They stayed in Kempsey until 1913. Their second child, Severin, was born there

in 1911. In that same year, George bought his first car—perhaps indeed the first car ever seen in Kempsey. A car, in those days, was a miraculous and 'magical object' (Barthes, 1993: 88).

Like Toad of Toad Hall in *Wind in the Willows* (Grahame, 1908), who fell in love with the first car he ever saw, the first encounter with a car was, no doubt, for George, magical. There is a doubly magical element to this photo for me— the magic of this new machine that was to replace the horse and buggy, and, also, the glimpse of a moment in *placetime*, inside the life of this family.

Most of the public horse drawn coaches ceased operating in New South Wales in 1897 but it wasn't until 1917 that motor vehicles took their place. The very first cars in rural New South Wales made their appearance in 1904 (de St Hilaire Simmonds, 1999). The only way to get to Kempsey in 1911, when this photo was taken, was by boat or by horse drawn drays on the rough road between Kempsey and Armidale. Although there were some short roads north and south, the Pacific Highway linking Sydney and Brisbane only came in 1930, and rail did not arrive in Kempsey until 1915. The car thus potentially transformed Jean's and George's lives.

On the back the photo is inscribed, by Jean, "Tom as a toddler". That is a curious inscription, given the significance of the car itself as the subject of the photo. Instead of the car, or herself, or baby Severin in the back with the nanny, Tom was what Jean saw when she looked at the photo; Tom, the apple of her eye.

What is most startling for me about this photo, is that Jean could be me looking out from under that hat. Her expression is one I know well, of outward calm and deep inner trepidation. The photo reveals that George and Jean were sufficiently well off to employ a nanny and to have a car at a time when that was exceedingly rare. George was earning £250 a year, but cars at that time could cost much more than that, so the funds for the car most likely came from inherited money.[2]

---

2   George's mother, Maria Louisa, had inherited some money from George Salting in 1910, but she had died in 1906 and Alfred in 1908. Alfred's will left everything to his unmarried daughters. Since none of them was unmarried, the estate was divided among all the children, with Evan as executor taking a percentage. An extract from George Salting's will stated: "I give and bequeath unto the daughters of the late Mr. Elberling of Denmark nieces of my mother the sum of Ten thousand pounds to be divided equally amongst them and to my cousins Maria Davies, Catherine E. Fraser and Louisa Turner, the sum of Ten thousand pounds to be divided equally amongst them and further to my said cousin Mrs. C E Fraser the additional sum of Two thousand pounds". The will was approved 22 January 1910. As Maria Louisa had predeceased George Salting, dying in 1906, the money went to her estate and was divided amongst her children, including George.

George was sufficiently aware of the significance of the historical moment to go to the trouble of memorializing the journey with this photo as they set out from their home—perhaps for a visit to the seaside, or to visit distant relations.

George is in the driver's seat, with his firstborn son sitting up proudly beside him, and looking out at the photographer. On subsequent journeys, I imagine George sometimes sat young Tom up on his knee and let him take the steering wheel—an image so enduring for Tom, that I and my siblings each had a turn at sitting on his knee and steering his car over narrow winding dirt tracks, when he was on his way at the weekend to visit rural clients.

After baby Severin, came Colin in 1912. In 1914 the family moved south to Taree, a smaller town closer to the sea, where baby Llewellyn was born. His full name was Llewellyn Ford Hughes Davies. He was named Llewellyn after George's much-loved little brother, and Ford Hughes after the recluse back in Wales, who died that year, after having lost the Davies family fortune and disentailed what was left of it.

George and Jean, and the four children, lived in Taree for four years. The next move was to Cootamundra, a town quite close to Murrumburrah, and the farm of George's childhood. After Cootamundra they moved back to the outback, though not quite as far out as Bourke—this time to Dubbo, where they stayed for another four years. Their youngest daughter, Dorothy, my Aunty Doc, was born in Dubbo in 1922. In 1925, the family moved to Kogarah, in Sydney, for one year. That year was my Dad's only experience of the city. It was his final year of school, in which he sat for his Leaving Certificate exam at the selective high school Fort Street High. After Kogarah, in 1926, the family moved west, over the Great Dividing Range to Orange, where Jean had been born. That is where they finally settled down. There, Tom could work in a lawyer's office, and undertake his Articles, studying for his legal exams at night.

Jean's Past

Jean's history—or the absence of it—was a major force that had catapulted me into this project of exploring entangled ancestral tales. I had been teaching in Maynooth in 2011, and was spending a few days in Dublin before setting off on the next leg of my journey. Until that trip to Ireland I had never considered I might have Irish ancestors. But on that journey I felt a powerful connection to Ireland and to the Irish people, which took me by surprise and made me intensely aware of knowing nothing about my grandmother, Jean. In Ireland I had encountered a love of stories, and of the telling of stories that seemed

FIGURE 29   Jean, *c.* 1910

uncannily familiar. Though my father loved to tell tales of George, and of his Welsh ancestry, he spoke not one word about Jean. He didn't even tell us her name, though her name was a story in itself.

As a child, when I had been looking idly through the hundreds of unsorted photos in a large drawer in the oak sideboard in the dimly lit dining room, I was startled when I saw this photo of Jean.

She seemed so familiar and yet I had no idea who she was. "Who *is* this?" I asked my Mum. Looking around nervously, she told me to put it back, warning me I should be careful not to let Dad see it. Jean had died just before my parents' wedding, and Dad had not got over it, she said. Thirty years later, I asked my father why he never spoke about his mother. After a long silence, he said "I don't know", with a finality that declared the question closed. I later found out that she was Irish.

In that one photo of Jean that I had found, her face is turned away, averted even from the camera's gaze. She seems shy—a little embarrassed perhaps, but she is smiling. It's a gentle, perhaps even teasing expression. Her luxurious hair is beautifully coiffed.

On Andrew Barton's on-line family tree, Andrew, descended from my father's sister Severin, writes that Jean would never talk about her past with her daughter, Severin. The silence about Jean's history, then, had begun with Jean. In Chapter 10, I unravel some of this carefully guarded set of secrets. (Sorry, Jean!)

Jean died in 1938 of chronic dyspepsia and secondary anaemia at the age of 53. George was 68, and war was on the horizon. Two years later he had two new grandchildren, my sister Susanne and Severin's daughter, Lynette Hibble. His sons and nephews were of an age to enlist. The war occupied his thoughts, and he wrote his reflections on the war for a local newspaper; I include them in Appendix 1, along with a humorous short story that George had published. George's younger brother, Llewellyn, wrote to him, at that time, about all the things going wrong in his life over in Western Australia. He had arthritis so badly he could barely walk—and so much in his family was going terribly wrong. Llewellyn's daughter, Dorothy, wrote to me of her mother's terrible illness and the ravages of war on her brother Owen:

> 1941 was a very bad year for us, Mum was extremely ill, & wasn't expected to live, Owen had been severely wounded in Tobruk, Evan had died following on from a serious accident earlier in the year. Mum was still recovering in hospital when Owen arrived home on a hospital ship to be greeted with all that terrible news. I had been sent to an Aunt while they were thinking what to do with me should Mum not survive. However, Mum did survive & I returned home. One joy for us was the birth of the 1st grandchild. Owen, after 3 years in hospital gradually learnt to walk. He never regained the feeling in his legs and continued to suffer terrible phantom pain. He married and had 4 children.

Dorothy sent me the letter that George had written in reply. Reading that handwritten letter was extraordinary. I was holding the very paper he had held and written on, and I was reading the words his pen had formed on the page that told the thoughts running through his mind in response to his brother's tragic circumstances. He wrote his reflections on the war and his own children's engagement in it—and of their, and his, possible fates. The bombs were raining down on London; young men, born in Australia, were off to defend the mother country and to see the world that stretched beyond rural New South Wales.

Over the days of deciphering that almost indecipherable letter, I was carried back to the day he sat down to write to his brother, whom he hadn't seen since he had left for Western Australia as a young man, where he went after Alfred had had his stroke in 1898. It is a tender, funny, compassionate letter, weaving the threads of family together for his younger brother, thousands of miles away.

It was just 30 years since George had bought one of the first cars in the country, and he wrote of another possibility, of visiting Llewellyn by plane, flying across the thousands of miles of country that separated them. But the world was enmeshed in war; one of George's own sons, Llewellyn, had enlisted, and another, Colin, was planning to follow. His youngest daughter, Dorothy, was training to be a nurse—the first woman in the family to take up a profession. He reflected on life, old age and death, and on the war that enveloped all of them.

190 Summer St
Orange
20 2 41

Dear Llewellyn,
It certainly is stiff luck. There always is a fly in the ointment. But yours is more than a fly. It's catastrophe. As you suggest we are getting on in years, which is quite bad enough in itself without added 'inflictions'.

Well! Old Bird, repinings won't help. We all have to face the barrier sooner or later. When all is said and done, we both can say we have done our bit. Had a good time, more or less, brought up our families & what happens in the few years left is only of minor importance. Giving all that in, we like to do the final lap or two in comfort, and that's where it's 'tough' in your case.

Let's get on to something more cheerful. Dorothy landed in last week unheralded from Sydney all smiles. Passed her first nursing Xam and was given 3 weeks leave. So made a beeline for Orange. Is staying, but in the country with a girl friend.

Llewellyn my 3rd son, left by the Queen Mary about 3 weeks ago. And is now, so far as I know, somewhere in "Malaya". In amongst the malaria and tropical diseases generally. I don't think he will have much chance of doing any fighting unless the war in Europe takes a turn for the worse.

Unless and until Germany is winning the war, or Japan thinks she is. She (Japan) won't make any drive south. It is all German strategy to make us divert troops and ships from Europe —

Colin my 2nd son is down from Queensland and is at present staying with Tom at Tamworth. He talks about enlisting. Has 4 months leave.

Dorothy and her pal have fixed it all up. I am to drive them to Sydney on the 28th. Colin is to meet us in Sydney and drive me home on Sunday the 2nd. The alternative is that I am to pay Dorothy's fare back by train. The younger generation know their onions —I have *two* new grandkids, both girls, sponsored by Tom (5 months) and Severin Hibble (3 months). Tom's kid is to be christened "Susanne" & Severin's "Lynette", both very good specimens –

Tom's practice is still growing expects to top the fifteen hundred mark this year. Altho the new taxation will give him a nasty jolt. I asked Llewellyn if they called at Fremantle to look up Nelly,[3] but whether he got the chance or not I don't know. They dealt them out tropical uniforms & clipped all their heads, must have looked hard seeds. He takes a 7¼ hat so would be a bit conspicuous.

Now that there is a reliable air service to W.A. next year I may be able to slip over and see you all. But suppose everything will depend on the war. If the Germans win, it will be goodnight nurse. The Japs will annex this bit of the world. For me no pension no work. When we win, which may take some years, there is sure to be another depression. So don't build on seeing me too soon.

There will not be any chance at all of Pollie and Evan[4] paying you a visit. Talking to Pollie you'd come away wondering whether she would be able to finance another meal. She is the dizzy limit. Must be worth quite a wad of dough – Evan is still streaking around as lively as ever (76).

Llewellyn[5] had his photo taken in his military rigout. He only gave me one so I can't send it over. He is very like you in face and disposition, weighs about 11 stone, strong as a bus horse, good boxer and swimmer. Walks about on his hands and all that sort of thing.

The irony is that a bullet can sink him just as easily as a golon waster.

I am going to do my best to stop Colin going. His mental ability could be put to better use in the war effort than just plain cannon fodder.

I enclose some articles. I wrote an Australian short story, if published will send a copy. Love to Dorinda[6]

Fraternally yours

George

---

3 Helena, George's older sister.
4 George and Llewellyn's oldest brother.
5 George's youngest son, named after his younger brother.
6 Llewellyn's wife.

Colin went ahead, despite George's attempts to persuade him otherwise, and joined the AIF a month later. He was discharged on 14 December 1945, having spent more than four years as a soldier. Llewellyn was at the fall of Singapore. He had fought for less than two weeks before being packed into a boat and taken to a Japanese prisoner of war camp. He arrived home in 1945 weighing only six stone. Tom joined the Citizen Military Forces and was exempted from going to the war.

George's newspaper columns had the same authoritative tone that my father adopted when he was delivering his impromptu lectures in response to any question he was asked, and some of the same deep conservatism. George's columns reveal a passionate attachment to the mother country, an attachment that still runs deep, though not quite so taken-for-granted as it was then. They make for fascinating reading, revealing a social structure that places capitalism on the side of good, with its binary opposite characterised as the evil of unions and of communism. Safety, survival, principled living, decent people—all of these sit clearly, in his mind, on the side of capitalism.

My parents lived out that same binary logic, and they were horrified when I 'switched sides'. I hadn't dared to tell my parents of my commitment to Labor values and union action; but my six-year old son let the cat out of the bag, joyfully announcing the Labor victory when we arrived on their doorstep. "Gough got in!" he had said, smiling happily. I had neglected to tell him that what was joyful news of a Labor victory at home, in Armidale, would be unmentionable in the conservative home of his grandparents. His happy greeting was met with a shocked and hostile silence. So successfully had our family ancestry been expunged of its strands of poverty and hardship, that I grew up as a cuckoo in the wrong nest, with my, apparently, deeply alien sympathies and commitments. I was the first in my family to go to university, and I experienced something of the same gap Jean must have felt when she was among the first in her family to go to school.

The final piece George sent his brother was a humorous short story that suggests that the light-hearted fun-loving George that Llewellyn remembered was still alive and well, despite Jean's death, and despite his pessimism about the war. There are moments too in the columns that are tongue in cheek, making fun of his own prognostications by tying them to the ancient prophets. His newspaper columns and short story are included as Appendices 1 and 2.

Jean and George are buried together in the Church of England section of the Organge cemetery, right next to the Jewish section. Their shared grave is under some ghost gums in a peaceful bushland setting. There is one headstone which reads:

FIGURE 30   Jean and George's headstone
PHOTO BY HELEN BATHGATE

REMEMBRANCE
Elizabeth M. Davies
Died 13th July, 1938
George William H. Davies
Died 27th June, 1946

George died when the war was finally over, and so joined his beloved Jean. The shared grave and shared headstone make a vivid statement, written in stone, of their commitment to each other. I will come back to Jean's name in Chapter 10.

And so I leave George and Jean, for now, and turn to my father, Thomas Alfred Davies, known as Tom.

CHAPTER 5

Thomas Alfred Davies (Tom)

The love-child of Jean and George, Tom, was born on 28 February 1909. One day shy of 29 February, he would tell us, though actually 1909 was not a leap year. The stories of his birth never included the broken engagement, the family disapproval, his grandfather's stroke, or his conception out of wedlock. Instead we were regaled with the imagined near miss, which would have meant that he only had a birthday every four years.

If there had been good fairies at Tom's christening, they would have granted him beauty, cleverness, wit, determination and a strong heart. The wicked fairy countered that with contained rage. Tom's godmother was his Aunt Severin Campbell, the daughter of William Campbell who we will meet again in Chapter 8. She was a primary school teacher.

Severin loved to regale her godson with the fascinating legend of his grandmother's royal Danish ancestry, and the adoption of the Danish prince's child by the Campbell family. Young Tom embraced that story as the truth of his father's origins along with his story of being descended from the fourth son of the King of all Wales. These stories of royalty set him apart from the other boys growing up in the bush.

George and Jean believed, as had Alfred and Maria Louisa, in a great deal of freedom and autonomy for their children. They should be free to roam the countryside and to explore, and to learn from whatever adventures—and misadventures—came their way. They offered their children discipline leavened with humour, freedom marked by major challenges, and adventures in the wild, scored by very real dangers. One of the dangers young Tom witnessed in those wild childhood days, happened when they had just moved to Cootamundra. There had been three days of solid rain. Tom and his little brothers, Colin and Llewellyn, made their way down through the scrub, thick with newly blossoming wild flowers, to see what the flooded river looked like.

Some local boys had tied a long rope to the branch of an old River Red Gum that leaned out over the river. The parrots and lorikeets screeched and clamoured – bright smatterings of red and green in the cool, dappled shadows of the giant trees. The boys were egging each other on to see who could swing out furthest into the river. With each pendulum swing, the boys below would push harder, and the boy on the rope would swing further, and higher, until finally, on the peak of a high arc, he would let go, and fly, limbs spreadeagled, into the turbulent water below. The swim to shore was urgent and electrifying, as the swift current carried each boy downriver. As each one made it to the river bank and climbed out, there were raucous cheers from his mates.

Then, one more wild leap out into the saturated blue of the sky, a boy plummeting down into the shadowy brown water—and suddenly the world was shattered with a piercing scream. The flood had tumbled trees and branches and rocks down the river, and the unlucky daredevil had landed on a jagged branch just below the surface. Blood rose slowly to mix with the surface slick of the river as the boy alternately yelled and gasped for breath, then sank beneath the surface. Boys ran upstream and dived in to see if they could catch him and carry him to shore. Others ran for help—to the doctor, to the parents, yelling blue murder.

Tom and his little brothers, newcomers to the town, stood rooted to the spot as the drama unfolded. A fraction of an inch difference, the adults said, and he would have lost his testicles. He could have severed an artery. He could have been killed. He was a very lucky boy. The image of the wild exhilarating flight through the air and the plunge into the cold murky depths lodged an icicle of fear into young Tom's heart, as he contemplated what might have happened if it had been him. It was a story he went on telling for years afterward, and it never lost its horror for him. He never lost his intense fear of heights born on that day.

Tom was a clever boy, and on his second day of school, in February 1914, he lined up in the first-grade line, instead of the kindergarten line where he had been placed the day before. When his teacher kindly pointed out to him that he was in the wrong line, he held up his first-grade primer and told her, in a voice tinged with fierce pride, that he could read it. And so he got to start school a year early. That was in the small town of Taree. The kids in Tom's class were a year older than he was, and he was determined to be the best.

Later that year, on 4 August, Tom went out to collect the newspaper from the front lawn. The headlines announced that Britain had declared war on Germany. Australia was at war. He stared at those words, afraid of them, and at the same time, proud in his childish heart that he could read them. George did not have to go to war, as his job as Clerk of Petty Sessions counted as an essential service—the law-breakers would still, after all, need to be dealt with.

During that same year, Tom's youngest brother had been born, and named Llewellyn Ford Hughes Davies; Llewellyn after George's younger brother, and Ford Hughes after the great uncle in Wales – the one who held the family fortune entailed to the first son of the first son—which meant it should eventually have come to Tom, as his Uncle Evan had no sons.

Thomas Hughes Ford Hughes had changed his surname from Davies to Hughes in order to receive an inheritance from his maternal aunt. He died in Wales on 8 March 1914. He had once been a talented and successful young

FIGURE 31
Taree Public School
PHOTO BY JODY THOMSON

man, but in his 30s he became a recluse, and at the same time accrued vast amounts of property—and mortgages—the prize property being the original Nant Gwylan, which had been sold out from under his cousin's feet, to 'foreigners'. The Davies fortune was no longer tied to the succession of oldest sons. When Thomas died, his estate went to his sister Ellen, who outlived him only briefly, leaving what remained of the fortune to her cousin Emma White, Alfred Davies' sister. An early feminist coup of sorts initiated by Ann Hughes. The newspaper report of Thomas's death read thus:

Landowner's Death in the Workhouse(1914)[1]
Eccentric Recluse leaves £74,000[2]
Mr Thomas Ford Hughes, who died in the Carmarthen Workhouse on March 8, has left estate worth £74,000, and letters of administration have been granted to his sister, Miss Ellen Lloyd Davies of Carmarthen.

---

1   A workhouse was an institution where able-bodied paupers were kept, doing unpaid work in return for food and somewhere to sleep
2   The current day purchasing power of £74,000 is £6.5 million, while its economic power is calculated as £56.5 million. (Lawrence H. Officer and Samuel H. Williamson, 2017)

For many years, Mr Hughes had lived the life of a recluse in a cottage in Carmarthen which no one was allowed to enter. When he became seriously ill, he still refused all help and on March 2 last, the authorities made a forcible entry and removed him to the workhouse.

Mr Ford Hughes owned the Aberceri and Nant Gwylan estates in Cardiganshire as well as land in Pembrokeshire. He was born in 1840 and his original name was Davies, but he adopted that of Hughes by deed poll on succeeding to the estate of his maternal uncle.[3]

He lived a normal life until he was about thirty years old but then for some unknown reason he became addicted to solitude. He took a cottage in Carmarthen and when he visited his mansions he would hire a carriage and travel at night. After a time, he gave up even these visits and he never left the Carmarthen cottage after 1887.

For years no one visited his house except a barber, and when the barber died, Mr Hughes allowed his hair and beard to grow. His meals were sent in from hotels but nobody got further than the door.

The grimy windows of the house were familiar to the Carmarthen people for nearly thirty years. The town council often discussed the possibility of the sanitary inspector procuring a warrant to enter but no action was taken as no nuisance could be proved. Two years ago there was a fire at the cottage and persons who saw the interior declare that ashes had accumulated in piles around the fire and that newspapers and books were stacked to the ceiling.

When the authorities entered on March 2, the door of the bedroom had to be pushed back inch by inch as the ashes and rubbish were shovelled out.

And so the holder of the family fortune, Thomas Hughes Ford Hughes, lived in the workhouse for a week before he died, and his fortune, once the mortgages on the crumbling, neglected estates were settled, had substantially dwindled.

Great Uncle Llewellyn, George's younger brother, had visited Thomas Hughes Ford Hughes before he died. His daughter, Dorothy Parkinson, recalls his account of that visit:

Thomas welcomed him in to his apartment, which in itself was amazing, as only a very select few were allowed past the doorstep. The place was piled high with newspapers & books, on his desk were piles of cheques

---

3   He was born in July 1845 and his sister Ellen in 1843.

from his tenants, which he never banked, as long as they paid their rent he was happy not to cash them, which was either foolish or generous to his tenants; had he banked them he may not have ended up with a lot of heavily mortgaged properties. He hired a coach & took Dad to see all his estates including the one that had belonged to his Mother, which for some reason had to be sold (I think that is where the "Foreigner" bit comes in). There must have been a strong emotional tie to his Mother as he was determined to buy it back. When he did, he restored it to its former glory along with all the furnishings including a grand piano. Then locked the door. Once again amazingly he took Dad inside, Dad was totally taken aback. It had been shut up for years, and one can only imagine the state of decay. His other houses had caretakers living in them, but for this one he only had someone to care for the gardens.

Thomas's sister Ellen, visited him, I believe fortnightly, but she was unable to enlighten Dad as to why, other than that he chose to be alone, and that was his choice ...

Dad thought he was very happy with his lot although decidedly Odd. He gave Dad a warm invitation to visit again should he ever return to England.

In another version of this story the grand piano could not fit in through the door and so was left in the garden to rot. Thomas Hughes Ford Hughes told Llewellyn he would inherit money from the estate. His sister Ellen inherited what was left of Thomas's fortune, and she made a will in Llewellyn's favour, but was unable to sign it, being too ill. Llewellyn went again to Wales, to get to the bottom of what had happened to the inheritance, but there was nothing to be done. In contrast to the earlier welcome, the Welsh extended family no longer wanted to know him.

This was not a story Tom chose to pass on to his children. Like his own conception out of wedlock, this story of the mad uncle and his lost inheritance was not to be part of the stories he would choose to tell.

Tom was nine years old by the time the great war ended, and the family had moved yet again, this time to Dubbo. Tom was shy and a little socially awkward, though he was clever at school and good at sport. Dirty jokes and ditties were a good way to gain acceptance among the boys. Inside the family he was confident and cared for, and he loved his father's endless stream of bush lore, picked up in the court-houses in Bourke and Dubbo and Taree, and later in Kempsey and Cootamundra. In his later life he loved to tell such stories of men who were barmy coots, who'd shot through before the law could catch up with them; there were battlers and bible bashers and bludgers; there were drongos and galahs and silly galoots who had buckleys of saving their skins in court, or of earning an honest crust; there were those who steered away from hard yakka with no intention of bursting their poofoo valves for any bullying autocratic squire; and, blow me down, there was a lucky blighter, whose case was all baloney, but his brief who knew a thing or two — told him to wear his best bib and tucker, and with a few smart arguments saved him from the klink. Getting up early in the morning was to get up at sparrow-fart, and when your time was up, you kicked the bucket.

George and his family took delight in contemporary bush writers like Henry Lawson and Banjo Patterson, and together the family immersed themselves in that folklore. On Sundays, when everyone else went to church, they drove in their magnificent car to iconic bush landmarks like the statue of the dog on the tucker box at Gundagai, or the Jenolan Caves.

Although attendance at elite boarding schools had become a significant marker of social worth, Jean and George kept their family tight around them, not risking trouble with the priests by sending their boys to Anglican schools. They sent the boys fruit-picking in the holidays to learn the benefit of hard labour, as well as to learn to mix with others in their local communities.

For his final year of school his family moved to Kogarah in Sydney. He and Colin went to Fort Street High School, a selective public school. According to the Fort Street High website:

> As the oldest selective high school Fort Street has a unique place in history of the State of NSW, having educated and nurtured some of the most prominent and influential citizens in Australia. Fort Street is acknowledged as epitomising and espousing the following: academic excellence, individualism, multiculturalism, tolerance, social and political awareness and responsibility, the liberal tradition of a broad based education and educational philosophy, and a strong sense of tradition, embodied in the saying, Once a Fortian, always a Fortian. (http://www.fortstreet.nsw.edu .au/School/History/)

The subjects Tom had been studying in Dubbo were different from the subjects he must now enrol in for his final year. As he travelled by train each day from Kogarah to Petersham, he swotted up on all the fourth year work he had missed. It was a stressful year, but one that he was proud of—two years of work in one, and he had succeeded. Fort Street's status, he would tell us, was equivalent to that of the elite private schools insofar as it guaranteed access to the upper echelons of the colony. After the year at Kogarah the family moved to

FIGURE 32   Tom aged 18, 1927

Orange, where Tom worked as an articled clerk, doing office work by day and studying by night.

This beautiful photo of Tom (*above*) was taken in Orange. He is focussed and he gazes intently at something to the left of the photographer, but his gaze also seems inward, almost mesmerised, as if gathering all his inward strength, so he is totally contained. He is stable, enduring; he knows his place in the world— or will make his place in the world. There is at the same time a softness about him. He has been well cared for. He is well-groomed.

Twelve years later, after finishing his articles and moving to Tamworth where he set up his own legal practice, he was married to Norma Blomfield— that bright-eyed laughing girl from the bush, with her virginal halo hat and her elegant lace dress.

I've had this next photo blown up from a tiny black and white snap. Tom and Norma and baby Susanne are on holiday at Manly. Tom's smile is a burst of sun-shine. He is secure and loved and surrounded by family. George is there, and sister Sev, as well as his godmother, Aunt Severin Campbell. His law practice is thriving, and though his Mum has gone, and the war is on, he is safe, holding his baby and smiling at Norma holding the camera.

When I look at this photo, I feel desperately sorry for all the unhappiness that was to come.

FIGURE 33   Tom with baby Susanne, 1940

In the photos of him holding me as a baby, four years later, on the day of my christening, he holds me away from him, but looks at me and laughs with me—we both laugh.

In a second photo with me, he turns to look at Norma with an expression of pride—as if to say look at what we have produced! But his forehead is lined, and the pure joy of the earlier photo with baby Suzanne is gone. There is a question, a vulnerability in that look toward Norma—something unresolved between them.

And yes, two years earlier, Tom had a fling with one of Norma's friends who lived across the road. Norma was staying with her mother, having a holiday after the birth of baby Tony. When Tom started to tell her what had happened, she had said "Stop! What I don't know won't hurt me". But something new was now present. Hidden. Yet another secret not to be spoken about. In public and with her siblings and Dad's siblings she was still the romantic, bright-eyed, laughing girl.

In the years that followed, Tom bought Norma a mansion to live in, with her own car and a full-time maid, and later a holiday house at the beach and each child sent to a prestigious boarding school in Sydney. But it was never enough—what about the overseas trips he had promised, she would ask. Tom buried himself in work to keep all the mortgages and school fees paid. He was often absent. After work he would go to the Men's Club. He was not the prince in shining armour that she longed for—no longer the young man with a smile that lit up the universe.

As I think now about my father, all these years later, I remember a man who was tightly controlled and afraid of chaos—of falling or drowning. When we

FIGURE 34A-B
Tom and Bronwyn, 1945

drove over the mountains to the beach, we (that is, we kids and our Mum) loved to stop and look at Ebor Falls, one of the highest waterfalls in the state, but Tom couldn't bear to go anywhere near it. Seeing us look over the waterfall made him sick. Even seeing us go close to the edge of the veranda at home was stressful. And if we came to a flooded creek, when driving to our seaside holidays, he would simply stop the car. Norma would goad him into driving through by getting out of the car and walking into the flooding water. She would test how deep it was, and if she could walk through it, he could drive through it she said—and so he had to, with four children sitting in the back. The tension in his body along with the smell of cigarettes, and the dust of the unsealed roads, made me acutely, perpetually, car-sick.

Tom was respected in his community—generous to the poor, mixing with elite men at the Club, playing snooker, exchanging vital information, along with jokes. The men at the Club laughed together, and they established the nature of the world together—with wives at home and in their place, and children who should be seen and not heard. On coming home from the Club, he exercised extreme discipline at the dinner table. He closely monitored how his children ate and spoke. We could not begin eating until everyone was seated. At that point we unfurled our linen serviettes and placed them on our laps. The salt and pepper were passed around. Even so, throughout the meal you must pay attention to what others might need at the table, offering the salt and pepper or butter or jam to anyone who might need them. If anyone had to ask you for anything to be passed to them, it meant you had failed in your duty to pay attention to others' needs. If you wanted anything yourself that was out of reach you may ask for it to be passed to you, but better still be silent, as asking was to rudely draw attention to the other's failure to notice that you might need it. Further, we must follow my father's example of putting a little of everything onto the fork, not too much, just a little of everything, using the knife to add a little salt from the neat pile on the side of the plate, then lean forward slightly, over the plate, keeping your back straight, and move the loaded fork tidily to your mouth. You must chew each mouthful thirty times, with your mouth, of course, closed. The entire meal must be consumed in this way. You must not cut up the meat, American style, and lay your knife down and move your fork to your right hand. You most certainly did not hold your knife like a pencil. At the end, to signal that you were finished, your knife and fork must be placed together, side by side on your plate vertical to the table's edge with the handles balanced over the lip of the plate. You wiped your mouth, delicately, with your fine linen serviette, which rested on your lap, and when everyone was finished you rolled your serviette neatly and replaced it in your silver serviette ring beside your plate. There would be no food spilled in your lap or wiped off with your hand, and there would be no food left on your plate at the end of the meal. At the same time, when Tony nervously jiggled his knee so that all the cutlery on the table rattled, it was understood that no mention should be made of that sound, and that Tony should not be asked to stop.

Once, when he wasn't looking I snuck out to the kitchen, with the thick fat from the loin chops still on my plate, and scraped the fat into the garbage bin. When I returned to the table without my plate, Dad made me go and get the fat back out of the bin and eat it. My only consolation was that I left some of the fat in the bin and he didn't notice.

Sometimes, though not often, Tom could be extremely funny. He once put a piping hot forkful of steak and kidney pie into his mouth, and immediately dropped it back out onto the plate, exclaiming "some bloody fool would have swallowed that!" That still makes me laugh.

There was never to be any argument at the dinner table, and certainly no speaking with a mouth full of food. As children, we were sometimes allowed to speak, and if we were particularly witty or wise my father would remark humorously 'out of the mouths of babes and sucklings'. But mostly it was my father who spoke, or there was silence. We learned not to ask questions, as his answers were long-winded and ponderous with many long pauses that could not on any account be interrupted. Debate was not possible under his rules, as that would count as interruption. It was at the table that we learned that, according to the laws of physics, men would never be able to fly to the moon, and that there could never be a Catholic Prime Minister, though in fact there had already been several. For him, the Church of England Church was more a matter of class than of religion, and it was only from the upper classes, he believed, that a Prime Minister might emerge. He believed one of his sons would be a Prime Minister.

Over the years Tom's containment became encrusted and solidified. His anger over my mother's perceived frigidity had a very tight lid on it. After all, in those days, men were legally entitled to claim their "conjugal rights". But men of character could not, in his view, resort to violence. When I was a Psychology student I practiced doing the Rorschach test on him. For each ink blot, he would say 'nope' or 'nothing' until right near the end he saw two sides of a chasm screaming at each other. The sides of the chasm were inert rock. The scream nevertheless erupted from both sides, and echoed in the empty space in between. It was a terrifying image of suppressed rage.

That suppressed rage and his disappointment with Mum translated into a serious misreading of the violence in my marriage. He thought I brought it on myself, as I was like my mother. But Larry's violence had nothing to do with sex, and at the age of 29 he killed himself in his car, on a lonely dirt road on the outskirts of the city where he had spent years in prison. I was a widow at 25, penniless, with three small children, and no support from my parents.

Dad's outbursts throughout his life were rare. The two sides of his chasm generally remained silent, and he soothed himself more and more often, as he grew older, with alcohol. Only in the extremes of his later alcoholism, which set in after he retired from his legal firm, did he develop the chutzpah that allowed him to say and do some of the things he'd only dreamed of earlier. One afternoon when Mum had invited friends over to play bridge, for example, he came into the room buck naked and asked if any of them wanted to give him a blow job. I'm afraid I find that story extremely funny, though I'm sure Mum and her bridge friends did not.

Apart from those bouts of alcoholism, about which he remembered nothing, everything about his body, as I remember it, was to do with containment—until finally his heart burst, on 31 October 1991.

There is a lot I have cut out of this chapter, deciding there is nothing to be gained in telling it. At the same time, I've shed quite a few tears for my father while writing about his life. I feel as though some tightness in my heart has unfurled in the writing. I am so sorry for his unfulfilled hopes, his grief, his anger, and above all, for the loss of that radiant happiness in the early days of his marriage. I spent a lot of years being angry with my Dad. I gave up on that anger when I turned 40. Now, in writing this, I've softened toward him much further. Writing about his life, and tracing the threads between my life and his, and between our lives and the lives of George and Alfred and Norma, I've begun to make sense for myself of those lives, entangled as they are in each other, and in the specificity of their places and times and social groupings. Those lives appear to me, now, as lives that are not mine to judge, but mine to be open to in their difference, in their varying, stuttering attempts to make what would count as a worthy life.

PART 2

Of Princes, Paupers and Soldiers: Stories of My Father's Family

∴

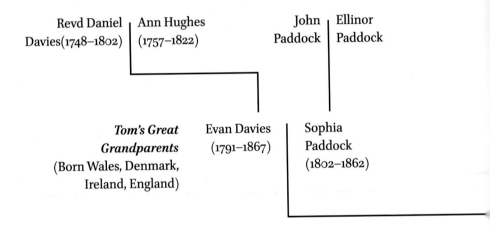

Tom's Great Great Grandparents
(Born Wales, Denmark, Spain)

Revd Daniel Davies(1748–1802) | Ann Hughes (1757–1822)

John Paddock | Ellinor Paddock

Tom's Great Grandparents
(Born Wales, Denmark, Ireland, England)

Evan Davies (1791–1867)

Sophia Paddock (1802–1862)

Tom's Grandparents
(Born Isle of Jersey, India, Ireland and England)

Tom's Parents
(Born at sea and in New South Wales)

FIGURE 35   Family tree of Thomas Alfred Davies

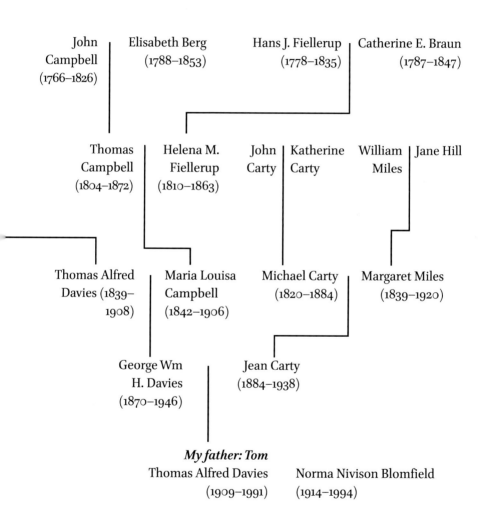

John Campbell (1766–1826)

Elisabeth Berg (1788–1853)

Hans J. Fiellerup (1778–1835)

Catherine E. Braun (1787–1847)

Thomas Campbell (1804–1872)

Helena M. Fiellerup (1810–1863)

John Carty

Katherine Carty

William Miles

Jane Hill

Thomas Alfred Davies (1839–1908)

Maria Louisa Campbell (1842–1906)

Michael Carty (1820–1884)

Margaret Miles (1839–1920)

George Wm H. Davies (1870–1946)

Jean Carty (1884–1938)

My father: Tom
Thomas Alfred Davies (1909–1991)

Norma Nivison Blomfield (1914–1994)

CHAPTER 6

Rodri Mawr, King of All Wales

The stories Tom most often told about his ancestors, as he sat with his family around the round oak dining table, were romantic tales of kings and princes. We were descended, he would tell us, from the fourth son of the King of all Wales. There were no details to this story, as to who the king was, or who the fourth son was, or when the king had ruled a united Welsh kingdom. I liked that story, even so. I was attached to the idea of being Welsh, because of my

FIGURE 36   The church at Troedyraur in North Wales, where members of Tom's family are buried
PHOTO FROM HELEN BATHGATE'S COLLECTION

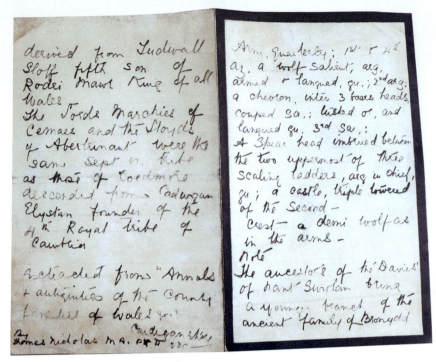

FIGURE 37   Genealogical memorandum

name. When I visited Wales several decades ago, I was greeted by the locals as someone who looked self-evidently Welsh. When I mentioned my father's story about the fourth son of the king of all Wales, however, hoping to get some clue about which king it might have been, I was told, with a laugh, that there never had been a king of all Wales—there had only ever been warring princes.

That was before the days of Google. So I put the story to one side as a mythical story. Tom was after all a teller of tall tales, though I had not heard this one as a tall tale when he told it.

Another fragment of the Welsh story was the importance of Nant Gwylan, the family home in Troedyraur, Wales—lost to the family, regained by Thomas Hughes Ford Hughes, then left to go to rack and ruin when he retreated into his life as a recluse and a hoarder (see Chapter 5). The Davies descendants who came to the colony called their homes 'Nant Gwylan'. We were the exception. Since *nant gwylan* meant 'home of the seagulls,' my mother would scoff, we could not name our house on the Liverpool plains, far inland and west of the Great Dividing Range, 'Nant Gwylan'.

The original Nant Gwylan is close to St George's Channel off the west coast of Wales. It is in approximately the same latitude as Cork in Ireland and Cambridge in England—almost exactly halfway between them. It could very easily be a place of seagulls. The Welsh *nant*, according to Google translate, means stream or brook, and *gwylan* means gull or seagull, but also, curiously, vagina—or birthplace.

Among the few documents that I found in my father's desk when he died, was a hand-written genealogical memorandum on a scrap of folded, black-edged paper, yellowed with age. It describes the family's coat of arms, and it names the king of Tom's story, and his son, though calling him the fifth, rather than the fourth:

> The ancestors of the Davies of Nant Gwylan bring a younger branch of the ancient family of Bronydd derived from Tudwall Gloff fifth son of Rodri Mawr King of all Wales... Extracted from "Annals & antiquities of the County families of Wales ( ) Cardiganshire" By Thomas Nicholas M.A.

Such tracing back of families through long lineages held enormous significance in the days when land ownership and political and legal privilege were closely tied to such lineages. I don't know who commissioned this research from Thomas Nicholas's Annals. Written before typewriters were readily available in the late 1800s it was probably commissioned by Tom's grandfather, Alfred, or perhaps his great grandfather, Evan Davies.

Many have assumed I would attempt to track my begats back to Tudwall Gloff. Apart from finding such research unbearably tedious and time-consuming, I can't actually see the point of it. My interest is in the fact that it exists as a family story. There is no class or financial significance, any longer, in being descended from kings. It is no more than a romantic family story, which might serve as a means of consolidating the bodily sense of rightful belonging among the rural elite of the colony.

I did often wonder when Dad told that story why it was the fourth son we were descended from, rather than his father.

Rodri Mawr (Rodri the Great) was the son of Merfyn Frych, King of Gwynedd. It was the marriage between Rodri and Angharad, daughter of Meurig, Queen of South Wales that created a united Welsh nation. From his father's death in 844 Rodri ruled over a realm stretching from Anglesey in the north, to the Gower peninsula in the south. He was a renowned warrior, famous for defeating an invading force of Danes at Anglesey in 856. The English were also a sporadic threat, invading and occupying Welsh land as early as 822. In 877 the two leaders, Rodri Mawr of Wales and Alfred the Great, King of Wessex, clashed, and Rodri and his youngest son Gwriad, then aged 10, were killed.

In Thomas Nicholas's Annals, Tudwall Gloff is the fifth son, rather than the fourth. Some sources cite him as fourth son and sometimes he is the fifth. His older siblings were Anarawd (b. 857), Merfyn (b. 859) and Cadell (b. 861). Tudwall was born in 863 in Caer Seiont, Carnarvonshire. The birth date of Aeddan is uncertain. Where it is assumed Aeddan was born in 862, Tudwall becomes the fifth son rather than the fourth. The pattern of births of his sons every two years suggests that Aeddan was born in 865, and the sixth son, Gwriad, in 867. In which case, our Tudwall was the fourth son of Rodri Mawr. However, some sources suggest that Queen Angharad was not his mother, that he was illegitimate, and that the other sons were his half-brothers. That would make sense of the story passed down emphasising descent from Tudwall Gloff, rather than Rodri Mawr.

United Wales lasted only for 33 years. After Rodri's death, his sons fought among themselves over the lands they inherited from him. Anarawd had become King of Gwynedd, Merfyn King of Powys and Cadell King of Ceredigion. Cadell killed his brother Merfyn, in an attempt to claim Powys. Tudwall, 14 years old at the time of his father's death, did not, it seems inherit land or title, perhaps because he was not a legitimate son. Three years after Rodri Mawr's death, Tudwall was wounded in a battle waged by his brother Anarawd against the invading English King of Mercia. His subsequent lameness, which gave him the name Tudwall Gloff (or Tudwall the Lame), disqualified him, under Welsh customary law—the *Cyfraith Hywel*—from ruling any territories.
Tudwall married Elen verch Aleth and their children were Alser and Arglwydd.

The story of romance and lineage that Tom evoked each time he repeated his story, would have been much more interesting if we had known those details, which the skin of time had grown over, smoothing and erasing the detail. The loss of Nant Gwylan and its re-purchase by Thomas Hughes Ford Hughes who then descended into isolation and madness takes on a new significance when linked to this story of its link to Tudwall Gloff.

We learned to revere Tom's Welsh grandfather, Alfred. Alfred's sword, his invitations to dine with the elite in India, his will, his retirement papers, and the memo about Rodri Mawr, were among my father's few treasured possessions, though Alfred died the year before my father was born. Alfred was born and grew up on the Isle of Jersey, where his father Evan had retired on half pay.

Evan was born in Wales in 1791 when Nant Gwylan was still safely in the hands of the Davies family. He was the son of the Revd Daniel Davies and Ann Hughes of Nant Gwylan, Troedyraur, in Wales.[1] Evan's wife, Sophia, looked very different from the Davies women—more like a Spanish gypsy, with her hooded eyes, high cheek bones and flower bedecked hair.

She was Sophia Paddock, from Antigua in the West Indies. Sophia's father, John Paddock, was a British ship's surgeon, and her mother, Ellinor, was of

---

1   It was Ann Hughes who left her estate to her nephew Thomas Hughes Ford Hughes instead of her own children.

FIGURE 38   Sophia Paddock, *c.* 1828   FIGURE 39   Evan Davies, *c.* 1850
            PHOTO FROM DAVIES   PHOTO FROM VENETIA
            FAMILY ALBUM   MCMAHON'S COLLECTION

Spanish/English descent. Sophia's family lived in St Helier on the Isle of Jersey, and had a house in St Malo, 12 miles across the Channel, in France. Sophia had been born in the West Indies in 1802. She married Evan Davies, then a naval surgeon, in 1828. Evan was 37 at the time of their marriage, and Sophia 26:

> British Embassy – Paris
>
> I hereby certify that Evan Davies, of Troedyraur in the County of Cardigan, in South Wales, Bachelor, and Sophia Paddock, of the Island of Antigua in the West Indies, Spinster, were married in the House of His Excellency the British Ambassador, the eighteenth day of March, in the Year One thousand eight hundred & twenty eight,
>
> By me N. H. Luscombe – Bishop
> Chaplain to the British Embassy at the Court of France
> Paris Augt 26-1828

The photo (above), taken much later, presents Evan as a serious man with a steady gaze, holding a book he appears to be in the throes of reading. It is a common complaint of these early photos that they make their subjects look too serious—not animated as they are in everyday life; but when I look at Evan's fantastically intricate comb-over, I catch, at the same time, the faintest of smiles lurking about his mouth and eyes.

Evan was the seventh child of the Revd Daniel Davies. He was the only one of the children to leave Wales, to become a ship's surgeon. When Evan's father died in 1801 his oldest son inherited Nant Gwylan. When he married Sophia in 1828 he settled in St Helier on the Island of Jersey.

Madeline Few, daughter on my great uncle Llewellyn writes that "Jersey, the largest of the Channel Islands, was just 12 nautical miles off the coast of France and had become, like France, a popular place for many Englishmen who found themselves on reduced incomes ... By 1840 no less than 5,000 British migrants were living on Jersey, mostly half-pay officers and their families" (Few, unpublished notes).

Evan regarded Wales as home. He and Sophia lived in St Helier where Sophia's family also lived, and where Alfred and his siblings were born. Their children were Evan John Edmund (1830–1853), Sophie Eleanor (1830–1831), Emma Frances (1832-1932), William (1834–1854) and Thomas Alfred, known as Alfred, my great grandfather, born in 1839. It was Alfred's sister Emma Frances, who inherited the remnants of Thomas Hughes Ford Hughes' fortune, though if it had still been entailed it would have come to Evan, and thence to Alfred, and then to my father (George's older brothers having no sons).

CHAPTER 7

Danish Princes and Princesses

Tom loved to tell the story of the Danish Prince who had secretly married a Lady-in-Waiting. It was a morganatic marriage—that is, a marriage between a person of higher rank and lower rank, where the low-ranking spouse cannot be elevated to higher rank through the marriage, and the off-spring cannot inherit property or title. The prince was obliged, so the story went, to divorce his wife and marry his cousin. Their child, Thomas, my father's great grandfather, had been adopted by the Campbell family, becoming Thomas Campbell (1804–1872).

There are websites that claim Elise Ahlefeldt Laurvig was the wife of this secret morganatic marriage to Prince Christian, but the Danish Royal Archives and historians say there is no evidence of a morganatic marriage to Elise or to anyone else. And no evidence can be found to support the family story. Madeline Few, daughter of my great Uncle Llewellyn, says that Thomas was born in November 1804 at Kronborg castle and adopted by John Campbell and his wife Elisabeth Berg.

The Berg family had an Inn at the market town of Lyngbye, which was close to Sorgenfrie Castle, the royal family's summer residence, which was at one time dedicated to illicit trysts. John Campbell, the adoptive father, a Scot, spoke and wrote fluent Danish, and his wife, Elisabeth, was Danish. He was later to become the Danish Consul in London. One plausible theory is that it was Elisabeth's sister who was the Lady-in-Waiting and the mother of Thomas. My attempts to find documentation to show that one of the Berg daughters had been a Lady-in-Waiting at the time, met with the same implacable resistance as every other query I or my cousins had made about Thomas Campbell.

When they adopted Thomas, John and Elisabeth Campbell already had two of their own children, Philip and Robert. Following the adoption of Thomas, Julia, Louisa, and Augustus were born. The details of the births of each of their biological children are registered in England, except for Louisa's. No record of Thomas's birth can be found—or has been released. Was Louisa's birth certificate buried for the same reason as Thomas's, I wonder?

According to the Danish Archives, when Madeline Few enquired, they could find no link to John Campbell or Elisabeth Berg in their biographical sources. The Danish archivist mentioned, in response to her query about John Campbell:

© BRONWYN DAVIES, 2021 | DOI:10.1163/9789004446717_007

... in 1816 John Campbell was acting Consul after Consul General Hornemann had been discharged following his bankruptsy. In Feb. 1821 Campbell applied for his own position as Royal Consul in London (refce. Dept.f. udensrigske Angliggender, England, ph 18.). He held this appointment until his death in 1826. Finally we can mention that Campbell's reports to Kommercekollegiets – of Konsulatsfag were written in faultless Danish – contrary to the reports from other Consuls. (Few, unpublished)

Thomas Campbell's descendants have nevertheless hung on to the story, and have elaborated it. George Salting, Thomas Campbell's nephew, reputedly in love with Maria Louisa, Thomas Campbell's daughter, attended a function at which Queen Alexandra of Britain (and Princess of Denmark) was present, and he remarked on the extraordinary likeness between Maria Louisa and Queen Alexandra, which, he observed, was not surprising since they were sort of cousins.

Owen Davies, son of my great uncle Llewellyn, was the great-grandson of Thomas Campbell. He had an uncanny resemblance to George VI of England—the grandson of Queen Alexandra. This story was told in a letter by Merthyr Davies to, Helen Bathgate in 2005:

> I must tell you too about the story of my brother Owen when he was about to embark overseas with the 2nd 28th Battalion AIF [WWII]. The Duke of Gloucester who was our Governor General at the time was inspecting the troops before departure when he spotted Owen and nearly "chucked a wobbly" as they say. He asked Owen his family history because he could not believe anyone could look so like brother George (the King).[1]

Dorothy, Owen and Merthyr's sister, suggests that Merthyr embroidered Owen's story somewhat—that although the Governor General did look startled when he saw Owen, it was his wife who stopped to talk to him, and then not about his resemblance to her brother-in-law George VI.

A major flaw in the story that Thomas Campbell was the son of the prince who was to become Christian VIII of Denmark, is that Christian is reputed to have had ten children outside of marriage. He is said to have carefully documented them and to have seen that they were treated well. It seems that

---

1   Prince Henry, Duke of Gloucester, was the brother of George vi. He was Governor General of Australia from 1945 to 1947.

FIGURE 40
Maria Louisa Campbell
VENETIA MCMAHON'S
COLLECTION

Thomas Campbell was not on the list—and nor was Hans Christian Anderson whose descendants and fans would also like him to be the son of the morganatic marriage that the historians say did not take place...

If Thomas was Prince Christian's son there needs to be some way to explain why this child, but not the others, was kept a secret—his life unrecorded in the royal archives, or if it is there, not released. The story was passed down to all of Thomas Campbell's children and grandchildren, always with the caveat that it was a secret. So secrecy on both sides is integral to the story.

In August 2015 I contacted a Danish royal archivist to seek help. I had become so convinced that the prince in question was Christian VIII from three separate sites online, which claimed that he had had a morganatic marriage in 1804 to Elise Ahlefeldt Lurvig, that I framed my question as a question about Christian VIII and Elise. The question was regarded by the archivist as too complex and he referred me to an expert on Christian VIII, Anders Monrad Møller. I provided Anders with all the detail I had, and he advised me that it was highly improbable that Christian VIII was the father of Thomas Campbell:

August 31, 2015

Dear Bronwyn,

Everything is possible, but the probability in this case is extremely small. There has been found no evidence at all of a secret marriage in 1804 and a forced divorce in 1806. As a matter of fact prince Christian as early as in august 1804 fell very much in love with his cousin Charlotte Frederikke and as you know they were married in June 1806. And it was certainly not because he at that time was likely to be king... [It was not until 1808 that he was] known to be the successor of Frederik VI ...

It is correct that Christian had a number of children outside marriage and that they were taken care of. That Thomas Campell is not mentioned is certainly an argument against the paternity of Christian.

As you can see there is so to speak no room for Elise Ahlefeldt. My conclusion is that prince Christian was not the father of Thomas Campbell.

Sincerely yours

Anders Monrad Møller

Putting aside my misgivings about any claim that starts with "as a matter of fact", especially given Prince Christian's multiple sexual liaisons and the fact that his marriage to Charlotte lasted only four years from 1806 to 1810, I further asked Anders if we could at least be sure that Thomas Campbell was born at the castle in Helsingør in 1804. He simply replied that "The parish registers of Helsingør are not complete for the beginning of the 19th century". This information from Anders seemed to bring the whole inquiry, yet again, to a dead end.

The genealogical strategy of searching for documentation through which the facts might be established was clearly only ever going to bring this story to a dead end. Rather than continue to pursue documentation that, it seemed, was being withheld, I decided to approach it in a quite different way.

I began again by looking for different entry points to the story.

I chose three anchor points:

1. George Salting's claim that Maria Louisa and Princess Alexandra were some sort of cousins, and looked very much alike;

2. The birth was top secret and still told as a secret when passed on to Thomas's children and grandchildren, a secrecy, moreover, that the royal archives seemed intent on perpetuating when I went there to make further inquiries;

3. The fact that Christian was open about his ten illegitimate children, makes it clear that there was no shame for a prince to have an illegitimate child and so no need for secrecy.

Taking these three points as my beginning, the question that became immediately obvious was: why so much secrecy, and *who* might be so undone by
this story getting out? Perhaps the parentage in question was not Christian the
prince, but a princess. Perhaps, even, Christian's younger sister.

Princess Alexandra, the "sort of cousin" was much the same age as Maria
Louisa, born two years after her in 1842. Alexandra's mother was Louise of
Hesse Kassel, born in 1817. Louise of Hesse Kassel had a remarkable resemblance to members of the Campbell/Davies family. Indeed the image I found
of her struck me with such force that I could not but help feel I was on the right
track—as if one of my spider's threads was wildly vibrating. This woman of the
extraordinary face, Louise of Hesse Kassel, was the daughter of Princess Louisa
Charlotte (*b*. 28-3-1789), the younger sister of Christian VIII.

Princess Louisa Charlotte (often only referred to as Princess Charlotte) was
fifteen and a half years old when Thomas Campbell was born on 8 November 1804. Could it be that Princess Louisa Charlotte had become involved in
Christian's assignations with his friends and mistresses at Sorgenfrie Castle?
An illegitimate pregnancy for Princess Louisa Charlotte, would certainly be
something that would have been kept secret.

Life in India

As a young man, Thomas was sent out to India as a cadet with the Anglo–Danish Company at Tranquebar. Tranquebar was successively a Dutch, Danish and
British colonial heritage town, situated on the Coramandel Coast in the Nag-
apattinam District in Tamil Nadu, South India. In Tamil, Tranquebar was Tha-
rangambadi, the land of the singing waves. At Tranquebar Thomas Campbell
met Hans Jacob Fiellerup (1778–1835), another Dane, and his wife, Catherine
Elizabeth Braun (1787–1847).

Hans Jacob Fiellerup and Catherine Braun had three surviving daughters:
Helena Maria (1810–1863);[2] Louisa (1812–1858) and Harriet (1821–1860). Their
daughter Angelica died at the age of seven and their son Charles lived for
only two years. Helena Maria was to marry Thomas Campbell. Louisa was to
marry Severin Knud Salting, who was to become the wealthy family benefac-
tor, and Harriet was to marry Emil Elberling, whose vivid memoir I draw on in
this chapter.

---

2   Both Helena Maria, and her daughter Maria Louisa were known as Maria. To avoid confusion,
    I continue to name them with both their first names.

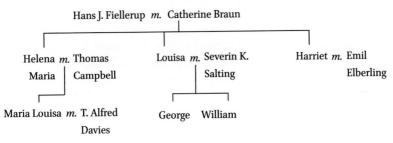

FIGURE 41   Family tree of Hans Jacob Fiellerup and Catherine Braun

When Thomas Campbell met 16-year-old Helena Maria Fiellerup, he was captivated. She accepted his proposal, and in 1826, when Thomas was 22 years old, and Helena Maria 16, they were wed.

Thomas and Helena Maria had twelve children, all born at Jellasore, Bengal:

- *Thomas* (1827–1871) married Matilda Forsythe (1827–)
- *David Henry* (1829–1885) migrated to New South Wales and married Amelia Briellat (1835–1870) then Louise Powell (1841–1892). Louise was the granddaughter of Richard and Christiana Brooks, my mother's ancestors.
- *Walter* (1831–1908) migrated to New South Wales and married Emma Briellat (1841–1929)
- *John Clemishaw* (1833–1857) killed in an uprising in India
- *William* (1835–1873) migrated to New South Wales and married Jane Grice. Their daughter Severin was my father's godmother.
- *Henry Fiellerup* (1837–1917) married Lina Johnson (1845–)
- *Edmund* (1840–1873) died of jungle fever
- *Maria Louisa* (1842–1906) my great grandmother, married Thomas Alfred Davies (1839–1908)
- *Catherine Elizabeth*, known as Kittie (1846–1911) married William Fraser (1842–1880) and migrated to South Africa.
- *Robert* (1846–1873) was attacked by a tiger and died from his wounds
- *Severin Alexander* (1847–1880) died young, at 33.
- *Louisa Harriet* (1849–1928) married William Turner (1837–1888)

The naming of Thomas's daughters revives my curiosity about his ancestry. If he knew he was the illegitimate child of Princess Louisa Charlotte of Denmark, he would have known it was a story that could not be told. Ten years after his own birth, Princess Louisa Charlotte's first daughter was born, and she called her Maria Louisa. In 1842 Thomas named his first daughter Maria Louisa. Princess Louisa Charlotte's second daughter was called Louisa and Thomas

FIGURE 42   Thomas and Helena Maria Campbell with their three daughters Catherine
             Elizabeth (Kitty), Harriet and Maria Louisa, *c.* 1840
             FROM ANDREW BARTON'S BARTON FAMILY WEBSITE

named his third daughter Louisa. It is possible Thomas was naming his daughters after his half-sisters. But his sister-in-law was also called Louisa—Louisa
Fiellerup.

   Louisa Fiellerup married Severin Knud Salting, and it was Salting who initiated the move to the colony of New South Wales. He asked Thomas Campbell
to join him on that venture, but Thomas had refused. Maria Louisa, Thomas's
first daughter, my great grandmother, explained, in an entry in the family bible,
his decision to remain in India:

He found life in India congenial, and enjoyed recreation with fowling piece and musket, and in later years taught my 8 brothers the uses of these weapons. As schools did not exist in India when we were children, and we were too numerous to send to England, he himself undertook our education, giving us useful instruction in the classics, history and science, while our mother attended to our religious exercises. He was so devoted to his home and family that when his brother-in-law, Severin Salting, invited him to partner him in a mercantile undertaking that they might try their fortune in the young colony of NSW (this was somewhere about the year 1833) he said 'I am comfortably provided for here, and a bird in the hand is worth two in the bush'.

Severin Salting's story is one of inheriting and losing a fortune, then re-making that fortune in New South Wales. Emil Elberling offered this account of Salting in his memoir:[3]

Salting was of Jewish extraction, which he never talked about. His parents died early and left him, their only son, a not inconsiderable fortune. He received a good education, became secretary to Councillor Malling and worked with him on the publication of Great and Good Acts, the best Danish reading book for schools at that time. As a young man Salting lived extravagantly, and got into debt. He had to be rescued by his Uncle and Curator, merchant Hallman. With Salting's consent he reinvested the capital of the Trust to achieve a higher return, enabling the debts to be repaid and the income to be maintained. Salting was overjoyed at this arrangement; instead of being admonished by his uncle, which he admitted he fully deserved, he was given the funds he needed to get him out of trouble with no loss of income. The joy was short-lived. Salting got into debt again, and went back to his uncle with a face like an undertaker. This time he was met with a sorrowful expression. Salting had prepared himself to promise that he would be more careful in future, but his uncle now told him that all the capital had been lost. The investments Salting's capital had been put into had failed and Salting was now ruined. Salting had to sell his belongings to pay off his debts, and avoiding his former associates, applied for references from Hamburg and London and sought new employment. He found a job in Hamburg as a copper trader...

---

3   The memoir was written in Danish and translated by Carl Wilhelm Kallenbach, dictated to Alan Fraser in Copenhagen in August 1999. The entire memoir is in the possession of Carl, who is descended from Emil Elberling and Harriet Campbell.

After working for some time in Hamburg, Salting was offered a better job through the Danish Consul Wilson ... in London.

With Salting's fortunes much improved, he made contact with Catherine Fiellerup and her two unmarried daughters, Louisa and Harriet. Emil continued:

> [In London] he became acquainted with his compatriot Mrs Fiellerup, my future mother in law. With her husband away in India, she was living in straightened circumstances with her two daughters Louisa and Harriet. He visited them frequently and did what he could to help. A first proposal of marriage to Louisa was refused, but he maintained his friendship with the family, and his second proposal was accepted.
>
> The firm of Arbuthnot which had affiliates in Madras, where my mother in law had known the manager since childhood, offered him a job in Sydney and helped him on his way. Salting and Louisa were married in September 1833 and left immediately for Sydney. My mother in law and Harriet returned via Denmark to Tranquebar where Fiellerup had a temporary job as book-keeper.
>
> Things went slowly at first for Salting in Australia. They had two sons, George, born 15 August 1835, and William born 18 January 1837. When the gold rush began [in 1850] and Sydney harbour was full of empty ships whose crews had deserted to the mines, and the farms were likewise robbed of their labourers, Salting went into partnership with an elderly ship's captain. They managed to buy a few ships very cheaply, and repaired them and sent them on whaling expeditions. They also bought grazing land. As a result of these ventures Salting was able to return to Europe a wealthy if not rich man.

Severin Salting made several trips back to New South Wales to look after his affairs there. His sons, George and William, went to school at Eton and then attended Sydney University where they took out numerous prizes. George took out Honours, and in the same year his younger brother, William, won the University Medal in English verse.

Back in London, Louisa had become seriously ill, and Severin and his sons must return to her bedside. Emil continues:

> His return to England in 1857 was on account of Louisa's health. She died on 24th July 1858, and Salting never got over her death. In 1859 he sent for Campbell's two daughters, Maria Louisa and Catherine to help with their education and to give them the opportunity of associating with other

young ladies. On that occasion he sent a letter to Harriet explaining why he had chosen Helena Maria's children and not hers. He assumed rightly that she would not want to part with any of her children and would prefer to receive an annual payment as usual.

Salting and I continued with a regular correspondence until his death on 14th September 1865. In his will he left £2,000 in trust with Flower and Co. to go on my death to my six daughters in equal share. His generosity made it possible for me to give my children more help than would otherwise have been possible, and will forever be gratefully remembered by me as well, I hope, as by my children.

Not only had Salting left money in his will to the children of Thomas Campbell, he had, as Emil reveals, paid them an annual allowance, and personally seen to the education of some of their children. He also sponsored the sons who migrated to New South Wales. By 1850 David Henry and William Campbell had begun a venture of their own on 'Goimbla', near Eugowra, but when that failed, they became managers of the Salting property, Cunningham Plains station. David Henry was paid an inordinately large salary, which Severin's sons continued to pay after their father's death.

But back to life in India ... Maria Louisa, when she was eight years old, wrote to her brother David Henry in New South Wales with news of home:

19 May 1850
My Dear David
As there is a ship going to Sydney I take this opportunity to write you a letter and tell you all the news. Papa got a letter from his mother [Elisabeth Campbell] a few days ago. She says she is in better health than she was before and also one from Louisitta [her aunt]. Mama is sending you some pickle and other things you asked for. Mr Alexander is passing – three days with us. Walter wrote to Mama yesterday. He went to Midnapore and passed a week with Mr Terry. Mama went to Balasere and took me with her. I enjoyed the change very much. Dr Chalmers has had a narrow escape from a Buffaloe. He was wounded in his stomac leg shoulder and face and has gone up to Calcutta to get a bone set which is broken in the face – I saw Mr and Mrs Allen at Balasere. Mrs Allen is a very pretty woman. He is also good looking. Mr Dicken sent us a number of playthings which are very pretty. Willy's birthday passed yesterday. Write me a long letter
Your affectionate Sister
Maria L. Campbell

Life, as we can glimpse it in Maria Louisa's letter, involved a great deal of letter writing, and visits to and from family and friends, and sometimes, considerable danger. Three of Maria Louisa's brothers died young in India. When her brother John was killed in the uprising, Thomas Campbell wrote in the family bible:

> *June* 21, 1857 – Our dear son, John Clemishaw Campbell met his death on this date, very cruelly murdered by Nana Sahib and his followers during the Indian uprising. It happened while he along with a number of his (compatriots) from the ill-fated garrison at Cawnpore proceeded down the Ganges on boats. Notwithstanding that the fiendish rebels had guaranteed a safe passage, no sooner had they embarked and dropped a short distance than they were fired upon and brutally massacred. A native who escaped told us that poor John died instantly without a groan, a musket ball having pierced his heart while gallantly returning fire on the miscreants. Peace be with him, a better or more affectionate son there could not be. (Family Bible)

Sixteen years later Robert died of his wounds after being mauled by a tiger. He was only 27. Edmund died in that same year of jungle fever, at the age of 33. Severin Campbell died seven years later, also at the age of 33.

Emil Elberling's Memoir includes the story of the death of his father-in-law, Hans Jacob Fiellerup:

> Fiellerup was a gentle and good natured man, with a poetic streak. He and his friend Rehling[4] used to take turns writing songs for parties – no better or worse than the usual party songs.
>
> Fiellerup had been a factor[5] in the Danish Asiatic Company, but he did not achieve any position of seniority until the company's business was in decline. The Company sent him on a mission to London to obtain compensation from the English Company for cash seized from the Company as war booty when Serampore was taken into possession by the English in 1801. Fiellerup was unsuccessful in his mission since it had been the Company's own employees who had handed over the cash without protest and without stating that the Company was a private trading company. The money had in any case been distributed to the Military.

---

4 A colonel in the British army.
5 A factor is a person who acts on another's behalf, especially transacts business for another.

Fiellerup returned to Serampore before going to Rio as supercargo[6] for a Spanish/Portuguese [ ]. He stayed with a family there for several years, and lost all.[7] He returned to England and Denmark, and obtained promise of employment in Tranquebar. Having taken up a post as accountant there, he brought his family out, but then was replaced in his job by [ ], which threw the family into desperate straits. The daughter, Harriet, was much criticised in these circumstances for attending parties and balls at Government House on the invitation of the Mouriers.[8] I can take some credit for coming to her defence, saying that the Mourier ladies were helping her escape from the sorrow and bitterness of her own home by taking her into their own family, and it was only natural for a young girl to participate in the pleasures and diversions offered to her.

One evening at the end of May Bock and I, returning from a party, saw several people hurrying across from Government House to the small dwelling in the square where Fiellerup lived. We followed and finding the house with windows and door thrown open, entered. Fiellerup was lying lifeless on a sofa in the middle of the room surrounded by his family and several others. He had collapsed with an apoplectic fit. The doctor, Christen, had been summoned, and arrived at the same time as we did, but nothing could be done. Fiellerup's wife and daughter were clinging distraught to his body, and I helped them away. Harriet fell unconscious into my arms. I took her, deeply moved, to an adjoining room where Miss Mourier soon arrived to look after her. This was my first close acquaintance with my future wife.

Hans Jacob Fiellerup died in 1835 when Harriet was 14 years of age. She and her mother, Catherine, went to live with Helena Maria and Thomas Campbell and their many children at Jellasore, Harriet taking up the role of governess to the children. Emil Elberling met her there again two years later, when he went on a visit to Thomas Campbell. He described being pleased by the happy intimacy of the Campbell family, though he admitted, that he found the children rather wild. It was on this visit that Emil proposed to Harriet.

After nearly three months stay I left Tranquebar for Serampore in a coastal boat in the company of Rehling, his wife and four children,

---

6 Supercargo is an officer on a merchant ship who supervises commercial matters and is responsible for the cargo.

7 In a shipwreck. Catherine and one of her daughters eventually went to fetch him and bring him back home.

8 Conrad Emil Mourier was Governor of Tranquebar from 1832 to 1838.

teacher Bjerring, secretary Rashid, and Mrs Fiellerup and her daughter who were bound for Serampore and then Jellasore where the eldest Fiellerup daughter, Helena Maria was married to the indigo planter Thomas Campbell...

[After some time in Serampore] I decided to go over to Jellasore to see Campbell... I found the happy intimacy of the Campbell family very pleasing, and I was especially struck with Harriet's loving patience in caring for and instructing her sister's rather wild children. It seemed to me that I could not find a better wife. I decided on the day of my intended departure to propose to her, and did so by letter which I put into a book which Harriet had asked to borrow, and I sent it to her by one of the children. I waited for the reply with beating heart which eventually came in the shape of a letter from Harriet's mother saying that Harriet felt she did not know me well enough to give an answer. I took this as a refusal, and sent a note to Campbell asking him to send my palanquin and belongings to meet me ahead as I did not wish to face the family.

Emil, not accustomed to having his desire thwarted, made a dramatic escape from the scene of his humiliation:

I climbed out of a window and set off across the fields, very miserable, to find my palanquin. After a few hours I was overtaken by Campbell on horseback. He did his best to comfort me, saying that Harriet's response had not been a definite refusal: she was just taken aback by the unexpectedness of the proposal. He urged me to return to his house and to leave again in a normal fashion, at least so as to avoid gossip. I accepted on condition that I did not have to take leave of the family. We got back after nightfall, and I set off again immediately. When I found a basket that had been left in the palanquin containing food for the journey I was further downcast, taking this as confirmation of the refusal of my proposal. I flung the basket out onto the road. By the time I reached Outecbarre where the way led upstream back to Serampore I had calmed down enough to read Mrs Fiellerup's note again. I now perceived in it the expression of a desire on Harriet's part to get to know me a little better. So on the boat I wrote to her again, repeating my patient prayer for a favourable answer.

With hope restored and feeling calm and contented, I returned to Serampore. On the 4th June I received a favourable answer from Harriet, and announced my happiness to my friends. This was received with comments to the effect that something of this kind had been expected as only a madman or someone in love could think of taking a journey when all reasonable people were seeking protection from the heat; I was asked why I had not told of the reason for my journey which was of course not made for the sake of one small law case. My assurances that I had not the least idea of making a proposal when I set out was met with disbelieving smiles.

[Colonel Rehling gave me permission to return to Jellasore and] I left immediately and was received with much affection. I used all my powers of persuasion to overcome the objections to an early union on the grounds that as Harriet was only sixteen the union should be postponed for a year. I overcame these objections and Harriet and her mother followed me to Serampore where they stayed with the Colonel (Rehling) and on the 10th July 1841 we were married in the Danish church by the Governor General's minister, Mr Wimberley.

While Emil had been making his emotional, dramatic exit from Jellasore, another suitor, sent by Severin and Louisa Salting from Sydney, had crossed his path:

On my way back from Jellasore in downcast mood after my first proposal I had crossed paths with a gentleman in a palanquin heading the other way. After our wedding Harriet told me that it had been a suitor from Sydney sent by her sister Louisa. He was a Mr Garrard, partner of Harriet's brother-in-law Salting [Severin Knud Salting], and had brought with him a letter inviting her and her mother to go to Sydney. He had been refused, and had left crestfallen. In December we received a letter from Louisa in which she said it had been her dearest wish to see Harriet united with a man who she knew and esteemed, and to be reunited with her and her mother in Sydney, and her regret at that time that this wish had been thwarted. Now she wished Harriet and me all possible happiness. So near had I been to losing Harriet. Was it providence that had taken me on the journey to Jellasore? Salting did not reply to my letter about our marriage, which was a disappointment to me. But I received a letter from him later with apologies.

The belief in providence occurs many times in these entangled tales. It is possible, Emil thinks, that God was looking after him, ensuring that he would marry Harriet and find happiness among God's chosen.

Their wedding was a sumptuous affair:

The Colonel gave a very nice party for us on our wedding day. But we had to cut short our time at table because of a plague of insects such as I had never before experienced. Instead of fried pigeon it was little winged insects that flew into our mouths, giving a very unpleasant taste to the food. It was impossible to avoid swallowing them. After we had done a tour with people wishing us good luck we had our first party ourselves which was much praised. We had amongst other things, ham and turkey. The ham, imported from Bayonne hermetically sealed, cost 20 Rdl. My mother in law [Catherine] who was now living with us was in her element, advised us on arrangements. She sat next to the Bishop of Cochin, China, who spoke to her now in English, now in Portuguese. The old man, who was usually silent at dinner as he did not speak English, was unusually vivacious; he was much delighted by a real expresso coffee (*poussé de café*) – and said that he had not enjoyed such a divine drink since leaving la belle France. The coffee was my mother-in-law's idea. It was served in small cups with a strong fine cognac slowly poured into it and ignited. We had had the servants practice making the coffee for several days before the party, and on the day they succeeded admirably. The Bishop had been Bishop of Cochin for many years. He had fled in fear of his life from persecution of Catholics. He stayed with us for six months while engaged in the publication of a Cochin China encyclopedia.

Emil was full of praise for Harriet's skilled and fearless horse riding. He was concerned, however, that she might be too relaxed a housewife if she followed the example of her sister Helena Maria. He enjoined her to be more disciplined, and to that end he recommended that she not read novels. He suggested, rather, that she should be guided in her reading by her wiser sister, Louisa Salting. Emil would offer her a sumptuous life of privilege, and in return she must tame herself, and become a disciplined housewife. He was a man used to having his way.

In the next chapter I turn to the story of two of Thomas Campbell's sons, David and William, who migrated early to the colony and took up land there called 'Goimbla' near the small town of Eugowra in mid-New South Wales and later took over the management of one of Severin Salting's properties on Cunningham Plains.

CHAPTER 8

David Campbell and the Bushrangers

In 1863 David Campbell shot dead the bushranger Johnny O'Mealley on his property Goimbla, near the village of Eugowra. Each account of that shooting differs in significant detail. In this chapter I use the differences in those accounts to explore both the elusiveness of what will count as history, and also to explore the entangled social threads that made up that time and that place. David and William Campbell, Maria Louisa's brothers, had been squatters on Goimbla since 1854. In that year David had married Amelia Breillat, daughter of the wealthy Sydney Merchant Thomas Breillat.

The British justice system was brutal in its punishment of the poor, and in particular the Irish poor. For minor infractions, both in the colony and 'back home' minor infractions could lead to the death penalty, to flogging, and/or to transportation. In New South Wales convicts were used as slave labour to build the colony. In the second decade of the 1800s, when governors like Macquarie and masters like William Cox gave them freedom and land in return for good work, the British government was incensed. They did not want the colony to turn into some kind of paradise. It must remain a place of horror that struck fear into the hearts of the poor who might be contemplating a life of crime.

The Bigge enquiry into the colony's governance re-established the division between gentlemen landowners with rights and privileges, and the poor, who had no rights and no privileges. This was music to the ears of the Exclusives—men like the hanging parson, Samuel Marsden, and pastoralist and magistrate John Macarthur. The Exclusives wanted to maintain the British class system in which the wealthy elite ruled, and the convict class was maintained as a form of cheap labour, obedient to its masters.

From the beginning of the colony in 1788, convicts had escaped into the bush, preferring to take their chances there rather than submit themselves to the brutal punishments of flogging and hanging. Some survived off the land, 'going native', some lived off wild cattle which had also escaped, and some became bushrangers, living off cattle duffing. Later in the 1850s, with the gold rush, they became highwaymen who held up coaches, including the gold coaches. Some convicts who had been given their freedom and small blocks of land had become the 'cow cockies' who scratched a poor living out of the ground. Those small landholders, and their poor friends and relations were friendly with the bushrangers and sheltered them when they could. Because

© BRONWYN DAVIES, 2021 | DOI:10.1163/9789004446717_008

the police were thus so often outwitted, it was made a crime to associate with anyone deemed to be a bushranger.

In 1861 the Robertson Land Act was passed to regulate who could own what land. Squatters found themselves having to buy up their 'own' land in multiple small blocks. Small-selectors could buy up pieces of the squatters' land. The squatters had to compete with them in order to retain their vast holdings and their control over water sources. All landholders, both rich and poor, were obliged, as a condition of purchase, to fence their land, build a dwelling, and clear the land, in order to prove they were genuine farmers. The blocks were small and the cost and the labour for small landholders of fencing, clearing, building their houses and buying stock and equipment, were considerable. And the resentment of the Exclusive squatters was considerable. The Emancipists (freed convicts and their supporters) opposed the British class system and fought for the right for everyone to have a 'fair go'.

Many of the small farmers did not actually own their blocks but were 'dummies' for the large landholders, sitting on their blocks for them and being paid £50 a year to stay there in order to meet the owner's conditions of purchase. Stock that had previously run free on vast expanses of unfenced land were now fenced in, at least in those areas that had been surveyed by the government surveyors and blocks of land put up for sale.

Before the work of the surveyors and the erection of fences, stock, including government stock, had roamed over vast tracts of land, sometimes finding new pastures for themselves, thus assisting the squatters in finding and opening up new pastures. The sheep were watched over by shepherds, usually the most lowly among the convicts, who lived lonely, isolated lives, guarding the flocks against dingoes and indigenous attacks. Some lost their lives in those attacks. Cattle, in contrast, could wander unseen onto neighbouring properties, or into as yet unexplored country. The accidental movement of cattle or horses from one station to another was common, and rebranding them, or branding them for the first time if they were clean-skins, was common. The Robertson Land Act in 1861 sought to bring order to this chaotic situation, which had, until then, allowed escaped convicts and their children to survive. There was, further, an increase made in the police force in rural areas. One such police officer, who features in this story was Frederick Pottinger.

Sir Frederick Pottinger had initially come to the colony in the 1850s to try his luck on the goldfields. Later he was to become Inspector of Police in New South Wales. In that capacity he became notorious for his run-ins with bushrangers, constantly frustrated by their skill in eluding him in the bushland that they knew much better than he did. That the elite prospered in New South Wales at the time is perfectly illustrated in Pottinger's story. According to the *Australian Dictionary of Biography*:

> Sir Frederick William Pottinger (1831–1865), police inspector, was born on 27 April 1831 in India, second son of Lieutenant-General Sir Henry Pottinger of the East India Co., and his wife Susanna Maria, née Cooke, of Dublin. Educated privately and in 1844-47 at Eton, Pottinger purchased a commission in the Grenadier Guards in 1850 and served in England until 1854. Active in social life, he lost much of his adoring mother's wealth on the race-course. In 1856 he succeeded his father as second baronet and soon dissipated his inheritance. Forced by debt to leave England, he migrated to Sydney. After failing on the goldfields he joined the New South Wales police force as a mounted trooper. A superb horseman, he spent the next few years on the gold escort between Gundagai and Goulburn.
>
> Probably because of conditions imposed by his family who still supported him with funds, Pottinger kept his title secret but in 1860 it was discovered by the inspector-general of police, John McLerie, and promotion came rapidly. In November he became clerk of petty sessions at Dubbo and on 1 October 1861 assistant superintendent of the Southern Mounted Patrol. Although determined to succeed in his career he was involved in a drunken brawl at Young on 20-21 December 1861. Sued, he received a public rebuke from Charles Cowper for his 'highly discreditable' behaviour. Posted to the Lachlan, he proved himself an indefatigable but unlucky hunter of bushrangers. (Selth, 1974: np)

Pottinger was notorious among bushrangers for his incompetence. His class background, however, meant that he could rise to a high-status position, however ill-deserved it might be. One of the men he had in his sights was Ben Hall.

Ben Hall lived on his own small farm, also near the village of Eugowra. According to Clune's ficto-historical account of Ben Hall's life, Ben was under suspicion because he had earlier been a friend of Frank Gardiner's, a notorious and elusive bushranger, and one of the few who did actually manage to escape to North America and make a new life for himself on the right side of the law.

Before Gardiner had made his escape, Ben Hall had been warned by the police not to associate with him. When someone who Gardiner had robbed saw Ben Hall soon after, he reported Hall as Gardiner's accomplice in the robbery. Hall was thrown into goal for a month until his case could be heard, and his name cleared. His wife left him during that period and later the police, who did not believe in his innocence, irrationally burned to the ground the hut he had built, as a warning that he should not take to a life of crime.

FIGURE 43
David Henry Campbell, *c.* 1860
PHOTO FROM DAVIES FAMILY
ALBUM

From Ben Hall's point of view, the fire was a declaration of war against him. He was left with no wife and child, and no home, and the police-force, led by Pottinger, was dedicated to his downfall. He took up a wild life, hiding out in the bush, eluding, out-riding and out-witting those intent on his downfall. He survived on his wits, and countered, wherever he could, the inequities between rich and poor. He was regarded by many as a gentleman who lived by a code of honour, not taking from the poor, not taking anything that was genuinely needed, and always treating people with courtesy, especially women. He would never take from the same person twice. As hefty rewards were put on the heads of Ben Hall and his associates, and as associating with them became a punishable offence, Hall and his men became, if anything, more daring. It was a high stakes game, with death as an inevitable outcome.

In 1863 David and William Campbell publicly committed themselves to assisting the police in hunting Ben Hall's gang down. Hall believed that this was unfair. It was not Campbell's war to fight, nor his job to hunt Hall down. He decided to pay him a visit to persuade him to back off. That visit went horribly wrong.

It seems from David's own account that he was not open to listening to what Ben Hall might have to say, and gunfight immediately ensued. In an attempt to get David to surrender the battle, Hall's men set fire to his barn containing not only the bales of wool and tobacco crop, and vehicles and equipment from the farm, but also David's favourite horse. In the blaze of light from the fire Johnny O'Mealley (pronounced O'Mailley), Hall's associate, was clearly visible when he stood up with the thought of returning to let the horse out of the barn. He was an easy target. On 19 November 1863, around 11pm, David Campbell shot Johnny O'Mealley dead.

A vivid and detailed account of this event by Edwin Rymer is re-told in Banham's (2007) history of Eugowra. Edwin Rymer's father had, in 1861, built the first of the hotels that features in this story. I have highlighted some of the elements of this story that appear to be quite different in subsequent accounts:

> *Edwin Rymer*: One morning early, Ben Hall with his gang of men including J. Gilbert, J. O'Mealley, J. Vane and J. Burke visited my father's hotel. After having two rounds of refreshments in the bar Hall asked for my father, who was absent in Molong on business. They told my mother they had no intention of interfering with the hotel or inmates and not to be alarmed. They left two half-crowns on the counter for their refreshments and went over to the other hotel about 100 yards distant, held up the inmates, took their money and also took all the money the butcher possessed. The butcher imagined there was something doing and was getting out the back door with his money when one of the gang came on the scene and demanded his roll of money. He took the gold and notes and returned the cheques to the butcher.
>
> Although Hall and his gang were classed as outlaws, there being a £1,000 reward offered for their arrest dead or alive, Ben Hall was an honourable man in many respects. He would not allow his men to interfere with women or take a life, as shown shortly after his visit to Orange. Burke was shot by Mr Keightley near Bathurst. Vane, being Burke's particular friend, desired to have revenge on Keightley but Hall decided to take Keightley prisoner with the object of getting a reward, and £500 for his release was demanded. Mrs Keightley quickly obtained the money and released her husband. Vane, being grieved over the death of his friend Burke, decided to leave the gang and give himself up, which he did with the hope of a better future.
>
> These were exciting days. David Campbell, the owner of 'Goimbla Station,' his brother and a station hand named Wilson volunteered to assist in the arrest of the bushrangers. This being whispered to Hall, he, with

Gilbert and O'Mealley paid a visit to Campbell's homestead with the idea of cautioning Campbell against taking such action. The time chosen was on a clear, summer, moonlit night. The walls of the building are of pisé with shingle roof and a lengthy verandah, with a garden in the front enclosed with a paling fence.

Outside the garden were cultivation paddocks and at the time of Hall's visit there was a growing crop of wheat or oats about five feet high. Hall and his men were on the verandah of the house and *could have shot Campbell through the window, but they had no intention of doing so had Campbell not shown fight. Campbell, on hearing footsteps, armed himself with a rifle and revolvers and Hall, seeing this action, retreated through the garden and got cover behind the paling fence in the growing crop.* Immediately Campbell came out onto the open verandah he was called on to surrender, but refused to do so. He was then threatened to be burnt out, but still he stood his ground.

There was a large shed at the homestead, well filled with bales of wool and bales of tobacco leaf that was grown on 'Goimbla,' vehicles, other equipment for station use and also a favourite horse of Campbell's. The shed was set on fire and burnt to ashes, even the horse, whose charred body was all that remained.

The gang then took up their position in front of the house and asked Campbell to surrender. He still refused *and firing then took place on both sides. This continued for some time and unfortunately for O'Mealley he was looking over the paling fence when he was shot dead by Campbell,* the bullet entering his neck just below the ear. *Campbell was not aware he had shot O'Mealley until next morning,* although there was a quietness following on the shooting. Hall and Gilbert took the dead body of O'Mealley a few yards into the growing crop and took his firearms and valuables he possessed and then took their departure, leaving their comrade's body.

During the quietness Campbell's brother slipped out of the door and walked nine miles to the police camp, then about one mile from the present town of Eugowra. Two mounted policemen arrived at 'Goimbla' during the night and next morning made a search, more out of curiosity. To their surprise they found the dead body of O'Mealley. Reports soon spread near and far of the shooting. I with others, only being two miles from the station, was early on the scene. Excitement ran high and hundreds of people viewed the dead body the following day.

O'Mealley was dressed as a true Australian bushman with high wellington boots, knee breeches, fancy vest and cabbage tree hat. His body was buried at 'Goimbla' but later was removed by O'Mealley's parents.

> *It seems likely that Campbell's brother stopped at his nephew's prop-
> erty 'Old Eugowra,' owned by Hanbury Clements (as later stated by his son
> Edgar), on route to the police camp. Mr. H. Clements is reported to have then
> taken the message to the police.*
>
> The body of John O'Mealley was buried at 'Goimbla.' I have it from a
> reasonably reliable source that after five to seven days it was exhumed
> by his father and brother, placed in a home-made coffin and transported
> on the back of a cart to Gooloogong, where it was buried in the family
> section of the old cemetery. This cemetery was below the sale-yards and
> towards the river. Many think he was buried at Forbes, but they lack proof
> to substantiate this fact. However, I do not want to get involved in any ver-
> bal battle on this point as my information came from one of the O'Meal-
> ley family. (Banham, 1994: pp. 24–6, emphasis added)

Some details to note from the highlighted passages:

> Ben Hall did not intend to kill anyone as he could easily have done so
> through the open blind; instead he retreated to the oat-field as soon as
> David Henry fetched his gun.

> David Henry was given ample opportunity to back down and to negoti-
> ate, but he refused.

> William either walked nine miles to alert the police that a bushranger had
> been shot, or he only went to Hanbury Clement's place (it will emerge in
> later accounts that William did go the 9 miles to the police calling in at
> Clements' on the way).

John O'Mealley was not always willing to abide by Ben Hall's code of conduct.
Ellis (2006) tells us more about him in his book *The Life and Times of Frank
Gardiner.*

> John O'Mealley was born in 1843, one of ten children to Paddy O'Meal-
> ley and Julia Downey, who kept an illegal distillery and shanty about ten
> kilometres from Sandy Creek, the property of Ben Hall and his brother in
> law John McGuire. The shanty was a well-known haunt of all the Weddin
> Ranges bad boys and also many of the gold diggers who passed between
> Grenfell and Forbes. O'Mealley was only a young boy when Gardiner
> began his career on the roads, growing up in the Weddin Mountains he
> quickly learned the best haunts and hideouts of the area. John O'Mealley

was like a half broken horse who had reverted to brumby, all the family seemed to be half wild and on the outer side of the law. He did not have the courtesy of Gardiner, Hall and a few other noted bushrangers.

Once he met a Mr Barnes[1] on the road, who had previously been robbed by the Hall gang and did not think it fair to go through another stick up. When O'Mealley demanded his saddle and bridle, Barnes refused and dug in his spurs, his horse quickly responding, however O'Mealley took aim and shot him in the back. Barnes fell from his horse and died as he lay on the road. O'Mealley stole the saddle and bridle.

After Gardiner's exit, Hall, Gilbert and O'Mealley became very active stealing horses, holding up people on the roads and attacking home-steads. They recruited several young men of ill character on some of their raids, amongst others John Vane and his young mate Micky Burke.

In October 1863 these five men robbed the homestead of a Mr Law-son near Carcoar.[2] Two days later the five notorious bushrangers attacked the homestead of Mr Henry Keightley, a gold commissioner who rented thirty acres of land on Bowman's station at Dunns Plains near Rockley. After a shootout Micky Burke was shot dead, and his friend John Vane was only just persuaded by Hall not to shoot Keightley, preferring to ran-som his life for £500.

So O'Mealley had witnessed a partner shot dead in front of him during the gun battle ...

About ten kilometres further upstream on the Mandagery Creek where the escort robbery occurred was the station homestead of 'Goim-bla', owned by brothers David and William Campbell. At about nine at night on the 19th November 1863, Hall, Gilbert and O'Mealley attacked them and during a fierce gun battle, O'Mealley was shot dead by David Campbell... (Ellis, 2006: Np.)

What is never questioned in any of these varying accounts of that awful night, is whether David could have listened to Ben Hall, in order to find out what he had come to say. Another curious feature of these accounts is the status of William. William was a squatter at Goimbla with David, but this fact regularly disappears from the various accounts.

At the magisterial enquiry next morning, David was found not to be culpable.

---

1 Barnes had set up one of the first stores at Murrumburrah, which is still standing, close to Cunningham Plains station.
2 Carcoar was, coincidentally, where my grandfather Euston Blomfield was born in 1877 four years after the shooting.

According to the *New South Wales Police Gazette* (1863: 368):

> About 9.30 p.m. on the 19th ultimo, the premises of David Henry Camp-
> bell Esq., Goimbla, Eugowra Creek, was attacked by the offenders Gilbert,
> O'Mealley, and Hall, who fired several shots into the house (one of which
> wounded Mr William Campbell); they also burnt down the out-buildings.
> Mr Campbell fired upon the offenders and mortally wounded O'Mealley.
> At a magisterial inquiry held on the 20th ultimo, at Goimbla, by William
> Farrand, Esq., P. M. Forbes, a verdict of justifiable homicide was returned.

In this police report we see the slippage of William, from co-squatter making
the heroic journey to get help, to incidental victim of little interest to anyone.
It is worth noting that it is only 'several shots' that are reported.

David was awarded £1000 reward for the death of O'Mealley by the New
South Wales government, and his and Amelia's portraits were painted, along
with the portraits of the Keightleys, as a commemorative act.[3]

Yet another version of this story appeared recently in the *Eugowra News*
in 2013. A century and a half later, the writer of the article has taken as fact
the clichéd version of the story that Hall and his associates were marauders
with murderous intent, despite evidence to the contrary. The article includes
an account of the event by Amelia Campbell herself, in a letter to her mother
written four days after the event. Amelia's own account further entrenches the
divide between the landed gentry and the bushrangers. She claims God was
the one who saved them from the murderous intent of the bushrangers. In her
account, too, the status of William is even further downgraded:

> Squatter David Campbell, his brother William and David's wife Amellia,
> along with servants and staff, were lucky to survive an attack when con-
> fronted by bushrangers Ben Hall, John Gilbert and Johnny O'Meally at
> 'Goimbla' homestead on the Mandagery creek just west of Murga on the
> evening of 19th November 1863.
>
> By the light of a fire which the marauders had set, burning stables, a
> barn, hay and a favourite horse the area lit well enough to set the scene
> for the shooting of O'Meally.
>
> A letter written by Mrs Campbell to her mother on 21 November 1863
> relates the story.

---

3 The portraits can be found on my ancestry.com site as well as at the National Library of Australia: http://nla.gov.au/nla.pic-an2293558

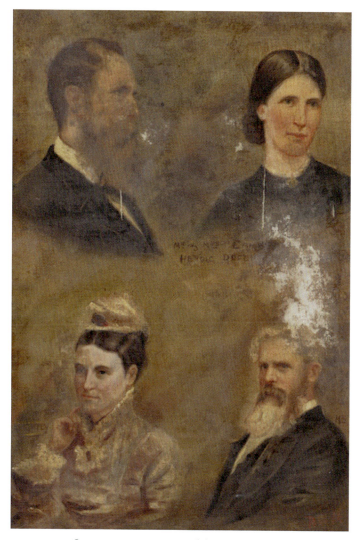

FIGURE 44   Commemorative portraits of the Campbells and the Keightleys

You will be anxious till you hear direct of our safety. It is indeed owing to the great mercy of God that the lives of David and William are spared. So many people have been here taking notes, that I doubt not you will read a most truthful account of all in the papers. I need not therefore weary you with another. We had no time for fear. The most dreadful part was the burning of the barn and stable. They are not much farther from the house than your stable; and at one part an outhouse, which is connected with the main building, is only divided by a road. You cannot imagine my agony while the flames were towering above us. Had the wind only blown towards the house all must have gone. The ground between the stable and out- house was strewn with straw from the haymaking; there was also a large heap of woolpacks and a cart, all of which were set on fire. I was in such deadly fear of its catching at this point, that I rushed out and succeeded in getting the road cleared with the assistance of the cook. By this time the roofs had fallen in, so that the danger was passed. I imagine the ruffians had also retreated. Mr. Campbell had ventured out to the spot where he had aimed at the man. He found his gun and hat, but not the body, for his mates had dragged it some distance away, and his idea at the time was that the man had merely been wounded, and would return for his things. A short while after we heard a rustling as of some one creeping stealthily through the oats, and were afraid to go out again lest the bushrangers should be lying in ambush. The men in the huts had now recovered from their panic, and came up to see what was going on. David stationed them at various posts, and they watched till morning. It was by this time 3 o'clock. I was very tired, went to bed and managed to sleep a little; but was awoke before dawn by the arrival of the police. They found the body, and I cannot describe to you the state of my feelings when I heard of it – heard that the unhappy man had been shot by the light of the fire which he helped to raise – for at the moment he fell the country round was as light as day. It appears the ruffians retreated to one of the huts, where they were cursing and swearing in a most fearful manner that they would yet have revenge; and I am grieved to add that a female servant heard one of them regretting not having shot the woman – meaning, I suppose, myself – but his comrade called out to him to hold his tongue, and mind what he was about. When the alarm took place, William rushed to the back door, not knowing that Mr. Campbell was in the house, and that the shots had been fired at him. William there received a charge of slugs in his breast, four wounds in all, but fortunately not deep. Startled, he staggered on, got outside of the place, and could not find his way back. He is now all right. (Cheney, 2013: 8)

Amelia's letter reveals her heroism—going out in the heat and glare of the fire to clear the road between the house and the barn of straw with the help of the cook. And it also reveals something quite surprising, that Ben Hall and his men had taken shelter in the servants' quarters. While Hall's men said they regretted that they had not shot her, such talk was regarded by Hall as unacceptable, suggesting they had not ever shot at her as other accounts say. Later we find that none of the servants had been willing to join the fight against the bushrangers, despite Amelia asking them to do so.

After the death of O'Mealley, the Campbell family were unpopular among many of the local people, including station hands and shearers. Alex Campbell, descended from David, notes that "the lower class people in the district, who were friendly with the bushrangers, made themselves objectionable to the family" (Campbell, 2017: 28). "Reputable people", however, the *Eugowra News* account continued, were jubilant:

> As soon as the excitement into which the colony had been thrown by the Goimbla incident had somewhat subsided, the public begun to discuss how best Mr and Mrs Campbell's bravery could be rewarded, and his losses made good. Public meetings were held, laudatory speeches were made and subscriptions were raised. The reward of £1000 offered by the government was, of course, handed over to Mr. Campbell, but the value of the property destroyed by the fire raised by the bushrangers was estimated at nearly double that amount, a goodly sum was raised, and 'every reputable person in the colony applauded to the echo the conduct of Mr. Campbell and his wife.' A huge Silver Epergne (dining table centrepiece) and Silver Coffee Urn were amongst the gifts which were also presented.
>
> Sadly, the lovely young Mrs Campbell died at 34 in childbirth, but she was certainly celebrated as a 'colonial heroine' for her bravery at the time of the siege. (Cheney, 2013: 8)

Amelia, it would seem from her letter, had no time for William, describing him as rushing about and getting lost—a far cry from a determined nine-mile walk after being wounded in order to alert the police. It seems the people in the district also overlooked him.

Yet another version of that awful night comes from Banjo Paterson in *Illalong Children*. As a boy Paterson had heard the story from the station-hand who had been in the kitchen at the time of the attack. Amelia's heroism is yet further enhanced in this story, as is the contempt for the bushrangers, though notably the station-hand was not interested in taking up the fight against them. In this account the dead body of O'Meally was found soon after he was killed. Paterson begins his account with a visit from Illalong to Cunningham Plains station:

> We were invited to stay in the house of a gentleman who had, in defence of his wife and family, shot a bushranger. It was at Cunningham Plains station, near Murrumburrah, twenty miles from Illalong, that we went to stay with Mr David Campbell, famous in the district as the man who shot O'Maley at Goimbla. He had later on removed to Cunningham Plains and

at the time of our visit he was living there with his second wife and three sons of his first marriage; neighbours were few and far between, so we were brought along to play with the little Campbells.

Mr Campbell was no two-gun man of the Wild West type. Shy, quiet-spoken and courteous, he left it to others to tell the story of the shooting, but an old station hand was still with him and had seen the whole thing.

'O'Maley and his mates,' he said, 'they had it in for the boss, I don't know why. Must have been something' he said about them and they got to hear of it. Anyhow, they came along to stick up Goimbla. It was just getting dark when they came. They must have reckoned they'd rob the place and get away without bein' reckonised. Mr and Mrs Campbell were in the house and the three kids were out in their room a few yards away from the house. The girls and I, we were in the kitchen at the back. You know in them days we were always on the lookout for bushrangers, and when we heard a rifle go off and the smack of a bullet agin a wall I says to the girls, "Here they are." No, I didn't go out. I reckoned it sounded as if that bullet was in a hurry. They thought the boss would come out and surrender when he heard that bullet, but he's a game man, the boss. He ran for his rifle and fired at the place the sound came from. And, if he was game, what about Mrs Campbell? She thought the youngsters would be frightened and *she ran down to their room, and the bushrangers fired at her as she ran down.* They were miserable murderin' hounds all right, shootin' at a woman. Then the boss sees, agin the skyline, a man's head lookin' over a fence and he fires at it. An' the next thing we hear is two or three horses gallopin' away, and there's no more shootin'. No one dared go out for quite a while, fearin' some trap. *And when we do go out, there we find O'Maley stone dead, shot through the throat.'*

Such was the saga of Goimbla, and we actually talked to the man who shot him, and were allowed to have pot shots at wild turkeys with the rifle which shot him. For weeks after we returned home, we gave a lifelike performance of the Drama of Goimbla, Jack and I taking it in turns to play the parts of Mr Campbell and O'Maley, while Flo and Jessie in turn played the part of the heroine Mrs Campbell, running down to the back room to the accompaniment of 'gunshot sound effects' produced by beating a roulade on a kerosene tin. (Paterson, 1983: 30–1, emphasis added)

That Ben Hall and his men were "miserable murderin' hounds all right, shootin' at a woman" is made less and less likely as the various accounts unfold. Amelia, it seems, went repeatedly into the line of fire without being shot.

So, finally, then, to the transcript of the magisterial enquiry held at Goimbla the following morning—with depositions from the police, from David and William, and from a gold-fields commissioner. Notably neither the servants nor Amelia were asked to give evidence; their views were evidently irrelevant in New South Wales law at the time, as were Ben Hall's. David makes no mention of Ben Hall's wish to talk to him, and he maintains the story that he did not know until next morning that Johnny O'Mealley was dead.

In the transcript we find William was indeed also a squatter at Goimbla, and he did indeed walk the nine miles to the police as well as calling in at Hanbury Clements' on the way *to tell him a bushranger had been shot*, who in turn conveyed the news to Pottinger. No clue is given as to why William walked, rather than riding his own horse (only David Henry's was burned in the barn), or why he did not borrow a horse from Hanbury Clements. Amelia's heroism shifts again in her husband's account, where curiously David feels compelled to add that she acted without his permission.

No mention is made of Ben Hall's attempt to talk to David about his decision to aid the police in hunting him down. Instead the encounter begins, in David's deposition, with close range shooting at his face. When the period of attempted negotiations is omitted from the account the shooting must be imagined to have gone on over an improbable two and a quarter hours from 8.45 until 11.00. even though it was only 'several shots' that were fired into the house. The story does not stack up, but no need is perceived for any further inquiry into the truth of what happened.

THE DEATH OF O'MEALLY MAGISTERIAL ENQUIRY
(*From* The Bathurst *Times own correspondent.*)
A ... Magisterial enquiry was held by Mr. William Farrand, Police Magistrate, Forbes, on view of the body of John O'Meally. *Sydney Mail* (NSW: 1860–1871) Saturday 28 November 1863 p 4 Article.

Michael Fagan, on oath, states: I am a senior-constable of mounted police, stationed at Eugowra. At two o'clock this morning *a messenger* arrived at the Eugowra police station and informed me that Mr. Campbell's station was in possession of the bushrangers, who were burning it down. I immediately proceeded to Mr Campbell's station, accompanied by two constables. I arrived about half past three o'clock. I met one of Mr. Campbell's men, who told me that he believed the bushrangers were in the house. When I reached the house, I saw Mr. Campbell, who told me that the bushrangers had left, and he showed me a place in the direction of which he fired, and where also he had found a carbine and a cabbage-tree hat. I found the spot to be in front of the dwelling, beyond a paling fence about forty yards from the house, near to which Mr. Campbell informed me he had found a carbine and a cabbage-tree hat. On this ground was a crop of oats - six feet in height. On examining the ground, I discovered a fresh track, which I followed up into the oats and I found the body of the deceased about ten yards from the fence. I searched the body and found two silk handkerchiefs thereon, which I produce. I found a bullet wound on the right side of the neck. The carbine produced I identify as a police carbine, and it is the same carbine which was pointed out to me by Mr. Campbell as the one found by him near to the spot where I found the deceased. I produce the cabbage-tree hat, aforesaid, which was handed to me by Mr. Campbell. I also produce a Colt's revolver, which was handed to me by constable Hogan who stated that he found it near the body. The revolver has six chambers, five of which were loaded.

Frederick William Pottinger, on oath, stated: I am officer in charge of police in the Lachlan district. On my way from Cowra to Forbes I met Mr. Hanbury Clements, at about twelve o'clock this day at Waugan who having informed me that Mr. David Campbell had shot one of three or four bushrangers who had attempted to stick up his premises on the previous night, I proceeded with Mr. Clements and my party of police to Mr. Campbell's. On my arrival the body of the deceased was pointed out to me, and I at once identified it as the body of John O'Meally. I have known John O'Meally off and on, for about three years, and I have frequently come into contact with him. I have apprehended him, and on one occasion he was in the Forbes lock-up for seven or eight weeks or more, and when in the course of prosecution of a case against him, I have had opportunities of watching him closely for hours together. I cannot, therefore, be mistaken as to his identity. The John O'Meally to whom I allude is the one who is known as the notorious bushranger, and for whom a reward of one thousand pounds is offered. On seeing the body I saw a bullet wound in the neck, after receiving which I feel sure that the deceased could not have lived many seconds.

William Hollister deposed : I am a senior-constable of mounted police. I have just seen the body of the deceased— the man said to have been shot by Mr. Campbell; I identify it as the body of John O'Meally, the notorious bushranger. I have known John O'Meally off and on since last July twelve months. I have seen him often, and have spoken to him frequently, and I feel that I cannot be mistaken as to his identity.

David Henry Campbell deposed : I am a squatter, residing at Goimbla, on the Eugowra Creek. I am a magistrate of the territory of New South Wales. About a quarter to nine last evening while seated in my dining room, I was startled by the sound of footsteps in the front verandah. I immediately grasped a double-barrelled gun, and proceeded to the door of my dressing-room, which adjoins my bedroom at the side of the house, when I was intercepted by a man at the doorway. *He instantly fired the contents of two barrels at my face, which I replied to by discharging one of the barrels of my gun.* The man immediately fled round the corner of the building and joined one or two others at the front door. I followed a short distance and seeing their strength, retired to my bedroom. The dining-room before mentioned was lighted up with a strong kerosene lamp, and the window blinds were raised. A spare gun was leaning in the chimney corner. My powderflask, containing some powder and some bullets, together with a box of caps, were lying on the mantel-piece. *Mrs. Campbell, whilst I was in the bedroom, rushed into the dining-room, and under the fire of the bushrangers from the front verandah, succeeded in securing the gun and ammunition before-mentioned,* which she brought to me, I immediately loaded the barrel which I had just discharged, and with the spare gun and ammunition rapidly passed through the dining room, and passing out at the back door took up my position between two slab walls which formed a passage from the back of the main buildings to the kitchen. I had not been there more than a quarter of an hour when a number of shots were discharged almost simultaneously from several directions, and one of the men called out, "If you don't immediately surrender, we will burn your place down." I replied "Come on— I'm ready for you," whereupon one of the bushrangers called out— "Is that it?" and a few minutes afterwards I saw flames arising from the barn, distant from the house about thirty yards. Mrs. Campbell had in the meantime, without my sanction, rushed across a paddock at the back of the house to the men's hut, distant from the house about 150 yards, for assistance, and was returning without success, and took up her position near to me with a servant girl. On the light increasing, consequent upon the progress of the flames, the bush-rangers retired behind a paling fence, about forty yards from the front of the house. Shortly after, Mrs. Campbell called my attention to a man with a cabbage-tree hat, looking over the said fence in the direction of the burning premises. I immediately ran round the end of the house, and from the front corner, took a deliberate aim at the man's throat. I fired, retreated, and re-loaded my gun. I should mention that, previous to firing this shot a number of shots were fired at the front door, with repeated calls to surrender, which I did not reply to. While occupied in reloading my gun, one or two shots were fired, and the bush rangers appeared to be retreating. About half an hour after—namely about half past eleven o'clock, I cautiously approached the spot at which I had fired, and discovered in the standing oats a single-barrelled carbine, and a cabbage-tree hat. I took possession of the same, until the arrival of the police, into whose charge I have delivered them. I identify the carbine and cabbage tree hat produced as the same I found in the oats. I kept watch until daylight, and then accompanied constable Fagan to the spot where we had previously found the carbine and hat. We followed a track in the oats about ten yards from the fence, when we discovered the body of the deceased. When I proceeded with Constable Fagan on to the oats, I found a pool of blood within a yard of the fence, as also a small pool near to where the body was lying. Immediately on my firing the man appeared to fall, but no sound was uttered. The back part of the cabbage-tree hat was dusty, as if the man had fallen backwards when hit, there was a small spot of blood inside the crown of the hat. I have no doubt but that the body of the deceased is that of the man at whom I fired. About a quarter of an hour after I obtained the hat and carbine, a Chinaman, whom I had set to watch the front of the building, reported to me that he had heard a rustling, as of a person approaching the spot where the body was found.

After the discovery of the body, I observed an indentation on the little finger of the right hand, as if a ring had been recently removed. Also, deceased's pockets had been turned inside out as if recently rifled I had never to my knowledge seen the deceased before. The bushrangers burned to the ground a range of stables containing eight stalls, and a large barn; the walls of the stable and the barn being of "Pisé " remain partially standing, but are rendered useless owing to the flames. The whole of the roofs were shingled and quite new. I estimate the cost of erecting the barn and stable at £400 sterling. The barn contained fifteen tons of hay, which I value at £50; and about five pounds worth of wool ready for the market. There was a new chaff-cutter in the barn, worth £20 sterling. In the stable was a favourite horse which I value at £20. The whole of the property above mentioned was entirely consumed.

William Campbell, on oath, states: *I am a squatter*, residing with my brother, the last witness. While in my bedroom about nine o'clock last evening, I heard three shots fired in quick succession, and immediately rushed into the dining-room, where several shots were then fired through one of the front windows. The room was lighted, and the blinds were up.

I therefore, immediately rushed out of the back door into the verandah. I there saw a man at my bedroom window (distant about five or six yards from where I stood), who fired two shots at me in quick succession, The first shot struck me in the chest, and I consequently stumbled and fell near to the step. So soon as I recovered I escaped through the back gate, and made my way through the standing oats at the back of the barn intending to make my way back to the house as soon as an opportunity presented itself. Very shortly afterwards a volley of a dozen shots were fired, accompanied by shouts from the bush-rangers, which to me were unintelligible. While still in the oats I saw the barn on fire, and saw two men passing the back wall of the barn rapidly, in the direction of the house. After the fire was lighted there was another volley fired towards the house from the direction of the barn. *This is the last firing that I heard, and I saw nothing more of the bushrangers ; and finding that all was quiet, I proceeded to the Eugowra police station on foot to give information to the police.*

William Browne, on oath, states: I am a Commissioner, in charge of the Lachlan Goldfield; I examined the body of the deceased, which I believe to be that of the well-known bush-ranger, O'Meally; I believe it to be his body from the countenance and the peculiar colour of his hair; he is however, much grown since I last saw him alive; I found a wound on the right side of the neck, which appears to have been caused by a bullet entering his neck under his ear, passing out behind the neck behind the vertebræ ; his death must have been instantaneous ; from the size of the wound I should think it was caused by an ounce ball; in my opinion the cause of death is so obvious that medical evidence is unnecessary.

A verdict of "Justifiable homicide" was returned, in accordance with the evidence.[4]

The findings of the inquiry would appear to have been a foregone conclusion. There was no attempt to find out why Hall and his men had come to Goimbla and certainly no attempt to ascertain whether David's refusal to listen to them had led to both the burning of the barn and the shooting, that ended in the death of O'Mealley. Once having put a reward on O'Mealley's head the killing of him would appear to be of almost no consequence other than the allocation of the reward.

---

4 This transcript was published in *The Sydney Morning Herald*, Friday, 27 November 1863. Retrieved from http://trove.nla.gov.au/newspaper/article/166656570 and *The Sydney Mail*, Saturday, 28 November 1983. Retrieved from http://trove.nla.gov.au/newspaper/article/13096315?

(In) Conclusion

So what was the spacetimemattering that made this event possible? The characteristics of colonial society at that time included the following:

- There was a category of person, including servants, on whom "reputable" people depended for the running of their domestic and work lives, yet who were not accorded names, who did not have a voice in legal matters, and who were subjected to brutal treatment for very minor and even non-offences, for example, the burning of Ben Hall's house.
- Women, even those who were counted as reputable, and even heroic, were not so respected as to have their voice heard in legal matters. For example, Amelia was not called as a witness at the hearing.
- The privileged, who have status through substantial money, landholdings, or title, or are connected in some way to the British ruling class, are able to maintain their status even when behaving extraordinarily badly and breaking the law. Pottinger was a perfect example.
- The treatment of convicts and bushrangers was brutal, and that brutality was taken-for-granted as the way things were. Their punishment was not taken to reflect badly on those who meted it out. David's shooting of O'Mealley was not seen by the officials, or his peers, as reflecting badly on him.

It has seemed extraordinary to me that the inquiry did not question the veracity of David's account, however improbable, or question his decision to move immediately to gun battle; nor did it try to get to the bottom of Ben Hall's intent on coming to talk to him. In this particular spacetimemattering, the possibility that Ben Hall had a legitimate voice that should be heard by David or by the police, was unthinkable. Once a claim had been made that he had been associated with Frank Gardiner, he was deemed to be a public enemy, even though his name had been cleared. His voice, and the voice of his men, was not able to be imagined by David, or by Pottinger, as something that anyone could or should hear.

The novelist Rolf Boldrewood/Thomas Alexander Browne, magistrate and gold-field commissioner, was a remarkable exception. Boldrewood himself would have been 37 years of age at the time of this event. He was married to Margaret Riley, the daughter of Honoria Rose Brooks. His account of the lives of men who fell outside the law, in *Robbery Under Arms*, is one of the most moving accounts I have ever read.

At the end of this chapter I find my heart aching for this terrible death. Johnny O'Mealley, 'half-broken horse gone brumby' was no hero. He did not have the social/cultural resources to make a different life for himself, as for example, Pottinger had had, or Frank Gardiner had when he escaped from the colony. I cannot help but grieve for the circumstances that made his life one that did not matter in the eyes of the graziers or the police.

Postscript: The Life of William Campbell

William was born in Jellasore Bengal on 18 May 1835, fifth son of Helena Maria and Thomas Campbell and younger brother of David, who had been born six years earlier. He was 28 at the time of the shooting. Ten years later, at the age of 37 he married Jane Grice. Their daughter, Severin Maud Campbell, was born at Wattle Flat Sofala. Severin was my father's godmother. William died in 1873. Severin was a baby, and William was only 38.

The only letter in my father's possession when he died was one from Severin(e), in response to his request that she become my sister's god-mother.

"Glenroy"
3 Rimmington St
Artarmon
20-8-40

My dear Tom,

My congratulations to you and Norma have been delayed, but you can't tell how pleased I was when Dorothy rang and gave the expected news. So you have a little daughter – it seems hard to realise how quickly the years pass – It is very nice of you to ask me to be a Godmother and I do appreciate the wish – but I think it should be someone much younger than I am – you see I am your God-mother and Dorothy's and I'm sure it would be better if Susanne Severin had someone more suitable – I'm glad you are giving her Severin for one of her names – it is uncommon – it is really a boy's name – a Danish name – I was called after one of my father's brothers and his [uncle was Severin Knud Salting][5] father of the two millionaires George and William Salting – George Salting was the owner of Cunningham Plains station which was managed by David Campbell and my father. Grandmother Campbell was a Dane – by the way the feminine spelling of the name is really Severine – but I always sign without the final e. I believe Hugh Stephens name is Hugh Severin – and his little girl

---

5 Amended from 'cousin was William Severin Salting'. This error of Severin's caused me many many hours of ineffectual searching.

at "Glenshaw" is Jill Severine – I don't think anyone else has the name[6] – Sue is a piquant little name – I'm glad Norma is so well. You must be pleased to have them home again. You will know you are alive now a baby rules the home – I am sending a little gift for baby – also a tiny thing for Norma and she will be able to see if Sue is as bonnie a baby as her father was – you say she has dark hair – well your curl is very fair – I've had the miniature and curl for many years. I was going to send them to Norma before but decided to wait 'till the babe arrived. It will be nice to see you all at...

The last page of her letter is missing, but in a collection of old photos I discovered it was Manly where she would see them, and where she would meet baby Susanne.

In the next chapter I turn to the story of David and William's sister, Maria Louisa Campbell and her husband Thomas Alfred Davies—known as Alfred. Maria Louisa and Alfred were my great grandparents. They migrated to the colony in 1870. By then David and William had moved to Cunningham Plains station to manage it for the Salting family. Alfred and Maria Louisa hastened to join David on receiving the news that Amelia had died.

---

6   Curiously she omits my father's sister, who was called Severin though she knew her well.

CHAPTER 9

From Soldier to Farmer to Magistrate:
Thomas Alfred Davies and Maria Louisa Campbell

Alfred was born on 18 February 1839, in St Helier, on the British island of Jersey, off the coast of Normandy.[1] When he was seven years old he wrote a letter from Margate, to his mother, Sophia, for her birthday. The letter was addressed to New St John's Road, St Helier, Jersey.

FIGURE 45   Letter from Alfred to his Mama
VENETIA MCMAHON'S COLLECTION

The fact that his dear Mama kept this small letter from her affectionate son, suggests he was very much cherished—and missed. This exquisite little letter carries me back to 1846, to the young Alfred on holiday, engaging in his labour

---

1   The letters and many of the images in this chapter come from Venetia McMahon's collection.

FIGURE 46   Alfred Davies *c.* 1853
             VENETIA MCMAHON'S COLLECTION

of love in writing to his Mama. The first three lines of his letter are perfectly and painstakingly written. That was no mean feat when writing with pen and ink, and at the age of seven. It is easy to imagine his pleasure in making the beautifully shaped letters and in perfectly spacing the words on each line. But on the fourth line disaster struck. His writing became messy, and the words didn't fit on the line. Was someone pressuring him to hurry up and finish his letter so they could go out to the seaside? As he squashes 'Mama' into the end of the line it is easy to imagine his distress at the wreckage of his beautiful letter. Whoever was pressuring him must have relented. On the fifth line his beautiful writing returns. But not quite. His line spacing is miscalculated and there isn't adequate room at the bottom for his signature. His Mama perhaps treasured this letter, as much as anything else for the drama she could see unfolding in his writing, between his desire for perfect control and his rising emotion.

A small watercolour painting of Alfred, when he was 12 or 13, still with his puppy fat, portrays him with a liquid softness—his eyes, the sea and sky behind him, all in the same pure blue of sky and water. His cravat and waistcoat, in contrast, are impeccably buttoned up, neat like the writing in his letter, this time with no slippages. As if in defiance of his own softness, Alfred sits upright; his expression is reserved, as if he is not at all sure he should be trusting the painter.

Alfred commenced a travel diary in 1856 when he was 17, where he kept a careful record of his travels. The entries are brief and give little of himself away. He records that when he was 18, he and his mother went to London, to pay a visit to Mr White, husband of his sister Emma, and then to Wales for several months, presumably to stay with family though he offers no details. A year later he recorded another visit to Wales, this time for six months, followed closely by a trip to Woodford in London. In 1859 he sought a commission in the army, and sat a four-day entrance exam from 7 to 11 February, at Burlington House in London. On 28 February he received notification that his exam was satisfactory, and in March, that he was appointed to the xxth Regiment and ordered to join the depot 1st Battalion at Chatham on or before 14 May. In 1860 he sailed for India, a trip of four months, calling at Portsmouth and the Cape along the way.

Once in India, he briefly recorded his various marches, and in 1862, he noted that the Delhi Gazette had announced his promotion to Lieutenant Vice. He did not, however, record the death of Sophia, his dear Mama, which occurred in that same year. He was remarkably consistent in not committing anything of emotional import to the page—the wariness toward the artist, it seems, was the same wariness he brought to imagined readers of his journal. The photo of him as a young man suggests the same caution and self-control. His friends in the

FIGURE 47
Alfred Davies
DAVIES FAMILY ALBUM

"Just before the Battle Mother"
a performed by Cornet Dickerson of
H.M. xx Regiment of feet. P.P.C.

FIGURE 48
'Just before the battle, Mother'

xx Regiment no doubt teased him mercilessly in attempts to break through his reserve. Among his possessions was a drawing entitled "'Just before the Battle Mother' as performed by Cornet Dickinson of H.M. xx Regiment of feet. P.P.C.".

They made fun of themselves and each other—these effete, highly cultured British soldiers, who must go out to battle, risking their lives for Empire.

In 1863, on 30 March, Alfred rode with his friend, Houghton, to Kumowhe where he was introduced to the Campbell family. Six months later, in mid-September, he took two weeks leave to go back to Kumowhe. He was in love with the beautiful Maria Louisa Campbell.

He plucked up his courage to propose to her, but when one of her brothers interrupted them, he had no choice but to put his proposal in writing. He was in agony, not only that she might refuse him, but at the teasing he might be subjected to if the letter were to fall into the wrong hands.

> My dear Miss Campbell
> You perhaps remember my saying some days ago what I thought of those who *wrote* such letters as this will be; I little thought then that I should be *compelled*, faute de mieux, to do so myself. I wish to tell you that *I love you*

better than any created being on the face of the earth. I meant to have done so yesterday morning had not your brother thought fit to do as he did. I am at a loss to determine in my own mind whether you feel for me anything but common friendship such as you would for any casual acquaintance. My love for you says yes, but my fears say no. I should never have written this but for one or two casual remarks of yours, as my circumstances at present are such as will entail the necessity of a long engagement until in fact I attain my company or at least am near doing so. But *if you do love me* that will not be an insurmountable obstacle.

The *small* events of the last few days have fully convinced me of the truth of the old saying that "the course of true love never did run smooth" and you can doubtless conceive the horrible state of doubt and anxiety I shall be in when I have given you this. I entreat you should you determine to refuse me to return me this letter that I may destroy it together with all my hopes of happiness as I could not submit to the jibes and sneers *of some* should this by accident fall into their hands. I wrote a letter yesterday but my courage failed me and my horror of what is commonly called a *snub* was ever present and deterred me from giving it to you. But on second thoughts I feel convinced that you will, should I be so unfortunate which God forbid, comply with my request about destroying this.

Believe me I am Yours devotedly
Alfred Davies 29th Sept /63

His journal gave no intimation of his anguish. He wrote, simply, at the end of his visit on 29 September: "Proposed to Maria Campbell that I should be her husband some day. She had no objection."

Thankfully, his letter was not destroyed.

A letter from Maria Louisa to Alfred written 12 months after the proposal and three months before they were married reveals a buoyant young woman. She is forthright and honest, chiding Alfred over a misunderstanding and commenting on the photos he had sent of himself which she found far too serious and unflattering. She knows the man behind the serious images he has sent her, and that is what she loves. She deals with his prickliness and his caution about expressing himself with loving good humour.

Gya 31st Aug [1863]
Darling Alfred,
I feel a little seedy and have a *headache* so you won't mind a shorter letter than usual. I have yours of the 26th and 27th before me enclosing the

FIGURE 49   Maria Louisa Campbell *c.* 1863
                        DAVIES FAMILY ALBUM

photographs. .... I wonder how it is but your likeness has the same fault
they say mine has, that is you have not your *own* jolly expression, and I
never saw you looking as you are in the picture. The likeness is altogether
very far from flattering but I like it all the same as I know what you are in
reality, dearest old fellow.

I see I made a mistake in quoting the Saturday Review but it is a shame, your spoiling the whole thing by a -- that should never have been in it. It is all a mistake!

I think your idea of being married at Benenes is the best after all...

The Gya place must evidently be knocked on the head as the Padre won't be able to come till December... but it can't be helped, and I don't so much mind as it struck me you did not *quite* approve of the place although you didn't say so. Can you tell me if diptheria is catching. Mrs B...bury's child is in a very dangerous state with it, and I stupidly sat with the baby for some time, I hope it is not because I hate the idea of getting anything the matter with my throat but I am not anxious about it.

I think I shall leave this note alone today and write you a longer one tomorrow. I don't think I *ever* told you I have got *such* a (huge) bath in my room. It is about 12 feet long and very deep. I can almost swim in it. I have had a pair of "swimmers" made as its a great amusement to *see* me perform my ablutions in the bath. It is such glorious fun I could be in it all day.

Remember you have promised to have a big bath built for me when I am Mrs Davies or rather before. Do you remember talking about it in the garden at Chanderapore.

This is a very stupid concoction but I can't help it. believe darling in the passionate and devoted love of
Your own wife
Maria

Two further letters survive, also from Venetia's collection, that Thomas Campbell, Maria Louisa's father, wrote to her in the months before her marriage. They offer a lovely glimpse of Maria Louisa's generous character and of the life of an indigo planter, and implicitly, the unpleasant and unsafe lives of those who worked in the factory:

Chanderapoorah
29th August 64

My dearest Maria
Your letter of the 25th convinces me that I acted judiciously in sending Robert to Gya without an hour's delay and I felt easy at the idea of his being under professional treatment, at the same time I hope soon to hear that Dr Banbury has been able to alleviate the symptoms and that no further mischief need be apprehended. – It is just like your kind self to

wish to be with me and enliven my solitude; but all things considered I think it best, though reluctantly, to forego the pleasure of asking you to join me here, the Season is bad for travelling and the discomfort of the vats at work in the compound together with the risk of a bad climate and no medical advice at hand we must let matters for the present remain as they are and I must content myself with endeavouring to be at Gya a fortnight or so before you are to be married and then lay plans for the future.

After writing the above I received the enclosures by the mail – it does not contain much news, we can however now make sure of seeing dear Kitty in November and we can by and bye settle who is to go down and receive her on arrival in Calcutta. – I am glad to see Robert's note of the 26th that he was better and now hope he will soon be all right. – With love all round

Ever Yours affectionately
Tho. Campbell

Robert did later die from wounds he received when he was mauled by a tiger.

In the days before the marriage Thomas Campbell wrote again to Maria Louisa on black-edged note paper from Calcutta, where he had gone to meet Kitty. He tells her of his deep melancholy on visiting the grave of his beloved Helena Maria, who had died a year earlier. He comforts himself with the belief, or trust, that her death was God's will:

Calcutta Nov 64

My dearest Maria
Your note of the 16th was handed to me by Miss Howe six hours ago when I called there. ...

There is no morning train through to Rajmahal on Sundays. My best plan therefore will be to take the 7am train on Monday and ---be with you all the same afternoon – please ask Walter to have a conveyance at the station to take us to his Bungalow. I have had the melancholy Trial today of shedding bitter Tears over your darling mother's Grave and you may fancy my misery, but God's will be done! The spot is in good preservation and a Marble Tablet placed on the headstone – but I cannot dwell on this mournful Subject.

Give my love to all and believe me
Your ever affe. Father
Tho. Campbell

Shoulders still bad – they wanted to galvanise me yesterday – but you know I am a stubborn patient – and of course declined the experiment.

Alfred and Maria Louisa were married on 28 November 1864, at The Kutcherry in Rajmahal, West Bengal. Alfred at the time of the marriage was a Lieutenant in the 1st Battalion. He was based at Rouker and she at Rajmahal. The witnesses at the wedding were Maria Louisa's sister, Catherine (Kitty), her father, Thomas, and A.J. Fraser.

Two months after the wedding Alfred's father, Evan, wrote from Jersey, a tender and affectionate letter, looking forward to meeting his new daughter-in-law, and re-connecting Alfred with news of 'home':

St Helier Jersey
Jany 31 1865

My dear Alfred
I have received your wedding cards to announce your marriage having taken place. I again reiterate my sincere hope that the event will be conducive to your future happiness. Also convey to my daughter in law my Congratulations and kind regards, Anticipating the time when I shall have the pleasure of being introduced to her! Have you yet recd. the £100 that I sent you? It was a bill from a bank in London made payable to yourself at the Agra Bank by the mail of the 1st of Nov last via Bombay in a registered letter ... which I trust you have received long 'ere this? And should it so happen that by any mishap that this has not come to hand write immediately to the Agra Bank on the subject. Your old friend the Revd. T. Davies of Treberflld has written me a letter of congratulations and at the same time making various kind enquiries about you and will no doubt write to you soon. As Emma is about to write have nothing further to add And am your affecte. Father
Evan Davies

For a time Alfred and Maria Louisa lived a high life in India. Their invitations to mix with high society included, for example:

Lieut and Mrs Davies invited to a Ball at Russapugla by Prince Gholam Mohumed to meet his Hon The Lieut Governor and Mrs Beadon 30-1-1866 (see opposite)

Mr and Mrs T. A. Davies invited to fancy dress ball at the Belvedere by the Lieutenant Governor 3-4-1866 *at* 9 *o'clock*

Their first child, Evan Alfred, was born in August 1865, in Dinapore. Alfred was posted back to the UK, and their daughter, Helena Maria (known as Nell), was born in Plymouth, in August 1868. Then he was posted to Ireland, where once again they mixed in high society:

Mr and Mrs Davies invited to dinner at Kilkenny Castle by Lord and Lady Ormonde 15th Jan c. 1867

In the UK Alfred's salary was insufficient to meet the social expectations associated with his position. It was a terrible ordeal for him to be unable to support his family in the way he believed he should, and in the manner to which Maria Louisa was accustomed.

They began to consider the possibility of migration to New South Wales. Both had parents and grandparents who had left their home countries and travelled to India, and to the West Indies. Maria Louisa's cousins, George and William Salting, had grown up in New South Wales, and three of her brothers, David, William and Henry had long since migrated there. With some trepidation about travelling into the unknown, Alfred and Maria Louisa decided to try their luck in the colony.

Alfred wrote to William Salting in 1869 about the difficulty of making the decision to go out to the Colony when he knew so little about it. A draft of that letter survived:

My dear Salting
I have been wavering for a moment in my decision to go out. In fact the more I look at it the better I like it.
   It may be that I am taking a leap in the dark not knowing what I am going to and in this outlandish place there are no means of getting books or anything else to enlighten one – but one thing I do know viz which I am leaving behind; and I am content. I don't think I shall be ever likely to try the experiment of trying to live on an insufficient income in the United Kingdom again – I have had enough of that for my lifetime.

To meet His Honor
The Lieut. Governor and
Mrs Beadon
Prince Gholam Mohumed
requests the company of
Lieut and Mrs Davies —
at a Ball on
February 30th 1866 —
at 9 P. M.
Russapugla
an answer will oblige.

FIGURE 50   Invitation to the Ball

I think I shall be able to start in July, unless I wait a little longer to get my step on retirement. But I shall soon know if I am to get it within a reasonable time and if not I shall retire as I am.

[The draft ends with a small ink drawing of a small thatched cottage with coconut palms—perhaps Alfred's idea of what life in the colony will be like.]

Maria Louisa and Alfred set sail from Plymouth on board the *Paramatta*, on 4 September 1870. Their third child, George William Hope Davies, was born on that journey. They arrived in Sydney on 12 December 1870.

They were welcomed by the Breilatts, who gave them the terrible news of the death of their daughter, Amelia, the wife of David Campbell. She had given birth to twins on 24 May. Only one of the twins survived. Four days after the birth Amelia died from peritonitis. Maria Louisa and Alfred gave up their own plans in favour of going to Cunningham Plains to help David with the management of Saltings' property, and with the care of the children. Maria Louisa wrote to her sister Catherine, telling her the news:

My dearest Kittie

Here we are at the end of our day – at last after being on board ship for more than three months and no one was more thankful than I was to get to the end of it, although as far as my confinement went and everything that went with it, nothing could have gone on more satisfactorily in any way. The little man came into the world just off the Cape of Good Hope and is a fine sturdy little Monkey. I got on capitally. I never felt even the ordinary (   ) that follow these affairs, of course having the care of the children without a servant was very hard work but the passengers were almost excessively kind – and Alfred you know how good and thoughtful he is when I am needy; now I think I have said sufficient about myself personally. The Breillats [Amelia's parents] came on board to meet us and invited us to stay with them, which we were very thankful to do for it seems so wretched to come to a place where you know nobody. They are all painfully kind and make us feel quite at home, Poor David I believe is dreadfully cut up at Amelia's death and to add to his misfortunes, he has himself met with a severe accident by a fall from his horse and is now under the care of a clever medical team at Yass. He wrote me a very kind letter and he seems to look forward to having us with him –I believe we are to stay with him now.

This is a change in our affairs, however of course I am very glad and I should do the same for his children as I should do for my own, one of the twins is alive and they have all experienced hurt. I'll take care of all the children - from what Mrs Breillat says he has a very comfortable house and I have no doubt we shall be very happy there.

We are both quite delighted with the look of Australia. I think the climate is perfect. It feels so very much like much of India seeing all the tropical trees and fruits and at the same time it is very like home.[2] It seems to be a mixture of the two climates. We only arrived the day before yesterday so have not had much time to see the place.

I was so glad to get your letter on our arrival – Your poor boy must have had a bad illness, but I trust he is well again – I know what an anguish though it is to have a child seriously ill so I quite feel for you... [Maria Louisa tells at length of 5 year-old Evan not being as robust as he likes to be and how he has a continuing discharge from his ear which she hopes will not leave him deaf]—the doctors say it is just a matter of time so I must wait patiently –. Poor David seems to have been very unfortunate

---

2   "Home" was England, where her Danish father had grown up, and where she had spent time as a young woman with the Salting family, and then as a young married woman with Alfred.

altogether with his family but Mrs Breillat says that both his wife and children would have been alive now if they had had medical advice for them, poor Amelia had neither doctor nor nurse to attend her. Her life would likely have been spared if she had been able to have ordinary treatment from any doctor. Poor David was almost out of his mind with grief and Mrs Breillat says that time does not seem to soothe him. It is really such a shocking tragic affair in every way.

I had not time to finish this letter the children being peevish and fretful. Poor Nellie and baby are quite upset from the sudden change from on-board ship life. We had to call in Dr Alloway but he seems to think it is nothing but the change – we will probably leave this 'morrow or the next day for David's place and I will write you a long letter from there – please pass this on to Papa for I have no time to write by this mail to him –

The Breillats are to have a large dancing party tonight – you have no idea how I have lost all pleasure in these affairs and do not care a button about them. I called on Mrs R... and Mrs McDonald both of whom I like. They seem ladylike and quiet, they asked affectionately after you and pleased to hear of your welfare.

Lady Manning[3] told Mrs Breillat that she hoped I would call on her, but I do not know if I shall go.

Give my love and kisses to the bairns – and the same to yourself – from ever yr afft. Sister

Maria Davies

The plains country they travelled into, west of the Great Dividing Range, was extraordinarily beautiful. The distant hills shifted in colour with the movement of clouds, sometimes soft flesh coloured, sometimes sky blue, sometimes disappearing into the sky or the plain.

Cunningham Plains station, an enormous holding, with "60,000 sheep and 80 employees, the number doubling in the high season" (Kass, 2009: 14), was near the tiny townships of Harden and Murrumburrah, west of Goulburn and north-west of Canberra. On the Station, David was in process of building a magnificent house on a block he had purchased with Saltings' approval. It was built of pisé, or rammed earth—a skill he learned from a Chinese man who worked for him and which he had used at Goimbla. It was there, following the months long sea voyage, that baby George first learned of life in the colony—life filled with tragedy and beauty and wealth.

---

3   The wife of Sir William Patrick Manning

FIGURE 51A-B   Cunningham Plains, 2017
                 PHOTOS BY ROGER BOYD

FIGURE 52   Homestead at Cunningham Plains station, now called Yarrawonga Merino Stud,
              2017
              PHOTO AUTHOR

At first things went well at Cunningham Plains, so much so that Alfred and Maria Louisa decided to set up their own property nearby. In 1872 David completed his beautiful house and married Louise Powell.[4] William Campbell left Cunningham Plains and married Jane Grice and moved to Sofala. Alfred and Maria Louisa bought their first block of land which they registered as 'Cunningham Plains Nant Gwylan'.

The Robertson Land Act, passed ten years earlier in 1861, led to the surveying of the vast acres of land which had until then been leased, or squatted on, by the graziers. It was divided into small blocks which could then be bought by small farmers, known as selectors. The graziers had to buy land from their own runs, block by block, in competition with the small selectors and sometimes with each other. There was a risk in this process that they could lose vital sources of water, and links between various parts of their properties if they did not take the matter of purchase very seriously. Purchase of the blocks was conditional on "improving" the land by clearing and fencing it, and on building a dwelling on it. The sale could not be completed until it had been certified that these improvements had taken place. Successive acts were passed in the 1860s in an attempt to engineer a successful outcome. One such act was "the 'Homestead Selection Act' which specified perpetual residence on each block" (Banham 1994: 16).

To manage the residential requirement the graziers developed a strategy of paying a man, known as a 'dummy', £50 per annum to live on it. In some cases the dummy's name was on the conditional purchase document. There was a lot of room for things to go wrong. Graziers purchased blocks in each of their children's names and in the names of trusted workers. The code of honour developed among the squatters was that they would not purchase blocks on each other's runs.

A great deal of responsibility fell on the shoulders of managers like David Campbell. The inroads of selectors on Saltings' stations led to a halving of their productivity. Absentee landlords were also vulnerable to their own managers, who might buy up vital pieces of their land with the aim of displacing them.

New South Wales had thus embarked on a radical programme of rural social change. The interior was to be populated. The town nearest to Cunningham Plains station and to Nant Gwylan was Murrumburrah. It had a population of 182 in 1871, but by 1881, with the influx of selectors and small businesses, the population was 1,620. It had both a Catholic church and a Church of England Church, and with the coming of the railway, there was a bank, a court of petty

---

4   Louise Powell thus married into my father's family. She was the grand-daughter of Richard and Christiana Brooks, who were my mother's great great grandparents.

sessions, a school, and a pub built by David Campbell himself in 1881. The town was divided between the pastoral elite and the new labor-voting railway workers, many of whom were Irish (Kass, 2009). This programme of rural social change threatened those Wiradjuri people who had survived the Black War, as they could no longer live on those areas unoccupied by the large landholders. The increasingly dense settlement on blocks of land, that were cleared and fenced and built on, made them increasingly dependent on work or charity from white settlers (Kass, 2009).

Between 1873 and 1875 Alfred bought successive parcels of land to make up a viable grazing property. His carefully laid plans depended on sharing Cunningham Plains station's shearing shed and equipment. Since its manager, David, was Maria Louisa's brother, and since Cunningham Plains station was owned by Maria Louisa's cousins, the Saltings, that was a reasonable expectation.

In 1874 Alfred was invited to become a "magistrate of the colony" in Kitarah, near Murrumburrah. These regional magistracies were unpaid positions allocated to the landed gentry whose task was to manage the legal affairs of their region. His work included inspections to establish whether selectors were following the requirements of the various acts. He was sympathetic to the difficult lives of the selectors. In part, he agreed to take up the position, because he saw them as vulnerable to the men on the bench, who were all members of the rural elite. In a letter to George Salting in December 1874, he wrote: "I have just been requested to accept the honour of being a magistrate of the Colony – I declined soon after I came out, but now a poor cockatoo has no chance with only squatters on the bench, so I shall have J.P. tacked to my name." A cockatoo, or cocky, was a term for poor farmers who scratched a living from the earth on their small blocks.

By the time George was four years old, he had two new sisters, Alice and Lillian, and then another brother, Llewellyn, born in 1875. His little sister Madeline was born several years later in 1878.

David Campbell meanwhile was tempted by the opportunities the new laws presented him with. He had more than once owned his own station and had lost what he invested in them. The Saltings had given him the position on Cunningham Plains because he was a member of the family who needed help. They paid him handsomely, at £1000 a year, and they covered all the costs related to the station, which had "60,000 sheep and 80 employees, the number doubling in the high season" (Kass, 2009:14). With the new laws David saw his chance to make good again. He bought blocks for himself, and set up a horse breeding stud, but in the process, it seems, he failed to look after the Saltings' interests.

The previous manager of Cunningham Plains station, J. Macansh, who had moved on to become a landholder, was alarmed at the state the station had fallen into. He wrote to the Saltings and told them their property was going to ruin. George Salting then wrote to Alfred to ask his advice, hoping what Macansh had said was exaggerated. Alfred wrote a long reply, in December 1874, asking that his reply remain in confidence since things were already bad enough between himself and his brother-in-law. He detailed all that he saw going wrong.

David, he said, had created very bad feeling in the rural community by free selecting 320 acres of a neighbour's run. As Alfred explained, referring to a map of the region:

> The original farm you permitted him to purchase is marked 1, upon which he has built. Next comes No. 2 a free-selection of 320 acres, upon Mr Weltman's run in the name of one of your oldest and most trustworthy servants on the station (old Bishop). There is an old saying that dog cannot eat dog, it is a point of honor among squatters not to take up land on each other's runs, unless they quarrel when it becomes a weapon of war between them – ie DC's proceedings have caused a great deal of ill feeling & heat -- which will bear fruit yet – I only hope you may not be again the victim.

Alfred was deeply affronted by David bringing Cunningham Plains station into disrepute. He also believed that not only was David's selection of dummies causing potential harm to the Saltings, but the land David was selecting for himself was at their expense, and in one case at Alfred's expense as well:

> Some of your dummies are men I would not trust for a moment, others children who cannot transfer the land until they become of age, and may then refuse to do so. Your manager naturally picks the best and most trustworthy men for himself and you, ie the station, gets the remainder. Nos. 3 & 4 are two selections, one of 200, the other of 40 acres adjoining each other, right in the centre of your purchased land and which will next to ruin the paddock he is about to fence for you there, with a *view to making you pay half the value of the fence he is putting around his own ground* – And finally No. 5, a selection he took up a few days ago with the avowed intention of cutting me off from 320 acres I had recently bought and marked W. Which has compelled me to buy another selector out at his own price to block him and keep the communication open with W lest D.H.C should get hold of him before me; in fact he tried and failed, not knowing the people. So I had at once to purchase it. But it is a contest that I cannot maintain. When I take up land, I have at the same time to take a man to employ & give him 50 pounds a year. He takes a man in your employ, paid by you, & doing your work, makes a dummy of him for

himself & at no cost to himself. In short, the direct enemy I have & who is using his utmost endeavours to ruin me, & using both his own & your capital to do so, besides the influence of the large establishment he is at the head of its unlimited capital, is your manager, D.H. Campbell ...

Alfred continued with his long litany of David's wrongdoing, carefully documenting each point. After a sustained effort to make an impartial account, his emotions got the better of him:

The management of Cunningham Plains is the laughing stock and scorn of the whole countryside, the manager does absolutely nothing, is universally hated for his mean grasping and ungenerous nature and little want of consideration for those whom he dares to bully – added to his helpless incompetency and the complete state of muddle he gets the sheep into whenever he chances to go among them *by himself*...

What I cannot stand in the man is his fearful selfishness. The station, his wife, children, all may go to the devil, so long as his hide is safe & his pocket untouched; and his conceit is something stupendous; once he gets an idea into his head he cannot be wrong...

Then with regard to work, he does, beyond marking out that big return he sends you every quarter, absolutely nothing. Usually of a morning his horse nicely groomed, with bright bit and stirrup irons is brought round by his groom, that you pay for under the impression that he is the man about the place... He takes care to be back comfortably by dinner after which judging by appearances he is not fit for any useful work for a couple of hours or so & then the buggy and pair will be brought round and his lordship will drive out in state for a constitutional with Madam.

David, for his part, hated Alfred with a passion. When David's sheep manager, Wilson, arranged with Alfred to have his sheep shorn in the Cunningham Plains shed David flew into a terrible rage. Though Alfred had a verbal agreement with him, that for the first two or three years of setting up his farm he could use the Saltings' shed, David was no longer willing to co-operate with him.

George and William Salting were alarmed at Alfred's letter, though George thought he had perhaps been a little spiteful. William, though, was confident that Alfred was a man of honour and integrity and that his judgement could be trusted. Given that Macansh had reported some of the same problems in his earlier letter, they had no choice but to act. The process of review went on during 1875 and early 1876. In April 1876, William wrote that the independent review "fully endorsed the charges made by Davies". He noted further, with

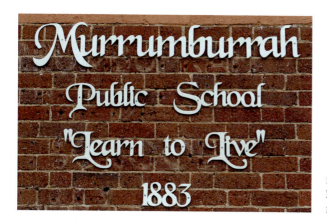

FIGURE 53
Murrumburrah School
PHOTO BY ROGER BOYD

alarm, that they are about to lose Wilson, the overseer at Bouyeo, who, according to the report "will be an immense loss to us, as he is a most efficient and hard-working man, and to him is due, and not to Campbell, that the station has been kept in anything like order. For while Campbell is riding and driving about with ladies and playing in polo matches Wilson will not remain [even if we increase his salary] under such a manager ...". The Saltings had been so careful of David's feelings, that he did not realise he was not only under review but that his position as manager was no longer secure. He made an offer to George and William that they should go into partnership with him. But rather than agree to partnership, they required him to give up his horse breeding enterprise and to sell his selections, and on those conditions, they kept him on as manager.[5]

Alfred meanwhile was closely involved in the community and in setting up his farm. He was appointed to the Public School Board in Cunningar, for example, in 1875. In 1877 he registered his stock brand xx. In that same year the railway came to Murrumburrah. By 1879 many of the squatters/graziers on their vast landholdings had largely been replaced by selectors on smaller freehold properties (Kass, 2009).

As the population of Murrumburrah and nearby Harden grew, public order issues arose. "The Anglican Minister William Cocks pleaded for the extension of the Police Act to the town to ensure that unsanitary practices such as keeping pigs and the disposal of butcher's offal onto vacant land was controlled to prevent the spread of typhus. The towns people were described as being of a very primitive character. The Police Magistrate agreed and the Police Act was

5 Curiously, in the account of David Campbell's life written by his descendent Alex Campbell (2017), none of this dramatic interlude is included. Perhaps David never understood what had gone on behind the scenes.

FIGURE 54   David Campbell's headstone
             PHOTO BY ROGER BOYD

extended to the town in Sept 1880" (Kass, 2009, p. 22). In that same year the Court House was built, an Assembly Hall erected, and the newspaper *Murrumburrah Signal* was established. In 1883 the school was built in Murrumburrah.

A further major change that was instituted at that time was the appointment of full time paid police magistrates. From 1881 to 1886 Alfred was appointed as police magistrate at Kempsey. He continued to do the earlier inspection work and was reported in the *Burowa News* 20-3-85 as making depositions at the Land Council on holdings just north east of Murrumburrah.

In 1885 he applied for a transfer to Cobar, just south of Bourke. He took up the position of Police Magistrate there on 22 May 1885. He was also appointed warden of mining in June of that year. David Campbell died that year, and Alfred took leave from his position at Cobar to go to Cunningham Plains to support his family.

The enigmatic message on David's gravestone tells a multitude of possible stories. It was erected by his employees, they say, "as a slight token of esteem".

In 1886 Alfred was transferred back to Kempsey. In 1887 he became an honorary churchwarden at the West Kempsey Church of England Church, appointed by the Bishop of Grafton. In 1887 the positions of District Registrar in Bankruptsy, Mining Warden, Licencing Magistrate, Deputy Sheriff and Visiting Justice to the Public Works Prison at Trial Bay were added to his duties. He was also a member of the Local Land Branch. In 1896 the geographic region for which he was responsible was extended to include Camden Haven and Port Macquarie.

In that first decade of paid magistracies, the work loaded on to the magistrates expanded in a way that paid no attention to what it was actually possible for one man to do. As I read of each additional responsibility added to Alfred's already demanding schedule I thought it would surely all break; not only Police magistrate in Kempsey, but also in Camden Haven and Port Macquarie, plus District Registrar in Bankruptcy, Visiting Justice to Trial Bay Prison, Mining Warden, Licencing Magistrate, Deputy Sheriff, Member of the local Land Board ... I know only too well what it is to persist in managing a workload that is unmanageable, at considerable personal cost. For Alfred it all broke with a massive stroke in 1898. He was totally incapacitated and unable to speak for the final decade of his life.

For some years after his stroke, Alfred and Maria Louisa lived in Walcha with their daughter Alice, who had married the Walcha GP, Sam Stephens. They bought the house next door to them, and they lived there until Maria Louisa became ill. She had cancer of the uterus and could no longer manage the care of Alfred in his incapacitated state. Eventually they both moved into Ermelo in Marrickville, where they could receive full time care. Maria Louisa died on 28 July 1906, and Alfred died two years later, on 31 May 1908.

Their oldest son, Evan, was the executor of Alfred's will. After he had been paid his commission, the estate of £514 was only worth, in 1912, £270—about $30,000 dollars in today's terms.

The house Alfred and Maria Louisa built is no longer standing; only the chimney remains. Nant Gwylan doesn't feature in any of the histories of the area, and it was difficult to find when I went searching for it with Helen Boyd and her son Roger. We found it a few kilometres up the wheat silo road. It had a lost, abandoned look about it. The name is spelt incorrectly on the rusting metal sign. Even so, my heart stopped when we found it, and I was able to begin to imagine the life that Alfred and Maria Louisa and their family had lived there.

At Nant Gwylan the plains open up into a vast flat landscape made up almost entirely of sky. The hills and mountains are distant and the sense of space, and of silence, inspires awe.

FIGURE 55   The author at front gate of Nant Gwylan
             PHOTO BY ROGER BOYD

FIGURE 56   Flat plains of Nant Gwylan, 2017
             PHOTO BY ROGER BOYD

CHAPTER 10

Small Selectors: Margaret Miles and Michael Carty

My grandmother, Jean, was an un-storied presence in my life until I began this project. My father, her first child, never spoke about her or her history. The first story I found, when I began this project, was an anti-story—that Jean would not discuss her history with her daughter Severin. All my subsequent attempts to find anything about her kept coming to a dead end. I discovered, toward the very end of this project, that it was not only my father's silence, and Jean's silence, that had defeated me, it was also her indulgence in name-changing that had led me on a series of wild goose chases.

Jean was born Eliza Carty, on May 20 1884. On her marriage certificate, she registered her name, not as Eliza Carty, but as Elizabeth Mary McCarthy, changing both her given name and her family name. Still further, on her marriage certificate, she registered her mother's maiden name as Margaret Stephens. But Margaret was the daughter of William Miles and Jane Hill, William a convict and Jane the daughter of one. Margaret Miles (1839–1920), had never been a Stephens. I was able to discover those facts through a surprising DNA match. Vicki Fisher drew my attention to the fact that we had a match. We found we were both descended from William Miles and Jane Hill. Their daughter Eliza Miles was the sister of Margaret Miles, Jean's mother. Margaret's sister, Vicki's great great grandmother, had not hidden the details of her ancestry. At last, through Vicki's research, I could begin to find my way into Jean's ancestry.

Even in the absence of stories, I had felt myself drawn to Jean. She died six years before I was born. Yet when I first saw the photo of her, and then the second photo of her in the car with George and the two children and their Nanny (Chapter 4) I had a compelling sense that she and I were of the same matter.

Margaret Miles married Michael Carty (1820–1884). Michael was Irish, and it was in Ireland that my sense of connection with the land itself and the people was so strong that, even in the absence of any story connecting me to them, I felt compelled to begin this entire ancestral project. The shared love of stories, perhaps particularly stories of death and of ghosts, was more than a random connection. Our DNA is entangled in the lands we come from, not so separate from them, and each other, and not so impervious to the events in our lives as our liberal humanist mythologies would have us think. If this project can be said to have had a beginning, that beginning was in Ireland, through a great grandfather I was yet to discover.

Michael was born into a catholic family in 1820, in Emgillavr (pronounced a little like MacGillvrey), in County Cavan in Ireland. A common cultural/historical thread that links Australia and Ireland, is our shared history of British colonisation. Cavan, the city in which Emgillavr is situated, escaped colonisation for quite a long time. It is the oldest inland town in the north of Ireland. Whereas Dublin had been controlled by the British since the invasion of 1169, Cavan remained under Irish control through the Middle Ages, and had little commerce with the outside world. It had an oral culture; business was conducted not through administrative structures, but through face-to-face meetings. Migrants to Cavan were attracted there from Dublin and Drogheda by trading opportunities set up in the mid-fifteenth century by Eoghan O'Raghallaigh, who set up a market below his castle on Tullac Mongan hill.

In the early seventeenth century Cavan was taken over by the English, and the territories of Eoghan O'Raghallaigh's descendants were confiscated and made available to English and Scottish settlers. In the subsequent century Cavan's economy flourished; money was invested in the building of roads to facilitate communication between the multiple small centres and the markets flourished. The farming of flax, and the making of linen was by then a thriving industry.

Despite the flourishing economy, the small farmers and factory workers lived in relative poverty. Their houses were mud-walled, thatched cabins. Only the wealthy could afford to build stone houses with slate roofs. Scattered among the thatched cabins were shops and taverns, and service industries like blacksmiths and harness-makers. The regular fair days attracted buyers and sellers from far afield. After all the buying and selling at the fair there was a great deal of drunken revelry. It was on such a fair day that Thomas Hardy's Michael Henchard, an itinerant, out-of-work hay-trusser, in a drunken fit of rage sold his wife and child to a passing sailor (Hardy 2012 [1886]).

By the time Michael Carty was born in 1820, Cavan had jails, military barracks, apothecaries and printers. A local middle class was emerging of businessmen, notaries and administrators. Not long before Michael was born, Lord Farnham set about beautifying Cavan, building boulevards, with beautiful houses on one side, and parks and fountains and walkways for the leisure of the gentry on the other. Such 'boulevardisation' served to further emphasise the gap between the rich and the poor. The Farnhams also built a fine parish church, attached to which was the Farnham (Catholic) National School.

There was already a great deal of poverty before the linen-making industry moved to Belfast in 1825. A mechanised factory had been built there, which made the production of linen cheaper and less labour intensive. A further blow was delivered to the people of Cavan when the Belfast factory began to source its flax locally, and the flax farming in County Cavan was annihilated. Further, with the end of the Napoleonic wars, there was less demand for the market goods sold in Cavan. When famine came, the poor had few resources to fall back on. Cholera hit the community in 1832 and the population of Cavan, through mortality and emigration, dropped by 20 per cent.

Although the English presence in the form of traders, soldiers and tourists had been a long-term presence in Cavan, Michael's first language is unlikely to have been English. He may well have been literate in Gaelic though it seems he never learned to write in English. He left a country riven by class and racial bias, suffering the collapse of local farming and industry, and plagued by cholera. The chance of a free ticket to New South Wales, with the promise of work, and the possibility of eventually owning your own land in the Colony, was a chance many of his compatriots were taking.

Michael migrated to New South Wales in 1841 through the Bounty system, which paid ship's captains as much as £19 for each suitably skilled worker they 'introduced' into the Colony; workers such as shepherds, ploughmen and agricultural labourers were in short supply in the colony, as were tradespeople like brick-makers, carpenters, blacksmiths, tailors and needlewomen. Young single people were preferred along with young married couples. Michael was described as married, with the comment on the ship's register stating "In good health and should be useful", suggesting he was a young man who was multi-skilled and not afraid of hard work.

Michael was 21 years old, and accompanied by his wife, Helen, whose parents were Anne and James Rickle, also from Cavan. He was responsible on the journey for the care of four other young Bounty migrants on the ship, who were much the same age as he was. They were Rose Cook/Cooke (aged 20, from Elphin, Rosecommon), Elizabeth and Mary Sharp/Sharpe/Shapp/ Sharpet (aged 20 and 23 of Drumgoon Cavan) and Thomas Sharpe (aged 20). The scribe, whose task was to enter the details of each passenger into the ledger, obviously had enormous difficulty decoding their Irish accents. While Michael was Roman Catholic, and was recorded as unable to read and write, the four young people under his care were Protestants, and all of them could read, and two could write. Michael's accent too was impossible for the scribe who made two stabs at the written form of Emgillavr: he wrote "Enigillavr? Enigivlavin?" knowing neither was correct. They arrived in New South Wales on the *Lady Clarke* on December 26, 1841.

A photo of Michael's son Christopher gives a clue to what Michael might have looked like. Strong and handsome, Christopher looks at the photographer with an intense gaze and a lurking humorous smile. His dark-hair, dark-eyes and olive skin mark him as one of the "black Irish". The rural idyll in the background of the photo, and his hand resting on a book, suggest at least a fantasy of a life of wealth and well-being; it is a photo of a man who has established himself in the world and who is just a little startled at finding himself there.

Looking at the childhood photos of me, I wonder whether Michael would have recognised me as one of his, one of the black Irish, so different from my angelic looking blond siblings.

I have found no further trace of Michael's wife, Helen Carty, beyond the ship's log. She was born in 1822 and was 19 when she left Ireland. If Michael and Helen had children I have found no trace of them, and I have begun to wonder whether they were even actually married. Sixteen years after arriving in the colony, on 4 January 1857, Michael married Margaret Miles. On the wedding certificate he was recorded as a bachelor, rather than a widower. As a Roman Catholic he would not have been able to divorce. A less likely possibility is that Helen had been deemed insane, and institutionalised. If that were so, then Michael would have been a Rochester who got away with it (Bronte 2014 [1847]). Helen's disappearance from the records remains one of the many puzzles I have no answer to in this story.

Michael and Margaret were married in Orange, in the catholic church, when he was 37 and she was 17. She had converted to Catholicism in order to marry him. They both signed their marriage certificate with an 'x'. Curiously, they both left blank on the certificate the names of their parents and the places they were born. Were they too engaged in disguising their origins? Prejudice against the Irish and against convicts and children of convicts were rampant at the time. Were they already hoping for something new for themselves at the time of their marriage, or were they just sick of the scribes who always got it wrong?

Michael was to become a farmer, buying multiple small blocks of land as they became available with the passing of the Robertson Land Act. The block they lived on for much of the 27 years of their marriage bordered Boshes Creek, north of Orange. Boshes Creek is a tributary of the Macquarie River. It is possible to get a glimpse of the land they lived on, since Boshes Creek is now a flora reserve within the Mullions Range State Forest. The reserve is 183 hectares of relatively undisturbed dry sclerophyll forest. It was, and is, a dramatic and beautiful landscape, steep, east facing and well-watered. It is described in a *Forests NSW* report:

> The reserve occupies part of a steep sided valley on the eastern fall of the
> Mullions Range and is drained by Boshes Creek which descends some 120

FIGURE 57   Sue, Bronwyn and Tony, 1946

metres within the Reserve over a distance of about 1.5 kilometres. This creek flows except in exceptionally dry times and even then the larger holes will still contain water. The valley sides are dissected by numerous steep gullies connecting with the main creek. The landscape is broken and rugged. Altitude varies between 670 metres and 850 metres. ...The area has a temperate summer climate and a cold winter. Frosts are of frequent occurrence in winter with occasional light snowfalls on the higher sections. (*Forests NSW*, 2011: 2)

The reserve is rich in biodiversity; the trees include Brittle Gum, Scribbly Gum, Red Stringy Bark, several kinds of Box, Peppermint, Candlebark Gum, Peppermint, Black Cypress Pine, and numerous kinds of wattle. The native animals recently observed there include the black striped wallaby, squirrel glider and spotted tail quoll. It is regarded as original forest, which suggests Michael allowed his sheep and cattle to wander in partially uncleared land, although the conditions of purchase mandated the ecologically unsound requirements of clearing and fencing.

Michael and Margaret had 13 children. The 13th was Jean (Eliza). Often when their births were registered the names were not yet chosen, so the constructing of the following details comes from a wide range of legal and other documents:

- Michael *b.* 1857, became a farmer at Euchareena north of Boshes Creek, *d.* 1943 aged 86;
- Male child *b.* 1859 and died young;
- Mary, *b.* 1861 married Denis Callanan in 1891, aged 30 and was widowed in 1894 with 2 children, d. 1928 aged 67;
- Nora *b.* 1863 married Patrick Lawrence, stonemason, in 1886;
- Ellen *b.* 1865, did not marry, was a cook/domestic and died of gastric influenza, 21.4.19 aged 54, leaving an estate of £100.9.0;
- James *b.* 1867 became a farmer, but died in 1885 aged 18;
- Peter *b.* 1871, died aged 17 in 1887. He was often left out of lists of children who could, for example, inherit from their father's estate, suggesting some kind of difference that led him to being discounted;
- Daniel *b.*1875 was a station-hand and dealer. He married Sarah E. Jennings in 1892. He died 3.1.1946, aged 71, leaving an estate of £78.4.2 to his son Leslie;
- Christopher, christened Christmas, *b.* Christmas Day 1878. His twin, Margaret, died in that same year. He became a successful blacksmith at Cobar. In 1904 he married Ethel D. Orr. They had seven children, and Ethel died young, aged 42. In 1927 he fell in front of a train breaking his left arm and crushing his right arm which had to be amputated. He died in 1944 aged 66;
- Alice *b.* 1880 married Leonard H.M. Newton, bank clerk, later bank manager;
- Margaret Jane *b. c.* 1882, married Edgar Hurford in 1901. She died in 1921 aged 39;
- Eliza *b.* 20.5.1884, married George William Hope Davies in 1908, when she gave her name as Elizabeth Mary McCarthy. She was known as Jean.

In his own name Michael acquired 380 acres of freehold land and 700 acres of conditionally purchased land. In his sons' names he had purchased considerably more. In James' name, for example, there were 380 acres of freehold land and 160 acres of conditionally purchased land. Some of the conditionally purchased blocks were selections from the large estate called Kangaroobie, which had many blocks selected out of it after 1861 by the selectors—small farmers who could buy blocks of land from the squatters' vast estates. Michael ran 1,600 sheep on his own blocks, and 26 head of cattle. Two horses were also purchased in his name. It was a dead sheep, however, that was Michael's ignominious undoing:

> Mr. Michael McCarthy, a sheep farmer, residing at Boshe's Creek, died from blood poison, caused by the skinning of a dead sheep. The deceased went to skin a sheep that died the previous day, and whilst so doing was stung on the arm by a fly, the impression made being painful; but, being a hearty old man, he sucked the wound, and treated it lightly. On the

following morning imflammation set in, and although everything was done to alleviate his sufferings he died in great agony from the effects of the wound. The deceased was about 70. (*Freeman's Journal* [Sydney], citing the *Western Advocate* [Orange], Saturday 12 April 1884)

Six weeks after Michael died, baby Eliza was born on 20 May 1884. In the following year, James also died, followed by Peter, only 16, in 1887; Nora and baby Margaret had died some years earlier. Not only did Jean's mother, Margaret, find herself widowed, with a baby and so many children to support, and so many losses to endure, but for four years she had to wrangle with the legal system. Both Michael and James died intestate. It was not until 1888 that she could sell their blocks of land. Part of her argument to the court in seeking permission to sell the land, was that the three surviving children who had now come of age, Michael, Mary and Ellen, had requested payment of their share of the inheritance. Another aspect of her request was that Michael had a debt to the Commercial Bank of £555 that had to be paid. There were also substantial fees from doctors, lawyers and funeral directors.

The deliberations of the court were complicated by the requirement first of establishing that all the blocks owned by Michael and James had been accounted for, and then to assess their value. Further, the court was intent upon setting up a legal mechanism to ensure fair distribution of the property to the surviving children. It appointed Margaret as administratrix, but required her to employ bondsmen to invest the money along with her, in order to give her an income with which to raise the remaining children. Burke and Coulson, auctioneers, were to act as her bondsmen. The specific allocations to her and to the children were, by court order, to be calculated by an actuary. He would presumably calculate what she was likely to need to live on and raise the children, and what each of the children could be said to need when they came of age. Ellen had £100 when she died in 1914, which may be the portion she inherited. She had worked as a domestic servant in Orange, where she had lived in, and had free board and keep.

In 1885 the value of the two sets of holdings was estimated as: James' land £968; Michael's land and animals £1295.

Margaret purchased a small two-bedroom house in East Orange, in McLachlan Street, which Jean and her siblings were to grow up in. Michael Jnr was by then away from home on his land at Euchareena and James stayed on Boshe's Creek until he died in 1885. There were seven children to squeeze into that tiny house. Margaret lived there for 35 years until her death in 1920. It was described, at that time, by the auctioneer and valuator Harry Chandler as:

> Lot 11 section 4a ... having a frontage to the west side of McLachlan Street, of one chain with a depth of two chains and twenty five links [a quarter acre block]. [It has] slab walls on the front and sides with a brick wall at the rear. There are four rooms in the main building partly ceiled with wood and the remainder hessian and lined with the last named material. There is a kitchen attached with wattle and daub walls, unceiled, iron roof and a small laundry and two small outhouses and paling fences.

Wattle and daub is made from a woven lattice of wooden strips called wattle, which is daubed with a sticky material, usually made of some combination of wet soil, clay, sand, animal dung and straw. Chandler estimated the house was worth £200 in 1920. The household furniture at that time consisted, in the front room, of a piano made by Gilmore and Co London, worth £15, a cedar safe, a pine table and cover, a sofa, five cedar chairs, a clock, pictures, a Jardiniere, a whatnot and sundry ornaments. In the first bedroom were a double bed, a single bed, a rocker, a small chest of drawers, a commode, and a washstand. In the second bedroom was a double bed. In the dining room, a dining table and three chairs. In the kitchen was a table, a dresser, three chairs, a small table and singer sewing machine. The total value of the furniture was £30.

When the family moved there 35 years earlier, the boys most likely slept in the outhouses, and the girls in the second bedroom, while Margaret and the baby, and perhaps little Alice, shared the first bedroom. I imagine the back yard had a clothesline, propped up with long thin wooden poles, a chook pen up the back, as well as a dunny, a veggie garden and some fruit trees, with the front garden reserved for flowers. It was a humble dwelling.

At the time they moved to Orange, three of the children were of preschool age, Jean, Margaret Jane and Alice, while Christopher, Patrick and Daniel may have been the first children in their family to go to school. The older boys stayed on at Boshe's Creek and Euchareena. Although Margaret never learned to read or write, she ran a household that enabled her children to gain the skills she and her convict parents hadn't had access to, and to acquire some of the graces, like playing the piano. The three oldest of her children, already adults when Michael died, could read and sign their names, albeit in wobbly, awkward hands. The presence of the piano suggests music rather than literacy was at the heart of family life.

I have wondered whether Jean felt distant from her mother when she learned to read and to write. Her teachers and the books she read opened up worlds to her not available to Margaret. But when I think of that crowded household, with a family living in town for the first time, and everyone developing new skills and contributing to the family's collective survival, I imagine

she had little time for self-indulgent reflections as she carried out her household tasks, negotiated her relationships with all the others, while completing
her homework and her piano practice.

At the same time, it is also true that Jean did position herself in the world
differently from her mother and her numerous siblings crowded into that tiny
household. She changed her name, and she made up a different name for her
convict grandparents. She called her father a grazier. While that term is correct
insofar as it refers to someone who fattens a large number of sheep or cattle for
market, 'grazier', in the Colony, was reserved for wealthy gentlemen landholders, who socialised with each other and with elite businessmen and profession-
als in the city. Michael was a small farmer in comparison, despite the multiple
blocks he and his sons had managed to acquire. He would more appropriately,
perhaps, be called a 'cocky' – a farmer scratching a livelihood out of the soil.
He had 1,600 sheep, compared with the Saltings, for example, who had 60,000
sheep. Though curiously, his holdings were comparable to Alfred's. Alfred's
elite background, however, and independent means, meant that he could (and
did) call himself a gentleman, rather than grazier, and in being appointed as
magistrate, he became one of the elite landholders who looked out for men
like Michael Carty.

Alice, Jean's sister, also gave her family name as McCarthy, rather than Carty
on her marriage certificate, entering his status as grazier, and her own status
as Lady. Unlike Jean, though, she did give her mother's maiden name as Miles.
She married Leonard Newton, an accountant in Victoria who later became a
bank manager back in New South Wales, in Drummoyne. It seems the change
to the name McCarthy was a sign of upward mobility.

I feel a strong affinity with Michael Carty. In my childhood and young adult-
hood I experienced a growing mistrust of the rural elite. My first taste of the
class position they so jealously guarded was at a rural dance party. A young,
handsome, well-dressed station hand, who was not from the rural elite, was
invited into the party by some of the rural sons, who realised that he was stuck,
hanging about in the cold, dark night, having to wait for the party to finish
before he could get a lift back to the station. As soon as he came in he was
ordered to leave by the scandalised parents, and we, in training to become the
next generation's elite, had to swallow the shame we felt at their snobbery,
and say nothing. I grew bored and impatient with the sons of graziers, so sure
of their entitlements and so apparently uninterested in thinking outside the
position they had been born into. I was outraged by the degree of passivity
that was expected of us, as rural wives in training. One of those sons rejected
me out of hand because I asked him to dance, instead of accepting my place
among the hopeful wall-flowers. I was impatient with mindless authority and

had no patience with my mother's refrain "What will people think?" I went so far as to drop my middle name, Nivison, because I didn't want to be branded as belonging to people who had what seemed to me such an unwarranted certainty about their superiority. I became active in the academic union and in the feminist struggle for social change. All of this my parents found both shameful and incomprehensible.

I wonder if Michael would have recognised me as one of his own. Even though I was not catholic, and even though I had a passion for learning and had developed a deep scepticism about the institution of marriage, we might have had some interesting conversations and stories to tell.

Despite the rigid social divisions between the largely Protestant elite, with their impeccable forebears and their English accents, and the workers, who were largely Irish and Catholic, class boundaries were sometimes crossed. James Dalton, for example, who bought Boshes Creek, moved from convict status to becoming a grazier. That movement across class boundaries was a complicated one to accomplish. There were petty signifiers of class that only the elite knew about; if you held your knife the wrong way, like a pencil, you could not be accepted; and you must have mastered the use of the serviette rather than wipe your hands on your trousers.

There was a multitude of other minor niceties at the dinner table, and the elite would not share their table with anyone who had not mastered them. Even worse, if you had not been to the right boarding school and did not have the right accent, your chances of being accepted were slim indeed. To be recognised as a grazier, or as one of the elite, you would have spent time studying abroad; and you would go to a Protestant church. You would necessarily be highly literate, and live in a magnificent house. You would have interesting house-guests and dinner parties and balls. In David Campbell's case, you rode about in your carriage, and bred horses and played polo, in preference to working on the farm. The elite employed others to do the hard work; and they were given positions as magistrates, with the power to decide the fate of the workers when they broke the rules.

While it is unlikely that Michael had made himself over into that version of an Australian gentleman grazier, still signing his name with a cross, and living in a humble dwelling at Boshes Creek, he may yet have been a respected, astute businessman and farmer. He had accumulated land for himself and his sons. The newspaper report of his ignominious death, however, makes no mention of personal qualities, other than his being "a hearty old man". And skinning a sheep already dead for a day, suggests he did not have men to work for him, and that he could not afford to let anything go to waste.

Jean did make her way across those class boundaries, changing her religion to Church of England, and marrying George. Her changes of name from Eliza, to Elizabeth Mary, to Jean, and from Carty to McCarthy, and her changing of her mother's maiden name to hide her convict ancestry, are the only remaining traces of that struggle to remake herself as someone appropriate for George to marry, in defiance of his family's opposition.

Five of Margaret Carty's children died before her: Jane, James, Peter and Ellen, and Christopher's twin who had died as a baby. Margaret lived for 35 years after Michael's death. She was ill for six months before she died. Two years before her death, on 24 September 1917, she made a will leaving everything to her daughter, Mary Callaghan, then a widow and living with her in the McLachlan St house. Mary had been widowed young and had raised her two children on her own. She had recently come to live with her mother and her Uncle John, as their carer. She was Margaret's sole beneficiary and executrix, and her inheritance was "absolutely for her own absolute use and benefit". The house and its contents were what Mary inherited, presumably along with the care of her Uncle John.

In Margaret's obituary, something interesting emerges. Some of the details in it are startlingly incorrect. Margaret was quite long-lived for those times, at 81. The obituary writer magnifies her age, saying she was 93½. The family generally were very vague about their birth dates and their ages, Ellen, for example, on the legal document in which she requested her share of the inheritance, claimed to be 21, when actually she was 20. But an additional twelve (and a half) years signals not an error, but a family given to the telling of tall tales. Had Margaret, in her pride at reaching such an old age, increased the number to make her longevity even more impressive?

My father was a master of tall tales, and I am intrigued that he might have learned that skill from the mother and grandmother he never spoke about. At the dinner table, he would spin stories with unbelievable elements, as if they were true or factual, sometimes including an element of truth in exaggerated form. He was also fond of shaggy dog stories, which derive their humour from the fact that the story-teller holds the attention of the listeners for a long time for no reason at all, as the end of the story turns out to be pointless. He would offer fabricated accounts of family origins, telling them with such seriousness that everyone listened with rapt attention, only to discover at the end of the story, when he started to laugh, that our legs had been collectively pulled.

Other fabrications in Margaret's obituary were that she had been born in Wales, instead of New South Wales, and that Michael had owned the vast station called Kangaroobie, when he had owned only a few small blocks of it:

OBITUARY
Margaret Carty

After an illness extending over a period of six months, the death took place at her residence, McLachlan Street, Orange East, on Friday last, of one of the oldest and most respected residents of the district, in the person of Mrs Margaret Carty, relict[1] of Michael Carty, who predeceased her in 1888.[2] The old lady, who was 93½ years of age, was a native of Wales, and for 60 years had resided in and around Orange, 35 of which had been spent in the cottage in which she passed away. In the early days her husband was the owner of Kangaroobie and Boss's Creek properties, which he disposed of later to Messrs Dalton, Bourke and Coulsen.[3] The late Mrs Carty was of a kindly and hospitable nature, and, though her death was not unexpected, it will be regretted by her numerous friends and acquaintances. She leaves the following family to mourn the loss of a loving mother: Messrs Michael (Euchareena), Daniel (Gregrn), and Christopher (Manildra), Mrs D. Callaghan (East Orange), Mrs Davies (Kempsey), Mrs Newton (Melbourne), Mrs. Hurford (Sydney), and Mrs P. Lawrence (Armidale). The only surviving brother is Mr. John Miles, who resided with the deceased at East Orange. The funeral took place yesterday afternoon, the remains being interred in the R.C. portion of the local cemetery.

William Miles and Jane Hill

Margaret's father, and one of her grandparents, came to New South Wales as convicts. Her mother was Jane Hill, born in Glasgow, in 1811. Jane was the sixth of nine children and her father, William Hill, had been transported in 1825. When Jane came to New South Wales she was a widow, called Jane Stimson. She came on the Spartan in 1838 as a free immigrant.

William Miles/Myles, the man who was to become Jane Hill's second husband, was a convict. His parents were Charles Miles and Rebecca Cotner, from Bristol. When William was 16 years old, he and his friend Will Rushton had been

---

1 'Relict' is archaic for widow—the left-over remnant or fragment of her husband!
2 In fact he died in 1884
3 Margaret sold those blocks to James Dalton who owned the surrounding property; Burke and Coulson were her bondsmen and auctioneers.

charged with stealing 4 promissory notes worth 4 guineas. William was sentenced to death—and the sentence later commuted to transportation for life.

William was transported at the age of 18, but even age was slippery in that spacetime. Without access to literacy, written records don't carry much weight. William was also recorded as being 21 and sometimes 16. In the ship's log he was described as 4'11", swarthy, with black hair and hazel eyes, sounding like another of the black Irish, though he lived with his parents in Bristol. He was transported on the convict ship *Asia*, arriving 29 April 1825. There were 200 male convicts who boarded that ship, and 197 who arrived in Sydney. Two had died, and one had escaped. A 'good trip' by the day's standards. Once in New South Wales, William was sent to Minto to work for a short time, and then to Bathurst to work as a stockman for Henry Perrier on his property Winslow.

On Jane's arrival, she and William applied for permission to marry, and were wed on 9 January 1839, in Bathurst, in the Church of England Church. They both signed their marriage certificate with an 'x'. Their surviving children were Charles, Margaret (Jean's mother), William, Thomas, Jane, John and Eliza.

William had been given a ticket of leave, on 15 August 1837, which meant he could at last begin to establish his own life and livelihood. He was later given a conditional pardon in 1844, and a full pardon in 1846. He became a farmer in his own right at Rock Forest and later Emu Swamp. Like those farm workers described by Banjo Paterson, he had had a hard life, and would probably become a hard father. He died, aged 50, on 28 April 1859 at Emu Swamp, of a disease of the lungs. Jane died 11 years later on 1 April 1870 of cancer of the womb. She was 59 years old. She lived, at the time of her death, at Boshes Creek with Margaret and Michael and the children. On her death certificate, Jane's oldest son, Charles, signed his name with an 'x'. The hard life of the sons of convicts, in his case, had left no room for schooling.

Reflections

It is ironic that the ancestors I most hoped to find, throughout this project, were ancestors with a passion for writing. The feeling of being out of place in my parents' household was, in large part, their lack of interest in books and ideas. Dad read the daily newspaper, and most enjoyed the comic strips, the weather report, and column eight in the *Sydney Morning Herald*, a column full of small quirky stories. What I hadn't imagined I would find, were convict ancestors, and ancestors who could neither read nor write, and yet with whom I would also discover a powerful affinity. Michael Carty from Emgillavr in Ireland, William Miles and Jane Hill, and their daughter Margaret, had had tough lives, and were not of the elite, with their presumptions of superiority. My impatience with the elite finds a home with Michael and Margaret—a comfort from them; our shared DNA suggests that all those feminist battles fought, all that championing of just causes was in my blood, just looking for its means of expression. I have loved finding Margaret, who, like me, found herself widowed with small children to care for, and who managed anyway.

As I contemplate this chapter, and its hardships, and the drawing to a close of all these stories of my father's ancestors, I find myself breathing that involuntary ragged in-breath that comes after a massive bout of weeping. It is an in-breath that says, in spite of all this, one may survive, despite a world that is too often inhumane and brutal.

PART 3

Of Judges and Surveyors, Sailors and Soldiers, Convicts and Farmers: Stories of My Mother's Family

∵

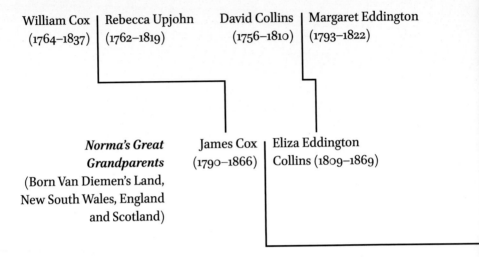

Norma's Great Great Grandparents
(Born England)

William Cox | Rebecca Upjohn
(1764–1837) | (1762–1819)

David Collins | Margaret Eddington
(1756–1810) | (1793–1822)

Norma's Great Grandparents
(Born Van Diemen's Land, New South Wales, England and Scotland)

James Cox | Eliza Eddington
(1790–1866) | Collins (1809–1869)

Norma's Grandparents
(Born Van Diemen's Land and New South Wales)

Norma's Parents
(Born New South Wales)

FIGURE 58   Family tree of Norma Nivison Blomfield

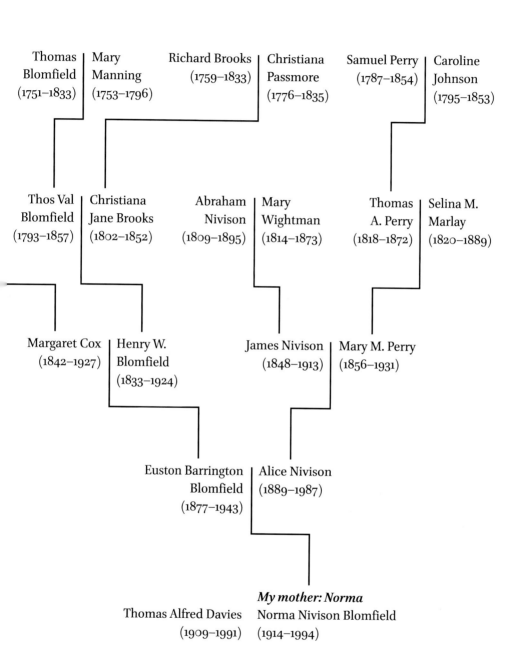

Introduction to Part 3

The five of my maternal great (x3) grandfathers whose stories I tell in this third part of the book are David Collins, Thomas Blomfield, Richard Brooks, William Cox and Samuel Perry. They lived their adult life in Jane Austen's England, each of them born in the two decades before Austen's birth. David Collins worked in New South Wales as Judge Advocate from 1788 with one trip home after nine years, before returning to establish the colonial settlement in Hobart, in Van Diemen's Land. Thomas Blomfield was the only one not to leave Britain; it was his son, Thomas Valentine Blomfield, who came to the colony in 1817 as a soldier in the British army having earlier fought in the Peninsular Wars. William Cox migrated in 1799, and Richard Brooks in 1814, both taking up substantial farming land. William Cox built the first road over the Blue Mountains in 1814. Samuel Perry migrated from England in 1829 to become the Deputy Surveyor General. Later arrivals (my great (x2) grandparents) from Scotland were the Nivisons, who came in 1840, and who also took up substantial land.

While a great many traces of these men's lives can be found, almost none exist of the women's lives. The exceptions to this are Richard Brooks' wife Christiana, and their daughter Christiana Jane Blomfield. The two Christianas wrote letters to each other and to their friends, and to family back in England.

There are personal dilemmas that I have encountered in writing their stories. In mapping out the specificity of each of their lives, I seek to tell them, as far as possible, from their own points of view. I continue to engage in the ethical principles I outlined in Part 1, in which I refrain from moral judgement, asking, rather, of each of them, 'What is it to be this'? In coming to know them, and in coming to care about them a great deal, I find myself deeply confronted by their sometimes brutal treatment of the convicts, and their near-obliteration of the indigenous custodians of the land. I don't shy away from that brutality, however much it distresses me; rather, I set out to get inside the spacetimemattering of British life at that time, as it was experienced by them. Through their lives I have been able to encounter the act of colonisation from inside itself, as it was lived and as it was understood by those who, in the name of God and of King and country, appropriated the land that belonged to others and set convicted men and women to work as slave labour in building up their fortunes. I thus seek to take the reader inside that spacetimemattering of colonisation, through the specificity of the entangled lives of my ancestors. In Part 3, I thus return to "the ligaments of power, sentiment, and moral conduct that constitute the heaving form of the social body" (Luxon 2016, 2) as it was,

© BRONWYN DAVIES, 2021 | DOI:10.1163/9789004446717_011

during the expansion of the British Empire. The past times that I write about are not static, but open to change.

I begin this part with David Collins, first Judge Advocate of New South Wales, who came here on the First Fleet in 1788. I delve into his life before coming to New South Wales and then travel with him on that long journey and into the first decade of the life of the colony.

CHAPTER 11

The First Fleet. David Collins: Buried in Oblivion?

> ... the past was never simply there to begin with and the future is not
> simply what will unfold; the 'past' and the 'future' are iteratively reworked
> and enfolded through the iterative practices of spacetimemattering.
>
> BARAD (2014: 181)

∴

As a young man David Collins (1756–1810) was a soldier fighting against the
rebels in the American War of Independence. He was horrified by the sav-
agery of war, and relieved when his father made it possible for him to take up
the position of adjutant, which involved him in more bookish and reflective
duties. After the devastating battle of Bunker Hill, where, in true British style,
row after row of soldiers in their red coats had been mown down by the rebels,
the British withdrew to Halifax.

There, in June 1777, not long after his 21st birthday, David married Maria Stu-
art Proctor. She was from a wealthy Halifax family and had high expectations.
Her father had died three years before and his fortune was soon to collapse
entirely. The independent income she had thought to bring to the marriage did
not materialise. David had a strong sense of his place as a member of the gentry, as did Maria, and once Maria's inheritance evaporated they did not have
the necessary independent income to sustain their lifestyle. This lack of capital
had a profound effect on the rest of their lives. Back in England, after that war
was over, with no independent income, their way of life was unsustainable:

> [Maria] was particular about her social connections and sensitive of the
> stigma attached to impecunious people in the circles in which the Col-
> linses moved. David himself was acutely aware of his social status as the
> eldest son of the commanding officer of the division and of the need to
> maintain the lustre of the family name. He was made even more painfully
> aware of his situation by the fact that his younger brother George, after
> serving with the marines in the West Indies, had married Mary Trelawney,
> the heiress of a prosperous family, resigned from the corps, and gone to be
> a well-to-do farmer in Devon. Marriage to Maria, however, had brought

David no such dowry. Some cataclysm had destroyed Maria's prospects, and Collins's only expectation of his in-laws was the privilege of having at some time to help support Maria's widowed mother, Margaret Proctor. To assuage his pride he tried to maintain their lifestyle by borrowing money, a fact which he concealed from his wife. (Currey, 2000: 27–28)

David could find no suitable employment at home, and he found himself with no option but to take up the offer of the position of Judge Advocate in New South Wales, where Maria would be unable to join him because of her fragile health. It had not been David's lot, with Maria, to re-create an intimate family circle. After the death of their baby daughter, Maria was advised she could have no more children.

Born to the Blood and Glory of War and a Love of Letters

David's grandfather was Arthur Collins, famous as the author of the influential *Peerage of England, or an Historical and Genealogical Account of the Present Nobility,* a work that had served to buttress the pretensions of the wealthy, "entrenching the adulation of lineage and breeding" (Currey, 2000: 8). David's mother was Henrietta Caroline Fraser of Kings County Ireland, and his father was Tooker Collins, a highly regarded marine, who had devoted his life to heroic defence of his king.

David had been educated at Exeter Grammar School, and at 14 his formal education had ended when he was appointed ensign in his father's division of the marines. A year later he had been promoted to second lieutenant, but his love was for words, rather than the blood and glory of war. He wrote to his mother from the warfront, urging her to send him the reading matter she had promised him:

> I must thank you in my own and father's name for the entertaining news you have given us in every letter. But above all I must thank you for the two pounds of green tea, and the very fine cheese, sent out by Thompson, and which I received yesterday. But my dear mother where are the magazines and newspapers you tantalised me with? I would gladly give you back the cheese for the thirteen *Critical Reviews*… (David Collins to Henrietta Collins 15 August 1775, Currey, 2000: 24)

David was much better suited to peace than to warfare. Years later, he mused in a letter to his father, written from New South Wales:

I have always thought that nature designed me for the tranquil, rather than the bustling walk of life. I know I was meant by that unerring guide rather to wear the gown than the habiliments of a soldier. Nature intended and fashioned me to ascend the Pulpit – there I think I should have shewn ability—there, or in some learned profession. (Collins to his father, 12 September 1791, Collins Papers, 1: 58).

Judge Advocate and Man of Letters

A decade later David published an extraordinary journal, of more than a thousand pages, describing the first ten years of the Colony: *An Account of the English Colony in New South Wales. With remarks on the dispositions, customs, manners etc. of the native inhabitants of that country.* The *Account* begins with the journey of the First Fleet, with himself and his fellow travellers sailing toward a place, and a life, that "the mind hardly venture[d] to contemplate" (*Account:* 1). It contained, he wrote, "a review of those hardships which in common with his colleagues he had endured and overcome; hardships which in some degree he suppose[d] to be inseparable from the first establishment of any colony" (*Account:* xxxvii).

The First Fleet's Journey and the Opening of New Horizons

The proposal that had been drawn up and presented to Cabinet in London, was that the Colony would serve as "a remedy for the evils from the alarming and numerous increase of felons in this country. It may also attend to the possibility of procuring masts and ships timber for the use of our fleets" (Guilford, 2007: 14). And David added: "beside the circumstance of its freeing the mother country from the depraved branches of her offspring, in some instances reforming their dispositions, and in all cases rendering their labour and talents conducive to the public good, it may prove a valuable nursery to our East India possessions for soldiers and seamen" (*Account:* xxxix).

The First Fleet was made up of eleven vessels; two naval war ships, the flagship *Sirius* and the sloop *Supply.* The rest were converted merchantmen. 1500 people were crammed onto those vessels. Captain Arthur Phillip, on board the *Sirius,* was commodore of the First Fleet, and Governor of the territory of New South Wales.

David travelled on board the *Sirius.* It was a small ship "crammed with stores and humanity: some 150 people tucked away in a claustrophobic wooden barrel 100 feet long, 30 feet wide and 24 feet deep... He was allocated accommodation on the gun-deck, the level marked out by the golden stripe along each side of the ship" (Currey, 2000: 32). He slept in a canvas hammock, two feet wide, and shared this space with three other men and with the ship's 20 guns.

Its ceiling was only five feet four inches high, but he had easy access to the deck and to light and fresh air. There, he began his journal, taking up his quill to record his story of colonisation.

The Collins family was embedded in the British Establishment, loyal to the King and committed to the values and practices of the Church of England. On the journey, when David found himself in Catholic Santa Cruz on the island of Teneriffe, on the holy day of Corpus Christi, he was fascinated by the glittering spectacle, and curious about what was common between the two religions:

> Those officers, whose curiosity led them to observe the religious proceedings of the day, very prudently attended uncovered, and knelt, wherever kneeling was required, in the streets, and in their churches; for, when it was considered that the same great Creator of the universe was worshipped alike by Protestant and Catholic, what difficulty could the mind have in divesting their pageant of its tinsel, its trappings, and its censers, and joining with sincerity in offering the purest incense, that of a grateful heart? (*Account:* lix)

Similarly, he did not judge the women in Rio for their looser attachment to chastity: "If frozen chastity be not always found among the children of ice and snow, can she be looked for among the inhabitants of climates where frost was never felt? Yet heartily should she [i.e. chastity] be welcomed wherever she may be found, and doubly prized if met with unexpectedly" (*Account:* lxxiii). An enigmatic comment that hints, perhaps, at an overture rebuffed.

At the Cape of Good Hope David and the other officers lived comfortably in the town. Despite a recent famine there, they ate well, took on adequate supplies of food and of livestock and plants for the remainder of the journey and for the establishment of their own farms and gardens in the colony. Acquiring knowledge of how to create their own gardens appears to have been startlingly happenchance, yet true to the adventurous spirit of that *spacetime*. They believed that any necessary skills could be learned whenever they were needed:

> As it was earnestly wished to introduce the fruits of the Cape into the new settlement, Captain Phillip was ably assisted in his endeavours to procure the rarest and best of every species, both in plant and seed, by Mr Mason, the king's botanist, whom we were so fortunate as to meet with here, as well as by Colonel Gordon, the commander in chief of the troops at this place; a gentleman whose thirst for natural knowledge amply qualified him to be of service to us, not only in procuring a great variety of the best

seeds and plants, but in pointing out the culture, the soil, and the proper time of introducing them into the ground. (*Account:* lxxix)

As it was, their crops failed, and they continued to depend on the unreliable arrival of ships carrying food supplies from home.

Although David had enjoyed his stay at the Cape there were some aspects of its systems of punishment that he found horrifying. He reports, for example, a Malay man running amok under the influence of opium, killing and maiming several people. So great was the fear of this man that the soldiers had been ordered to shoot any Malay person on sight. When he was captured he was "immediately consigned to the death he merited, being broken on the wheel, and his head and members severed after the execution, and distributed in different parts of the country" (*Account:* lxxxi). Although David believed that the Malay man's death was merited, he was appalled by the savage implements of torture that he saw at the prison:

> Within the walls were to be seen (and seen with horror) six crosses for breaking criminals, a large gibbet, a spiked pole for impalements, wheels etc, etc together with a slight wooden building, erected for the reception of the ministers of justice upon execution days... The bodies of those broken on the wheel were exposed in different parts of the town, several instances of which, and some very recent ones, were still to be seen. (*Account:* lxxxi–lxxxii)

When they set sail, he reflected, without any apparent irony, on his feeling that they were now leaving civilisation behind, travelling outside the known world and into the land of 'savages'. His unquestioning belief in the 'truth' that Great Britain and its Empire were at the pinnacle of the civilised world, overrode the evidence before his eyes, of British brutality and lack of civilisation when it came to the treatment of convicts and of the natives of colonised countries. As they left the Cape he wrote:

> It was natural to indulge at this moment a melancholy reflection which obtruded itself on my mind. The land behind us was the abode of a civilized people; that before us was the residence of savages. When, if ever, we might enjoy the commerce of the world, was doubtful and uncertain. The refreshments and pleasures of which we had so liberally partaken at the Cape, were to be exchanged for coarse fare and hard labour at New South Wales. All communication with families and friends now cut off, we were leaving the world behind us, to enter on a state unknown;

and, as if it had been necessary to imprint this idea more strongly on our minds, and to render the sensation still more poignant, at the close of the evening we spoke (to) a ship from London. The metropolis of our native country, its pleasures, its wealth, and its consequence, thus accidentally presented to the mind, failed not to afford a most striking contrast with the object now principally in our view. (*Account:* lxxxv–lxxxvi)

Sailing across the Indian Ocean, and south of the Australian continent they encountered storms, rogue waves, and the extraordinary navigational challenges of charting their course in unfamiliar waters. There were deaths, attempted escapes, insurgencies, and, to his delight the luminous phenomenon of the *aurora australis,* with its "lights floating on the surface of the water" (*Account:* lxxxviii).

When eventually they arrived at the southernmost tip of New Holland David contemplated the perspective of the unknown others who lived there: "At night we perceived several fires lighted on the coast, at many of which, no doubt, were some of the native inhabitants, to whom it was probable our novel appearance must have afforded matter of curiosity and wonder" (*Account:* lxxxix). Although he had characterised them as savage in his mind's eye on leaving the Cape, his first impulse in this first encounter at a distance, was to look at the Fleet from their imagined point of view. It's a complicated story.

On the journey northward along the east coast they were plagued by foul winds and heavy sudden squalls which made for slow progress. When at last they arrived safely at Botany Bay, David was amazed at the good fortune that, with the blessing of God, had enabled them to arrive safely at their destination. The belief that God, through his Providence, had blessed their voyage and brought them safely to the Colony, was integral to the dominant discourse through which the act of colonisation and subjugation were justified:

Thus under the blessing of God, was happily completed, in eight months and one week, a voyage which, before it was undertaken, the mind hardly dared venture to contemplate, and on which it was impossible to reflect without some apprehension as to its termination…. [W]e had sailed five thousand and twenty-one leagues; had touched at the African and American continents; and had at last rested within a few days sail of the antipodes of our native country, without meeting with any accident in a fleet of eleven sail, none of which were merchantmen that had ever before sailed in that distant and imperfectly explored ocean: and when it is considered, that there was on board a large body of convicts, many of whom were embarked in a very sickly state, we might be deemed peculiarly fortunate, that of the whole number of all descriptions of persons coming to form the new settlement, only thirty-two had died since their leaving England, among whom were to be included one or two deaths by accidents; although previous to our departure it was generally conjectured, that before we should have been a month at sea one of the transports would have been converted into a hospital ship. But it fortunately happened otherwise; the high health which was apparent in every countenance was to be attributed not only to the refreshments we met with at Rio de Janiero and the Cape of Good Hope, but to the excellent quality of the provisions with which we were supplied... the general joy and satisfaction which immediately took place in finding ourselves arrived at that port which had been so much and so long the subject of our most serious reflections, the constant theme of our conversations. (*Account*: 1–2)

'Only' 32 dead. This, perhaps more than anything he wrote, reminds me just how difficult this task is of imagining, and bringing to life the spacetimemattering where these lives and deaths were being played out.

Invasion

On finding the ports of Botany Bay and Sutherland unsuitable for the establishment of the settlement, a group that included David set out in three boats to look for a more suitable location, holding themselves at the ready to fight off any locals who might not welcome them:

The governor set out on Monday the 21st, accompanied by Captain Hunter, Captain Collins (the judge advocate), a lieutenant, and the master of the Sirius, with a small party of marines for their protection, the whole being embarked in three open boats. The day was mild and serene, and there being but a gentle swell without the mouth of the harbour, the excursion promised to be a pleasant one. Their little fleet attracted the attention of several parties of the natives, as they proceeded along the coast, who all greeted them in the same words, and in the same tone of vociferation, shouting every where 'Warra, warra, warra' words which, by the gestures that accompanied them, could not be interpreted into invitations to land, or expressions of welcome. It must however be observed, that at Botany Bay the natives had hitherto conducted themselves sociably and peaceably toward all the parties of our officers and people with whom they had hitherto met, and by no means seemed to regard them as enemies or invaders of their country and tranquillity. (*Account*: 2)

Yet they were indeed invaders.

That invasion, they believed, had the blessing of God—how else could they ever have arrived safely? Furthermore, and contrary to the image of invasion, was the idea that the establishment of a colony in the antipodes would contribute to the glory and might of empire. When reports later came to them of Britain's glorious efforts in support of William v of the Netherlands, David reflected on the potential lack of glory, in contrast, that their own heroic efforts in the colony attracted:

> We trusted, however, that while differently employed, our views were still directed to the same object: for, though labouring at a distance, and in an humbler scene, yet the good, the glory, and the aggrandizement of our country were prime considerations with us. And why should the colonists of New South Wales be denied the merit of endeavouring to promote them, by establishing civilisation in the savage world; by animating the children of idleness and vice to habits of laborious and honest industry; and by shewing the world that to Englishmen no difficulties are insuperable? (*Account:* 55)

Moreover, by way of self-justification, they had every intention of a *friendly* invasion, imagining that if they were successful they might accomplish a harmonious and respectful co-existence.

That was not, of course, to be. David later reflected, with profound regret, that their friendly reception had been unwarranted:

> How grateful to every feeling of humanity would it be could we conclude this narrative without being compelled to say, that these unoffending people had found reason to change both their opinions and their conduct! (*Account:* 3)

In January 1788, however, they were still buoyed by joyful optimism and excitement:

> The governor, with a party of marines, and some artificers[1] selected from among the seamen of the *Sirius* and the convicts, arrived in Port Jackson, and anchored off the mouth of the cove intended for the settlement on the evening of the 25th [of Jan]; and in the course of the following day sufficient ground was cleared for encamping the officer's guard and the convicts who had been landed in the morning. The spot chosen for this

---

1 Artificer: a skilled craftsman, clever or inventive designer, or serviceman trained in mechanics (Collins English Dictionary)

encampment was at the head of the cove, near the run of fresh water, which stole silently through a very thick wood, the stillness of which had then, for the first time since the creation, been interrupted by the rude sound of the labourer's axe, and the downfall of its ancient inhabitants; a stillness and tranquillity which from that day were to give place to the voice of labour, the confusion of camps and towns, and the 'busy hum of its new possessors'. That these did not bring with them, 'Minds not to be changed by time or place,'[2] was fervently to have been wished...
(*Account:* 4)

David thus characterised the local inhabitants as living in the unsullied tranquillity of nature in her purest garb. The newcomers' transformation of the landscape was a violent confrontation between nature and culture. As ancient trees were felled and the land cleared, space was opened for creating the semblance of culture, of British civilisation, where the British outcasts they carried with them could be transformed through learning the "habits of laborious and honest industry" (*Account:* 55).

The men who were in charge of this complex act of expanding the Empire were soldiers, schooled in decades of bloody wars. For the most part, the labour was to be carried out by convicts who had little reason to love the values of the Empire that had spat them out. David feared that the convicts would sully the purity of nature by introducing vice, profanity, and loose morals. Believing, nevertheless, that such sullying was inevitable, he hoped that in his role as Judge Advocate he might reduce their negative impact, by opposing "the soft harmonizing arts of peace and civilisation to the baneful influence of vice and immorality" (*Account:* 4).

David had repeatedly, since the age of 14, been exposed to the brutal excesses of war, and now, so recently, he had observed the brutality of western civilisation in its systems of punishment at the Cape. It seems extraordinary that he could, nevertheless, and without apparent irony, characterise European civilisation as offering the "soft harmonizing arts of peace". He believed (though hoped would perhaps be closer to the truth) that it would be through the rule of law that they would establish a stable foundation for the colony, "a foundation that was established in the punishment of vice, the security of property, and the preservation of peace and good order in our community" (*Account:* 11).

---

2 An approximate quote from Milton's *Paradise Lost*.

At the very beginning, with the industry of clearing ground, and making roads and shelters, it seemed as if a comforting, recognisable kind of order and regularity could be created out of the impossible chaos of nature:

> The disembarkation of the troops and convicts took place from the following day until the whole were landed. The confusion that ensued will not be wondered at, when it is considered that every man stepped from the boat literally into a wood. Parties of people were every where heard and seen variously employed; some in clearing ground for the different encampments; others in pitching tents, or bringing up such stores as were more immediately wanted; and the spot which had so lately been the abode of silence and tranquillity was now changed to that of noise, clamour, and confusion: but after a time order gradually prevailed every where. As the woods were opened and the ground cleared, the various encampments were extended, and all wore the appearance of regularity. (*Account:* 5)

The hubris of Empire fuelled the newcomers' faith in their capacity to recreate the order of European civilisation, despite their limited knowledge both of the geography of the place they had come to, and of the arts of food cultivation. In the middle of an antipodean summer, they began transplanting the "Old" into the "New":

> Some ground having been prepared near his excellency's house on the East side, the plants from Rio-de-Janiero and the Cape of Good Hope were safely brought on shore in a few days; and we soon had the satisfaction of seeing the grape, the fig, the orange, the pear, and the apple, the delicious fruits of the Old, taking root and establishing themselves in our New World. (*Account:* 5–6)

Establishing the Colony

David approached his work in the colony with high ideals. The convicts were thought to be "past the probability of amendment" in their home country, yet David hoped that his work with them might lead to their reform—to their cherishing of "the seeds of virtue" (*Account:* xxxviii). In this hope he drew on Dr Johnson (1750: 292) who wrote "Let none too hastily conclude that all goodness is lost, though it may for a time be clouded and overwhelmed; for most minds are the slaves of external circumstances, and conform to any hand that undertakes to mould them ... ".

FIGURE 59   'A Night Scene in the Neighbourhood of Sydney', engraving from Collins' *Account*,
2: 150
"Savage as these beings were toward our people, and to each other, yet they
could unbend, and divert themselves with the softer amusements of singing and
dancing. The annexed engraving represents a party thus occupied, and gives a
correct view of their persons and manners. The figure leaning upon his shield,
the attitude of the women dancing, and the whole group, are accurate delinea-
tions of a party assembled by the light of the fire at the mouth of one of their
excavated rocks. It might be supposed, that with this exercise, and the company
of their females, their angry and turbulent passions would be at rest, and that
the idea of murder could not enter their minds; yet have they been known to
start away, in search of some unsuspecting object of their revenge or hatred, who
before the morning has received a dozen spears through his body: and this is
man in his uncultivated state." (*Account* vol 2: 149–151)

David brought high ideals to his encounters with the custodians of the land
that they were appropriating. He hoped that his anthropological documentation of the local language and customs would bring powerful friends to the
native inhabitants of the colony.[3] The *Account* has an Appendix with twelve
chapters, devoted to an account of the local custodians' culture and manners,

---

3   Linguistic note: "Native" was a positive term at the time, in contrast to "savages", and referred
    simply to the country one was born in. David referred to himself as a native of England, and
    people born in New South Wales were later to be called natives of that country.

including some extraordinary engravings. The Appendix was at first intended to become an independent book about the people of Sydney Cove. When John Hunter published his book on Eora language, he drew extensively on David's work.

Overall, David's *Account* is an attempt to make sense of the encounters between three groups of people with incommensurable ways of seeing the world; the officers, the convicts and the original custodians of the land. It provides a window onto the troubled history of settlement, and to the *spacetimemattering* of 1788. David's investment in the writing of the journal became integral to his own individual mattering. Should it be well received, he reflected, its publication would be, 'the most fortunate circumstance' of his life (*Account*: xxxviii).

The reformist ideals David held in relation to his work with the convicts were undermined by the fact that neither he, nor Governor Phillip, nor perhaps any of the other officers, knew what conditions they might offer the convicts that would enable the "seeds of virtue" to germinate in this new place. They relied on British law with its threefold rationality of punishment, deterrence and rehabilitation, which no more worked in the colony than it had back home. What "clouded and overwhelmed" the minds of the convicts could not be mended through brutal punishments, or the deterrent effect on others of those punishments. Rehabilitation, the third arm of British law, depended on the convicts being able and willing to become hard workers, willing to work for no more than food and shelter.

The convicts were granted a great deal of autonomy, out of necessity, and things constantly went awry when spirits were brought on shore by the sailors, and drunken revelries ran out of control, or when they were attacked by the local custodians of the land when "straggling"[4] out into the bush, looking for vegetables, or game, to supplement their inadequate rations.

If there was a failure of understanding between those in power, and the convicts, there was an even greater failure to understand the perspective of those whose land they were occupying. The officers' orders were to establish friendly relations. When the natives were aggressive, attacking convicts who were out foraging for food or collecting building materials, this was interpreted, to begin with, as retribution for bad behaviour on the part of the convicts, despite their claims to the contrary. Fundamental to this misreading were the officers' enduring contempt for the convicts, and their unwavering belief that the desired friendship with the locals would be on the newcomers' terms. Those

---

4   To straggle: to go or come or spread in a rambling or irregular way, to stray, to linger behind or wander from the main line.

terms included, for example, that the local custodians, while not being recognised as people under British law, and not able at law to represent themselves, would nevertheless be subject to retributive justice under the British
legal system. Further, in co-inhabiting the land, that land would be made productive, not as it had been for thousands of years, but through British modes
of farming and commerce. The newcomers failed to recognise that if this was
to work, the local people must be treated as equal under the law. As the law
stood, they could not represent themselves in any law court or give evidence as
witnesses. And the words of one white man could override any number of the
indigenous people.

A Forgotten Man?

David Collins' fate, as one who might be forgotten, "buried in oblivion", was
intimated by his wife, Maria, four years after the First Fleet set sail in 1787.
Maria suffered from severe asthma and epilepsy and her doctor had forbidden
further pregnancies after the baby died. Presumably that had meant the end
of sexual relations between them. A wry comment by James Finucane in 1809
shows the intimate link assumed at that time between marriage and child-bear-
ing: "My chief clerk ... was married this morning to an amiable young lady, who
has already given proof of her aptitude for matrimony by having had last year
a child by her husband's predecessor" (Whitaker, 1998, p. 87).

Maria's letters to David make regular protestations of love and devotion, but
they are also bitter and carping. She was lonely and unhappy, and living in genteel poverty supported by a portion of David's salary. She constantly pressured
David to come home. She wrote to him about the stress that waiting to hear
from him caused her fragile body. She reminded him that she was a good wife,
sending him the newspapers and clothing that he needed. She offered, in the
event that he could not secure a job in England, that she would go anywhere
in the world with him—though that was clearly impossible given the state of
her fragile health. She threatened that she would grow indifferent to him in
response to his own apparent indifference. She promised that she could learn
to live frugally if need be. And she told him that running that 'infernal place'
– a Colony full of convicts – was perceived as so lowly an occupation back in
England that he was already being forgotten. His name was no longer being
spoken, she told him. His friends were disappointed in him. She was vulnerable and depressed. She ended one such letter, pleading "Come home then my
dearest love and resume your place in the world, and no longer be buried in
oblivion". She reiterated her own deep dejection and disappointment: "I know

not what you might say hereafter, as my heart is disappointed, and I care not how matters go now I no longer have any expectation of seeing you" (January 1791, Currey, 2000: 74).

In contrast with Maria's dire predictions of his being buried in oblivion, Fletcher, the editor of the 1975 edition of David's *Account,* claims he was highly regarded for his work in the first years of the Colony: "between 1788 and 1796 he performed his judicial duties to the complete satisfaction of his superiors who came to regard him as indispensable and prevailed upon him to stay for longer than he intended" (Fletcher 1975: xvii). Fletcher also wrote that David's character was similar to that of Governor Phillip's: both men displayed "courage, diligence, high sense of duty, integrity, an unusual measure of honesty which prevented them seeking any gain from office, the capacity to bear hardship uncomplainingly and to inspire others by the force of their example" (Fletcher, 1975: xxxi). Fletcher continues:

> Collins, though cast in a similar mode to the first Governor, was not so aloof and distant a figure as Phillip. A large, broad-shouldered man, over six feet tall, he had an open friendly expression, golden curly hair and the fine forehead of the scholar. He was a man of warmth and feeling, gregarious by nature and fond of conversation. Like Phillip he earned the respect of those with whom he worked, but he also aroused affection. (Fletcher, 1975: xxxi)

David was a man who longed both for adventure and for a warm loving family; he longed both for a quiet reflective life, and for recognition and a place in society; he was an idealist, and he was often outraged by those who could not live up to his ideals.

His sojourn in the initial settlement lasted for nine years, though there were times when he felt unappreciated and longed to be home. He wrote to his father:

> I find I am spending the Prime of my Life at the farthest part of the World without Credit, without Profit, secluded from my family, my connections from the World, under constant Apprehensions of being starved. All these considerations induce me to embrace the first Opportunity that offers of escaping from a Country that is nothing better than a Place of banishment for the Outcasts of Society. (Guilford, 2007: 19)

His father, the family patriarch, advised him to come home, telling him that his time in the Colony would not serve his career well. But despite his longing, and his father's advice, and despite Maria's pleading, he did not come home. Instead, he diligently applied himself to his work as Judge Advocate, and as Secretary to the Governor. Whenever the opportunity arose, he engaged in research and documentation of the local inhabitants' language and culture. He also started a small family with the convict Ann Yeats. Whereas at home in rural England it was "a truth universally acknowledged, that a single man in possession of a good fortune, must be in want of a wife" (Austen, 1968: 15), on the high seas, and in remote colonies, it might more accurately be said that a truth universally acknowledged was that a man in a red coat, or a sailor, or even a vicar, if not accompanied by a wife, must be in want of a mistress.[5]

Ann Yeats, aged 22, a Yorkshire milliner, had been charged with breaking and entering, and of stealing 36 yards of printed cotton valued at £5. At the age of 17 she had been sentenced to be hanged, then given a reprieve and sentenced to seven years transportation. She had sailed on the *Lady Penrhyn,* where she became pregnant to one of the seamen, Joseph Theakston. She had given birth to their baby not long before arriving at Botany Bay. She was well-regarded as one of the better and most trustworthy of the convicts. While Joseph Theakston departed on the *Lady Penrhyn* for China, Ann opted to stay in Sydney Cove, not taking up the offer of going to Norfolk Island where a small number of the most trusted convicts were sent soon after arrival.

When she began her affair with David in 1789, Ann was still living in the convict quarters. David lived in Government House, where he stayed even after his own house was built. He preferred Government House not just for the company of the governor, or the better food and service, but also because he needed to be frugal, since half his salary went directly to Maria. His reason for staying in Government House may also have been that Ann, as one who was most trusted among the female convicts, worked in Government House. On 13 September 1790, their daughter Marianne Collins was born.

Their little family, as he called them, soon included their son George. David gave Ann his 100-acre land grant on the Hawkesbury River.

David's *Account* is written in a formal impersonal style, while his letters reveal an emotional, home-loving, tender being. In his letter home to his mother, for example, when he was a young soldier fighting the Americans in the War of Independence, he wrote first of his concern for her health, and then turned, tenderly, to each of his siblings:

---

5 Baird (2017), in her biography of Queen Victoria, notes that Whig gentlemen in particular were expected to have a mistress or mistresses. Victoria's husband, Albert, was regarded as very odd, and even suspect, when he did not take a mistress.

THE FIRST FLEET. DAVID COLLINS

FIGURE 60   Government House, drawing by Samuel Perry, 1859, in the Mitchell Library,
Sydney
REPRODUCED IN OPPENHEIMER, 2009: 119

When you write to [brother George], if he is in England, assure him of my
love. Tell him I often think of Gandy's Lane and Exeter. I have got the pencil case he gave me, and it is of use to me here. Before I get home Nancy
will I dare say be grown a fine girl improved in everything that is necessary [and] accomplishing. She may probably be pleased to hear that I am
well and have not forgotten her. How does Will go on at his book, does he
still intend to be a ... hearty, plodding fellow, or has the red coats and the
fife and the drum enlivened his ideas? As for Atty I am convinced he is
the admiration of every body at the barracks. I daresay he has forgot me
by this time... Pray for me my dearest mother. (Letter to Henrietta Collins
15 August 1775, Currey, 2000: 23)

The fear of being forgotten was already tangled up in his affections. Another
letter, a year later, reveals the longing he experienced for family and home:

I am very glad to find that Nancy and Billy come on so well in their writing.
I think Bill writes the prettiest hand of the two. Nancy must mind her
spelling, and not stick her letters too close together, nor too upright, but
give them an easy inclination to the left ... You cannot conceive my dearest mother with what pleasure I read those passages in your letters that
treat of yourself and the little ones. Oh how I long once more to clasp

them to my bosom ... (Letter to Henrietta Collins 11 November 1776, Currey, 2000: 24)

This tender young man was also a man who, positioned as Judge Advocate in the colony, handed out brutal punishments for what seem now to be minor infractions. As I said, it's a complicated story.

Much of the suffering endured in the early years of the colony came from the failure of the crops, the loss of animals from drought and from the failure of anticipated supply ships arriving from England. The drought compounded the problem for the natives, whose food supply was depleted through the depredations of the newcomers who were destroying the habitat, as well as hunting, gathering and fishing to supplement the salted beef and biscuit they had brought with them. The food supplies brought with them from England were inadequate and many of the convicts were seriously ill with scurvy, and venereal diseases. The work needing to be done by the colonisers in order to establish themselves, was seriously compromised—not just by illness, but also from some of the convicts' unwillingness—or inability—to become the good citizens David dreamed of them becoming.

Dispensing Justice

As soon as sufficient order was established after arrival in the colony, a ceremony was held for the reading of King's orders. The newcomers assembled in a circle around the governor to hear the details of the King's claim on the land:

> As soon as the hurry and tumult necessarily attending the disembarkation had a little subsided, the governor caused his Majesty's commission, appointing him to be his captain-general and governor in chief in and over the territory of New South Wales and its dependencies, to be publicly read, together with the letters patent for establishing the courts of civil and criminal judicature in the territory, the extent of which, until this publication of it, was but little known even among ourselves. It was now found to extend from Cape York (the extremity of the coast to the northward) in the latitude of 20° 37′South, to the South Cape (the southern extremity of the coast) in the latitude of 43° 39′ South; and inland to the westward as far as 135° of East longitude,[6] comprehending all the islands adjacent in the Pacific Ocean, within the latitudes of the above-mentioned capes. (*Account:* 6)

---

6   That is, halfway across the continent to present-day Darwin, Alice Springs and Adelaide.

They had clearly heard the words "warra warra", spoken by the owners of the land, but those words had no weight against the might of the King's words. There was still a lingering belief in the Divine Right of Kings.

As well as laying claim to the entire east coast of the continent, and inland to 135° of East longitude the ceremony included exhortations to the convicts, who must, as a matter of urgency, be converted into a malleable, free workforce:

> ... the governor, addressing himself to the convicts, assured them, among other things, that 'he should ever be ready to shew approbation and encouragement to those who proved themselves worthy of them by good conduct and attention to orders; while on the other hand, such as were determined to act in opposition to propriety, and observe a contrary conduct, would inevitably meet with the punishment which they deserved.' He remarked how much it was their interest to forget the habits of vice and indolence in which too many of them had hitherto lived; and exhorted them to be honest among themselves, obedient to their overseers, and attentive to the several works in which they were about to be employed. (*Account*: 6)

The history of authoritarian, punitive methods of control, and of social conditions that made survival impossible *within* the law, made it unlikely that the governor's words would be heard as benevolent. Unsurprisingly, many of the convicts used their freedom to roam about, and to engage in often risky pursuits, whose singular intent was survival:

> The convicts had been mustered early in the morning, when nine were reported to be absent. From the situation which we had unavoidably adopted, it was impossible to prevent these people from straggling. Fearless of the danger which must attend them, many had visited the French ships in Botany Bay, soliciting to be taken on board, and giving a great deal of trouble. It was soon found that they secreted at least one-third of their working tools, and that any sort of labour was with difficulty procured from them.
>
> The want of proper overseers principally contributed to this. Those who were placed over them as such were people selected from among themselves, being recommended by their conduct during the voyage; few of these, however, chose to exert the authority that was requisite to keep the gangs at their labour, although assured of meeting with every necessary support. Petty thefts among themselves began soon to be complained of; the sailors from the transports, although repeatedly forbid-

den, and frequently punished, still persisted in bringing spirits on shore by night, and drunkenness was often the consequence.

To check these enormities, the court of criminal judicature was assembled on the 11th of February, when three prisoners were tried; one for an assault, of which being found guilty, he was sentenced to receive 150 lashes; a second, for taking some biscuit from another convict, was sentenced to a week's confinement on bread and water, on a small rocky island near the entrance of the cove; and a third for stealing a plank, was sentenced to receive 50 lashes, but, being recommended to the governor, was forgiven. (*Account:* 7)

David and the Governor were repeatedly puzzled by the failure of punishment to act as a deterrent, and they followed the egregious logic that more brutal punishment was the answer, since they were dealing with a different kind of people from themselves. Rather than admiring their adventurous and rebellious spirit, and working with it, they could only comprehend their activities as irrational or atrocious:

> The mildness of these punishments seemed rather to have encouraged than deterred others from the commission of greater offences; for before the month was ended the criminal court was again assembled for the trial of four offenders, who had conceived and executed a plan for robbing the public store during the time of issuing the provisions. This crime, in its tendency big with evil to our little community, was rendered still more atrocious by being perpetrated at the very time when the difference of provisions, which had till then existed, was taken off, and the convict saw the same proportion of provision issued to himself that was served to the soldier and the officer, the article of spirits only excepted. (*Account:* 7)

It is interesting to ponder on this dynamic from the point of view of the convicts. It seems obvious that they needed more food than the soldiers since they were to engage in long hours of hard physical labour. They took risks to get that food, just as many of them had been forced to do at home. Survival had, and still, necessitated such risk-taking. Many of them had spent their lives on the edges of a social order where the resources of the rich were apparently endless. Stealing from them was not only a way of surviving, but of fairly redistributing resources in a deeply inequitable world. But in the colony it was the government that had the resources, and they were not endless. Even those in power were going hungry.

Quite clearly David did not understand the experience of extreme poverty and hunger. Dickens was yet several decades away in opening up the world of poverty and hardship to middle- and ruling-class imaginations. The more hopeful David was of the convicts, in his own rational, educated, middle-class terms, the more negative he became about them, when they failed to respond to the fairness of his rulings and the governor's decision-making. It seemed to him that the food rations being given were both generous and fair. He was sometimes indignant to the point of outrage:

> It was fair to suppose that so liberal a ration would in itself have proved the security of the store, and have defended it from depredation; but we saw with concern, that there were among us some minds so habitually vicious that no consideration was of any weight with them, nor could they be induced to do right by any prospect of future benefit, or fear of certain and immediate punishment. The charge being fully proved, one man, James Barrett, suffered death: his confederates were pardoned, on condition of their being banished from the settlement. Another culprit was sentenced to receive three hundred lashes; but not appearing so guilty as his companions, was pardoned by the governor, the power of pardoning being vested in him by his Majesty's commission... [O]ne convict, James Freeman, was pardoned on condition of his becoming the public executioner. (*Account:* 7–8)

And so James Freeman found himself hanging his fellow convict, James Bennett, an eighteen-year old boy who had been transported for highway robbery, committed when he was sixteen. James Bennett had been flogged on board the *Friendship* for breaking out of his shackles and then again for stealing food from his fellow convicts. He came before David's court for stealing, and was sentenced to be hung:

> The month of May opened with the trial, conviction, and execution of James Bennett, a youth of seventeen years of age, for breaking open a tent belonging to the *Charlotte* transport, and stealing thereout property above the value of five shillings. He confessed that he had often merited death before he committed the crime for which he was then about to suffer, and that a love of idleness and bad connexions had been his ruin. He was executed immediately on receiving his sentence, in the hope of making a greater impression on the convicts than if it had been delayed for a day or two. (*Account:* 22)

And so, three months after their arrival, "James Freeman placed the halter around Bennett's neck and the handkerchief over his eyes. Bennett mounted the ladder, Freeman pulled it from under him" (Currey, 2000: 56–7).

What motivated James to confess, and so make the act of hanging him less shocking? Did he believe in the hereafter, where his confession might be taken into account, or more likely, did he hope, as sometimes happened, that the evidence of a conscience could win him a reprieve? If the latter, it was to no avail; no time was given for reconsideration or a pardon from the Governor. Immediately after his hanging, with the assembled convicts looking on, a group of men who had recently been found guilty of theft on less serious charges was led to the foot of the gallows. Their shirts were removed, their hands were bound and the flogger laid into their bare backs while the body of James Bennett turned slowly in the rain above them" (Currey, 2000: 57).

The convicts had spent the long journey confined, often in chains, and before that, many of them had been in prisons and on the hulks where they were treated in brutal de-humanising ways, inadequately fed, and exposed to contagious illnesses and the likelihood of death. On arrival in the colony they were needed as an active, willing, autonomous workforce.

By way of encouragement and in hope of rehabilitation, task work was instituted. Once the convicts had completed their set work tasks they were free to attend to building their own shelters. David was disappointed that they did not take up the transformation of themselves that such a system made possible: "for the most part they preferred passing in idleness the hours that might have been so profitably spent, straggling into the woods for vegetables, or visiting the French ships in Botany Bay" (*Account:* 11).

David believed, even so, that under the circumstances, the convicts were surprisingly well-behaved. The governor did not see it that way:

> Although several thefts were committed by the convicts, yet it was in general remarked, that they conducted themselves with more propriety than could have been expected from people of their description; to prevent, however, if possible, the commission of offences so prejudicial to the welfare of the colony, his excellency signified to the convicts his resolution that the condemnation of anyone for robbing the huts or stores should be immediately followed by their execution. Much of their irregularity was perhaps to be ascribed to the intercourse that subsisted, in spite of punishment, between them and the seamen from the ships of war and the transports, who at least one day in the week found means to get on shore with spirits. (*Account:* 20)

By June it became evident that the responsibility given to the convicts for managing their own food rations was leading to serious problems. The food supplies for people working hard all day were inadequate; hunger drove some to take risks foraging for food and stealing to feed themselves, and for one poor man, it led to a kind of mad, uncontainable desire to eat:

> Exemplary punishments seemed about this period to be growing daily more necessary. Stock was often killed, huts and tents broke open, and provisions constantly stolen about the latter end of the week; for among the convicts there were many who knew not how to husband their provisions through the seven days they were intended to serve them, but were known to have consumed the whole at the end of the third or fourth day. One of this description made his week's allowance of flour (eight pounds) into eighteen cakes, which he devoured at one meal; he was soon after taken speechless and senseless, and died the following day at the hospital, a loathsome putrid object. (*Account:* 26)

Interestingly research conducted during the Second World War on the effects of starvation found that starving people almost always steal food. It also found that indiscriminate introduction of food to a starving person can send their body into shock and cause a heart attack. More recently people starving as an effect of anorexia and bulimia have been found to steal food, even when they know they won't eat it (Wright, 2015).

Six months into the life of the colony, abhorrence and frustration began to overwhelm David's ideals. He did nevertheless struggle to understand the convicts' situation from their point of view. He was often unable to establish guilt, for example, due to the moral code among the convicts: "There was such a tenderness in these people to each other's guilt, such an acquaintance with vice and the different degrees of it, that unless they were detected in the fact, it was generally next to impossible to bring an offence home to them" (*Account:* 28). He also observed the difference in understanding of rules among those who had not had the opportunity to learn to read: "it was very common to have them plead in excuse for a breach of any regulation of the settlement, that they had never heard of it; nor had they any idea of the permanency of an order, many of them seeming to think it issued merely for the purpose of the moment" (*Account:* 44).

As the weeks and months passed the severity of the punishments increased. Despite that brutal regime, those of the convicts who survived did eventually manage to build a beautiful city and to establish thriving farms, where food could be grown, and both they and their masters could flourish. Others had absconded to become bushrangers in defiance of the extreme punishments being handed out.

Settling in and Expanding Westward

At first the encounters with the local people seemed to go well:

> Governor Phillip, having been very much pressed for time when he first visited this harbour, had not thoroughly examined it. The completion of that necessary business was left to Captain Hunter, who, with the first lieutenant of the *Sirius*, early in the month of February, made an accurate survey of it. It was then found to be far more extensive to the westward than was at first imagined, and Captain Hunter described the country as wearing a much more favourable countenance toward the head or upper part, than it did immediately about the settlement. He saw several parties of the natives, and, treating them constantly with good humour, they always left him with friendly impressions.
>
> It was natural to suppose that the curiosity of these people would be attracted by observing, that, instead of quitting, we were occupied in works that indicated an intention of remaining in their country; but during the first six weeks we received only one visit, two men strolling into the camp one evening, and remaining in it for about half an hour. They appeared to admire whatever they saw, and after receiving each a hatchet (of which the eldest instantly and curiously showed his knowledge, by turning up his foot, and sharpening a piece of wood on the sole with the hatchet) took their leave, apparently well pleased with their reception. The fishing-boats also frequently reported their having been visited by many of these people when hauling the seine [*a vertical net*], at which labour they often assisted with cheerfulness, and in return were generally rewarded with part of the fish taken. (*Account:* 12)
>
> Every precaution was taken to guard against a breach of this friendly and desirable intercourse, by strictly prohibiting every person from depriving them of their spears, fizgigs, gum, or other articles, which we soon perceived they were accustomed to leave under the rocks, or loose and scattered about upon the beaches. (*Account:* 13)

Despite these warnings, their belongings were stolen by the crew from the transport ships still in the harbour. These thieves were driven off by the

indigenous people when they attempted to land in a small boat. When retalia-
tory stealing took place—some tools from Garden Island—the soldiers fired at
them to warn them off, and one was shot.

> To such circumstances as these must be attributed the termination of
> that good understanding which had hitherto subsisted between us and
> them, and which Governor Phillip laboured to improve whenever he had
> an opportunity. But it might have been foreseen that this would unavoid-
> ably happen: the convicts were every-where straggling about, collecting
> animals and gum to sell to the people of the transports, who at the same
> time were procuring spears, shields, swords, fishing-lines, and other arti-
> cles from the natives, to carry to Europe; the loss of which must have
> been attended with many inconveniences to the owners, as it was soon
> evident that they were the only means whereby they obtained or could
> procure their daily subsistence. (*Account:* 13)

Some of the sailors had been punished for purchasing such articles from the
convicts, but the trade continued secretly, with those who purchased goods
soon travelling northward and bearing none of the consequences of these depredations. To make matters worse, the French, who were carrying out research
in Botany Bay, had taken to firing on the local people whenever they thought
they were behaving in an unacceptable way:

> We also had the mortification to learn, that M. De la Perouse had been
> compelled to fire upon the natives at Botany Bay, where they frequently
> annoyed his people who were employed on shore. This circumstance
> materially affected us, as those who had rendered this violence neces-
> sary [i.e. the natives] could not discriminate between us and them. ...[We
> were in no doubt that] he forebore using force until forbearance would
> have been dangerous... (*Account:* 13)

The French were thus given the benefit of the doubt. To begin with, in marked
contrast, the convicts were not. What ensued then, was a profound failure of
communication with the local custodians only one month after arrival:

> In the course of this month [of February] several convicts came in from
> the woods; one in particular dangerously wounded with a spear, the oth-
> ers very much beaten and bruised by the natives. The wounded man had
> been employed cutting rushes for thatching, and one of the others was
> a convalescent from the hospital who went out to collect a few vegeta-
> bles. All these people denied giving any provocation to the natives: it was,

however, difficult to believe them; they well knew the consequences that would attend any acts of violence on their part, as it had been declared in public orders early in the month, that in forming the intended settlement, any act of cruelty to the natives being contrary to his Majesty's most gracious intentions, the offenders would be subject to a criminal prosecution; and they well knew that the natives themselves, however injured, could not contradict their assertions. There was, however, too much reason to believe our people had been the aggressors, as the governor on his return from his excursion to Broken Bay, on landing at Camp Cove, found the natives there who had before frequently come up to him with confidence, unusually shy, and seemingly afraid of him and his party; and one, who after much invitation did venture to approach, pointed to some marks upon his shoulders, making signs they were caused by blows given with a stick. This, and their running away, whereas they had always before remained on the beach until people landed from the boats, were strong indications that the man had been beaten by some of our stragglers. (*Account:* 18–19)

Interspersed with these violent, sometimes lethal, attacks by the local custodians, were friendly exploratory visits:

> ... a party of natives in their canoes went alongside the *Sirius*, and some submitted to the operation of shaving: after which they landed on the western port of the cove, where they examined every thing they saw with the greatest attention, and went away peaceably, and apparently were not under any apprehension of resentment on our parts for the murders above-mentioned. (*Account:* 24)

And some of the convicts struck up convivial relations with some of the local people, without apparent risk:

> In one of the adjoining coves resided a family of them, who were visited by large parties of the convicts of both sexes on those days in which they were not wanted for labour, where they danced and sang with apparent good humour, and received such presents as they could afford to make them; but none of them would venture back with their visitors. (*Account:* 29)

Despite David's view that hostility from the natives was most likely justifiable, the governor wanted to bring their attacks under the control of British law. He initiated several punitive expeditions, which ended in failure when the culprits couldn't be found:

> *June* 1788 The governor, however, on hearing that the two rushcutters had been killed, thought it absolutely necessary to endeavour to find out, and, if possible, secure the people who killed them; for which purpose he set off with a strong party well armed, and landed in the cove where their bodies had been found; whence he struck across the country to Botany Bay, where on the beach he saw about fifty canoes, but none of their owners. In a cove on the sea-side, between Botany Bay and Port Jackson, he suddenly fell in with a party of armed natives, in number between two and three hundred, men, women, and children. With these a friendly intercourse directly took place, and some spears, etc. were exchanged for hatchets; but the murderers of the rush-cutters, if they were amongst them, could not be discovered in the crowd. The governor hoped to have found the people still at the place where the men had been killed, in which case he would have endeavoured to secure some of them; but not having any fixed residence, they had, perhaps, left the spot immediately after glutting their sanguinary [bloodthirsty] resentment. (*Account:* 24–5)

As winter set in, the presence of the newcomers began to cause more serious harm to the original custodians of the land, with habitat destroyed, game and vegetables depleted, and hunting implements stolen:

> The cold weather which we had at this time of year was observed to affect our fishing, and the natives themselves appeared to be in great want. An old man belonging to them was found on the beach of one of the coves, almost starved to death.
>
> The natives, who had been accustomed to assist our people in hauling the seine, and were content to wait for such reward as the person who had the direction of the boat thought proper to give them, either driven by hunger, or moved by some other cause, came down to the cove where they were fishing, and, perceiving that they had been more successful than usual, took by force about half of what had been brought on shore. They were all armed with spears and other weapons, and made their attack with some shew of method, having a party stationed in the rear with their spears poised, in readiness to throw, if any resistance had been made. To prevent this in future, it was ordered that a petty officer should go in the boats whenever they were sent down to the harbour. (*Account:* 28–9)

The bloody conflict continued into August. Quite unreasonably, the governor was outraged by the theft of a goat, not willing to recognise how many of the local people's animals they had plundered:

> On the 21st a party of natives landed from five canoes, near the point where the observatory was building, where, some of them engaging the attention of the officers and people at the observatory, the others attempted forcibly to take off a goat from the people at the hospital; in which attempt finding themselves resisted by a seaman who happened to be present, they menaced him with their spears, and, on his retiring, killed the animal and took it off in a canoe, making off toward Lane Cove with much expedition. They were followed immediately by the governor, who got up with some of the party, but could neither recover the goat, nor meet with the people who had killed it. (*Account:* 32)

This pattern of hostilities continued through the following six months until in December the governor decided it was necessary to kidnap some of the local people in order to make a dialogue possible through learning their language and thus finding the means to convince them, ironically, of the newcomers' good intentions.

> It being remarked with concern, that the natives were becoming every day more troublesome and hostile, several people having been wounded, and others, who were necessarily employed in the woods, driven in and much alarmed by them, the governor determined on endeavouring to seize and bring in to the settlement, one or two of those people, whose language it was become absolutely necessary to acquire, that they might learn to distinguish friends from enemies.
>
> Accordingly on the 30th a young man was seized and brought up by Lieutenant Ball of the Supply, and Lieutenant George Johnston of the marines. A second was taken; but, after dragging into the water beyond his depth the man who seized him, he got clear off. The native who was secured was immediately on his landing led up to the governor's, where he was clothed, a slight iron or manacle put upon his wrist, and a trusty convict appointed to take care of him. A small hut had been previously built for his reception close to the guardhouse, wherein he and his keeper were locked up at night; and the following morning the convict reported, that he slept very well during the night, not offering to make any attempt to get away. (*Account:* 40)

The man they captured was Arabanoo. While captive they treated him well, by their standards, washing him, cutting his hair and beard, dressing him in British dress and feeding him large quantities of food at a side table to the governor's dining table.

The process of learning language was thus begun. Arabanoo was civil and affable and made friends with his captors. They treated him like a favourite pet, and displayed their friendly intentions by taking him on a lead to show his people that he was alive and well. It is impossible not to cringe with shame at such details, told, as they were, without any apparent embarrassment or shame.

During Arabanoo's captivity smallpox began to ravage his people, causing widespread death. In April 1789:

> ... either in excavations of the rock, or lying upon the beaches and points of the different coves they had been in, [they found] the bodies of many of the wretched natives of this country. The cause of this mortality remained unknown until a family was brought up, and the disorder pronounced to have been smallpox. It was not a desirable circumstance to introduce a disorder into the colony which was raging with such fatal violence among the natives of the country; but the saving the lives of any of these people was an object of no small importance, as the knowledge of our humanity, and the benefits we might render them, would, it was hoped, do away the evil impressions they had received of us. (*Account:* 53)

Of those people they brought in, two children survived; a girl who then lived with the clergyman's wife, and a boy who went to live with the surgeon, Mr White. Arabanoo's deep distress at so many people dying had moved his captors to see him differently:

> From the first hour of the introduction of the boy and girl into the settlement, it was feared that the native who had been so instrumental in bringing them in, and whose attention to them during their illness excited the admiration of every one that witnessed it, would be attacked by the same disorder; as on his person were found none of those traces of its ravages which are frequently left behind. It happened as the fears of everyone predicted; he fell victim to the disease in eight days after he was seized with it, to the great regret of everyone who had witnessed how little of the savage was found in his manner, and how quickly he was substituting in its place a docile, affable, and truly amiable deportment. (*Account:* 54)

After his death, the experiment was repeated with the capture of Bennillong and Cole-by.[7] Cole-by escaped first. Bennillong demonstrated the same willingness as Arabanoo to mimic English ways and to learn English language and manners, all the while being kept on a leash.

He soon came to regard the principle Europeans as his friends. He addressed Phillip as *Beanga* (father) and in turn liked to be called *Dooroow* (son). Collins was *Babunna* (brother). But unlike Arabanoo Bennillong was not content to be a captive, and in May 1790 he tricked his attendant, jumped from a water barrel over the paling fence around the governor's house, and disappeared. (Currey, 2000: 89)

When he was later sighted with a group of his people at South Head, the governor made haste to go there to meet up with him. It was September 1790. Governor Phillip approached the men with great friendliness and unarmed. Bennillong expressed great pleasure, in particular, in seeing David Collins again. He began to introduce his companions, but trouble struck quickly. When Phillip stepped forward toward Wille-me-ring, with his arms outstretched:

> The savage not understanding this civility, and perhaps thinking he was going to seize him as a prisoner, lifted a spear from the grass with his foot, and fixing it on his throwing stick, in an instant darted it at the governor. The spear entered a little above the collar bone, and had been discharged with such force, that the barb of it came through on the other side. (*Account:* 111)

The newcomers made a hasty retreat. After breaking off the very long spear, and firing shots from the boat, they rowed for two hours back to the settlement. The wound was not fatal, and Phillip ventured out again after two weeks. He was at great pains to assure Bennillong that he desired no retribution, except for the punishment of Wille-me-ring. Since that was not the local people's approach to retribution, which could spread to the family and friends of the perpetrator, this was an interesting cultural exchange.

The British conception of justice, in which only the wrong-doer should be punished, gave way when the governor's gamekeeper, who was in the woods hunting game for the settlement, was dangerously wounded by Pe-mul-wy. Phillip ordered swift revenge, ordering not just that Pe-mul-wy be brought in, but that the punitive expedition either capture, or if that was not practicable, kill, six of Pe-mul-wy's companions. Phillip, David explains, had never wanted to spill the local people's blood: "in his own case, when wounded by

---

7   I am using the spelling Collins adopted in his journal.

Wille-me-ring, as he could not punish him on the spot, he gave up all thoughts of doing it in future. As, however, they seemed to take every advantage of unarmed men, some check appeared absolutely necessary" (*Account:* 118). The game-keeper had of course been armed.

Following the Governor's orders, an armed group of 52 men, accompanied by two doctors, set out on the three-day journey. Kate Grenville's (2008) fictional version of that savage hunt, which ended without success, is brilliantly, chillingly told. Her story captures the doubleness of the newcomers' attitude: while some of them had established cordial relations with the local people, once they were positioned within the well-oiled British killing machine, they were willing to carry out Phillip's bloodthirsty orders.

Three years into the settlement it was clear to the British officers that the local custodians did not accept the dispossession of their land. Their early fantasy that by learning the local language they could reconcile the people to their presence had faded. Further their gift-giving had backfired in unforeseen ways:

> *January* 1791 It was much to be regretted that any necessity existed for adopting these sanguinary punishments, and that we had not yet been able to reconcile the natives to the deprivation of those parts of this harbour which we occupied. While they entertained the idea of our having dispossessed them of their residences, they must always consider us as enemies; and upon this principle they made a point of attacking the white people whenever opportunity and safety concurred. It was also unfortunately found, that our knowledge of their language consisted at this time of only a few terms for such things as, being visible, could not well be mistaken; but no-one had yet attained words enough to convey an idea in connected terms. It was also conceived by some among us, that those natives who came occasionally into the town did not desire that any of the other tribes should participate in the enjoyment of the few trifles they procured from us. If this were true, it would for a long time retard the general understanding of our friendly intentions toward them; and it was not improbable but that they might for the same reason represent us in every unfavourable light they could imagine. (*Account:* 122)

And so I must break off from this disastrous scene, left wondering how it was that otherwise decent people could, in that spacetime, get things so terribly wrong. Their good intentions put me in mind of a young woman in New York who told me, not long after 9/11, that the attack on the twin towers had occurred because Americans had not worked hard enough to let the world know how good they were. American dominance, she thought, was unquestionably based on their superior values. Just so, my invading ancestor, and his compatriots, did not question God's Providence, which had brought them there, nor the glory of the self-sacrifice in the endeavour of expanding the great British Empire. Nor did they question the concept of *terra nullius*, which defined as unquestionably right the conversion of all land into productive land at the hands of hard-working men. At the same time, men like David saw the havoc they had wrought with some considerable anguish.

When David returned to England, he completed and published his *Account*, telling the story of the first ten years of the Colony. It was as he had hoped, well received. But still there was no offer of suitable work at home. He would eventually take up the post of Lieutenant Governor in Hobart, Van Diemen's Land, further expanding the Colony on that southern island. I will tell that story in Chapter 15. For now, I turn to my great (x3) grandfather Thomas Blomfield, whose story lends some insight into the lives of the Irish, so many of whom were to become convicts in the colony.

CHAPTER 12

The Irish Uprising: Thomas Blomfield in Ireland

> Memory does not reside in the folds of individual brains; rather, memory is the enfoldings of space-time-matter written into the universe, or better, the enfolded articulations of the universe in its mattering. Memory is ... an enlivening and reconfiguring of past and future that is larger than any individual.
>
> BARAD, 2007: IX

∴

While David Collins was working in the colony of New South Wales, extending the British Empire and putting the convict outcasts to work to that end, another of my ancestors was involved in quelling the Irish uprising. Captain Thomas Blomfield (1751–1833) was from Suffolk, in England. In this chapter[1] I work with one letter he wrote back home to his daughter when he was stationed in Ireland in 1799.[2]

The letter was written from Dundalk, north of Dublin, and just south of the border with Northern Ireland. Thomas wrote about what he observed there, and how he felt about it. The letter in this sense works with his immediate memories—with what had made a vivid impression on him, and how it had affected him. His memories are intimately recorded, through his goose feather quill scratching words onto the page while he sits in his tent, with his son Barrington sleeping beside him. He writes of what matters to him, but more broadly, what is being made to matter at that time, in that place.

I ask here, in this chapter, what was the spacetimemattering that Thomas Blomfield's letter mobilised and wrote into in his letter? What was his entanglement and responsibility in the quelling of the Irish uprising? How did he affect it, and how did it affect him?

---

1 A longer version of this chapter was published as Davies, 2017.
2 The letter is one of a collection of letters written by Thomas Blomfield and his son Thomas Valentine, and Thomas Valentine's wife, Christiana. They were transcribed and printed by the *Armidale Express* in 1926 as *Memoirs of the Blomfield Family*.

© BRONWYN DAVIES, 2021 | DOI:10.1163/9789004446717_013

The letter was written in response to a request from Matilda that he make an account of himself. When she received her father's letter, she would have read it to her assembled family, bringing to the words on the page, not only sound and intonation patterns, but facial expression and bodily posture. The assembled listeners may also have imagined the sound of the quill scratching the words onto the page, the sound of the flap of the tent blowing in the breeze, or the voices of the men in the camp, drifting in on that breeze. They might have imagined the sight of Thomas's 15-year-old son, Barrington, asleep beside him. Those members of the listening family might also have had in mind the sight of Thomas's face, his bodily posture at his writing desk, the detail of his uniform. And he, when he wrote, had them in mind—knowing that his letter would be read out loud and passed from one to another, exclaimed over and pondered upon. He could not have imagined I would be poring over it still 220 years later.

The words on the page of the letter, now, invite us (that is, you as reader and me as writer) into different forms of existence—into an encounter in which we will each be affected. When I began to think about bringing Thomas's letter to life in writing about it, I was first thinking about how to analyse the letter, I was focused on the work I would need to do to bring the words on the page to life—to animate them. But, as I worked my way into it, it became evident that the letter itself was alive, animating me, affecting me. Reading the letter carefully, and making my way into it, had something of the same impact on me as reading good literature, or going to see a Shakespearean play, or a Verdi opera on stage.

As Achilles says of literature: "The writing of literature is to trace new lines, lines that amount to a whole cartography—that in turn becomes a geology. For Deleuze we are able to flee via these new cartographies; we are able to find what Deleuze and Guattari refer to as lines of flight" (Achilles, 2012: 6). Thomas's letter, like literature, had the power to take me on a line of flight into the spacetimemattering of Dundalk in 1799.

In becoming audience to a play, we come to know the characters, and to know them through the words they utter to other characters, and to us as audience. As audience, we witness the bringing to life of the material specificity of each character on the stage, the actors breathing life into the words on the page, inviting us into the emergent multiplicity and the flow of forces that animate them. Animation works both with the material specificity of a subject *and* with the emergent, multiple intensities and flows through which humanity is constituted. Shakespeare's characters endure, for example, because in the specificity and intensity of their passions as they emerge on the stage, they offer a reading of the human condition, of its struggles, its passions, its divisions, and its limitations. In our encounter with the characters, as audience, we expand our experience and our knowledge of what it is to be human in our own material specificity, and also in the multiple contradictory folds of ourselves, of the events we are part of—the emergent multiplicity of ourselves.

In a family history, written by another one of his descendants, Thomas Blomfield's life is primarily told in terms of his military career:

> Very little information about the early life of Thomas Blomfield, grandfather of the Australian family, can be found. The 'Ipswich Journal' in June 1833 said: 'On the 4th inst. died at Haughley highly respected in his 83rd year, Thomas Blomfield, Esq., many years Captain and Adjutant of the 10th Suffolk regiment of Militia.' He was gazetted lieutenant in 1778, Adjutant 1797 and Captain 1798 of the Western battalion of the 10th Suffolk Militia and served for a few years in Ireland at the end of the century during the rebellion. (Blomfield, 1950, Chapter 2, Part 3: 14)

The author of this family history, E.V. Blomfield, goes on to say he searched in vain for Thomas's birth details in no less than 67 parishes. More recent family searches have located Thomas Blomfield as the illegitimate son of Mary Blomfield. Mary lived from 1719 to 1784, and her life was unusual, to say the least. She was one of two daughters of Barrington Blomfield and Mary Wingfield. Her son, Thomas, was born in 1751, when she was 32 years old. She remained single until Thomas was 11. When both her parents died she and her sister, Elizabeth, inherited substantial property.

Shortly after her parents' deaths Mary married, in fairly quick succession, three men considerably younger than herself. First there was John Edwards, who was 16 years younger than she was. Then Charles Aldrick, who was 22 years younger. Charles was co-executor with her of her first husband's will. Then in 1772, at the age of 53, Mary married John Stanford, who was only 22 years old—only one year older than her son Thomas. When Mary died, John Stanford was married a second time to Amy Fowler (née Alexander). His third marriage was to Matilda, Thomas Blomfield's daughter—the recipient of the letter Thomas wrote from Dundalk. With that marriage to Matilda, John Stanford became both Thomas's step-father and his son-in-law.

Thomas Blomfield, like his mother Mary, and like his third step-father, John Stanford, had three marriages. He married Martha Jordan (1750–1777), with whom he had his daughter Matilda (b. 1774). Matilda had been born when he was 23 years old, and perhaps a little prior to his marriage to her mother. When Martha died three years later he was a widower for six years before marrying Mary Manning (née Seaman) with whom he had his son Barrington (b. 1784), who he had with him when he wrote the letter from Dundalk. He had named

Barrington after his maternal grandfather, Barrington Blomfield, thus securing the link with his family's heritage that had potentially been broken by his own illegitimacy. Louisa and Thomas Valentine Blomfield were also children of that marriage to Mary Manning.

One of the things I have loved about opening this space of my Blomfield ancestors, is that they were unpredictable. They never quite did what you might expect of the law-abiding and god-fearing family they were, who were recognised as respected members of their communities. Their family network was later to include Charles Blomfield, the Bishop of London who officiated at Queen Victoria's coronation in 1838, and Sir Reginald Blomfield the renowned architect whose major architectural works are listed in the book *Sir Reginald Blomfield: an Edwardian architect* (Fellows, 1985).

There were powerful forces of normalisation at work on and through members of polite society in that spacetime. Those forces have been depicted in intimate detail by Jane Austen. The lives of the Blomfields, nevertheless, take very surprising turns—like a step-father becoming a son-in-law, or a great (x4) grandmother having an illegitimate son and then marrying three young men after she came into her inheritance. The Blomfields make my own moments of non-normativity seem quite acceptable; to be a Blomfield descendant is not necessarily to fit within the normative lines of force that dictate how the lives of gentlemen and gentlewomen should be lived.

For the 100 years before Thomas Blomfield found himself in Ireland as part of the British force quelling the Irish uprising, Ireland was dominated by the Anglican Church of Ireland. The Church was made up of families whose English ancestors had taken up land in Ireland after its conquest.[3] Ireland was nominally an autonomous state, but in practice it was controlled by the King of Great Britain and supervised by his cabinet in London. It had been thus for 100 years since the defeat of the Catholic Jacobites in the Williamite War in 1691.

In 1799, the year Thomas wrote his letter from Dundalk, the people of Ireland were mostly Roman Catholics, who were excluded from political power and from land ownership under the British Penal Laws. Many of the Irish leaders had converted to Protestantism to avoid the severe economic and political penalties imposed by England on Catholics. The great bulk of land-owners were the Anglo-Irish families who were often absentee landlords, with Catholic peasants carrying out the labour on their farmlands under conditions of extreme poverty.

The Tory statesman Edmund Burke, an Irishman educated at Trinity College Dublin, said of the Penal Laws: "It was a machine of wise and elaborate

---

3   David Collins' mother (Chapter 11), was almost certainly part of that English gentry's colonisation of Ireland.

contrivance, and as well fitted for the impoverishment, oppression and degradation of a people, and the debasement in them of human nature itself as ever proceeded from the ingenuity of man." Dr Johnson described the Penal Laws as "more grievous than all the pagan prosecutions of the Christians" (cited in O'Shaughnessy, 1988: 12).

Twenty years earlier, in 1778, the *Catholic Relief Act* had been passed, partly as a reward to the Irish for not having joined the Scottish uprising (which had been supported by the French army), and partly in the vain hope of preventing the Irish from making an alliance with the French in the way that Scotland had done. Further, the British army had been in need of more soldiers to quell unrest in India; the Relief Act removed restrictions that had prevented Irish Catholics from joining the British army and from entering the professions. It gave them equal voting rights to Irish Protestants, though not the right to stand for parliament. The Act did not serve to alleviate the extreme poverty of the landless peasants who could barely survive on the alienated lands.

Joseph Holt, who appears in Thomas's letter as the Rebel General Holt, and who will appear in later chapters, was one of six sons of John Holt, a farmer in County Wicklow. The Holt family was Protestant and loyalist and had come to Ireland under James I. In 1797 Joseph Holt changed allegiance and became a member of the Society of United Irishmen. In May 1798, his house was burned down by the loyalist Irish Militia of Fermanagh. In Holt's memoir he tells how during the early 1790s there had been "many outbreaks of resistance which were ruthlessly put down by the British forces. Lord Movia, speaking in the House of Lords on 22 November 1797, protested that the mere suspicion of arms in a house provided 'sufficient grounds to burn it'. Finally, in May 1798, open rebellion broke out" (O'Shaughnessy, 1988: 12).

After the burning of his house, Holt fled to the Wicklow Mountains where he gradually assumed a position of prominence with the United Irish rebels. Avoiding pitched battles, he led a fierce campaign of raids and ambushes against loyalist military targets in Wicklow, reducing government influence in the county to urban strongholds.

Meanwhile at Vinegar Hill, on 21 June 1798, over 15,000 British soldiers launched an attack defeating the rebels there. Following their defeat, the surviving rebels headed toward the Wicklow Mountains to link up with Holt's forces. Holt was given much of the credit for the planning of the ambush and defeat of a pursuing force of 200 British cavalry, at Ballyellis, on 30 June 1798. Holt and his rebel soldiers continued the United Irish guerrilla campaign, eluding large-scale sweeps into the mountains by the British army. He had a steady supply of recruits, many of whom were deserters from the British militia.

The news of the British defeat of the French at Ballinamuck, in September 1798, meant the United Irishmen could no longer depend on aid from the

French army, and Holt negotiated the terms of surrender. Dublin Castle was eager to end the rebellion in Wicklow and allowed him exile in New South Wales, without trial. Unfortunately he failed to negotiate safe passage for his men.

According to O'Shaunessy (1988: 11), who edited Holt's memoir:

> Joseph Holt had many faces. He was a mountainy, lion-hearted, humane, indignant man, with an abiding love for his family. He was also a sanctimonious, strutting, vainglorious man, a canny opportunist looking for the nearest way, a warrior with the heart of an accountant. Joseph Holt was a survivor, a reluctant rebel. An informer? Never to be trusted? That last question would, after 1798, become a thorn in his side for the rest of his life.

Thomas Blomfield's letter from Ireland was written some months after Holt had capitulated. The first part of his letter tells of the fate of two of the rebels who had been captured after the surrender. Thomas's words to his daughter tell of his horror and sorrow at their execution. He writes of his melancholy, and his emotional entanglement in their deaths, and of the burden of responsibility he felt in overseeing those deaths. Melancholy was a condition that manifested itself in tears at that time in Britain (Dixon, 2015). And those tears were read as a sign of true spirituality, understood as a capacity to be moved by the sorrow of the crucifixion.

At the same time, as Captain of his troops, he must pull himself together. He must, in literary terms, be both Shakespeare's weeping Titus Andronicus and his more rational brother, Marcus:

> [Titus Andronicus cries out] "If any power pities wretched tears, To that I call". Marcus is the voice of reason, telling his brother to calm down: "do not break into these deep extremes", "let reason govern thy lament". (Dixon, 2015: 45)

And now to the letter itself:

> I am seated, my dear Matilda, with an intention of complying with your request, viz., to give you some account of myself since I last wrote to you, but from the multiplicity of regimental business which passes through my hands, I am so perfectly confined that I have not had one opportunity of examining any part of this country, therefore what information I shall

be able to communicate will be dearly purchased by the postage of my letter. First I shall present you with a melancholy event, a sight which in all probability you will never witness a similar one, and I sincerely hope such another will never occur to me.

The 5th, or Royal Regiment of Irish Dragoons were quartered with us in this Garrison and neighbourhood, but from the improper behaviour of a part of the Regiment the General who commands this district has got the whole removed and they are at this moment on their passage to England. Two privates of this Regiment about four months since deserted and joined the Rebels, but since the famous Rebel General Holt surrendered many of his followers have been given up, and information being of these two they were soon apprehended, tried by a general court-martial, and sentenced to be shot at the head of the Regiment. On the 23rd ultimo this sentence was put into execution upon the beach of this Bay.

The Dragoons were drawn up on each side of the two prisoners and our Regiment in line directly in front, at about 20 yards distance. After the proceedings having been read to the regiments and prisoners—they were allowed their own time to pray, confess, etc., etc., to their priests— they were then blinded and, kneeling by their coffins, received the fire from nine of their comrades who were chosen for this occasion. One died instantly, but the other received several single shots before he expired. They were Roman Catholics and brothers, names Patrick and Michael Freeney. Thus ended this duty; though necessary, yet the most awful and painful in which officer or soldier can be employed, and I hope the dreadful example will have the desired effect upon the regiment and point out to those who have had an inclination to swerve from their duty to their King and country, the danger which they have avoided and the disgraceful and untimely death which awaits every traitor.

The deaths of Michael and Patrick Freeney had cast Thomas into a state of deep melancholy. He had been forced to oversee and to witness something he found unbearable. These rebels had thrown in their lot with Joseph Holt to fight for Ireland's freedom from English domination. Such rebels might have found a place in history as heroic freedom fighters. Instead, with the defeat of the French army, and Holt's terms of the negotiated peace, which protected him but failed to protect his soldiers, they were 'given up', 'apprehended' and shot as traitors and deserters.

In the last six lines of this passage Thomas recovers himself with military rationality; he hopes their horrible deaths will act as a deterrent, preventing others from being disloyal to King and country. With these few lines Thomas recovers his positioning as the Captain of his men, and as loyal and dutiful soldier. In so recovering himself as Captain of his Battalion he mobilises the absolute right of the power of the colonizing force, whose terms allow no legitimate loyalty to Ireland, to Holt, or to the Irish people. It is in writing to Matilda that the melancholy of the event could be allowed to emerge in his own body, and tears could perhaps be wept for the cold-blooded killing of two brave young men.

In the next paragraph of his letter Thomas changes the subject away from the melancholic deaths of the rebels, and the necessity of duty to King and country, to the polite intercourse of family and society, almost by way of repairing the social fabric that such events and his melancholy might be felt to disturb. In this part of his letter, which could almost have been written by Jane Austen, he re-territorialises himself as a gentleman, with an unassailable place in the networks of polite English society.

> To change the subject. In this regiment, strange as it may appear, I [nearly] met with a person who is almost a relation. Her maiden name Alexander, a daughter, I believe, of Mr Alexander who lived at 'Yarmouth' or 'Lowestof.'[4] Her present name Bamford. Her husband is a cornet and acting Adjutant. Unfortunately I never had an opportunity of being introduced to the lady. I had a very distant invitation, or, rather, no invitation from the husband. He said he should be glad if I would take tea with him, but never mentioned time. I saw him every day, but no second offer upon the subject escaped his lips; and their route for England coming very suddenly, away she went, and I know not what sort of person my cousin is, whether tall, handsome or otherwise. Barrington says she has been upon the stage.

So even while he recovers himself within military/colonial discourses, he admits to an 'almost relation' who has been upon the stage, a profession not altogether approved in the polite circles of Suffolk. Even so, with this small story Thomas brings himself back to Matilda and her husband John Stanford, and to the entangled family networks in which they are mutually embedded.

He then turns to a discussion of John Stanford's new uniform, of which, teasingly, and with tongue-in-cheek, he disapproves on aesthetic grounds. At

---

4   John Stanford's second wife (after his marriage to Thomas's mother and before his marriage to Thomas's daughter) had been born Amy Alexander—hence the reference to the person he failed to meet as an 'almost relation'.

the same time, he positions himself as one with rank over Mr Stanford, as the one who will be doing the inspection of his Corps, adding yet another dimension to the complexity of this relationship. And in animating that space of his relationship with John Stanford he falls into an acute longing to be home:

> I should be very pleased to have an opportunity of seeing Mr. S. in full uniform. At the same time, with all due deference to his choice of dress, I cannot bring myself to imagine it a becoming one. Blue and black is a very singular and particular uniform, and only worn by engineers. Surely blue with scarlet cuffs and collar, blue lapels, pocket flaps etc., etc., edged with white or scarlet, would have been a much lighter looking dress. But dress is all mere fancy, and a man can fight in one colour as well as another. I hope to have the honour of reviewing the Corps on my return to England, and I doubt not but I shall be highly satisfied with their performance. In April we expect to be recalled. How happy shall I feel myself once more to set foot on my native soil, for the longer I stay in this country the less I like it, and I am wishing away the days and nights with more earnestness than I ever before did. Lord Euston is come to England and will not return, except anything particular occur in this country.

Then, once more, he recovers himself from melancholy, this time with a small story that John Stanford will find interesting:

> We are very quiet and as well or better situated than any regiment. The barracks are very good, and commanded by Major-General Lord Charles Fitzroy (Lord Euston's brother), who keeps an excellent table, at which some one or other of us take our beef and claret every day in great comfort. Barrington and myself dined with him on Saturday.

In marked contrast with such luxury was the life of the Irish peasants, who Thomas turns to in the second half of his letter. Here he takes up the discourse of early anthropological writing, that is, a discourse of colonial power documenting alien and inferior species in the lands they have conquered. Early anthropology, having emerged from natural history, regarded "human primitives" under the rule of colonial administrations much as if they were part of the natural flora and fauna. As such, parts of their bodies and their artifacts were collectable curiosities for scientific study. Thomas's account takes up these anthropological modes of intelligibility, thus animating another line of force integral to colonial power at that time and in that place. In this account, it is no longer melancholy that overtakes him, but horror. His account performs in Barad's words 'the enactment of boundaries—that always entails constitutive exclusions' (Barad, 2008: 122). He treats what he writes about the Catholic Irish peasants as a reality that is independent of himself as observer. He is not aware that his horror is instrumental in the constitutive work of separating them out as another kind of being from himself.

For want of a better subject I will endeavour to describe an Irish wake, alias funeral. One happened some little time since near the barracks, at a house, or rather cavern. Very few of the houses of the peasants have any chimney. They burn turf and make the fire at one end farthest from the door, out of which issues the smoke, and the family so completely enveloped in it that they cannot be seen. Persons (as you may suppose) unaccustomed to such infernal vapour cannot for a moment stand it, and when by chance any of the inhabitants come to the door they look as brown as any old wainscot table you ever saw. When the smoke is not much and you have an opportunity of looking in, you will see man, wife and children, hogs, cow, cocks and hens all mixed in one room. This I assure you is quite common, and it is also as common to see the hogs, etc., with the children eating boiled potatoes out of the same wooden bowl. More of this some other time, and now I turn to the wake.

The corpse was rapt up in a clean sheet and laid upon a kind of form, a very little distance from the ground, surrounded by men and women. One of the latter—who is hired for the occasion and by custom taught a solemn chant, or, rather, howl—gives the signal, and they all bow themselves down over the corpse and take hold of the sheet or whatever covers it. She begins her howl, in which the rest immediately join and begin clapping their hands, and a more savage, hideous noise cannot well be conceived. This is repeated during the night at short intervals, which intervals are filled up by smoking tobacco and drinking whiskey—a spirit peculiar to Ireland and which is distilled from barley. In fact they make a perfect frolic and sometimes get completely drunk. I have seen in Dublin about 11 o'clock in the morning a funeral procession preceded by a person with a large pitcher of liquor. The bearers were so completely intoxicated as to stagger from one side of the street to the other, and every moment I expected to have seen the corpse dashed upon the pavement. Every person, both bearers and followers, was making as much noise as is heard at a bull-baiting in England. This savage, indecent mode of burying their deceased friends is peculiar to the Roman Catholics. Protestants observe the same decorum and solemnity as in England upon the occasion.

Thomas's account is not simply descriptive—it vividly *constitutes* the imper-meable boundaries between himself as English and Protestant, and the Irish Catholic peasants. The smoke in their houses is 'infernal', the children eat with animals, the funeral chant becomes a 'howl' so 'savage' and 'hideous it 'can-not well be conceived'. They get 'completely drunk' and become both 'savage' and 'indecent'. He constitutes the boundary by abjecting the other—that is, through a horrified expulsion from himself of whatever it is they are. It is thus a performative account in which Englishness, Protestantism and gentlemanli-ness are accomplished for himself, and for the readers for whom his letter was intended. Their collective identity is secured in its difference from the primi-tive other.

In the next passage, he mentions a skull that will become a specimen for science, taken back to England in the same way Aboriginal skulls were being removed from Australia. Yet once again his horror finds expression, not at the appalling poverty that the peasants have been trapped in by British rule and land ownership, a depth of poverty that makes grave robbery one of the maca-bre methods of survival. He doesn't see the implicit power he wields as Captain in the British army. His descriptions of the peasants are written as if this is what they are by nature, and by their own peculiar norms. The boundaries that separate them are thus constituted as impermeable and fixed. Although he may not have intended such a reading, he is nevertheless mounting an implicit argument that justifies the colonial power of which he is part, and that makes sense of his own performance of domination as Captain of his Batallion. He continues this justificatory stance:

> As a further proof of their disregard to their dead, in a burying ground about two miles from this place, called Castle Town, are to be seen 40 or 50 skull bones strewn about looking as white as snow, one of which, having some peculiar marks, Dr Freeman intends to secure and bring to England. The remains of the dead strewn about this Romish consecrated ground are not confined to skull bones, but every other bone—and you may absolutely see pieces of flesh adhering to the sides and bottoms of broken coffins. In short, my dear Matilda, they are not the most pleasant of beings to reside amongst, and I shall be very happy to get out of the country. You would be surprised to see in what filthy manner these peo-ple live. Even farmers who have land sufficient to employ seven or eight horses take scarcely any other food but potatoes, sour butter milk, and barley and oat bread. Knives and forks are not very common and by most not thought necessary.

Thomas's longing to escape from this association with people living in these dreadful conditions, and his position of power, override the possibility of questioning the conditions of intelligibility through which he, and in contrast they, are making sense of the world (Davies, 2008). In not questioning those conditions of intelligibility, however, he succumbs ever more deeply to the event through which the continuation of the domination of Catholic Ireland by Protestant England is effected; the words that circulate from one to another in letters and in conversation, reiterate the conditions of intelligibility; they are a constitutive part of the event, in which exploitation and oppression of a people remains thinkable as legitimate practice.

Thomas concludes his letter with a passage about the dangers of travelling by sea and a sense of his own vulnerability, combined with his dependence on God's Providence for his survival. Providence, in that placetime, "referred firstly to the immutability of the Lord's eternal and unchangeable decree ... [and] was the single teleological thread which wove together past, present, and future, the blueprint for human history drawn up in the beginning" (Walsham, 1999: 9):

> We have had a great deal of bad weather, high winds and very stormy, since our arrival here. A great number of vessels have been driven on this coast and completely lost. Last week two were totally wrecked within two miles of the town and every person perished; and this afternoon six recruits arrived belonging to the Lancashire Dragoons who sailed last week from Liverpool, in company with four more vessels with troops. Just within two miles off Dublin Bay a sudden storm came on and the other four ran upon a rock and went down with every soul on board. Thank God that we were so far from land at the time we were caught in the storm when coming to Ireland, or we must have shared the same fate, and I pray to God that we may have His gracious protection on our return, and that He will so rule the hearts of our domestic and foreign enemies that we may soon return to the enjoyment of our domestic concerns and comforts.
>
> As I cannot conclude with a subject more interesting to my feelings, nor one in which (I conceive) you can join with me more fervently, I shall lay down my pen, when I have assured you that I am, affectionately yours, T.B.
>
> P.S.—Barrington is fast asleep, but he has desired me to say that he begs his respects, love, etc., to all.
>
> Love to Mr. Stanford and respects to all my friends.

It is to John Stanford, curiously, that he sends his love, to Matilda he sends affection, and to his friends his respects, while Barrington sends 'love, etc.' to all.

In animating Thomas Blomfield's letter, and responding to its animating force, I have explored the constitutive flows in between specific human subjects, material objects, and a range of onto-epistemological lines of force—such as religion, class and colonialism, through which the British Empire gathers its force. I have explored the constitutive work that produces the specificity of Thomas Blomfield, at the same time that it constitutes those others he encounters. I have looked at how the words on the page of his letter invite his audience into different forms of existence—permeating their, and our, indefinite boundaries—and, also, re-citing (re-cementing) those boundaries that make oppressive social relations possible.

CHAPTER 13

Richard Brooks: A Tragic Journey

Two years after Thomas wrote his letter from Dundalk, Richard Brooks, in 1801, became captain of the convict transport ship *Atlas*. He was to become infamous among historians for being the brutal captain of a ship on which one third of the convicts died. Richard Brooks (1765–1833) was born into an English seafaring family on his father's side, and ministers of the church on his mother's side. His paternal grandfather, Nathanial Brooks, made a fortune in the cod-fishing industry in Newfoundland in the mid 1700s. A harsh industry, cod-fishing depended on Irish workers, who were press-ganged when willing workers weren't available, or taken from the gaols with the connivance of the Irish authorities.

In the 1760s, during Richard's early childhood, the British fishing industry in Newfoundland came under attack from the French navy. The French burnt the British processing factories to the ground and sank their ships. Richard's grandfather, Nathanial, made a daring escape, sailing off to bring the British navy to their rescue (Maher, 2016). Richard's father, Henry Brooks, continued fishing in the Newfoundland fishery despite the French attacks. Meanwhile Richard's mother, Honoria, whose father and grandfather were vicars, raised Richard and his brothers in the genteel atmosphere of the vicarage. In the mid 1770s, around the time Richard first went to sea, his father miraculously survived his ship being wrecked in a storm.

Two decades later, in 1790 and following the American War of Independence, the English were banned from fishing around Newfoundland. Richard's oldest brother, named Henry after his father, continued fishing there, and continued, to his ultimate detriment, in the oppressive treatment of his Irish workers. Rebellion against their oppressive colonial masters was on the rise in Ireland, and Henry's men rose in mutiny against him, murdering him with an axe and throwing him overboard (Maher, 2016). Henry's murderer was hanged, and the three Irishmen who aided him were transported to New South Wales. The justice system, in true Dickensian manner, cut no slack for the poor, or for those who rebelled against abusive forms of employment and of colonial power. It was illegal to form a workers' union, for example, and forming or joining a union was punishable by imprisonment. The value of the lives of the poor, and of the Irish weighed very little on the scales of justice in the late 1700s in Britain.

© BRONWYN DAVIES, 2021 | DOI:10.1163/9789004446717_014

FIGURE 61   Richard Brooks, portrait by Augustus Earle, n.d., in the
             National Gallery of Victoria

The end of the cod-fishing industry led to many bankruptcies. Richard's
father's estate, after his death, was declared bankrupt, as was the estate of Richard's uncle, Nathanial Jnr. Richard's early work life, in his teens, had been full of
risk and adventure. It was supported by the taken-for-granted exploitation and
brutal treatment of workers. Nevertheless, major global changes made his life
increasingly economically precarious.

Following the collapse of the fishing industry Richard became, for a brief
period a privateer (a government sanctioned pirate who captured foreign

trading ships), and then a merchant mariner, plying his trade between England, India and China. All trading activities at the time, however, were heavily circumscribed by the power of the wealthy East India Company, to whom the British government was entirely beholden.

In 1796 Richard married Christiana Passmore (1776–1835). At the time of their marriage, he was described as being '6 ft high' and 'very handsome' and full of activity and vigour' (Maher, 2016: 20–1). Christiana was from a family of gentlemen and gentlewomen. She was interested in politics, music, theatre, and in education for girls. Their first child, Henry was born in 1798, with her daughters Christiana Jane, Mary Honoria, Jane Maria, Honoria Rose and Charlotte born every two years from 1802. As her daughter Jane remembered it (Cox, 1912), Christiana and her children lived in a cosy house with a beautiful garden on The Crescent in Greenwich. Christiana had no interest at all in going to sea, content with her autonomous life in London where she could pursue her own interests.

The American War of Independence had not only put an end to the fishing industry in Newfoundland, but to convict transport to America. By the late 1700s trade with India and China was also becoming less accessible and by 1800 the colony of New South Wales offered new trading opportunities. Since 1788 convicts had formed its primary cheap labour force. The convicts cleared and farmed land for those gentlemen who had taken up large tracts of land east of the Great Divide. They built roads, they mined, and they built new towns and cities. The growing colony was urgently in need of household, personal, agricultural and industrial goods. The most lucrative trade in Sydney in 1800 was the trade in alcohol, which served as the local currency, the British government not having foreseen the need the colony would have for its own currency. The import of 'rum' required a licence, as well as the Governor's permission to land it. Leading merchants in the colony, D'Arcy Wentworth and Robert Campbell, had made their fortunes through the rum trade, and Richard Brooks set out to do the same, combining that trade with convict transportation.

In 1801 Richard Brooks became captain of the convict transport ship *Atlas*. One third of the convicts died on that journey. The historians Bateson and Ahearn have claimed that those deaths were caused by Richard Brooks' inhumanity.

When I first encountered those historians' accounts, the knowledge of such an evidently flawed ancestor weighed heavily on me—binding me unwittingly into the historians' moralistic, judgemental interpretations. It took me a while to realise that I needed to tease out the entangled lines of force at work, which made those deaths possible.

The archives offer, if one looks carefully at the detail, a quite different story from that of the historians. That different story dismantles their narrative structure that divides the world into binaries of guilty/not guilty, humane/inhumane, or hero/anti-hero, and it enables me to approach Brooks and the journey diffractively – that is, as if there is not only one linear, causal story to be told, but, rather, entangled, multiple agencies and forces affecting each other, and folding into each other. Those entangled agencies include not only the characters of the individuals involved, but the British concepts of masculinity, class and religion; they include the recent uprisings of the disenfranchised Irish against their English colonial masters, the American war of independence and the ongoing war with France; the material conditions on board the ship; and the regulations controlling the treatment of prisoners. These were some of the many entangled lines of force that were integral to what was made to matter on that fatal journey.

Transportation

In the 80 years between 1788 and 1868, 158,702 male and female prisoners arrived in New South Wales. Many more had embarked on those perilous journeys. Some escaped, but many died, most of them from the contagious diseases they brought on board from the prisons. The much-cited authority on convict transportation, and one of the historians who accuses Brooks of inhumanity, Bateson, observes of the transport of convicts:

> Disease took by far the heaviest toll. Scurvy, dysentery, typhoid fever, smallpox and other diseases were commonplace, especially in the earlier years of transportation, and effective measures to combat them were introduced but tardily.
>
> For a long time no real effort was made to ensure that the convicts embarked were physically fit to withstand the rigors of the long voyage through varying climatic conditions. The medical examination prior to embarkation was perfunctory, and, indeed, was for many years a useless formality ... The result was that many convicts, having already spent months in the insanitary, fever-ridden gaols or in the noisome hulks, were sent aboard the transports in a sickly and emaciated state and, often enough suffering from a contagious complaint. (Bateson, 1974: 4)

The Journey of the Atlas

In 1801, 151 male convicts and 28 female convicts were loaded onto the *Atlas* in Dublin and Cork. Many of them were seriously ill with typhoid and dysentery. One that the ship's surgeon sent back died before he reached shore. Others died before the Atlas set sail across the Atlantic. Three escaped in Rio. Only 85 men and 26 women reached New South Wales (Bateson, 1974).

The *Atlas*'s sister ship was the *Hercules,* captained by Lucklyn Betts.[1] Between Cork and Rio, Betts faced an uprising among his prisoners, leading to substantial loss of life. Bateson, blames the uprising on Betts, accusing him of being too soft, and for failing to take the rumours of an uprising seriously. Ahearn (2013), who has also written at length about the *Atlas* and *Hercules* journeys, agrees with Bateson on this point. The rush to take up a position of moral judgement and blame is seemingly irresistible. They condemn Betts even while acknowledging elsewhere the difficulty of the task all captains faced in deciding how to respond to rumours of an uprising from among the prisoners. Rumours will be rife, Ahearn says, but punishment of prisoners, he also adds, could not be given without good reason.

When it comes to the *Atlas*'s journey, in contrast to the *Hercules'*, both historians blame Brooks for taking the rumours of an uprising too seriously, so treating the prisoners with unreasonable severity. They also accuse Brooks of overloading the ship with his own trade goods, leading to the cramped and airless quarters of the prisoners, which further contributed to their ill-health.

There is no doubt that the *Atlas* was overloaded, but why it was so cannot so simply be attributed to Brooks' inhumanity or greed as Bateson and Ahearn claim. They claim, without reliable evidence, that the goods stored in the hospital, preventing proper attention to the convicts' health, were Brooks' private trade goods. That those goods belonged to Brooks, was asserted by Jamison, a free passenger on board the *Atlas* for the first two months of its journey. Jamison himself was, in no small part, responsible for the ship's overloading.

The *Atlas* and the *Hercules* commenced their journey on 29 November 1801. They should have sailed in September to avoid the fierce November weather in the North Atlantic. But transport ships must wait upon the arrival of the convicts from their various prisons and hulks. The November storm that they struck on setting out, took more than two weeks to blow itself out, damaging the *Atlas*—springing the mizzen mast, carrying away the bowsprit bitts, and damaging the food and water supply.

The ship's surgeon, Elphinstone Walker, who was responsible for the health and well-being of the convicts, was unable to fulfil his duties during the storm due to his own illness, an illness that appears to have continued intermittently throughout the seven-month journey. Their care was left in the hands of one of the convicts, Sir Henry Browne Hayes.

After the storm had blown itself out, Brooks encountered a problem with the Sergeant and some of the soldiers. Reliable soldiers had been difficult to find, given the British engagement with Napoleon's troops in Egypt and Syria,

---

1   Sometimes transcribed as Luckyn.

and in Spain and Italy, as well as the military engagement in India. The guard on board the *Atlas* was drinking heavily and becoming quarrelsome, unwilling to carry out their duties. Brooks wrote in his log on 9 January 1802:

> A complaint from the Prisoners of their Provisions being Improperly Cooked, with their suspicions of their not getting the Quantity Allowed by Government Also from the Soldiers of their Allo'e of Liquor – for their being frequently drunk. Stopped it Entirely.

Trouble continued with the guard. On 3 May Brooks' log noted he had disciplined Sergeant Champion putting him "in irons for disobedience of orders and making mutinous language on the main deck". The soldiers on board the transport ships at the time were as like as not to join in rebellion with the convicts under their charge, or equally likely, to refuse to supervise them if they came up on deck for air and sun. Sergeant Champion later tried to jump ship at the Cape (Maher, 2016).

By the time the ship called at Rio for repairs, two months after embarking, on 2 February 1802, 70 of the *Atlas*'s prisoners were seriously ill. They were removed to an island off Rio to give them a chance to recover.

On that two-month journey, the passenger Jamison and Richard Brooks had several serious altercations. The hostilities between the two men began in Dublin when Jamison attempted to bring on board, with himself and his family, ten tons of goods. His contractual allowance was for two tons. Brooks himself had been granted 'privilege' to carry his own trade goods and these had already been stowed on board. The *Atlas* was loaded close to its proper limits, and Brooks suggested to Jamison, and one other listed passenger, that they might sail on another ship that had room for them both, including room for Jamison's ten tons of goods. While the other passenger agreed to the transfer, Jamison refused, on the grounds that he was a King's Officer, who was entitled to the passage that had been booked for him (Maher, 2016).

Failing to resolve their dispute, Brooks closed the matter by setting sail for Cork, where he was to pick up further prisoners, leaving Jamison and his ten tons of goods behind. Infuriated, Jamison travelled overland and caught up with the *Atlas* in Cork. In Cork, without Brooks' consent, he managed to get his family and five tons of his goods on board—three tons more than his allowance. Brooks was furious that his ship was now clearly overloaded and that his authority had been so blatantly flouted.

Once on board, the sources of Jamison's fury multiplied. The best cabin, which he had expected to be given on the basis of his prestigious upcoming appointment as New South Wales Surgeon, was occupied by a wealthy convict,

Sir Henry Browne Hayes, who had paid handsomely for it. The cabin Jamison
and his family were allocated was cramped, and was, furthermore, used to
store some of the ship's food stores including sugar drums stored under his
bed. Between Cork and Rio the relations between the two men grew worse as
the journey progressed, with Jamison's avowed contempt for the other passengers, Sir Henry and Mrs Atkins, wife of the New South Wales Judge Advocate,
generating a great deal of friction.

At Rio, Jamison and Brooks had a further major falling out, when Jamison
was found bringing customers on board, to whom he was selling the personal
goods he had brought on board at Cork. Outraged, Brooks ordered the customers off his ship. The following night, Jamison came back on board drunk and
aggressive. There are several versions of the fight that ensued, each varying
in significant detail, Jamison saying Richard Brooks had beaten him savagely
while his mates held him down, others saying Richard Brooks was ill at the
time and although the two men began to fight following Jamison's drunken
and intemperate behaviour, kicking and breaking open the case belonging to
the first mate, the other men pulled them apart. The upshot was that Jamison
was transferred (or transferred himself) to the *Hercules*.

Outbursts of rage punctuate the lives of men in the early days of the colony. They drank a great deal of alcohol, it being a lot safer than water at the
time, and they ate a great deal of meat, since live animals and salted meat
were easier to store than fresh fruit and vegetables. It is little wonder they were
occasionally liverish and given to rage. Issues of status and honour also fuelled
their rage; privileges were granted according to status and honour, and so these
were fiercely guarded. On board ship the Captain had total authority, a fact
that was galling to Jamison whose status on land was well above that of Brooks'.
Sir Henry Haye's ambivalent status as both convict and an Irish knight also
made for complex transactions.[2]

The accounts made of the conflict on board offer a fascinating insight into
the way in which status, power and privilege were made to matter in that
spacetime. Jamison gave his version of the final conflict with Brooks that had
led to his removal to the *Hercules* as follows:

> I came rather late in the Evening on board the Ship Atlas on Saturday the
> Twentieth day of February in the Year One Thousand eight hundred and
> two, said Vessel then lying in the Harbour of Rio Janeiro, on descending

---

2 Sir Henry was accused of abducting a Quaker heiress. After evading court for some time, he
   decided to give himself up rather than have his name continually besmirched in the press.
   There are multiple conflicting accounts of what actually happened, but nothing conclusive.

the After Ladder, I found the Steerage so blocked up that the way to my cabin was utterly impeded by Packages stowed there; I endeavoured with my foot to remove them, but not succeeding in my efforts to obtain a Passage; by pushing out of my way a Case which effectually prevented my progress, I laid hold of it with my hand, when the part I held broke off, – and with much difficulty, I at length reached my Cabin. Shortly afterwards (having undressed) I put on my dressing gown and went on deck. Mr. Byron first Mate of the Atlas addressed himself to me, Ironically saying he was much oblidged to me for breaking open his Case, (meaning the Case I had removed) and exposing his property to the Sailors in the Steerage: I told him in reply that he was not obliged to me, and that there was no personality intended by me in removing the Case in question, as it prevented my going into my cabin; Mr. Byron, in a style of much haughtiness demanded to know, If I wanted to Command the Ship; I replied that I neither wanted to command, or to interfere in anything relating to the Ship; but as the Atlas was in His Majesty's Service, and myself a King's Officer and ordered a Cabin in her for my accommodation, I of consequence expected a passage to it: ... Mr. Richard Brooks Master of the Atlas being then in his bed, called out from the Cabin where he lay, and asked what noise that was on deck; Mr. Byron replied that some words had taken place between him and Mr. Jamison, Mr. Brooks then said, Mr. Byron put that mutinous scoundrel (meaning me) in Irons; irritated by such illiberal language I told Mr. Brooks he lied, and that I was neither Mutinous nor a scoundrel, without further altercation Mr. Brooks came out of his Cabin, struck me repeatedly and to prevent all possibility on my part of resistance or defence, I was forcibly held by Mr. Byron, Mr. John Willen, and others; I was knocked down on the deck by Mr. Brooks, and being down, then overpowered by him and his adherents, in such defenceless situation, with unmanly violence he made repeated blows at me, until he had vented his savage, and brutal passion, when he returned again to his Cabin. (HRA Series 1 Vol iii: 708–709)

On the one hand Jamison reports the thrashing as a cowardly and savage act on Richard Brooks' part, beating a man who is being held down, and on the other hand his story asserts his own innocence. He makes no mention of his trading activities earlier in the day, such activity generally being considered well beneath someone of the status of Principal Surgeon. Nor does he make reference to his own five tons of goods contributing to the clutter on board the ship. And finally, he makes no mention of his own state of inebriation, or of having kicked others' containers and breaking them open.

Sir Henry made at least two accounts of the altercation, in which, far from being held down, the men on deck were seeking to pull the two men apart. He wrote to Earl Hardwicke, Lord Lieutenant of Ireland on 26 October 1802, of Jamison:

> In Rio Janeiro this man was generally inebriated and during this temporary privation of his senses was unremittingly asserting his importance in the Scale of Society, he being a New South Wales assistant surgeon. In one of those frantic sallies he abused Captain Brookes, who was then exceedingly ill and hardly able to walk, in the grossest manner. Blows consequently ensued to prevent which I exerted myself assisted by two strange Gentlemen, who happened to be on Board, in separating the combatants he then issued forth a torrent of the most vile abuse against me, and made use of many improper expressions to excite me to quarrel with him likewise. Having met him the next day on shore at a Coffee Room, I sent one of the above mentioned Gentlemen to him to know if he recollected any part of the language he made use of the preceding day, he being then likewise drunk with all the arrogance and self sufficiency of a New South Wales task master returned as answers 'that he would grant no audience to a Convict'. I came up to him and called him a coward and a Poltroon and expecting a suitable chastisement he exclaimed "O Sir Henry, I am beneath your notice" which effectively disarmed me of Resentment. The Captain not being able to endure further repetition of his Insolence had him removed to the Hercules. (http://www.sirhenrybrownehayes.com/dark-times.html)

Sir Henry further wrote to Lord Hobart in the Department of Colonies in London on 6 May 1803:

> The Transport Board had also by letter ordered Captain Brooks to receive on board his ship a man named Jamieson. Would your Lordship wish to know him? In figure he resembles a hackney chairman, in behaviour a clown; illiterate beyond measure, stupid when sober, and when drunk outrageous. While we lay at Rio this man in one of his drunken fits quarrelled with Captain Brooks and they actually fought on the quarter deck. Compassion for a moment superseding contempt engaged me to join the company in separating them. Our kindness procured us all, and me in particular, a volley of abuse in terms not calculated to escape notice. On the shore the next day, when the fumes of his liquor were dissipated, I requested an apology, and obtained satisfaction. The steps I then took

were universally approved of. He went on board another ship and I forgot him. (Historical Records of New South Wales, henceforth HRNSW, vol 5: 104)

While Sir Henry had been disarmed by Jamison's words to him in the Coffee Room, Jamison avenged himself on Sir Henry once he arrived in the colony. His report to Governor King led to Sir Henry being sentenced to six months' gaol for his "improper" language to Surgeon Jamison. He was further subsequently forbidden by Governor King to come to Sydney to retrieve his personal goods. Richard Brooks' own account of the dispute to the Commissioners of Transport was as follows:

> April 14 1802
> I am sorry to Report the Ill conduct of Mr. Jamison. Having a few days before I left Rio been obliged to Order Two Men out of the Ship who were then in the lower Cabin on the point of purchasing Goods from him of all Kinds, which were taken on board as Cloathing, he seemed to be much hurt at the time. The day after he came on board late in the evening intox-icated, and abused my Officers, and at the same time made use of that horrid kind of language which I was not accustomed to, and forced me from my bed when laying ill on the quarter Deck, which caused a fight. He has also behaved very ill to the Two Women passengers. Every indulgence that was possible was done for him. We had some Altercation before we sailed from Cork, because I would not take more goods on Board. I told him my Orders from Capt. Raines was not to exceed more than Two Tons, and by some means or other he has got on board near Five Tons, which I will send you the measurement of in my next Letter. (HRA Series 1 Vol iii: 572)

On arrival at the colony, Jamison had also written to Lord Hobart in London, making the case that, out of moral duty, he must report that it was Richard Brooks' trade goods that had caused all the problems on the *Atlas*, including the typhoid and dysentery.

> Were I tacitly to pass over the complicated abuses committed on board the Atlas Transport, I should consider myself highly reprehensible. A due sense of moral duty urges the information contained in this letter, and I shall neither exaggerate or diminish the facts it states, but detail the circumstances I communicate truly as they occurred in the hope that if attended to I may be the instrument of future benefit to His Majesty's

Service, *in preventing a repetition of abuses disgraceful to humanity, by bringing the offender in the present Instance to such just punishment as the nature and extent of his offences may seem to deserve.* (HRA Series 1 Vol iii: 704, *my emphasis*).

Clearly Jamison did not recover his equanimity on the remainder of the journey on board the *Hercules*. In his report to Lord Hobart he asserted that the crowding of the hospital and the prison was the fault of what he called Richard Brooks' illegitimate merchandise (though Brooks had official permission to carry his trading goods). Jamison made no mention of his own five tons of goods loaded without Brooks' consent, or of his own trading activity. His attack on Brooks goes so far as to claim that Brooks *willed* the illness of the prisoners:

> A dangerous fever and dysentery appeared amongst the convicts, to which numbers fell victims; nor were the necessary means adopted to check the progress of this destroying Malady used; on the contrary it should see, from the conduct pursued, that *it was intended to aid the baneful influence of this harbinger of Death...* (HRA Series 1 Vol iii: 704, my emphasis).

This is clearly a wild accusation, not least because from 1800, the payment for convict transport was calculated not just on how many embarked, but on how many arrived safely and ready to work.

Jamison further accused Brooks of using false weights, short-changing the convicts of their share of food and water so he could sell their food on arrival in the colony. Brooks himself had noted this complaint from the prisoners, that false weights were being used. He wrote in his log (9 January 1802): "A complaint from the Prisoners of their Provisions being Improperly Cooked, with their suspicions of their not getting the Quantity Allowed by Government Also from the Soldiers of their Allo'e of Liquor – for their being frequently drunk. Stopped it Entirely". Fair weights were the responsibility of the ship's surgeon, Elphinstone Walker. Although Walker was intermittently ill, there is no reason to believe that Brooks did not order that correct weights be used after receiving the prisoners' complaint.

Jamison, notably, did not step in to assist when Surgeon Walker was ill during that first two months of the voyage. His report doesn't mention Surgeon Walker's illness, and neither does it mention the water casks that were washed overboard in the storm, or the animals drowned. He not only makes no reference to the fact that the prisoners were already seriously ill when they came on board, but claims that their illness was *caused* by Richard Brooks;

and that the shortage of food and water was due to Richard Brooks' avarice and cruelty.

Jamison's submission, made from a sense of 'moral duty' and 'truly' stating the facts can be read as a vengeful diatribe, and as a means of covering up his own culpability in bringing his own five tons of trade goods on board when the ship was already fully loaded.

Sir Henry Brown Hayes, who had stepped in when Surgeon Walker was ill during the storm, wrote to the authorities in London complaining that Governor King was not fit to govern, boasting as he did that he was beyond the law; King, he observed, had no-one who would support him, except for one of his cronies, Surgeon Harris, and now Surgeon Jamison, the three of them forming a powerful triumvirate.[3]

It is extraordinary, and in the final event inexplicable, that the historians Bateson and Ahearn, in constructing their anti-hero narrative of the "inhumanity of Captain Brooks", look no further than Jamison's account. They don't mention the nature of Jamison's conflict with Brooks, even though it is of immediate relevance to any reading of his version of events. Further, they ignore, for the purposes of their moral judgement, the *spacetimemattering* of the journey. Instead, they construct the characters they write about, based on a handful of unexamined clichés—imputing motives and desires that depend on a narrow theory of personhood, ignoring the entangled agencies of which they demonstrate full knowledge in other parts of their writing.

As it turns out, the ship's surgeon, Elphistone Walker, also made an account of the voyage, which offers vital clues as to what was going on, on board. As ship's surgeon, it was Walker who was responsible for the health and conduct of the convicts. In his letter to the Commissioners for Transport in England, written the day after the arrival of the *Atlas* in Port Jackson, he emphasised the illness of the prisoners when they came on board. His letter puts the lie to Jamison's account that they had become ill after coming on board, or as a result of Brooks' having placed them in irons when mutiny was threatened.

---

3   A colourful portrait of Governor King written by O'Shaughnessy in his introduction to Holt's memoir (1988: 22) reads: "a harsh, uncouth man, plagued by bouts of ill-health, subject to violent and unpredictable outbursts, 'God-fearing', eccentric and sometimes given to alarming 'practical jokes', Governor Philip King was not, I suppose, a bad man. He had done his best to curb the rum trade but was himself addicted to the bottle. Horrified at the sexually licentious ways of the colony he had found that the spirit was willing but the flesh weak. In the early 1780s, King being a married man, had sired two children through a convict woman on Norfolk Island—the penal settlement he had founded soon after Phillip had landed at Port Jackson. A tyrannical man, King had yet resisted the attempts of John Macarthur to limit the rights of the emancipists. And he had pressed Westminster for trial by jury".

Bateson ignores the account of Surgeon Walker, the person, after all, most likely, given his duties and responsibilities, to know if there was a threat of mutiny. To Brooks, the Transport Commissioners had made Walker's role clear:

> Mr Elphinstone Walker, having been appointed Surgeon Superintendant of the Convict Ship Atlas, we *direct you to comply with such Regulations, as he may think necessary, respecting the Management of the Convicts and their treatment while on board*; and it is absolutely necessary that the said Vessel should be furnished with a sufficient number of Scrapers, and everything proper for keeping her sweet and clean, the better to preserve the health of the Convicts and Passengers during their voyage to New South Wales ... : and we inform you, *that you are every day, when the weather will permit and the Surgeon requires it*, to cause a number of Convicts to be brought upon Deck for the benefit of Air, and see that their berths are properly cleaned and ventilated ... ("Transport Commissioner. Instructions to Richard Brooks, Ship's Captain" cited in Ahearn, 2013: 368, my emphasis)

To Elphinstone Walker the Transport Commissioner wrote very specific instructions: he was solely responsible for the care and management of convicts; he must ensure that no goods were brought on board not approved under the contract (that is, it was Walker who should have prevented the loading of Jamison's five tons of goods); he was responsible for water and for rations and good preparation of meals for both crew and passengers, making sure both were sufficient; he was to ensure that meat bought at any port was both good quality and good price; he was to ensure that sufficient lemon juice and sugar was loaded for all on board to have a daily dose over a period of six months; he was to visit the sick twice a day and to see both to medical treatment and management of diet as well as seeing to their comfort; he was to visit the healthy convicts daily, to listen to their complaints and to check for any signs of illness and ensure immediate treatment; he was to bathe the sick weekly, and with those removed to the hospital they must also have their hair removed and their clothes washed and fumigated; he was to keep the cabins and the hospital clean and aired and dry; he must keep a daily journal recording the sicknesses, the treatments and the deaths; he was to be economical in his use of medicine; he was to record any ideas he had about better care of convicts; and finally he was to record any unusual or interesting events on board.[4]

---

4   The full transcript of his instructions is available in Ahearn 2013: 369–371.

These instructions make it clear that management of the prisoners rested with the Surgeon; the Captain was to agree to their coming out on deck when weather permitted and when the Surgeon required it. What should happen when the weather was poor and the Surgeon himself was ill was not specified.

Bateson takes no notice of Walker's account of the illness of the prisoners when they first came on board, nor does he take account of Walker's failure to stock the ship with adequate scorbutics for the prevention of scurvy. He ignores Walker's account of the poison the prisoners smuggled on board at Rio, and his concern about reports of a planned mutiny. Bateson further ignores Governor King's reliance on Jamison's account and he ignores the friendship between Governor King and Jamison.

Instead Bateson asserts that:

> There is no evidence beyond the master's own statement, that the prisoners had attempted to seize the *Atlas*, and Governor King certainly considered that there had been no attempt at mutiny. *We are justified in fact, in concluding that Brooks invented the story of a mutiny and of the poisoning of the soldiers' coffee* so as to have an excuse for calling at the Cape. At Rio he had learnt that European goods were a glut on the Sydney market, and *his motive* for calling at the Cape was to try and find an alternative market for his private trade. (Bateson, 1974: 184, emphasis added)

So the historian, it seems, is not beyond invention himself, claiming that there was no evidence beyond Brooks' account, when clearly there was, and claiming to know, with no evidence, what Brooks motives were, and why he acted as he did.

The authorities at the time regarded the length of the transport journeys as crucial. To that end ships' captains were instructed not to make any stopovers but to sail without delay to Port Jackson unless they had very good reason to stop—for repairs or supplies. The Governor's committee to enquire into *Atlas*'s journey took their main task to be to consider whether the stopovers that were made were in fact necessary (HRA series 1 vol III: 555–6). The very terms of the Governor's inquiry implied that there was a causal relation between Brooks' trade goods and the convict deaths. Governor King reported the findings of the inquiry to the Transport Commissioners stating that: "The master of the Atlas having such a quantity of private trade and spirits on board, appears to have produced most of the bad consequences complained of in that ship" (9 August 1802 HRA series 1 vol iii: 554). The Committee was, notably, not asked to investigate Jamison's goods, or the veracity of Jamison's account.

Governor King, it would seem, colluded with Jamison's quest for revenge. To this end he also refused permission to Brooks to offload his spirits other than some he allowed him to sell to the French exploration ships in the harbour. The documentary records are silent on how Brooks did finally manage to off-load and sell his trade goods—quite possibly in Van Diemen's Land.

The Committee's decision that Brooks had not been justified in calling at the Cape makes it evident that they too had ignored the report of the ship's surgeon, and had ignored Brooks himself, whose letter to Governor King stated that they "arrived at the Cape of Good Hope on 12th April to get a supply of Bread and Water owing to the quantity of Bread being damaged from the badness of the weather we experienced on our first sailing" (HRA Series 1 Vol III: 554).

The committee found that while Brooks had been justified in calling into Rio for repairs, he had been under no necessity to call at the Cape. After leaving that port, furthermore, he had not used every exertion to expedite the voyage. The mortality, in the committee's opinion, informed, it would seem, solely by Jamison's account, and by Governor King's support of that account, had not been caused by disease carried aboard when the convicts had embarked in Ireland, but had resulted from "the want of proper attention to cleanliness, the want of free Circulation of Air, and the lumbered state of the Prison and Hospital" (HRA series 1 vol iii: 556).

Current quantitative analysis of those convict journeys finds no correlation between long journeys and death rates. They find that stop-overs actually aided survival, since food and water and medical supplies could be replenished. Maxwell-Stewart and Kippen (2014) test various theories about what caused the deaths on all the convict transport ships, including not only the length of the journey, but also overloading, weather patterns and climate. The *pattern* they find of sudden spikes in deaths on individual ships is identical to the pattern of epidemics. In other words, the claim by both Brooks and by Surgeon Walker, that the most significant problem was the contagious diseases brought on board in Dublin and Cork, was most likely correct.

The entangled fortunes of Richard Brooks, Sir Henry Brown Hayes, Thomas Jamison, Elphinstone Walker, and later Governor King, cannot be so readily untangled in the way the historians have suggested. The causal agents in that entangled mess include the characters of those on board the ship, and the collusion between Jamison and Governor King once they had landed. But the entangled lines of force in the spacetimemattering of the journey include much more:

Space includes here the physical place of the small ship and the material conditions on board, the Atlantic and its fierce November storms, and the material conditions in the original prisons and hulks where epidemics were allowed to rage.

Time. 1801 was the aftermath of the Irish uprisings. Integral to that time was the oppressive attitude of British government toward Irish catholics, which at that time was enshrined in unjust and brutal laws and practices. The ongoing war with the French led to poor quality guards being sent on the transport ships; and the necessity of trade in the establishment of a distant southern colony meant that convict transport ships must double as trading ships. The monopoly on trade held by the East India Company was pushing trade further afield. Finally, the American War of Independence, which led to the end of convict transport to America, necessitated the off-loading of prisoners in the far distant colony—the excess of prisoners having been caused in turn by the extraordinarily punitive laws used in the management of the poor and of the rebellious in England and Ireland.

Mattering. The policy of offloading those who ran foul of British law (law heavily prejudiced against the poor, against Catholics, and against the rebellious) was one in which the lives of the convicted barely mattered except as they could be used as slave labour for building the new colony; trade mattered in bringing new and exotic goods to the wealthy in England from far off exotic countries; class mattered at law and in everyday practice, meaning that gentlemen's lives mattered in a way that others' lives did not; the forms of masculinity practiced by British (usually Anglican) gentlemen mattered both in terms of their efforts at securing their ongoing recognition as gentlemen, entitling them to good treatment. That better treatment of the elite, had, as its underbelly, acceptance of colonial oppressive practices. The treatment of Sir Henry Brown Hayes, a convict, to first class travel on board the *Atlas*, and sharing the Captain's mess, is a case in point. As O'Shaughnessy (1988: 12–13) observes of the entrenched attitudes to the poor:

> The British government countenanced the most savage atrocities, and ... turned a blind eye to torture. Here are some of the comments made by British and Irish statesmen and politicians at the time:

> Among a people hardly yet emerged from barbarity, punishments should be more severe, as strong impressions are required. The Marquis of Beccaria

> It is unmanly to deny torture, as it was notoriously practiced. John Claudius Beresford

The man who would balance the slight infractions of the Constitution in inflicting a few stripes on the body of a perjured traitor, and the loss of many lives and property, must renounce all pretensions to wisdom and patriotism. Sir Richard Musgrave, member of the Irish Parliament.

I want to turn, finally, to the practice of flogging that existed at the time. Ahearn accuses Brooks of flogging the convicts without sufficient cause—since in his view the rumours of uprising should not have been taken seriously. Flogging, in all its brutality was not, I suggest, a symptom of Brooks' abnormal character, but, horrifically, of his normality within the spacetimemattering of the British (in)justice system in the early 1800s. Excessive punishments for the poor, compared to relatively minor punishments for the same infractions on the part of the gentry, were commonplace (Golder, 1991).

Subsequent Voyages

Brooks made several more trips to the colony before moving there permanently with his wife and children in 1814. In 1806 he was re-employed as a ship's captain of the convict transport ship, the *Alexander*, which he brought safely to Port Jackson with only two deaths. The historians, in their dedication to the storyline of Brooks as anti-hero, are at a loss to explain the success of that voyage, resorting to platitudes such as "perhaps he had learned his lesson". In fact, following the inquiry, he had faced no more than a minor fine, and the irritation of Governor King, who refused to allow him to land his trade goods in Sydney. What had changed between 1801 and 1806 were the rules regarding the health of prisoners who could be sent on transport ships to the colony. The medical examination could no longer be perfunctory or a useless formality. The prisons could no longer offload the sick and dying onto the transport ships. The lines of force came together to effect that one significant change following the fatal journey of the *Atlas*.

The emotional burden for me now, is no longer the thought that I have one inhumane ancestor, but an intimate knowledge of the harm humanity is capable of perpetuating, when it is caught up in unjust, self-serving regimes of power. The world's inhumanity touches me much more deeply since I have been brought face-to-face with it on exploring the tragic journey of the *Atlas*; I am made more vulnerable to inhumanity; the borders of my physical being have been made more permeable through this journey; I have become less able to ignore my own implication in whatever is being made to matter globally, and in the lives of those who are close to me.

When I ask of Richard Brooks "What is it to be this?" I am immediately in awe of his skill as a sailor, and his capacity to command that impossible journey; I am held apart by his life-long refusal to talk about the journey, and can only wonder at the pain of it, the frustration of it, and the anger he sometimes let loose; and I am in awe of the adventurous spirit that enabled him to undertake many future journeys, some of them so heroic they defy imagination. Maher (2016) tells, for example, how on being shipwrecked on the Falklands due to the ship's captain being drunk and incompetent, Brooks, with the help of Joseph Holt, saved the passengers, setting them up on an uninhabited island. He then set out in the longboat with six men, rowing thousands of miles up the coast of South America in perilous seas to initiate a rescue mission for the stranded survivors.

I can weep for Richard Brooks now, and for myself, as he turns the question back to me, back to myself, and asks me, what is it to be this, now, in the world I am enmeshed in?

While Richard was making successive trading trips to New South Wales up to 1814, when he eventually migrated with his wife and children, the war with Napoleon was being fought by many of the young men who would eventually make their own way to New South Wales. In the next chapter I look at the letters written by Thomas Valentine Blomfield, written from the warfronts in Portugal and Spain, to his sister Louisa and to her husband John Edwards, and to his father, Thomas Blomfield. The wars with the French were a massive drain on Britain's economy, which increased the desperate straits of the poor and therefore their chances of running foul of the law and being banished to the colony. The soldiers too often fared badly, abandoned without food or shelter or transport. Fighting in service of the King was seen as a noble service, but there was little that was noble about their lives at the various fronts.

CHAPTER 14

Thomas Valentine (Val) Blomfield: At War with Napoleon

Thomas Valentine Blomfield (1793-1857),[1] son of Thomas Blomfield, arrived in New South Wales on 3 August 1817. He had sailed on the *Dick* with a detachment of the British 48th Regiment of Foot. He later settled in the colony, selling his commission in the army, marrying Christiana Jane Brooks (1802–1852), and taking up life as a gentleman and farmer. I will explore their life together in the early colony in Chapter 18. In this chapter, I tell the story of his life on the battlefields of the Peninsular War.

Thomas Valentine Blomfield was born on Valentine's Day in 1793. He was known as Val, and sometimes as Tom. When his father wrote to his daughter Matilda from Dundalk in 1799, Val was six years old, and growing up in her care. In 1800 his father married Sarah Kimmance. The seven children from that marriage, born between 1800 and 1815, remained separate from the children of the first and second marriages. Val never mentioned Sarah or her children in his letters, though he continued to write to his father.

After their mother died, Val, Louisa and Edwin, the children of Thomas's second marriage, turned to each other, and to Matilda, and to Matilda's husband, John Stanford. Later Louisa's husband, John Edwards, became an integral member of that small, intimate family circle. In the letters that have survived, which Val sent home from the warfronts in Spain and Portugal, he addressed himself to his sister Louisa, to her husband, John Edwards, and to his father. He consistently sent love and affection in his letters to Louisa, Matilda (Mrs S) and John Stanford (Mr S), as well as to John Stanford's son by an earlier marriage,[2] Wingfield, who was similar in age to Edwin and Louisa. Edwin was also at the warfront, and Val mentioned, more than once in his letters home, his desire to be in touch with him.

Val entered the army as an ensign in 1809 when he was 16 years old. He was appointed Lieutenant two years later while fighting against Napoleon's invading forces in Spain and Portugal. These were known as the Peninsular

---

1   The letters in this chapter can be found in *Memoirs of the Blomfield Family,* The *Armidale Express,* 1926.

2   After his first wife Mary Blomfield died, John Stanford married Amy Alexander. Amy died in 1795. Louisa Blomfield, his first wife's grand-daughter, was his third wife.

© BRONWYN DAVIES, 2021 | DOI:10.1163/9789004446717_015

Wars. Such appointments were not based on merit as we now understand it. Commissions in the army for higher rank were bought, on the understanding that those with wealth were the educated classes, and that education and birth were the best indicators of competence to hold higher office. Those commissions could later be sold on leaving the army, as Val was much later to do. He was awarded the Military General Service Medal with clasps for Busaco (1810), Albuera (1811), Ciudad Rodrigo (1812), Badajoz (1812), Salamanca (1812), Vittoria (1813), Orthes (1814) and Toulouse (1814).[3]

The letters home to Framlingham are dated from 1810, when Val was 17, to 1813 when he was 20. Two further letters were written from Ireland, where he had been posted in 1815. His letters take us inside the experience of a young man fighting year after year in bloody battles. They re-animate the war as it works its way on and through his body and into his ways of being in the world; at the same time, they animate his bonds with his family. In the act of writing to them and receiving letters back from them, in the intensity of remembering them and longing for them, and in his simultaneous concern at growing different from them, he inevitably changed—becoming different in the spacetime of life on the battlefields.

Animating Bonds with Family: Being English and Becoming Not-English

In Chapter 12 I left Thomas Blomfield, Val's father, in Dundalk, yearning to be home among his family and praying "to God that we may have His gracious protection on our return, and that He will so rule the hearts of our domestic and foreign enemies that we may soon return to the enjoyment of our domestic concerns and comforts". Eleven years later, Val wrote to John Edwards, Louisa's husband, from Alamedilla, a small village in Granada in the south of Spain, of his longing for home, and his fear that war was making him unfit for the genteel company of women:

> This time two years I landed at Lisbon, after having a fine tossing in the Bay of Biscay. I heartily wish I was there now, running before the wind at ten knots an hour on my way to Old England. I hope that time is not far off, but I am sorry to say I do not see much likelihood of it. When I do get there I shall want a little polishing before I can go into any company, or I shall be very apt to make use of some of our soldierlike expressions,

---

3   See http://dagworth.steventon-barnes.com/Blomfield.html

MAP 3   Spain and Portugal

and as to conversing with a lady, I think that would be entirely out of the question, as I have never spoken to any English lady since I left my native shore ... (Alamedilla, southern Spain, September 1811)

He often wrote of his fear that warfare was making him unfit as company for the polite English society he yearned for. He worried that being a soldier had transformed not only his language, but also his body in unacceptable ways. English gentlemen, at that time, should not look, he feared, as he now looked. Jane Austen, writing at just that time, had one of her characters, Sir Walter, speaking as a landed gentleman of independent means, express his revulsion for men aged by the weather. Such a man would become "prematurely an object of disgust to himself" said Sir Walter, and he would want nothing to do with him—he would not even consider, he said, leasing his property to one so weathered (Austen, 2012: 26).

It is, in Barad's (2007) terms, a precarious onto-epistemological shift that emerged in Val's writing, a shift in his language and his body that cut him off from home even while he longed for it—a cutting together-apart (Barad, 2012). Just as the habituated practices of English society had begun to erase themselves from his mind, so the familiar comforts of home had begun to seem strange to him, as his body accommodated itself to the harsh conditions of war. He could no longer imagine sleeping on a feather bed, though he could still imagine going out with his brother-in-law shooting for game. He concluded this letter to John Edwards with all these contradictory forces running through him—the longing for the same old familiar life among his loved ones, a life that had become strange to him in his soldier's hardened body, and his fear that he will have become a stranger to them—a doubled strangeness—estrangement—from his intimate family circle:

> How happy I shall be when I see myself amongst all my friends at Framlingham. It will appear to me as a new world. I am sure I shall not be able to sleep on a feather bed. I mostly sleep sound between my blankets on the bricks, with my leather portmanteau for a pillow. I wish I was with you, going out to shoot. I have a hare today for dinner; an officer of ours killed 2½ brace yesterday. Remember me to all, and believe me, yours sincerely T.V.B. (Alamedilla, southern Spain, September 1811)

Nine months later, his awareness of the difference between himself and those at home seemed to have become even more intense. He wrote to John Edwards, for example, that he was pleased to hear that the girls at home were well, then warned that his own transformation was so great that they may not even *want* to know him when he eventually does arrive home:

> Remember me kindly to them all [the girls] and tell them I am quite sure they would not now look at me, as I am as brown as Mahogany. I have now reason to expect to be soon with you, as we have had eight officers landed at Lisbon for us, and don't be surprised if you have a brown looking fellow walk in at your door one of these days. I fear you would not own me. (Rueda, north of Salamanca, Spain, June 1812)

He edges his fears with humour, making light of them, envisaging himself as a "brown looking fellow". At the end of this letter he worries that the vital link between them will be further erased by the illegibility of his letters. Even this concern he managed to make light of, with an amusing image of himself composing his letter in his underpants:

> I fear you will not be able to make either head or tail of this scrawl, but I am really so very hot that I am hardly able to hold my pen, though I have

nothing on but my shirt and drawers. (Rueda, north of Salamanca, June 1812)

Sometimes, though, his humour deserted him. Three months earlier he had written to Louisa of the precarious nature of his existence. He could not bring himself to tell her the detail of his hairsbreadth escapes, and he found himself with nothing to say. Perhaps he sat there a long while, pen in hand, struggling to find the words that would bind him together with Louisa, and not set them apart. But suddenly the Drum major was there and he must bring his letter to an end:

> How happy I shall be when I see myself seated amongst you all, and tell-ing you my hairbreadth escapes, etc., etc. I believe I have nothing more to say at present.
>
> Remember me to Mr. E. [John Edwards], Mr. S. [John Stanford], Wing-field, and my good friends at Tannington, particularly to the female cre-ation.
>
> I will write again to some of you when this business is over. I fear there will be a great many lives lost before we can call this place ours. The Drum major has now come for the English letters.
>
> Adieu, my dear Louisa. Remember me to all friends and relations, and believe me to be, your affectionate brother T.V.B. (Alamedilla, southern Spain, March 1812)

In other letters Val had joked about death, hoping he would not get "the leaden fever", or saying he would write more if he had "time and a whole skin". But here in this letter to Louisa the thought of death weighed on him in anticipa-tion of the lives about to be lost. He bade her "adieu my dear Louisa", a farewell redolent of the fear of never meeting again. He asks her to *remember him* to family and friends. While this is his usual way of ending letters, it seems espe-cially poignant here. Remember me... and believe (in) me, he asks.

In this and other letters I have broken his letter into paragraphs to make the reading of them easier, though the original letters had no such breaks; the scarcity of paper meant that every bit of space must be used, letters must be written on both sides of the flimsy page, cross-hatching each page with a sec-ond set of lines running vertically. Each letter Val sent would have taken hours to decipher by those who sat around reading it, connecting themselves to him through his words on the closely written pages, imagining the vivid scenes he described for them, laughing at his jokes, and praying for his safety.

In March 1813, one year after that letter to Louisa, Val recounted in a letter to John Edwards the horrors of being put in charge of the sick. He had sufficiently recovered his humour to make an entertaining story of his own precarious struggles for survival:

> Being with the sick I was much better off. I had, to be sure, a great deal of trouble during the day but then at night I mostly had a house to go into and sometimes a good bed, and in general plenty to eat, but the poor men that I had charge of (which were about 150) had scarcely anything to eat, so that they are actually dying every day through starvation. I should have almost starved myself but that the woods between Salamanca and Ciudad Rodrigo are plentifully stocked with pigs and, of course, I helped myself. None of us had any rations after we left Salamanca until we came to Rodrigo, which was eight day's march. It was one continual wood all the way. The poor pigs suffered very much; shooting them was like a smart skirmish, which lasted all day. The Marquis of W. hung two men whom he caught shooting them.
>
> The letter which you mentioned was addressed to the army by the Marquis, and was a very unjust one. He says the troops suffered nothing neither from the fatigue nor anything else. He says we were the worst army he ever heard of or served with. Now, it is a known fact that the army was harassed with very bad marches and very little to eat, and that the sick died like rotten sheep, and many other evils.
>
> However, with the assistance of a little pork I arrived at Rodrigo, from whence I was sent to Ceclavin, where I remained on duty for nearly a month and then joined my regiment. (Esealhao, north-east Portugal, close to the border with Spain, Portugal, March 1813)

When he himself became sick six months later, his father, Thomas, feared he was malingering. There could be no tolerance as far as he was concerned, for men who could not endure the rigours of war. Val wrote back, reassuring his father that he was up for the fight, at the same time bidding him *adieu* and asking him to tell the people of his home town not to forget him:

> At that time I had every reason to expect being in England long before this, and had the ship sailed from thence a day or two after I embarked I certainly should have got leave for England on my arrival here, but we were three weeks on board before we sailed, on account of bad weather. I had a very strong certificate from the surgeon of the regiment to say it was necessary for me to be sent to my native country for recovery ...

The cause of my late indisposition was not what you hinted. I must now soon think of returning to the fatigues of war, and not indulge too much in the good bed I have at present, for I don't wish to be thought a skulker. This paper will not stand crossing, so for the present I must bid you adieu. Remember me to all friends and inquirers. Tell the people of Framlingham not to forget me.

Believe me yours affectionately T.V.B. (Santander, Spain, Nov 1813)

Val was indeed very ill. A friend, Charles Crowe, had written three months earlier:

> 12th August [1813]
> Visited my poor friend Close who is again ill, and conveyed to a house in Lesaca. I was rejoiced in finding him better, and preparing to go to the seaside. Accompanied by Lieutenant Thomas Valentine Blomfield of the 48th Regiment who is also in a very precarious state of health. Most fervently I do hope that these two worthy fellows may speedily recover! Blomfield – or Old Val – as we facetiously call him – volunteered from the West Suffolk Militia... Val has seen much service and is highly esteemed by everyone. (Peninsular Journal of Charles Crowe of Coddenham, Suffolk, Soldier 1785–1854)

By the time Val finished his tour of duty in Portugal and Spain, and was posted to Ireland, his use of humour as a strategy for dealing with the overwhelming impact of so many deaths had taken a macabre turn. Now at the age of 22, having been a soldier for six years, he wrote to John Edwards from Limerick of looking forward to the novelty of witnessing the hanging of men in the Irish gaols who would soon be on trial:

> The gaol here is full of prisoners. The Assizes will be held in about a fortnight. I believe a great number will have their necks stretched. It will be a novelty to me, as I never saw a man hung, at least not in a regular sort of manner. I have seen rascals belonging to the army hauled up to a tree... (Limerick, Ireland, Feb 1815)

Legend has it that Australian male identity was born one hundred years later, on the battlefield at Gallipoli. In reading Val's letters, I can't help wondering if it was forged much earlier. The transformation of himself, and the dilemma which that transformation confronts him with, runs all the way through his letters. He is English, and at the same time is becoming not recognisably English.

He wrote, for example, of being repelled by the women he had met in Spain and Portugal, even while being fascinated by them, and even while fearing that English ladies will not now look at him. He writes his way into this dilemma, knowing his dear Louisa will not approve of what he writes:

> I believe I need not be much afraid that any Spanish or Portuguese lass should run away with my heart. Certainly there are some very pretty, but then they are always spitting and belching, which to an Englishman is rather disgusting; and if a person has a mind to kiss them, why he stands a chance of getting an immense puff of garlic, which is enough to disgust any person; they use an immensity of it. The Spanish girls dress uncommonly pretty. They mostly have small feet and walk uncommonly well, but it is rather a rare thing to see a pretty face except in large towns. There are a great many pretty faces in Badajoz[4] – at least there were when I was there. I think I like the Portuguese lasses better than the Spaniards, as I have been more amongst them. I understand that the girls of Andalusia are the finest in the world, but for my part I am sure I should like none so well as those of my native soil. You see I am rather at a loss to fill up my paper, as I have nothing extraordinary to relate. You must not show this to my sister, as it is such nonsense. (Alamedilla, southern Spain, Sept 1811)

In writing of women in this way, Val cannot help but admit he is straying outside the rules of polite English society and he asks that his words be dismissed as nonsense—and not even read. Eighteen months later, he wrote again to John Edwards, of being fascinated by the "pretty Spanish girls" who do not reject him, and of the mysterious elusiveness of the "better sort of women" in Portugal:

> You may suppose how sorry we all were to be obliged to leave Madrid, and the fine country about it, where we were so well received and treated in the best manner possible, and to be obliged to leave behind all the pretty Spanish girls, who all thought it an honour to walk with a British officer; but in this abominable mountainous country the better sort of women are never seen, except when they go to church, and then it is almost impossible to get a peep at their faces, as they always wear a large black mantle which they put over their heads, with a large kind of hood and some black crape which cover their faces. Sometimes they peep at the lattice windows, but on the appearance of an officer they immedi-

---

4   Badajoz is in Spain on the border with Portugal, 100 miles or so east from Lisbon.

ately go away. (Esealahao north-east Portugal, close to the border with Spain, March 1813)

Animating the Peninsular War: Tales of Battle and Hardship

In his letters Val reported the details of battles and the physical duress he and the men suffered as they marched hundreds of miles through forests and mountain ranges while carrying heavy weights; they were often without adequate food; men died of starvation; and some of the animals too dropped dead from carrying heavy weights and having no fodder. He wrote of the physical duress of the war as if he could hardly believe that he and the troops must suffer such shocking conditions. I include three such letters here, in their entirety; I have chosen one to John Edwards, one to Louisa, and a third to his father.

From Sarzades, then, in Portugal, in 1810, Val wrote to John Edwards who had just become his brother-in–law. His letter commenced quite formally, focussing on the business of war, and his promotion to light bob or light infantry—the soldiers who provide a skirmishing screen ahead of the advancing army, harassing and delaying them, and screening their own heavy infantry and cavalry from enemy fire. He laughs scornfully at the reports of some British volunteers back home experiencing minor hardship and being lauded for it in the papers, when their hardships are nothing compared to what Val and the soldiers at the front are experiencing. Only in the last part of this letter did his voice become more intimate as he expressed his delight that Edwards was now married to Louisa.

> My dear Sir,
> The orderly corporal has just been to inform me that the post goes out to Lisbon at 3 o'clock. It is now almost 10. You wonder, I dare say, that I did not write before. I received [a letter from my] sister at Portalegre about the beginning of July, and since that time we have been continually marching, sometimes in pursuit of the enemy and sometimes retiring. The enemy that we have to oppose in this part of the country are now increased to more than double our number, so that we have retired to this place, it being a very strong position amongst an immense chain of mountains, and if the enemy do attack us and we find it necessary to retire we have a very strong pass across the mountains to retire upon, but this position being so very strong I think they will not dare to attack us. They have an immense number of cavalry, but they would have no affect

on us. We have a Portuguese division with us and all commanded by Lieutenant General Hill.

We have lately had a new General join us. He is a terrible fellow. His name is the Hon. W. Stewart, who was once Colonel of the 95th regiment, and as the country here is very much adapted for light troops he has formed another light company from each battalion, so that now each Battalion has two light companies. I am appointed to the one in our regiment, but we do not wear a light bob's dress, and are merely distinguished by a piece of lace around the right arm above the elbow. I have now plenty of work – four hours drill every day, running up and down immense hills.

We have been in this camp about a fortnight and I have been in a tent but a very little while, and before I used to sleep under trees if I could get one. We have been miserably off since we have been here in this camp, as the town we are near has not half a dozen inhabitants in it. Of all the miserable places that I ever saw this is the most so of any. It was deserted when the French came this way before and the inhabitants have never returned to it since.

We have been lately living upon a very bad chocolate without sugar or milk. Our ration bread is a pound and a half a day, and sometimes as black as your hat. We used to eat some of that and drink some of the abovementioned for breakfast and for dinner our ration beef is a pound a day, boiled, and sometimes without salt or vegetables. But now, as we have been here a short time, supplies have reached us – both provisions and money. For the last three weeks, ten dollars would not be collected from the whole Battalion, and as for my part I have not had a Farthing this long time but as soon as I have finished this scrawl I shall get my month's pay from the paymaster.

The last papers we received gave an account of a sham fight in London with the Volunteers, which you may be sure amused us very much. It ended with saying that the poor fellows got wet through and that they went through all their hardships without a murmur. Poor fellows, I pitied them very much. I wonder would they go through a day's march of 30 miles with 60 rounds of ball cartridge, besides the other things, and when they got to the ground where they were to halt, and then scramble to get the best tree, and perhaps as soon as they had got off their packs it began to rain in torrents, and then had to cook a piece of sorry tough beef – I wonder would they like that.

In one four days' march there was a Sergeant and eight men dropped down dead from different regiments and another day five. The days are intensely hot and the nights very cold. At the camp we came from to this we had two days' immense rain, and to see the poor men then stand without a cover really was shocking; I cannot describe it. After that you may suppose how I pity those poor volunteers of London who, after a little fatigue, go home, change their clothes, and then sit down to a comfortable meal. I now know what it is to get up from dinner hungry, but I have my health very well.

We have very little news from the main army in the Alps, and only that they frequently have skirmishes. You know, of course, that "Ciudad Rodrigo" has fallen long since and the army are now besieging "Almeida". I dare say his Lordship will not try to relieve it, and it seems to be the great general impression that there will not be a general engagement this summer, so that we are likely to be another year in this country.

I have very little more to say, only that I am very happy to have the pleasure of writing to one who I esteem so much, as a brother. As you say, little did I think when I left you at London that within a twelvemonth I should write to you as a brother.

Give my love to Louisa and tell her I hope she is a good housekeeper, and should ever I come home I shall feel great pleasure in visiting two sisters in one town, and in a town that I like so much. Tell her when I come she need not be particular in making me a bed – my bed now consists of a little straw and a large cloak. Give my love to Mrs. S. [Matilda] and tell her that she must write to me very often, and likewise Louisa, as the letters cost nothing.[5]

Louisa will write to my father and tell him to write to Captain Garnham, or else he will think I have forgotten him. I would write to him now but for want of paper. It was a great favour that I got this sheet, and that was one of the reasons that I did not write to you before. Tell Louisa that she must tell my father not to forget to write to Captain G., and likewise that I wrote to him from Portalegre. I must now end my nonsensical epistle. I trust you will excuse it. Remember me to all friends both at Framlingham and Tannington, to Mr. Wingfield, Mr. S. and to every friend, and believe me, I remain yours very truly T.V.B.

P.S. – Have the goodness to write frequently, as an English letter is a great treat. I wish I could get one every day. I think you would not know me, as I am brown as a Portuguese. If I have forgotten to mention anything excuse it, as there is a talk of marching tomorrow. Our advance

---

5   In a subsequent letter he apologised for this mistake; while the postage costs him nothing, his family still have to pay for the postage.

posts [the light-bobs] frequently have skirmishes with the enemy. Farewell. (Military camp near Sarzades, mid-east Portugal, August 1810)

Two months after writing this letter, Val wrote to Louisa from Bucellas, southwest Portugal, just north of Lisbon, expressing at the outset his keen disappointment at not hearing from her, and on the other documenting in vivid detail the action he has been engaged in.

My dear Louisa,

Each packet that arrives is a disappointment to me. I begin to think that you have all forgotten me. I have not received a single line from anyone since yours from London. We are at last got into quarters after having lived for three months like Gipseys, and not even so well; for three months I have not even seen the sight of a bed. My clothes likewise have not been off me for that space of time except when I could get a clean shirt and stockings to put on, and it is not always I can get them.

I wrote to my father in a very great hurry from "Pena Cova," not knowing hardly what I said. Two days before that I had been witness to an action; although not actually being engaged, a few shots and shells came over our heads, which of course did no harm. The 45th behaved extremely well three times repulsing an immense column of the enemy who attempted to ascend the hill, which they very near did before our troops knew it. The Portuguese troops behaved extremely well, and even the peasantry armed themselves and joined in the action.

The battle continued the greatest part of the day, beginning before it was quite daylight, and while the enemy were engaging our centre they likewise sent another large force to get around our left, so as to get between us and Lisbon. This movement of the enemy's obliged Lord Wellington to fall back upon the position we now occupy. It was impossible for them to make us quit our position with plain fighting, and so they found it. We were actually in the clouds. Very few of the officers have anything to put on to keep them dry or from the cold. We were three days in that situation. On the nights of the 28th and 29th it rained in torrents.

We now occupy a position that is impossible for the enemy to get round either our right or left as our right is on the Tagus at Alhanbra and our left extends to the sea. We have near 500 pieces of heavy cannon alongside our position, besides an immensity of field pieces. Our right is also defended by gunboats to the amount of between 20 and 30, manned by English sailors. Our position is immensely strong. Our light troops and cavalry are continually engaged, and I believe as often successful. Our left division the day before yesterday were almost surrounded by the enemy's columns. Notwithstanding, they engaged them, and a company of the 95th carried off 200 prisoners, and our cavalry took a whole regiment of the enemy with the exception of a man or two; in fact the enemy's horse are not able to meet ours in the field.

We have just received information that an English Brigadier with Spanish troops surprised and took 4,000 of the enemy in the town of Combie; in fact there is not a day or night but what there is an action.

We are up every morning at 3 o'clock and marched to our alarm posts, to await the attack of the enemy until it is light. We are not sure of an hour and are always ready now. For ten or twelve days I have been wet to the skin and up to my knees in mud, and often marching day and night in going to our alarm posts. This morning it rained in torrents, and we were all wet through in a minute. Besides, as I am acting light bob, I was sent out in front with the rest of the light companies, and to add to my comforts had to ford a river nearly up to my sash. As the rainy season is now set in, we shall have shocking work of it. You may, I think, soon expect to hear something decisive as the enemy are very near us, and are concentrating their forces so as to attack us at one point...

Remember me to Mrs. S. [Matilda], Wingfield, to Mrs. May and all my friends at Tannington and elsewhere, and accept yourself the love of your affectionate brother, T.B.

NB. I should like to hear from Edwin.[6] (Bucellas, south-east Portugal, October 1810)

Eighteen months later Val, now a lieutenant and 19 years of age, wrote to his father from Povoa, in north-west Portugal, again with vivid detail of the fall of Badajoz and the subsequent horrifying chaos as the British soldiers ran amok, looting, raping, destroying:

My dear Father,
I am well aware that you expected to hear from me long before this. I should have written to you immediately after the fall of Badajoz, but had no time. My servant was wounded and everything in confusion. However, I will proceed to give you a description of the siege and assault and likewise what I have been doing since the fall of Rodrigo, and then I think you will see I had sufficient excuse for not writing before.

---

6   Several times Val mentions his desire to make contact with Edwin, who is also at the front, but he does not have information on where he is stationed.

After the fall of Rodrigo we remained in quarters in some miserable villages in the north until the 27th February, when we commenced our march for Badajoz,[7] but most of our regiment unfortunately having the itch we were halted after the first day's march for six days to get rid of that unpleasant companion, and then we proceeded on our way to the above mentioned place, where we arrived after a very pleasant march by ourselves, except the last four days that were wet. However, we were too late to help our brave lads to open ground, as that was done on the night of the 17th.

We had very bad weather for about a week, so that we were seldom dry. We had only three divisions employed in the work, which were the 3rd, 4th, and light, so that we were very hard worked, relieving every six hours. Some poor fellows, in fact most of them, had not a night's rest out of seven. They [the French] did not fire so much from the garrison as at Rodrigo, but they contrived to destroy a considerable number of us. I had, of course, many narrow escapes. One morning in the main breaching battery one shot and a shell that were thrown nearly at the same time killed and wounded 17 of the party that I had at work. I received no injury except a crack in the head by a stone, which rather stunned me.

Our works were remarkably fine. As well as I can recollect, our flanking batteries opened on the 23rd and our breaching one's a few days after. An incessant fire was kept up until the 5th, when the breaches were thought practicable, and we received the order to storm that night at ten o'clock, but the order was countermanded and our batteries directed to breach in another part of the wall, which was effected by the evening of the 6th, the wall being very soft in that part. The columns were put in motion for the assault at dusk. The 3rd Division were directed to escalade the Castle, and the light and our division (the 4th) were ordered to storm the breaches. One brigade of the 5th division escaladed on the left of the town near the Guadiana. We all started to our different points of attack about 9 o'clock.

The garrison very soon found that we were coming and opened a tremendous fire on us. The grenadier companies of our division lead the van. The night being very dark it looked as if the Heavens were on fire. It was the grandest sight I ever saw. We had made three breaches and they had 1,000 men at each, and notwithstanding the immense fire that had been kept up from our batteries they had contrived to cut the breaches completely off from the town. They had also finished breastworks at the top of the breaches and immense chevaux-de-frizes and loop-holes made

7   In south-west Portugal.

in the house, near the breaches; in fact they left nothing undone that they thought would impede our progress. They had also planks stuck full of iron spikes laid on the slant of the breaches at the top, and on the top of the wall very large shells ready to light, which I saw them do, and roll them down on us.

We moved up in very good order under immense fire into the glaci,[8] and there we remained for a length of time and could not get on. We at first had to get down over the palisade and then by ladders into the ditch, which was wet. I was standing up to my breech in water for two or three hours. I made an attempt at all the breaches, and did all I could to get up, but they knocked us down as fast as we ascended. I was knocked down several times by the poor fellows who were killed. My cap was knocked off my head and torn to pieces, and the breast of my jacket was also torn. We had such obstacles in our way that it was impossible to surmount them, and were obliged to retire out of the ditches in complete confusion, the two divisions being quite intermixed.

However, the 3rd Division succeeded in gaining the castle, or we should not have taken the town that night. But the enemy had not the least idea the castle would be attacked, as it was the strongest part of the town, and therefore were not so well prepared, having the greatest part of their force at the breaches. We had ladders 40 feet long for the castle. The strength of the garrison when we commenced 5000; they lost 200 during the siege, which was a considerable number. As soon as they found the castle was in our possession they were panic struck and almost immediately threw down their arms. We then all got in and secured the prisoners.

Then the town was given up to plunder for 24 hours, and such a scene I never before saw. Every door that was fastened was immediately opened by firing into the keyhole. Some fellows loaded themselves with church plate, others with doubloons, dollars, and other kinds of coin and others making off with horses, mules, etc., etc.

If I had not been a great simpleton I might have got several horses or mules. I might have bought them of the men for a very few dollars – they sold fine horses for 6, 10, and 20 dollars each, which were worth 100 and more, but not having any money in my pocket I could not purchase, as the fellows wanted ready money. However, I thought perhaps I could find one myself, and away I started. It was not long before I fell in with a cavalry mare, ready saddled. I directly mounted her and rode off to my tent. I still have her. She is rather clumsy but suits me very well.

---

8   An artificial slope that is part of a medieval castle.

The soldiers very soon got drunk and things were carried to a pretty pitch, committing rapes, murder and plunder – in fact every sort of devastation was going on. They even shot one another, and it was impossible for any officer to interfere. As to the plunder they well deserved all they got, but it is impossible for me to describe the scene to you. It was four or five days before we could get the men into any kind of order at all. We had 3 officers killed, 10 wounded (one of which – a captain – is since dead), 29 men killed, 116 wounded, beside 6 sergeants. Of course many of the brave fellows are since dead...

The country about here is very mountainous and the villages very miserable. The French have never been here. Wine is very cheap – about 4d a pint. It is astonishing to see the dirt and filth the inhabitants of this part of the country live in, and their habitations – I cannot call them houses – so very uncomfortable, although they have plenty of money. I wrote to Louisa a day or two after I arrived at Badajoz. I think I told her I was a Light Bob. I am afraid I shall not be able to come to England for some time, as we have so few officers in the regiment. I have had the command and payment of the light C for the last two months. T.V.B ("Povoa" northeast Portugal, May 1812)

Plunder, as Val observes, was regarded as legitimate practice by soldiers, as a way of celebrating victory and supplementing their meagre incomes. Val had described his own difficulties in surviving during these battles. His income, even though he was an officer, must all be spent on uniforms, on supplementing the inadequate food supplies, or buying horses and mules to do the army's work. It was not until 1899 that the Hague Convention ruled that military forces, far from destroying enemy property, should defend it (Hoffman 2006). He regarded himself as a bit of a fool for not joining in the plunder, though the job of the officers was to stop the wild excesses of rape and murder—not join in. But Val had become pragmatic enough to find himself a horse, even if it was one that was not very good.

In case it seems that Val was losing his sense of humanity, I include an excerpt from a letter written soon after, about the fall of Salamanca. He wrote to John Edwards from a camp near Rueda, just north of Salamanca:

Salamanca is by far the best place I have seen in the country, not excepting Lisbon. Some of the buildings are uncommonly fine, particularly the large Cathedral and the old college. It has likewise a most elegant square, the streets are wide and clean, and a great number of all sorts of shops. The part of the town near the fort is very much destroyed, including many fine buildings, and one very good square. It is said upwards of 100 families went away with Marmont.[9] After the fall of the fort the enemy retired, first setting fire to three or four villages and destroying the property of the inhabitants. How would Framlingham look on fire and plundered by the enemy? What the poor people suffer is beyond any description. We are now close on the river Douro and the enemy on the other side. They have destroyed all the bridges on that river, so that we are again looking at each other across a little river. (camp near Rueda, mid-north Spain, June 1812)

Val's letters thus re-animate the war as it worked its way on and through his body and into his ways of being in the world. At the same time his letters kept alive his bonds with his family. He remembers them and longs for them, and he depends on them to remember him. One of the things the letters make visible, 200 years later, is his concern at the growing difference between himself and his life back home. In the theatre of war he was inevitably changing—sounding less like an Englishman and strangely familiar to me—as if he were already becoming Australian—laconic, tough, funny, and pragmatic. He doesn't mention any mates, though, and perhaps mateship was impossible, at that time, across the firmly fixed class lines. His servant remained invisible throughout his letters until he was injured. That attitude to servants was typical of the times—they were literally required to be invisible to those who employed them (Dawes, 1989). That invisibility remained in my family 150 years later.

The complex emotional dilemma of being the same yet different from the family members he was close to—the people who had sheltered him and cared for him after his mother's death and while his father was absent. They have, throughout the war, believed in him, and remembered him; they have read his letters and responded to him. They have provided him with a lifeline throughout the war. But he found himself changed and sometimes doubted if they would any longer want to know him.

I quoted the fictional Sir Walter early on in this chapter who would not move in the society of men who had served in the navy or army; he particularly objected to men in the navy due to their weatherbeaten faces. I return to Sir Walter's other point of objection, the loosening of the British class system that war was creating. It is, he pompously asserts, "the means of bringing persons of obscure birth into undue distinction, and raising men to honours which their fathers and grandfathers never dreamt ... A man is in great danger of being insulted by the rise of one whose father, his father might have disdained to speak to ..." (Austen, 2012: 28)

---

9   The French General and nobleman who became Marshall of France and Duke of Ragusa.

Val was afraid not so much of mixing with men of obscure birth, but that he had fallen in the eyes of the young English ladies he might have wanted to marry, ladies who presumably mixed with the likes of Sir Walter. His place in English society seemed fragile. So the colony eventually beckoned him, as a place where such social niceties were no longer quite so firmly in place. There, the multiple and emergent ways of being served to open as-yet-unknown possibilities. He had not been able to imagine taking a Spanish wife. They were pretty and walked beautifully, and were honoured to walk out with him in his officer's uniform. But their differences he could not tolerate. The young women in New South Wales, it would turn out, were also happy to walk out with him, and, significantly, they carried English manners and morés with them. This is not to say that Val did not also carry all sorts of class and religious biases with him into the life of the colony—not least his dismissive attitude toward men of lower orders. The colony was, after all, British. While it has preferred to think of itself as egalitarian, what will emerge in the chapters that follow is that it was no such thing. Val's attitudes to gender might also be thought of as foundational to early Australian masculinity. Women must be decorous and uphold the manners of polite society, and become good housekeepers.

In Chapter 18 I return to Val and to his life with Christiana Jane in the 1830s, on their farm in New South Wales. But first, I turn back to David Collins. The British were worried that France would begin to claim land on the south of the Australian continent. They wanted settlements at Port Phillip Bay, current-day Melbourne, and on Van Diemen's Land, in order to defend Bass Strait and keep it open. David, still unable to find work at home, took up the task of forming one of those settlements.

CHAPTER 15

Lieutenant Governor of Van Diemen's Land: David Collins and His Descendants

David Collins (1756–1810) left New South Wales on 29 September 1796, sailing on the *Britannia*. It was nine years since he had left home to become Judge Advocate in the colony. The new Governor, John Hunter, was appalled at the prospect of his departure. David had not only acted as Judge Advocate in both civilian and military courts but also as Secretary to each of the Governors, Phillip and Hunter. Hunter had written earlier to the Duke of Portland of David's "meritorious exertion and diligence" adding "if he were now impatient to quit the colony, I could not without exposing it to the most manifest injury, give my consent to his doing so" (Currey, 2000: 128). When Hunter finally consented to David's departure he wrote strong recommendations for him, including a letter to John King, the under-secretary at the Home Office: "You cannot conceive, sir, how very much this settlement will suffer in the department of the law by this gentleman's return home ... a circumstance which very much increases the dutys of the governor," and he added how important it was that David be replaced by someone with a very high level of competence, "on whose knowledge and ability he can with confidence rely" (Currey, 2000: 131).

David arrived home to find his wife Maria in a very weakened condition. He wrote to his mother "I have found my dearest wife ill and weakened beyond anything I could have imagined." A month later he wrote again, indicating Maria had impressed on him his own culpability: "I trust in God she will soon be restored to her former health, which I fear my absence robbed her of" (Currey, 2000: 135, 136). The only way David could have supported Maria in the manner to which she was accustomed was for him to take up the position in New South Wales, and the only way he could have had a family was with a mistress. But it was hard for her not to blame him for the misery that both of these facts made her feel.

Ann Yeats, David's mistress, and their two children had travelled home with him. Ann wanted to catch up with her family and friends in Liverpool. Managing his two families was a delicate business. He had supported both Ann and his wife on his Judge Advocate's salary, and had given Ann his grant of 100 acres on the Hawkesbury River. He had lived frugally, staying in Government House rather than setting up his own household, and he had incurred debts in honouring both sets of obligations.

© BRONWYN DAVIES, 2021 | DOI:10.1163/9789004446717_016

FIGURE 62   Engraving of David Collins on the box cover of his *Account* published in 1798

On returning home his salary was now one quarter of what it had been in New South Wales, and he and Maria found themselves in dire straits. Maria was aware of Ann and the children, and keen to remind David that not everyone would tolerate such a situation; she wrote to him of people who had received him in London, that they must be "ignorant of your unhappy connection, as I know enough of him and his lady to think he would [not otherwise] introduce you to her, or she receive you, as they are people of strict principle" (Currey, 2000: 140).

The taking of mistresses seems to have been extraordinarily common among the ruling elite of the time. Even Revd Knopwood, who was later to travel with David to Van Diemen's Land, engaged in it, and Phillip Gidley King, when Commandant on Norfolk Island, despite having his lively, supportive wife Anna Josepha there with him on the Island, had children by more than one mistress. Those children were adopted by Phillip and Josepha and taken with them when they returned to England.

Three decades later, when the young Victoria ascended the British throne, it was regarded as very odd when her husband Albert chose not to have a mistress. People suspected there was something wrong with him that he did not. Baird, her biographer, comments that it was more a Whig than a Tory practice to see the keeping of mistresses as not only normal but normative. Lord Melbourne, for example, Victoria's first Prime Minister, had a wife who strayed, having many lovers and several children with them:

> What was surprising was that Melbourne stayed faithful to his cuckolding wife. According to his biographer David Cecil, a married man was then thought peculiar if he did not have a 'sprightly, full-bosomed' mistress. As for married women, 'the practice was too common to stir comment'.
>
> But most people outside of the world of the Whigs condemned their sexual indulgence. They risked ridicule and, for the women, ruin if their amours were exposed in the press or in court. (Baird, 2017: 87)

On his return home in 1797, David's hopes of an appointment in London were not fulfilled, despite the strong recommendations and promises he had received. There were many naval and army officers looking for similar positions. His case was not helped when Governor Hunter was sent home in shame for not reining in the colony's expenditure. In 1800 Phillip Gidley King, who we encountered in Chapter 13, was appointed Governor in Hunter's place. King was to remain in New South Wales until he was replaced, in 1806, with William Bligh, against whom the military of New South Wales would rebel. Bligh was later to cause David a great deal of grief.

Both King and Hunter gave David access to their own records of the colony. The complex task David faced in writing his *Account* was to make the experiment of colonising New South Wales one that was successful, and both interesting and saleable (this in the face of Maria's continued assertions that it would be of no interest to anyone, and would be waste paper after nine months). He wanted to give due credit to the men who had suffered very real hardships in the task of establishing the colony. He wanted to signal as well that there were problems—that the project of turning the natives into replicas of themselves had not succeeded, since in the end, they preferred, and reverted to, their old ways.

Bennillong, the man in whom they had placed so much store, taking him to England, and housing him in Government house on return, moved between his two worlds, not fully accepted in either place. He was no longer regarded as a leader among his own people, and in the ensuing conflict he became understandably angry. His access to spirits in Government House no doubt exacerbated the ensuing violence.

David and his colleagues had developed close friendships with some of the indigenous people, like Bennillong, learning their language and attending their ceremonies. David had even been secretly gifted with the tooth of one of the boys being initiated. But he had come to realise that the language they shared referred to everyday objects, and not to the abstract principles that would be necessary to form a treaty. When the indigenous people fought to take back their land, burning homesteads and killing the inhabitants, the full force of the punitive British law had been brought down on their heads.

This punitive response was not just because the British newcomers gave unquestioned loyalty to the British hierarchy and its growing love of empire, but because they saw it as a matter of their own survival. They were so often on the point of starvation and death; they had, for the time being, no ships and thus nowhere else to go, and must forcefully persuade the natives to respect the newcomers' property and lives.

Even now, some Australians believe, as David and his associates did, that bringing British civilisation to the "savages" was a gift. By the time David was writing his *Account*, however, he had come to believe that the colony could do no good for the local custodians, other than to leave them alone, to live in harmony with nature—a possibility the colonial experiment had in fact deprived them of, though that fact was difficult for the newcomers to understand. While admitting these problems in the *Account*, he wanted to argue for the success of the colonial experiment. The transportation of convicts, he argued, had opened up the possibility of redemption, making it possible for many of those sent to the colony to lead good and productive lives. He also argued for the economic advantages the colony could bring to Britain if the sealing, whaling and forestry industries were developed. As it turned out, none of his recommendations were ever accepted.

With Maria's help David completed and published the *Account*. It was a success insofar as it received the positive attention he had hoped for. But its success was not sufficient to solve his financial problems, and not enough to secure him the administrative post in the city that he so much desired. He says very little about his own health at this time, except in private letters, but it seems clear the ordeal of 9 years in the colony had taken their toll. He had no desire to leave home again, but was forced, out of his own penury, to agree to take up the task of creating a settlement at Port Phillip, on the northern coastline of Bass Strait. Establishing a British settlement there was seen as necessary, now that the Strait had become navigable, to prevent the French from taking up land or blockading the Strait. Such a blockade would give them the strategic power to interfere with the shipping between Europe and New South Wales.

David set out, once more, on April 24 1803 on HMS *Calcutta,* with 308 convicts, a number of free settlers, 17 wives and 18 children. Revd Knopwood, who was to act both as a minister of the church and a magistrate, sailed with him. While some historians tell the story of David's parting with Maria as a sorrowful leaving of a loved one, others see those protestations of love as a genteel fiction.

Ann Yeats had already returned to the colony with her children. On board the *Calcutta* David took up an affair with Mrs Power. Her husband, Matthew Power, was a convict, and his wife, a free woman, was travelling with him to the new outpost of the colony. Matthew Power was given unusual freedom and privileges on board, and later in the colony—in return for turning a blind eye to his wife's affair. On this second trip to the Southern hemisphere, David was open about his relationship with the Powers in a way he had not been about Ann Yeats. His friend Revd Knopwood supported him entirely, while others were affronted, not so much by the affair, but by the open nature of it.

Another of the other convicts on the *Calcutta* was James Lord, who was doing seven years for stealing oats and for using force of arms. James Lord's son, David, was to become the richest man in Van Diemen's land, and James Lord's grandson, Edward, would eventually marry one of David Collins' grandchildren.

Revd Knopwood, who was to become a close associate of David's, kept a daily journal of the journey of the *Calcutta.* He wrote as if he was the one in charge of all the doings on board the ship. He sounds like a fussy busybody minding everyone's business except his own. I pick up his account, briefly, sailing across the Tropic of Cancer on the way across the Pacific to Rio:

> *Friday 10th* Wind S.E. b S. A.M. Steady fresh breezes and clear. At 10 Old Neptune came on board. Such persons as had never crossed the line were compelled to undergo the ridiculous ceremonies of shaving, &c., which those who were privileged were allowed to perform. P.M. The day was conducted with much myrth: at 3 moderate and clear wr.
>
> *Saturday 11.* Wind S.S.E. A.M. moderate breezes and cloudy: 30 past 10 saw a sail to the S.W., standing to the windward, set t. gl'nt. Sails. P.M. – do. wr.; at 1 shortend sail and boarded *Rio Nova*, from Africa to Demarara

with 325 slaves, men and women; took three men out of the above ship for mutiny, and confind them; quarter before 3 in boat and made all sail; we got parrots, &c., from the ship; half-past 11, Mary Wiggins was deliverd of a son, wife of a Colonial marine.

Sunday 12 Wind S.E. A.M. Steady fresh breezes, and clear; 30 past 9, musterd by divisions; 10 performd divine service to all the convicts, &c., &c., as before. P.M. – 40 past 5 spoke [to] the *Ocean*; enquired after the health of the people; was informd they were all well, but that Mr Hartley, a settler, had behaved ill on board. The evenings are dark at 6, nor light till near 6 in the morning.

Monday 13 Wind S. b. W. A.M. Moderate wr.; at 9 released and sent to duty the three men from the Rio Nova. P.M. – do. Wr. Ocean in company.

Divine service for the convicts was something so taken for granted by Knopwood that he barely mentioned it, bypassing any detail with "&c., &c.,". The weather in contrast was of primary interest and was given detailed attention morning and night. He recorded the *Calcutta*'s stopping to talk to other ships, and also, later, its fleeing from an enemy ship. What was of no moment to Knopwood, it seems, from his account, was the practice of slavery, other than to mention the numbers carried on any specific ship. Yet slavery was being much debated at the time. In 1787, 16 years earlier, The Society for the Abolition of the Slave Trade was founded in Britain; the French had declared in 1789 that men are born and remain free and equal in rights. And in the same year that Knopwood was writing this journal, Denmark–Norway had banned the slave trade and ended the importation of slaves into Danish dominions. Knopwood was not, apparently, concerned with such ethical issues; he was more focussed on punishment of individuals for mutiny.

In the following passage, he reveals himself as a lady's man, smitten by the beautiful Antonia, whose 'fruits' she had given him. "The convent of D. Ajuda, or of Assistance, received as pensioners, or boarders, the widows of officers, and young ladies having lost their parents, who were allowed to remain, conforming to the rules of the convent, until married, or otherwise provided for by their friends" (Collins *Account* lxx).

At Rio de Janeiro Knopwood wrote:

Friday 8 wind vble. A.M. Moderate and clear. I went on shore and see the town and convents; I see a very beautiful girl at the Convent D. Yuda, from her I received fruits, &c.

Saturday 9 Wind vble. A.M. Do. Wr. This morn Col. Collins, Lieut Huston, and self, went to breakfast at the Monastary of Franciscans with

Pater George Bunden, he was an Englishman and had been there a long time; he shew us all the Convent which was very grand. Received fruit, fresh beef, water &c., for the ship's company and convicts. P.M. – Continuel lightning.

Sunday 10 Wind vble. A.M. At 9 went on shore, and see High Mass performed at the Monastary D. Franciscans and I visited the Convent D. A. Juda and see the *charming* girl Antonia. [Here he reports going to the theatre, seeing some negroes dancing, and going shooting, and details the stores brought on board. Then it is time to set sail.]

On Sunday 17th I visited D. Ajuda for the last time. The Carmelites had a great feast this day in the eve, great fireworks; Capt. W., Col. Coll[ins].; Lieut. Huston, and self on shore, and returned late on board with the Capt. &c., &c.

I see Antonia this eve at 5, and we took leave of each other with Regret. Vale!

Knopwood's casual attitude to slavery was still the dominant discourse in 1803, and portended ill for both the convicts and the indigenous people of New South Wales, who were looked upon by many, like Knopwood, in terms of the unpaid labour that might be extracted from them. Henry Reynolds observes:

> When New South Wales and Tasmania were settled, slavery was still practiced throughout the British empire although increasingly questioned. The enslavement of millions of Africans was justified by their putative racial inferiority seen as being related to the colour of their skins. The emerging theories about racial hierarchies placed Tasmanians on the same level as Africans, even below them ... If the Aborigines were beneath the reach of European conscience, then anything was possible; atrocity had automatic and prospective legitimation. (2012: 34)

As it turned out David found the location of the projected Bass Strait settlements, first on Port Phillip Bay and then the River Tamar, unsuitable to establish a colony, even though they were much more suitable locations for trade, now that ships were making their way through the Bass Strait, and much more useful in terms of the requirement that the Strait be protected from the French. The soil at Port Phillip he deemed unsuitable, and on the Tamar, the Aboriginal people of the north midland nation had made a show of great hostility to the would-be settlers, and David had no stomach for confronting them.

In consultation with Governor King, David negotiated the alternative site on the Derwent River, at the place that was to become Hobart. In the beginning of this settlement, once again, the crops failed and no help came.

MAP 4   Van Diemen's Land

According to Currey, David's biographer:

> Early in 1807 the residents of Hobart Town were still surviving from hand
> to mouth, and madness was in the air. In the absence of wheat, what
> little bread was baked for the public ration was made from Cape Barley.
> It was such a miserable concoction that the marines one day pelted the
> commissary and his clerks with the barley cakes they had been given. The
> inedible missiles 'rolled like shot', John Pascoe Fawkner observed, 'only
> not quite so hard'. (Currey, 2000: 247)

Eventually supplies did come, first rice and cattle and rum from India, and
then a trickle of food sent by Governors King, then Bligh, from Sydney. "And
while Bligh kept supplies coming, the land slowly began to yield its bounty"
(Currey, 2000: 247). David decided to consolidate that bounty and ordered several hundred breeding cows from Bengal with which to establish a pastoral
industry.

When David had first arrived on the Derwent, he failed to read out his
instructions to the assembled populace, which included the order that the
local people not be harmed. Lyndall Ryan (2012) judges him harshly for that

oversight. He did not attempt, this time, to make contact with the indigenous people, believing there were not many of them about and that they were peacable—not likely to be a source of conflict. Catastrophically, when a large group of them appeared with spears, evidently on a hunting expedition, the newcomers feared they were under attack and fought back with guns and a cannon, informing David only after a number of them had been killed.

Lyndall Ryan (2012) blames David for that unjustified attack. Although he did then read his instructions to the assembled newcomers, which gave the local people equal right to protection under the crown, that right was soon to be undone by Richard Atkins, the drunken Judge Advocate of New South Wales, who found that indigenous people could not be recognised as people under British law, and could not therefore bear witness in court against their assailants. Such a ruling, presumably, also made it impossible for the indigenous people to participate in signing a treaty—should that ever have come up as a serious proposal. At the time, the poor, and women, were also not recognised at law as people, let alone as citizens. Only men of property possessed any rights of citizenship in Britain or in her colonies.

In the early years the new settlement on the Derwent was dependent on food from England and also from Sydney—from Governor King, until 1806, and then from Governor Bligh.

David's requests to London for urgent supplies, such as the parts to build a mill to grind their own wheat, fell on completely deaf ears. London was preoccupied with the war against Napoleon, and the little settlement on the Derwent was of no interest to them. Others had had to be sent to establish settlements on Bass Strait. In Hobart Town, the convicts got about naked after their clothes fell apart, and they were often close to starvation. Several convicts had escaped to live in the bush, setting themselves up in competition with the indigenous people for their food supplies and shelter. David, too, had no choice but to hunt for kangaroo, further depleting the food supplies of the local people.

There were some entrepreneurial characters in the settlement who profited from the shortages, charging inflated sums for simple necessities. David was appalled by such marketeering, and wanted nothing to do with it. He lived in a small cottage that did not keep out the wind and the rain, he owned no land, and his debts increased to the point where his financial agent refused to honour his payments. He was adamant nevertheless that he would not stoop to unethical trading, writing to his brother George:

> I am endeavouring to live here as economically as possible, and avoiding drawing upon my agent, which are the sole means I possess of liquidating my debt with him, for to enter into a disgraceful traffic I will

never consent to. I should ill have profited from my father's example, if I did, and have too great a respect for his memory to disgrace it. I know you will applaud these principles, and though a few hundreds would be extremely useful, yet my gratification will be, when I resign my office, to lay my hand upon my heart, and say I never appropriated a sixpence of the government money to my own use. (Currey, 2000: 260)

While David lived thus, adhering to his own high standards, his ex-mistress, Ann Yeats was living in some luxury with her husband James Grant "in a 'commodious' brick house in Chapel Row, Sydney ... [while] Collins did not even own the five-acre plot on which his cottage stood, though his civil officers between them had grants totalling eight hundred acres, and even Mathew Power had fifty" (Currey, 2000: 248–9). David nevertheless ensured his two children with Ann had a good education. They eventually made their way south to join him.

When the British government eventually decided to pay attention to David's letters of demand and of complaint, they were eager to deny any wrong-doing. They misinterpreted what he had said, telling King, when he returned, that David was accusing him of neglect in his position as Governor. King, a volatile and pugnacious man, was outraged, and angrily turned against David. David in turn was now accused of negligence and mis-management. He now had few friends he could rely on, and he counted Bligh amongst them. The new Lieutenant Governor, sent to replace Bligh when he was deposed, also turned against David.

Before he was deposed, Bligh was ordered to oversee the closure of Norfolk Island:

> In Oct 1807 ... Collins received from Bligh a despatch from the latest colonial secretary, Wm Windham, telling him that the government wanted the entire population of Norfolk Is removed to VDL. Bligh told Collins that nearly 400 people ... had elected to move to Hobart Town and could be expected to arrive soon. ... The first of the islanders—thirty four individuals—arrived in the Lady Nelson at the end of November, and they were followed by further contingents during the next twelve months. (Currey, 2000: 254–5)

Absurd promises had been made to the Norfolk Islanders, who did not want to leave their island paradise. William Windham, the Colonial Secretary had promised them

> ... two acres of land for every acre of cleared land they had occupied on the island and one acre for every acre of uncleared land. Houses equal to

those they had occupied were to be built for them at government expense and they were to be given any tools and implements they required. Settlers and their families were to be fed and clothed for two years; they were to have the labour of four convicts for nine months and two for the ensuing fifteen months; any livestock they were forced to leave behind was to be paid for in kind by the government, and under certain conditions compensation up to £1000 per person was to be paid. (Currey, 2000: 254)

These were ludicrous promises. David had no such resources to give them out of his own meagre government funding, and no additional funds were forthcoming from London. He offered them what he could, and in some cases that meant being billeted in the tiny cabins the convicts lived in. The islanders agreed to set up a settlement further up the Derwent River with their own labour, and with whatever meagre resources David could give them.

It was here, on this settlement, that David came in contact with Margaret Eddington (1793–1822), who was to become his mistress, and mother of my great great grandmother, Eliza. Mrs Power, though still a good friend, had gone to live with her husband.

Margaret Eddington and Norfolk Island

Thomas Eddington, Margaret's father, had been sentenced to transportation for seven years, on 5 or 6 July 1785 in the Berkshire assizes. His name was recorded as Thomas Heddington, and his age as 29. He had spent time on the *Ceres* hulk before being put on the *Alexander* on 6 January 1787 though they did not set sail until May. He had arrived in NSW in January 1788 as part of the first fleet, along with David Collins.

A month after the First Fleet arrived at Port Jackson, 23 settlers, 15 convicts and 7 freemen were sent to establish the settlement on Norfolk Island. Unlike the colony's mainland there were no indigenous people living there so they did not have to face conflict with the land's owners. Two years later, in 1780, when food supplies were desperately low at Port Jackson, Governor Phillip sent 281 more people, more than a third of the convicts, including Thomas Eddington—to Norfolk Island, on the *Supply* and the *Sirius,* to further develop the settlement there. Phillip Gidley King was its first Commandant.

Norfolk Island would be responsible for supplying the navy with its much-needed flax in desperately short supply since Catherine II of Russia had blocked supply of it to Britain, knowing there could be no navy without it. The crew's instructions on the *Sirius* were to proceed to Canton, after dropping its human cargo at Norfolk Island, in order to fetch desperately needed food supplies. But Norfolk Island had no safe harbours; the *Sirius* ran aground on the reefs off the island. Norfolk Island and Port Jackson were cut off from each other and from the outside world.

The Norfolk Islanders, all of whom had managed to reach land after the *Sirius* was wrecked, lived off mutton birds until they could successfully grow crops. In New South Wales, people continued to die of starvation. The anticipated supply ship from England had not come, as it had struck an iceberg. It was three years before the next transport ship, the *Lady Juliana,* arrived with food supplies, and a new batch of sickly, emaciated convicts, one of whom was Elizabeth Thompson.

Elizabeth was sent with other convicts to Norfolk Island, where Thomas Eddington had by now gained his freedom and a land grant of 12 acres (lot 59). He later leased another 12 acres (lot 50) in 1796. Thomas and Elizabeth married on 5 November 1791, when Revd Richard Johnson visited the island and married more than 100 couples. Their daughter, Margaret, was born in 1793, and their son John in 1795.

Thomas died in 1798 when Margaret was five years old. His headstone (number 153) is the earliest legible one that has survived on the island:

IN MEMORY OF

THOS HEADINGTON

WHO DIED 13TH JAN. 1798

AGED 40 YEARS

DEAR WIFE DO NOT GRIEVE

NOR CHILDREN, SHED A TEAR

FOR I AM GONE TO HEAVEN ABOVE

TO MEET SWEET ANGELS THERE

Elizabeth bought five more acres to add to the 24 Thomas had managed to accumulate, and there she supported the two children for the next ten years. When the island was to be evacuated, the livestock were slaughtered to prevent others being tempted to live there. Elizabeth's sheep were valued, on 30 December 1806, at £16.05.00.

By the time they left the island, Elizabeth's daughter, Margaret had grown into a fine young woman. At the age of 14 she had given birth to a son, whose father was the Island Commandant, John Piper. The age of consent at that time was 12 years, or puberty. It was not raised to 13 until 1875. Then it was only with scandals relating to child prostitution and sex slavery of children in the 1880s that the age of consent was raised to 16.

Margaret's baby was called John, and was adopted by Piper and cared for by another of his mistresses, Mary Ann, who was also the daughter of convicts. Piper took Mary Ann back to England with him, along with his children, and eventually married her.

When Margaret and her mother and brother sailed for Hobart Town, she was 16 and "it was rumoured that Piper had entrusted Margaret to Collins's 'protection'. Whatever the truth of the matter Margaret Eddington (a 'good looking, healthy, well made woman' according to Fawkner) had gone to live in Government House at Hobart Town shortly before the arrival of Bligh" (Currey, 2000: 278–9).

Although he could not marry Margaret, David treated her openly as his wife. According to Guilford (2007: 27) David "often appeared in public with Margaret on his arm and had her living at Government House".

William Bligh

Meanwhile Governor Bligh had been deposed and Foveaux had been sent to replace him. Bligh was under strict instructions from Foveaux to sail directly for England where the courts would hear the case against him. But instead of sailing through Bass Strait, and home, as he had agreed to do, he made his way south to Hobart Town. He believed he could depend on David's loyalty, and that David would help him win back his position as Governor. Finnucane, the assistant Judge Advocate under Foveaux, wrote:

> Sunday 16 April [1809].
> By a Bengal ship which arrived this day and which, on her way to India, touched at the River Derwent, we learn that Commodore Bligh, in further violation of his honor so solemnly pledged, has gone to that settlement and taken up residence there, in expectation of receiving instructions from England to return to Port Jackson with an adequate force to reinstate him in Government and to enable him to take ample vengeance on those who dispossessed him of it. (Whitaker 1998 70)

For David, the rebellion against Bligh had gone against everything he believed in. He thought King George would not under any circumstances condone it, since he had never condoned rebellion in the past. Further, Bligh was his only ally who might advocate for him, and at that time, without a sponsor no-one could survive. At the same time he could not afford to risk alienating those now in charge in Port Jackson, since he still depended on them for his supplies.

He found himself in an impossible bind. But Bligh, oblivious to David's precarious position, was outraged that he would not join forces with him to protest his eviction and support him in taking back his seat as Governor of the colony.

Bligh further deeply offended David by attempting to take over the running of the Hobart settlement on the grounds that he was David's superior officer. In retaliation for David not taking up arms for him, he had David's son unfairly court martialled, and he made strong objections to Margaret's presence in Government House. Further, to add to David's distress, letters were arriving from London that totally undermined his position. Foveaux had been sent to take over the rule of the colony until such time as Paterson (who had established the desired settlement on the Tamar) could take over. Foveaux was no supporter of David's, and went so far as to cancel the order he had made for breeding stock from India. He wrote reports home claiming that David was incompetent and had failed to establish the colonial outpost, which was, after all, of no "utility either to the Crown or the colony" (Currey, 2000: 267). Under all of this pressure, David became so ill that he evaded the requirement that he provide a medical certificate to the company insuring his life—a policy he had taken out to protect Maria in the event of his death.

The Birth of Eliza and the Death of David Collins

On 17 December 1809, the daughter of David Collins and Margaret Eddington, Eliza Eddington Collins, was born. Three months later, on March 24, 1810, David died at the age of 54. He had served for six terrible years establishing the colony in south Van Diemen's Land. The doctor had thought he just had a cold, underestimating the extent of the damage caused by the conflict with Bligh. Margaret, like her mother Elizabeth before her, found herself alone, with a baby to support.

Of David's death the *Derwent Star* wrote that "Deep and silent dejection seemed to take possession and nothing was heard but low voices of mutual condolence". On his coffin was inscribed on silver plate: "His Honour Lieutenant Governor David Collins and Colonel in the Royal Marine Forces departed this life March 24th 1810". Revd Knopwood read the service, and the procession to the graveside was attended by more than 600 people. St David's Church was erected in his memory.

After his death it was his human qualities, as well as his practical achievements, that were remarked upon by contemporaries. One described him as 'a most amiable and excellent man', another said he was regarded as 'the Father and Friend of all'. Joseph Holt testified that he 'had the good wishes and good

word of everyone in the settlement. His conduct was exemplary and his disposition most humane'. In similar vein John West wrote of 'his cheerful and social
disposition' (Fletcher, 1975: xxxi).

His body was placed in a sealed Huon Pine coffin, inside a sealed lead receptacle, which was sealed further in a second Huon Pine coffin. His body was
surrounded by leaves and herbs that would preserve his body. When his coffin
was opened 115 years later, on 25 March 1925, in search of missing documents,
David Collins was perfectly preserved:

> The witnesses found themselves face to face with a man who had been
> dead for more than a century but to all appearances might have been
> buried a week ago. He was clothed in a scarlet dress uniform as if, one
> witness would say later, he were about to take a salute. Medals and dec-
> orations were pinned to his breast; the brass buttons on his tunic were
> untarnished, and his officer's sword glinted at his side. ... He was full-
> faced, with fine features. He had been clean-shaven but a slight stubble
> had appeared after death. He must have once been handsome. (Currey,
> 2000: 2)

So David has lain there all this time, defying those who would forget him back
in England, and those of his descendants, my grandmother included, who were
to forget him. There were no papers to be found with him, and his coffin was
quickly sealed again and replaced in his tomb.

On his death Margaret returned to her family. Her brother, John Eddington (1795–1869), had been granted 35 acres in the Bagdad district and was
described as one of the first Publicans in Hobart town, authorised to sell liquor
at his *Bird in the Hand* establishment in Argyle Street. Her mother, Elizabeth
Eddington, had not remarried.

In 1811 Margaret found a new partner. George Watts was young and handsome, an ex-convict who had served his term. According to Guilford (2007: 31):

> He was a well made fine looking fellow, and his kind nature was evident
> in his open, friendly face. George built huts and worked on farms for
> which he was paid, and he saved his money and behaved well. He was
> trusted by the overseers and was allowed to hunt kangaroo during the
> famine of 1806 and 1807. By selling the meat he earned up to four pound
> a week and was often paid a further 15 shillings for grinding wheat for the
> bakers. By 1810 he had earned a considerable amount of money.

She married him, but the path would not run smooth. George had been sentenced in 1803, to seven years transportation. He had already served his term

when he married Margaret. But the lecherous Knopwood had designs on Margaret. As a magistrate, as well as a minister of the church, he had power to have George sent to do labour that got him out of the way. But Margaret alerted George to Knopwood's frequent visits, and he left the work he had been assigned in order to confront Knopwood, and throw him out of his bed and his home.

In revenge, Knopwood had George charged with being absent without leave from work, which he could not legally do since George's sentence had expired. He nevertheless sentenced him to a flogging. Rather than allow himself to be subjected to such public humiliation George escaped to the bush and made his life there as a bushranger in Van Diemen's Land. Whenever he could, he made his way into town to visit Margaret. But Knopwood was not done with George. He had him trapped and sent to the brutal coal mines in the Hunter Valley. George escaped even from there, and returned to his life as a bushranger, visiting Margaret and their baby Maria whenever he could. Maria had been born in May 1812, two and a half years after her sister, Eliza Eddington Collins.

The harsh, self-interested treatment that elite magistrates like Knopwood engaged in to further their own greedy interests makes for one of many shameful elements of the early Tasmanian story. Although Knopwood was an officious little busybody and an inveterate lady's man, and as the rest of his diary shows, a chronic hypochondriac, his treatment of Margaret, a beautiful woman in a colony where women were in short supply, was not only a sign of his character, but a sign of the times, and a sign of the darkness in humanity that can manifest itself when the times encourage it.

The domination and control of women, and the contempt for convicts, was so normalised in the early colony that Knopwood probably understood himself to be engaging in harmless seduction. The removal of George, as a mere ex-convict, could also have been seen by the magistracy as the reasonable domination by powerful men over a lesser man. That elite, white, male self-interest was integral to the British imperialism that sanctioned the occupation of land that belonged to others, and that sanctioned the racial hierarchy that validated harsh treatment, even enslavement, of "lower" classes or races. Eventually Knopwood's machinations were to lead to George's death.

Margaret married again, this time to Charles Connolly, a 32 year-old emancipated publican on 17 January 1819. Without a husband she would have had no means of protecting herself from Knopwood. Charles and Margaret had a daughter, Ann.

Margaret died in 1822 at the age of 29. At the time, Eliza was 12, Maria 10 and Ann 8. The wealthy David Lord, son of convict James Lord, stepped in and supported the three girls, ensuring they gained a good education and all the skills they needed to mix in elite circles.

Eliza married the grazier James Cox, Maria married Edward Lord, the son of David Lord, and Ann married Mr McGregor and was presented to Queen Victoria. Margaret's mother, Elizabeth Eddington, my great (x4) grandmother, died in Hobart on 10 April 1839, aged 92.

The Colony After David's Death

In the decades after David's death, Hobart and Launceston eventually began to thrive. Rural landholders and workers were threatened by bushrangers, as were the indigenous people. In 1824 Governor George Arthur was appointed, and after several years in the position he spent a large portion of his government funds to clear up the dual problem. He annihilated the bushrangers, and declared war on the indigenous people. The Black War was not to end until 1830, when the infamous black line, in fact three black lines, was implemented over a fifteen-month period. It was "the largest force ever assembled against Aborigines anywhere in Australia" and led to the end of the Black War (Ryan, 2013: 3). Once war was declared, as was also happening on the mainland, indigenous people could be shot or otherwise killed by any of the newcomers. The strategy of the black line, used throughout the empire, involved lining up all the white men, who would walk across the colony shooting or capturing the original owners of the land, successfully driving them off whatever land the newcomers were laying claim to.

By 1833 there were only 200 of the original custodians still living. Sponsored by Governor Arthur, the Christian missionary George Robinson persuaded them to surrender themselves to him, to be taken under his protection. He cynically promised that their lands would be returned to them. They were placed on Flinders Island and there they continued to die from white diseases and from sorrow. Robinson had imagined he would create a viable Christian community, but instead he oversaw their deaths. He sent each of their skulls to England for the furtherment of science, and was amply rewarded for his contribution to the genocide of the Tasmanian people.

Eliza and James Cox

The final part of my story in this chapter runs parallel to these terrible events. On May Day 1829, in St John's Church, Launceston, Eliza Eddington Collins married James Cox, the son of William Cox who built the first road over the Blue Mountains. James was a successful grazier and a member of parliament. He and his son John from his first marriage were unlikely to have escaped the requirement that they serve on the black lines.

Eliza was 19 years old, and brought to the marriage a property called 'Fern-hill', a 500-acre grant given to her when she was 10 years old. Eliza's bridesmaid was her 17-year old sister, Maria Watts, who came to live with James and Eliza.

James' first wife, Mary Connell, had died a year earlier, in July 1828. There were seven children to be taken care of, one boy and six girls, born between 1813 and 1828. The oldest of Mary's children, John, was just four years younger than Eliza. The youngest of them, Julia, died in 1829, leaving three-year-old Ann the youngest of Mary's brood, now the responsibility of their step-mother, Eliza, and her sister Maria.

Like Esther, in *Seven Little Australians*, Eliza entered into her marriage with seven, and then six, children to care for. Esther "was only twenty—just a lovely, laughing faced girl, whom they all adored" (Turner, 1894: 9). Eliza too was adored, and James, unlike the fictional tyrant Captain Woolcot, was a man beloved by everyone.

James' younger brother, Alfred, wrote of Eliza, she was "a good-looking bright clever little woman, the sunshine of her husband's life in his health and a very tender nurse in his failing years" (quoted in Whitaker, 2014: 118). Of James he wrote:

> By his family he was beloved and respected, for he was gentle and just to all, making no distinctions between them... Though not a conspicu-ous man in political life, he was the big man of his neighbourhood, and looked up to by his fellow settlers with something like pride. For a few sessions he sat on the Legislative Council of the Colony, but political life hardly suited him and he retired from the Legislature some few years before he died. In early life he had been too busy a man out-of-doors, and too practical to be able to adapt himself wholly to the sort of life that politics exacts of a man. (quoted in Whitaker, 2014: 118)

Alfred also wrote of James:

> I have always considered James, as of all my father's sons, most like his father. In face and figure, strikingly so in his last years. He had his father's energy, the same clear head, and as strong a determination when he took a matter in hand to go through with it, as his father always exhibited. (quoted in Whitaker, 2014: 117)

In the first years of James' marriage with Eliza, the work was completed on the magnificent sandstone mansion, Clarendon (*overleaf*), named after the Cox family home in Sydney. Of the Clarendon homestead, Alfred observed: "The

FIGURE 63   Eliza Eddington Collins, Clarendon. PHOTO AUTHOR, 2017

FIGURE 64   James Cox (1790–1866), portrait at Clarendon. PHOTO AUTHOR, 2017

Governor of the Colony at the time, Sir William Denison who had been entertained by him, spoke of the house and its appointments as the most English-
like and complete establishment that he had been entertained at, in any of the
Colonies" (quoted in Whitaker, 2014: 119).

The house, still standing, was built of sandstone, and of bricks made from
clay that was dug from a pit close to the house. That pit later became a lagoon
(*overleaf*) that attracted black swans and Cape Barren geese.

FIGURE 65   Clarendon

In the fields they kept fallow deer, emu and kangaroo. Their merino sheep stud was regarded as the best in the Colonies, and their Herefords won prizes at the Agricultural shows. Most beloved by James, though, was his stable of magnificent horses. It was on a visit to Clarendon, now a historic home, that I first heard about Eliza and David Collins.

On either side of the front door are the magnificent dining and drawing rooms, one with a black marble fireplace and the other with white. Further in are the library, a music room and official business rooms. The servants' quarters and working areas are all downstairs. Upstairs are the bedrooms and the nursery. White fireplaces signified rooms for girls and women, and black marble signified boys' and men's rooms. There was a bedroom for Eliza and one for James, joined by a shared dressing room.

With the race war over, and the bushrangers also obliterated, the children of Eliza and James could grow up in a romantic replica of the lives of the English gentry that their grandfathers David Collins and William Cox had left behind. They had a life that their grandmother Margaret may have aspired to when she got together with Piper and then Collins, though it was never to be, for her. Their great grandparents Thomas and Elizabeth Eddington, could not have imagined that their grandchildren would live in such wealth and luxury. The children grew up with no knowledge of the brutal past to cloud their pleasure in the rural landscapes they loved.

FIGURE 66   The lagoon
PHOTO AUTHOR, 2017

FIGURE 67   The house sits on a rise above the South Esk River and its flood plains, and has a
glorious view of distant snow-clad mountains
PHOTO AUTHOR, 2017

FIGURE 68   The morning light floods through the elegant windows surrounding the front
             door at Clarendon
             PHOTO AUTHOR, 2017

Eliza and James' three youngest children were Margaret, Cornelia and Rosa. Margaret Cox (1842–1927), was my great grandmother. She was Eliza's fourth surviving daughter, and the oldest of the three little ones. The three little ones were separated in age from their three older sisters, Eliza, Ellen and Francis, three children having died in between the first three and the last three. And they were younger by far than the children of James' first family with Mary, many of whom had already married by the time Margaret, Cornelia and Rosa were born.

The three girls played in the vast rambling, well-tended garden, and learned to carefully tend their own gardens. They had lessons together with a rather strict governess, and they played happily with their dolls in the nursery: "We had our dolls houses on a bench on one side of the room and had such happy times with them; we had parties, weddings and the dolls visited just like grown ups do" (Rosa, in Cox and Cox, 1988: 7).

It is this memoir, written by Cornelia and Rosa when they were much older, that vividly brings to life the happy childhood home that James and Eliza created:

We had a lovely garden covering four acres of ground in which all the vegetables were grown to supply the household; fruit trees were in abundance – apples, pears, cherries, plums, damsons, currants (white, red and black), oh! and the gooseberries, I had nearly forgotten these – they were so good! At the lower end of the garden was a small grove of nut trees and in autumn it was a joy to go and hunt for nuts among the fallen leaves. The garden beds were bordered with flowers in great variety; lovely old-fashioned Stocks, Peonies, Wallflowers, Carnations, Roses, Lilies, Pansies etc. In front of the house, in flower beds, were such pretty bulbs in the Spring – Snowflakes, Daffodils, Jonquils, Tulips, Hyacinths and others, while Cowslips, Primroses and Violets were in profusion.

Our house was on high ground and the garden sloped down the hill and as children I and my sisters loved to race down the centre walk. The fruit trees in blossom made such a beautiful picture – on one side of the path stood an almond tree with white blossoms and opposite one with pink blossoms, farther on a cherry plum tree which looked to me like a beautiful bride in her snow white dress and flowing veil. (Rosa in Cox and Cox, 1988: 8)

They tell how the garden was subjected to flooding when the mountain snows melted in Spring and the Spring rains came—the river would spread out for miles across the flood plains just below the house. The animals must all be got to high land. In one flood they thought the cattle were drowned, but they miraculously turned up after three days when the flood waters subsided. The children would help take up the flowers out of the way of the flood waters, and then re-plant them after the flood subsided.

Rosa and Cornelia also wrote of their happy memories of their holiday house, Marionvilla, 40 miles upriver from Launceston, near to George Town. They travelled there each summer by steam boat. There they gathered shells, and wild flowers for their sister Eliza, the oldest of Eliza and James' children. They gathered seaweed for her to preserve and send to London to the Museum:

On this beach very pretty stones were washed up by the tide and we used to spend most of the day hunting for 'gems' which were often found there. At the far end of the beach were charming little pools of water left by the tide in the rocks and there were lovely anemones, limpets and corals. (Rosa in Cox and Cox, 1988: 8)

They would watch the steam boats heading for the mainland, guided by the two white lighthouses, and the smaller fishing boats and sailing vessels. They went boating themselves, too, and had wonderful picnics with friends in the shade of trees by the beach, with a driftwood fire for boiling the kettle and for baking potatoes. Later they would sing songs and recite poems around the campfire, or go for long walks.

The Marionvilla garden too was a delight:

> There were a few large mulberry trees bearing fine berries and somehow we young ones always managed to get mulberry juice on our clean gingham dresses. The ripest sweetest berries [were high] on the trees so we couldn't resist climbing up to reach them when – down would come an over-ripe berry, flop onto the climber! (Rosa in Cox and Cox, 1988: 8).

When the girls had learned all their governess had to teach them, they went to board in Hobart to complete their schooling:

> My sisters and I were great chums but the time came when Margie and Corrie had to leave home and go to school as the English governess was not capable of teaching the more advanced branches of education which the girls were now old enough to learn, so my mother placed them with a clergyman and his wife, Mr. and Mrs. Davenport, who lived in Hobart, the Capitol of our Island... My sister Fanny undertook to teach me at home and my lessons with her were a pleasure. She was gentle, patient and extremely lovable, whereas our governess had been hasty and nervous, and often stricter than necessary... (Rosa in Cox and Cox, 1988: 9)

Cornelia takes up the story of her travel with Margie to school in Hobart:

> It was quite one of the sights to see the Mail Coach start with its team of well-matched horses, driven by a first rate whip, Mr. James Lord, and the guard blowing his horn, you can imagine what a tedious journey it was in the coach, the distance being 120 miles from town to town, of course there were frequent stoppages while the horses were changed, always four, and passengers got down from the top and from the inside to stretch their legs and get a good dinner, though a hurried one, and the call "all aboard" came far too soon, and while tea or coffee was brought it was so hot you could not drink it in the few minutes allowed...
>
> While we were at school at Hobart part of the Regiment was quartered at the barracks, so we often saw soldiers and heard the band play, and once a week we were given lessons in drilling by a Sergeant Major of the 12th Regiment, we used to like that very much. Then we had lessons in

dancing from Signor Carandini – so we thought we had enough to do besides our regular lessons, but they were happy days. (Cornelia in Cox and Cox, 1988: 4)

When Margie left school, it was Rosa's turn to join Cornelia at the school of the Davenports.

James Cox, like his father, was an Emancipist, not rushing to judge people for the harm that had befallen them at the hands of the harsh British class system. His preference, though, was for a colony of free settlers, and he was later to celebrate with his family the end of transportation to Tasmania in 1853 after some 73,000 convicts had been transported there. His youngest children remembered as school children being given a silver medal to commemorate the end of transportation (Cox, C. and R., 1988). Like his father, however, James demanded, and got, high quality work from his convict workers and for that he paid them well.

James and Eliza prospered. In 1838 they had 46 male and 27 female free settler servants at Clarendon and an average of 36 convicts during the period 1830–35 while their house was being built. In 1866 the farm workers moved off Clarendon to live in Evandale, the nearest small town, other than the village of Nile. During this period of prosperity northern Tasmania became the food bowl of Australia. James exported grain not only to New South Wales but also to India, Mauritius and the Cape Colony.

Margie married Henry Wilson Blomfield (1833–1924), the son of Thomas Valentine Blomfield and Christiana Jane Brooks. I have found nothing about Margie and Henry, except for another lecherous minister of the church, this time Archdeacon Reiby, who sexually molested Margie at his home, Entally House:

> In June 1868, certain improprieties were alleged to have taken place in the smoking room and billiard room of Entally, between the Archdeacon and Mrs Margaret Blomfield, formerly a Miss Cox of a highly respected family with which Mr Reiby was on intimate and trusted terms. Other events were reported as taking place between Mrs Blomfield and Rev. Reiby on 8 July 1868 at the Blomfield property 'Strathmore', which resulted in Mr Blomfield writing to and visiting the Bishop, accompanied by his wife. Blomfield also waited in the town of Launceston 'for a week, in order to horsewhip the Archdeacon in the public street'. (National Trust [n.d] 5)

Archdeacon Reiby took Henry Blomfield to court for libel, but he lost his case, and had to give up his ministry in the church. He later moved into politics where he had a successful career.

FIGURE 69
James Cox, portrait at Clarendon

The snow-covered mountains of Tasmania and the beautiful, open, sun-kissed fields, the site of the birth and happy childhood of my great grandmother Margaret Cox, is also the site of the darkest period of Australian history—the site of sometimes abominable treatment of convicts and ex-convicts, of women, and of the displacement and genocide of the indigenous people. Margaret and her sisters were to grow up innocent of the cultural monstrosity that had secured them the idyllic childhood they grew up in. That innocence passed down through the generations to me and to my siblings. We knew nothing of our brutal history when we grew up in our beautiful house and garden, and swam in the sea on our holidays. It is only in my research for this book that I have come to appreciate the full horror of it.

In the next chapter I go back to New South Wales and to James Cox's father William, and his building of the first road over the Blue Mountains.

CHAPTER 16

Opening Up the Interior of New South Wales: William Cox

William Cox (1764–1837) built the first road over the Blue Mountains. The mountains had formed an impenetrable wall for the newcomers between the east coast and the country's interior, until Blaxland, Lawson and Wentworth had discovered the way over them. William Cox was the only one of her ancestors my mother ever mentioned. I felt proud, in primary school, telling my teacher that William Cox was my ancestor, though I had no idea what role he had played or what building the road had entailed.

Early Life

William's biographers puzzle about his character. They find him an enigma (Whitaker, 2014) and contradictory (Cox 2012). But to me he seems familiar; he makes sense; I can imagine him as not unlike my grandfather Euston—both reserved and likable, gentle and adventurous. He grew up in England, where his father, Robert Cox, had been a master mariner. According to his biographers, William, like David Collins, was of the English gentry, but had no wealth of his own (Cox, 2012; Whitaker, 2014). His mother, Jenny Harvey, despite her poor income, placed a great deal of importance on her sons' education, and they attended the Queen Elizabeth Grammar School not far from where they lived.

William initially took up clock-making as his profession, and in 1789, at the age of 25, he married Rebecca Upjohn from a well-known clock-making family. When French invasion was threatened in 1793 William joined the Militia which were stationed across the south of England. He served in the Wiltshire Militia before being commissioned in the regular army as an ensign in the 117th regiment in July 1795, and then the 68th regiment in January 1796. In September 1797 he transferred to the NSW Corps where he was gazetted as Paymaster.

The Journey Aboard the Minerva 1799–1800

William departed England on the *Minerva* in 1799, on board the same ship as the Irish rebel leader, General Joseph Holt. Holt was being sent into exile, with some of his United comrades who, after his surrender, had been captured and

© BRONWYN DAVIES, LEIDEN, 2021 | DOI:10.1163/9789004446717_017

FIGURE 70   William Cox engraving *c*. 1824
             FROM COX 2012, FRONT PAGES

sentenced to death, and later had their sentences commuted to exile. William Cox was Captain of the Guard on the *Minerva*.

The Irish Rebellion had been carried out by men who wanted human rights for the Irish, but also, as Holt points out, by desperate men who wanted no more than a chance at life:

> Dispatch to the farthest ends of the earth some thousands of felons, along with a few hundred Irish political prisoners—many of those prisoners

faithfully enlisted in the cause of human rights for their own people, some little better than desperadoes looking for the main chance ... (Holt's memoir edited by O'Shaughnessy, 1988: 19)[1]

And who are they now, and what are their chances, he asked, now they have no choice but to serve their English masters in the colony, without hope of anything different. In retrospect, of the colony, Holt later wrote:

> Roughly one quarter of the inhabitants of the colony consisted of Irish people who had remote prospects of liberation from their abominable servitude. Their country's hopes had just been devastated by the disastrous rebellion of 1798, and seemed likely to be buried for ever by the Act of Union which incorporated Ireland in what was being called (of all things) the United Kingdom. (1988: 19)

The history of Irish oppression, enshrined in the Penal Laws, Holt saw as being continued in this forced exile, lived out on board the *Minerva*:

> For more than a century the forbears of these dispossessed Irish people had 'like the Egyptians and ancient Hebrews', suffered under the yoke of those Penal Laws which had debarred them from speaking their own language, from their own form of religious worship, from education and from the right to bequeath property to their own children; that is, when they happened to possess property. At this time, only about 5 per cent of Irish farmers owned the land which they tilled and grazed. Should they wish to sell a horse, the maximum price allowed them was £5. (1988: 19)

Their English masters, in other words, had the Irish in a mean-minded stranglehold, which led to the living conditions Thomas Blomfield described when he was stationed there. On the first leg of the journey to Cork, one of his messmates had shared his bed in the prison with Holt. The conditions in the prison were noxious:

> Mr Brady shared his coarse pillow with me, which was composed of a small lock of hay. The plank, on which was our gangway all day, formed our bed at night, and each motion of the vessel, the bilge water would flush under our sides. The deck should have formed our covering but the hatchways were left open—tho the fact is, were they shut, we should

---

1   All quotes from Holt come from his memoir edited by O'Shaugnessy in 1988.

have expired from suffocation and stench, as there was a large tub placed in the centre of the vessel. This tub was a receptacle to hold the excrements of 80 prisoners whom, being new sailors, resorted very often to it, this chamber not being discharged but every 24 hours, from the agitative motion of the vessel kept the contents in a state of continual evaporation which, to weak constitutions, was really noxious. (1988: 32)

Holt was sleeping in the prison, though he was a political exile and not a convict. Having shared the lot of the prisoners as far as Cork, he was vividly aware of the gratuitous cruelty of the ship's captain, Dobson, who had cut their rations to the point of starvation. "It was no use to seek redress, for any that did was chained to the deck" (1988: 32). Dobson refused to allow them to buy food even though many of them were starving, having been on the water, imprisoned, for 8 months already, "and hadn't the means of shifting themselves and was in an inexpressible state of torment, being covered with vermin" (1988: 35). Following Holt's written report four officers came on board and found the weights to be false and the conditions of the prisoners unacceptable, and Dobson was removed from the ship. Captain Salkeld was appointed in his place.

When Holt's wife and son came on board at Cork, they fell upon each other with joy. Hester had been able to join the ship through the good offices of Mrs LaTouche, who had earlier acted as an intermediary for Holt's surrender. She had induced him, he says, to resign his life in the mountains, precisely because it excluded him from the company of his beloved Hester who "was more dear to me than my life" (1988: 33). Holt paid 120 guineas for their passage and the carpenters made a small cabin from the steerage, which he and his family shared with Revd Henry Fulton and his family, who were being exiled for the same reason as Holt.

It was at Cork that Joseph Holt first encountered William Cox:

> Next morning I was addressed by William Cox Esq., who was paymaster to a military corps of South Wales, who shook hands with me, saying that he was sorry for my misfortune, next enquired for my family. I related Mr and Mrs La Touche's goodness to me, showing him her Ladyship's letter. He then asked me to his cabin, where he gave me refreshment. There I saw Mrs Cox, who is a respectable and amiable woman, with four beautiful children on board, namely Charles, George, Henry and Edward, and they ever after proved most affectionate to me. (1988: 36)

William Cox and Joseph Holt struck up a friendship on that journey. Both their wives gave birth on that journey, and both had left older children behind.

William and Rebecca had left behind their two oldest sons, William Jnr and James, to complete their education, and Joseph and Hester had, with great sorrow, left their daughter in the care of Mrs La Touche.

Before they set sail on the long journey, William and two other soldiers bade Holt dress in his finery and took him ashore. There he was offered, by 'a General and a Major' on behalf of the government, a bribe to leave the ship with his wife and to go into the employ of the English army. Holt refused their offer:

> "I ventured my life for many years for my King and country, and to support his Majesty's laws, and received bad treatment, so I must refuse all offers. The passage is paid for my wife and son, and I think I have earned mine better than any United man on the ship. So in the name of God, I will go and try my fortune in a country where I am not known."
>
> On which, Major Ross spake and said "You are a man of your word and resolution."
>
> Mr Cox repeated some certain facts that he had been told, which gave me a full character, on which the General directed Mr Cox to give his compliments to Governor King and hoped he would do something for me. This rested in the mind of Mr Cox and, in four years after, it met me with a pleasing return. (1988: 40)

Just before the ship set sail Mrs Holt was brought to bed:

> The State room was got ready when Mrs Holt wanted it, and she was attended by Mrs Hobbs. In Cove of Cork was seven children born for, between soldiers and prisoners, there was 34 women. Mrs Cox and my wife made 36 women, 132 men prisoners, 27 privates, 4 sargents, one lieutenant, 3 mates, 4 quartermasters, and 20 sailors.
>
> On 7th July, at 6 o' clock in the morning, Mrs Holt had a young son born and, on the 19th, he was baptized by Parson Fulton and Mr Harrison, William Henry Alcock and Mrs Hobbs stood sponsors for him; and on the 24th August we weighed anchor and sailed with a fair wind. (1988: 41)

Rebecca Cox too gave birth to a baby on that journey, but his name does not appear in any subsequent account of the Cox children.

The *Minerva* finally sailed for the colony, after many delays.

One of the features of those journeys was the opportunity to engage in trade along the way. William took advantage of his contacts in the clock-making industry, taking with him a collection of watches and other goods to sell in Rio.

He employed one of the convicts to embellish the watches to increase their
value, as Holt explains:

> Captain Cox carried with him a vast quantity of various merchandize
> such as watches, beaver hats, calicoes, shells, glasses of various kinds, cut-
> lery &c. which commodities he sold at Rio de Janeiro at a most incredi-
> ble benefit... There was a prisoner on board, name of John Austin, from
> Dublin, who was transported along with Marong, a French man. Their
> crime was for forging notes on the Bank of Ireland, to a large amount.
> Marong was, by trade, a jeweller, and Austin an engraver, so Captain Cox
> employed Austin to form various ornamental figures on the watches,
> which was a great inducement to his intended purchasers, though he
> confessed that their inside was not genuine, only best known by 'London
> Runners', as the Portuguese are a sort of people who much delights in
> brilliant objects, quite ambitious and possessed of plenty of money. So he
> got speedy and beneficial demand for his time-keepers. (1988: 42)

Holt was impressed by William's entrepreneurial prowess, but their friendship
was cemented when William sought him out to assist in taking care of the
prisoners:

> Reader I wish to inform you the manner in which I was treated by Cap-
> tain Cox on my passage, as he seemed to take more notice of me than any
> who were on board, which led us to a conversation at times of leisure.
> He would frequently say to our Captain: 'This is a fine day to let up the
> prisoners to wash and shave.'
>   Our Captain replied: My quartermasters are too busy'.
>   'I don't care for that' replied Cox 'I only want the keys, and I shall find
> a quartermaster of my own.'
>   He would then turn to me, saying: 'Will you act as quartermaster today,
> as you have some well wishers in prison, and you can give them a longer
> time than the rest?' which reason to serve my friends induced me to act
> as such.
>   So, getting the keys of the prison, I'd first release my friends, which
> created a great jealousy among the prisoners, which partiality I hope
> you'll excuse, as the United Crime I conceived was not so deserving of
> punishment as Robbing Criminality. Moreover I had Mr Cox to second
> my intentions. I gave my friends double time of liberty, the rest I was
> strictly punctual to their limited stay. Mr Cox would stay the whole time
> on deck, taking amusing conversation from the prisoners, and cautiously

speculating to have each man shaved and clean agreeable to his liking. This practice he most strictly observed during our passage. (1988: 42–3)

William offered Holt a chance to give favours to men who were loyal to him, in a way that benefitted both Holt and the prisoners. The system of favours worked at every level of society at that time. William emerges in Holt's account as someone who knew well how that system worked and how to put it to good use.

A particularly entertaining story in Holt's account, is that when the *Minerva* was under siege by two Spanish ships flying Portuguese colours, and all the soldiers were made ready to defend the ship, Holt was asked if he would man one of the cannons. When asked was he ready to fight he had said yes, and was invited to choose his own men. As it turned out the *Minerva* outran the Spanish ship, and the cannons were put away. Holt wryly pointed out later that he and his men might have taken the ship over at that point. He had, after all, only said he was ready to fight, but not against whom.

The *Minerva* made the fastest journey of any transport ship. Despite a massive storm in the last part of the journey that washed the lower quarter gallery away and broke the jolly-boat in two, the Minerva arrived in Port Jackson safely with only three passengers having died along the way—a very low number for that spacetime.

Life in the Colony—The Making and Unmaking of Fortunes

William made one mis-step with Joseph on arrival in the colony when he told him he had permission from Governor King to have Joseph work for him as overseer of the convict labourers assigned to him. Holt refused the job, indignant that permission had been sought from the Governor, who had no place to be assigning Holt, a free man, to anyone. William mended the breach and Holt eventually agreed to manage his farms on terms and conditions of his own choosing. He didn't want to be paid a weekly wage, but to be paid for the actual value of the work he carried out. Cox knew it was a hard bargain, but it was a contract that worked well for both of them. Holt's knowledge of farming was invaluable.

William temporarily lost Holt when, during a potential Irish uprising, Holt was being enticed to take the lead in the revolt. Although he had not yet agreed to lead the uprising, he was arrested and thrown in gaol. When William himself fell into trouble, as Paymaster, over his management of the New South Wales

Corp's funds, Joseph Holt was there to watch out for his wife and family and land. Holt stayed in the colony until 1812 when he sailed for London on the *Isabella* in 1812, a fateful journey, on which his fortunes became entangled with a third of my great (x3) grandfathers, Richard Brooks, when the *Isabella* was shipwrecked off the Falkland Islands.

Like many others in New South Wales at the time, William was intent on accumulating land. While he and his sons had land granted to them, he was also intent on buying good land when it became available. He used Holt's knowledge of farming to help him make good decisions. In his capacity as Paymaster he was able to borrow money from the Corps' funds to extend his holdings. While such borrowing was not illegal, he could not muster the funds from debtors in time to pay out a large and unexpected call on the funds. He was forced to declare himself bankrupt, sell up his Sydney properties and travel to London to face his creditors. Charged with "malversation", or professional misconduct, he was removed from his appointment as Paymaster.

Although he had declared himself bankrupt and sold most of his goods, he was able, during his period in London, to fund a commission for his oldest son William as ensign, and with his enterprising second son, James, and William's talented wife Rebecca running his affairs for him in Richmond, he was able to re-establish himself as a successful landowner.

He arrived home in January 1810, less than three weeks after the arrival of Governor Macquarie.[2] In October that same year Macquarie appointed William magistrate at the Hawkesbury. His homestead at Richmond, Clarendon, was built on the grant of land given to his sons James and William. He had begun work on it after he sold his Sydney property and before leaving for London. The house and farmstead were widely admired for decades to come:

> The original house was a large, rambling structure of one storey, built partly of stone and brick, the latter bearing that warm, red colour so often seen in buildings of the early days. The entrance-hall is stone flagged, and there are tall niches at intervals along the walls, where probably old fashioned lamps stood ... Rooms opened out on all sides, the majority containing fireplaces of generous proportions ... Doors, window frames, wainscots, mouldings, mantels, architraves are all cedar. (Fitzpatrick, 1923: 191–2)

---

2   Macquarie was Governor of NSW from 1810–1821. His appointment followed a period of rule by the soldiers after they deposed William Bligh. The period between Bligh and Macquarie was known as the interregnum and had lasted for two years.

His large estate at Clarendon near Windsor had all the appearance of a self-contained village. Over 50 convict servants acted as smiths, tanners, harness makers, wool sorters, weavers, butchers, tailors and herdsmen. Cox had steadily improved his flocks, which Commissioner Bigge described in 1820 as among the six best in the colony (Hickson, *Australian Dictionary of Biography*).

So what, so far, might we say William's character was? Through Holt's eyes we can see William as a humane man, committed to ensuring the well-being of the prisoners. He was, as well, an entrepreneurial man, a risk-taker, and a good negotiator. He was interested in men in all their diversity, not setting himself above them to judge them, but curious about what they were capable of. His conversations with the convicts on board the Minerva had pragmatic value. He had been able to employ Austin and Marong, for example, to further his trade in Rio. Among the prisoners there were skills and knowledges that William could put to good use in setting up his new life in the colony. He was clearly able to rise quickly in the face of adversity. His youngest son Alfred wrote that both William and his son James were men of energy and enterprise, with clear minds and a strong determination. If they took a matter in hand they were determined to go through with it. They were both, like the rest of the Cox men, non-talkative "little inclined to talk for talking's sake" (Whitaker 2014: 116, 117). Which is perhaps what made them good listeners. Governor Macquarie gave high praise to William when he wrote: "Mr Cox is a Sensible, intelligent Man, of great arrangement, and the best agriculturalist in the colony" (Governor Macquarie to Earl Bathurst recommending William Cox to be the commandant at Bathurst, 24 June 1815, HRA series 1, vol viii: 360).

A decade after his return to the colony, following the inquiry into the Corp's funds, both William and Governor Macquarie came under attack for their humane attitude toward convicts and the use of convicts' skills to build the colony. Lord Bathurst, back in London, was outraged that the colony, the purpose of which was to strike fear of transportation into the breasts of the lower orders, was being turned instead into a beautiful city and safe haven, where all people could have a chance at life. He had no interest in the hope, earlier expressed by David Collins in 1788, that convicts might better themselves and at the same time make a valuable contribution to their new community.

Commissioner Bigge was sent from London to engage in a major enquiry into the workings of the colony. William argued with Bigge that the accomplishments of the convicts hardly fitted with the home country's view of them as refuse: "Let a foreigner, a stranger, be told that it is the Convict, the refuse of our Country, that have performed nearly all the labour that has been done here in the short space of thirty years, and I think he would be astonished" (William Cox to Commissioner Bigge, 7 May 1820).

William did not treat convicts as refuse, either on the *Minerva*, or in his work with them in the colony. From the beginning, he understood the value of treating them with dignity and civility. Later, as magistrate he was able to find good men to work on his farms and on his various projects, at the same time protecting them from unreasonable or cruel masters. Some resented that he did not share the good convicts around more, accusing him of keeping them to work on his own farms and building projects.

William was a generous master, handing freedom to hard-working convicts. Commissioner Bigge took exception to such emancipatory values. As Hickson wrote of William in the *Australian Dictionary of Biography*: "Politically he was always a radical, signing many petitions for such reforms as representative government, repeal of taxes, and trial by jury, being 'firmly of the opinion' that 'Respectable Emancipists' would be worthy jurors".

The Road Over the Blue Mountains, 1814

It was in 1813 that Blaxland, Lawson and Wentworth found a way over the mountains. Until then, all attempts on the part of the British newcomers to cross the mountains had failed, and the colony remained confined to the narrow strip along the east coast. Macquarie funded William's road-building venture in a minimal way. He did not want to open up a highway over which convicts could escape. Nor did he particularly want settlement to spread out across the plains west of the mountains. The population was too small, he believed, and should not be spread more thinly than it already was, making it more vulnerable to attack from the natives. At the same time, due to droughts and caterpillar plagues there was a need for new pastures; and further, there would be something quite portentous and grand, for him, if he were able to make a grand tour across the mountain on a road he had commissioned. He would be able to send Earl Bathurst the kind of scientific report he desired— the "science" in this case being detailed documentation of flora and fauna that might be useful to the home country.

After the initial path-finding by Blaxland, Lawson and Wentworth, Deputy Surveyor Evans had mapped out the route that a road might follow, keeping to the ridges rather than following the rivers, as previous unsuccessful explorers had done. William kept a daily journal during the months of road and bridge building, which makes it possible to imagine, now, what building such a road entailed. His journal reveals the qualities his son Alfred wrote of—of energy and enterprise, a clear mind and strong determination, as well as the qualities Joseph Holt observed, of humane good will toward, and concern for, the

MAP 5   Cox's Road, New South Wales

well-being of the men working for him. And we can see a man taking enormous pleasure in accomplishing each stage of this extraordinarily complex task.

Working for him, he had an assistant, Thomas Hobby Esq, and a chief superintendent, Richard Lewis, and John Tighe, a guide who had attended Evans in surveying the road. These three were free men. He also had with him Samuel Ayres, a personal servant from his own household. Thirteen convicts had specific jobs such as leader of the road-makers; leader of the road-making gang; charge of the stores; rough carpenter; sawyer; quarryman; blacksmith; shoemaker; and bullock driver. Another 23 convicts were assigned as labourers to carry out whatever work needed to be done as the work progressed. At the completion of the road these men were given emancipation, or free pardon, or tickets of leave. Some were given emancipation before completion, and new men employed in their place. The free men, Hobby, Lewis and Tighe were given grants of land and cows and horses as a reward for their work. There were as well a troop of soldiers to act as guards, both in protecting the crew and its stores from hostile attacks, and also from overly curious tourists. The guards may also have been assigned responsibility by the Governor, for preventing the convicts from escaping, though such escapes appear to have been very unlikely, with all the men fully committed to their work on the project, no matter how difficult it became.

The names of the soldiers, unlike those of the workers, were rarely mentioned by William in his journal. It is as if he was determined to distance himself from the military nature of the project. The soldiers were mentioned simply as 'soldiers' when they were given a useful job to do that furthered the road building project, or when the possibility of hostile attack arose. When he borrowed horses and carts from them, he did record their names.

Whether he liked it or not, William and his road builders were moving into territory belonging to others, and they were dramatically transforming it, not least by removing the barrier that kept the Wiradjuri, custodians of the land west of the mountains safe from the newcomers. The newcomers were not welcomed by the Wiradjuri. One of the rare and ominous mentions William made of the possibility of violent resistance to the road was when he mentioned the blacksmith making pikes for self-defence.

If William did reflect on the virtue of Governor Macquarie's decision that a road should be built, or ponder on the harm British imperial expansion might cause to the people whose land was being invaded, he did not record that in his journal. Such reflections could at worst have been read as treason, punishable by death, and at best, could have undermined his capacity to work with Macquarie on future projects. There was no local power that could question the Governor's authority, except in the case of a military coup, such as Bligh had experienced. The Governor's orders were incontrovertible—they might as well have been orders from God.

In his journal, William maintained his gaze on the technical and logistical challenges of building a road across 100 miles of difficult terrain, and on the human challenge of his own personal endurance, as well as the endurance of the men who would carry out the physically demanding work under hard climatic and geographic conditions. Twice he mentioned Aboriginal men who had joined him, and who promised to work with him. They were men from the regions where he had his own farmlands. William was tuned into the skills indigenous men had, just as he was with his workers, on the one hand according them respect, and on the other, seeing how their skills made them useful in facilitating the project at hand.

William's journal makes for compelling reading.[3] I include excerpts from it to give a sense of the gargantuan road building task itself. Integral to that task was William's relationship with the men and with the country. None of those working on the road, including William, had been over the track mapped out

---

3   The journal in its entirety can be found in Whitaker (2014) and, also, in the Mitchell Library, at the State Library of New South Wales.

by Evans, except for Tighe, who had accompanied Evans. Their knowledge of
what was ahead of them, in terms of the work to be done to complete the
one hundred miles of road, was emergent. What tools would be needed, what
bullocks, what resources—all would be discovered as they went, William sending to the Governor for additional clothes (slops) and tools and bullocks, and,
on occasion, sending to his own farm, asking Rebecca to send additional food
when the government supplies for the 30 men had run short.

The work commenced in mid-winter, in fine clear frosty weather in 1814:

> *Thursday 7 July* 1814 After holding conversation with his Excellency the
> Governor at Sydney relative to the expedition, I took leave of him this day.
> *Monday 11 July* 1814 Began converting a cart into a caravan to sleep in, as
> well as to take my own personal baggage, which was completed on the 16th.
> *Sunday 17 July* 1814 Left Clarendon at 9 a.m.; arrived at Captain
> Woodriff's farm at noon. The carts from Richmond arrived at 2 p.m., and
> at 4 the 2 carts and waggon arrived from Sydney with provisions, slops,
> tools etc. Mustered the people and issued bread to them.

William began by assigning responsibility to the workers for the tools and,
also, for the preparation of their own food, which they managed within their
assigned groups. He made sure that each was adequately clothed, and work
began at once:

> *Monday 18 July* 1814 At daylight gave out the tools to handle and put in
> order. Issued half a week's provisions to the whole party. Began work at 10
> a.m. to make a pass across the Nepean River; the banks are very steep at
> the east side. In the afternoon issued to the workmen a suit of slops and
> a blanket each man (30 in number). In examining the slops 2 pair shoes
> and 3 pair trousers was deficient. Gorman, who had charge, states the
> case had been broken open when he took it out of the Parramatta store.
> Wrote to his Excellency the Governor for additional bullocks and some
> small articles of tools. Weather fine, clear and frosty.
> *Tuesday 19 July* 1814 Finished the road down the right bank of the
> river. The swamp oak on Emu side very hard to cut and root. In the after-
> noon began our operations on Emu Plains. A complaint being made of
> the pork, which was issued as six pound pieces, were very deficient.

William took the men's complaints seriously and ensured the food was adequate and the men well-fed. The blacksmith was kept constantly at work to

ensure there were good tools to work with. He was satisfied, from the beginning, with the quality of the men's work. His own work involved both ensuring
the effectiveness of the work being done on each site, often having more than
one site ongoing at any one time. He constantly explored ahead to plan the
next stages.

> *Thursday* 21 *July* 1814 ... Made good progress on Emu Plains; the men
> worked very well. Weather clear and frosty.
>   *Friday* 22 *July* 1814 ... Wind very high in the afternoon. One of the fell-
> ers, William Lonain, received a hurt in the face and shoulder from the
> limb of the tree falling on him. Hard frost and clear.
>   *Saturday* 23 *July* 1814 Hard frost and clear weather. ... Lonain, who was
> hurt yesterday, very much better. Wrote to the Governor for 2 more pit-
> saws, iron and steel ...
>   *Sunday* 24 *July* 1814 Examined the ground and marked the road from
> the creek on Emu Plains to the first depot (with Lewis). Gave a pound of
> tobacco to Edward Field for a lot of cabbage, which I gave to the work-
> men. ... The workmen exerted themselves during the week, much to my
> satisfaction. Examined the ground leading from Emu Plains and fixed on
> the spot to cross the creek at, as well as one to begin ascending the moun-
> tain ...
>   *Tuesday* 26 *July* 1814 Made a complete crossing-place from the end of
> Emu Plains to the foot of the mountains, and began to work up them. The
> ascent is steep; the soil very rough and stony; the timber chiefly ironbark.
> Sent the stonemason to the depot to build or line the chimney, as also the
> smith to put up his forge. Sent the superintendent with a man to mark
> the road from the depot through the brush to the next forest ground, a
> distance of about 5½ miles. Ordered the corporal and soldiers to prepare
> to remove in the morning from the bank of the river to the depot, with a
> cartload of provisions, and there to remain until further orders.

At the end of the first month William took a weekend off to go home to Clarendon, leaving Lewis in charge. The men continued well in his absence. On his
return he continued to give Lewis additional responsibility; the worker who
objected got short shrift.

> *Monday* 1 *August* 1814 Left Clarendon at 10 a.m. and arrived at the depot
> at 2 p.m. Found the road completed to the said depot, much to my satis-
> faction.

Tuesday 2 *August* 1814 The workmen go on with much cheerfulness, and do their work well. Gave them a quantity of cabbage as a present. After dinner I gave directions to Lewis to inform Burne he was to take the three forward fellers to fire-making. Soon after he, Burne, came to me and said he would not receive any orders from Lewis, but would obey any I gave him, on which I told him I should send any orders I had to give to him by whom I pleased. He went away but soon returned again and said he would leave us, on which I ordered the constable to receive his gun and ammunition, and he went away. Ordered him to be struck off the store and informed the party he was discharged from being a superintendent under me, and had nothing more do with either me or them.

Wednesday 3 *August* 1814 Sent the two working gangs with their bedding etc. 2 miles forward. Lewis was marking through a thick brush about 2 miles ahead. Heard the report of a gun, and soon after heard the chattering of natives on which they returned and reported the same. Gave notice to the sergeant to provide a corporal and three men to go forward and take up their quarters with the working men.

William kept the soldiers with the workers after this encounter, but no open conflict ensued.

Thursday 4 *August* 1814 Removed from the depot to 7½ miles forward, as also the corporal and 3 privates. Lewis got leave to go to Richmond and return again on Sunday next. The men at work in a very thick, troublesome brush. A fine day, but close. The wind in the evening got round to the southwards.

Friday 5 *August* 1814 Timber both thick and heavy, with a thick, strong brush, the roots of which are very hard to grub up, making it altogether extremely hard work.

Saturday 6 *August* 1814 ... The men all healthy and cheerful. Mr Hobby joined me last evening. The people all moved forward to the end of 9 miles...

Wednesday 10 *August* 1814 ... Kendall somewhat better and undertook the cooking for his mess.

Thursday 11 *August* 1814 Clear weather. The wind very strong from the westward made it dangerous in felling the timber, which is both heavy and thick. Workmen removed to 10½ miles. Water there to the right of the road. The smith set up his forge; employed in repairing tools. Mr Hobby with Lewis and Tye went forward 6 miles and marked the road for the fellers. Gave the people a quantity of cabbage.

Friday 12 *August* 1814 Mr Hobby went to Castlereagh. Fine weather with icy wind. Gorman reported there was not any meat and sugar arrived and that he had only 14 four-pound pieces left in store, and no sugar.

Saturday 13 *August* 1814 At daylight sent Lewis to the depot with a letter to Mrs Cox to send me out immediately 300 lb. of beef to serve to the people in lieu of salt pork. Gave orders to the corporal to send Private Ashford to the depot and for Sergeant Bounds to send me Carrol in lieu of him, the former being ill and not fit for the advance party...

Monday 15 *August* 1814 Fine morning, and being out of the brush had six fellers at work. At 9 a.m. arrived a cart from Clarendon with a side of beef 386 lb., 60 cabbages, two bags of corn, for the men.

Apart from the building of the road and the bridges and documenting the work itself, William's task was to make a recording of the landscape. He documented where good accessible water was to be found, where there was good grass and fertile soil. He noted what kind of wood was available and what purposes it might be put to, such as cart building, bridge building, and house building. He also documented what animals were present that might be hunted for food.

Wednesday 17 *August* 1814 Removed forward to a hill ahead of the workmen. Water at 11½ miles to the left; ditto at 12 to the right; ditto at 12½ to the left; ditto at 13½ to the right. At the three first places in very small quantities; at the latter plenty with a place fit to drive stock to water. The timber in the forest from 11½ miles to 13 very tall and thick. Measured a dead tree which was fell that was 81 feet to the beginning of the head, and at 13½ [miles] a blood tree 15 ft 6 inches in circumference. There is some good stringy bark timber on this forest ground.

Thursday 18 *August* 1814 The wind very high these last two nights, and this evening stormy but the wind blew off the rain. Measured the 13th mile this evening; just entered a scrub brush with stunted timber. Mr Hobby returned this day, got 2 lbs of shoemakers thread from Clarendon and put Henderson one of our men to repair shoes during the week. The smith employed this week in making and repairing tools and nails for the men's shoes. The stonemason went forward to examine a rocky ridge about 3 miles ahead and on Monday next he is to go there to work to level the ground.

Friday 19 *August* 1814 At 9 o'clock left the party for Clarendon. Mr Hobby and Lewis left in charge. Stephen Parker ran a splinter just under his ankle last evening; unable to work today.

After a week at Clarendon, William returned to find the sergeant in charge of
the soldiers had died. He sent for a coffin, but headquarters sent for the corpse
to bury it at Windsor. He turned his attention to the stores, and to the progress
on the road. He was satisfied with the progress, though Lewis had left due to
illness, and Hobby had continued alone. It was at this point that two Aboriginal men joined the team:

> *Saturday 27 August* Measured to the 16th mile, immediately after which
> the ground got very rocky, and in half a mile we came to a high moun-
> tain, which will cost much labour to make a road over. Got 2 natives who
> promise to continue with us – Joe from Mulgoa and Coleby from Rich-
> mond.

This is a curious entry. How did he 'get' them? Did he bring them with him
from Clarendon? What was the bargain he had struck with them? On the one
hand Joe and Coleby did not appear in the final tally of grants of land and animals given as rewards for the work; on the other, they were given names, which
is more than was given to the soldiers.

> *Monday 29 August* 1814 Commenced operations on the mountain, with
> all the men. Continued the same on Tuesday, except with the fellers who
> went forward on the next ridge. Had to remove an immense quantity of
> rock, both in going up the mountain and in the pass leading to the bluff
> on the west end of it. Examined the high rock wall and fixed on making a
> road off it from the bluff instead of winding round it. Began cutting timber
> and splitting stuff to frame the road off the rock to the ridge below it,
> about 20 feet in depth. The men worked extremely hard and smart to-day.

> *Sick List, Monday*
> Samuel Davis, splinter in his hand, Thomas Kendall, ill from a bad cold.
> Stephen Parker, from sick list to work this day.

> *Wednesday 31 August* 1814 All hands employed at the bridge.

As they moved into the mountainous terrain the difficulties inevitably multiplied. Accidents and illness increased, the bullocks became exhausted—with
food and water for them more difficult to find.

> *Sunday 4 September* 1814 ... No water for stock near the bridge, nor
> a blade of grass. The water we get is near a mile distant, and that in a
> tremendous gully to the right. Went forward to Caley's pile, and from

thence up the rock to Evans' cave. You get a view of the country from north-west round to south and ssw as far as the eye can carry you from hence. The land to the west is still higher. The country to the northward appears extremely hilly with nothing but rocks and timber. To the east there appears much level country. Windsor and various parts of cleared land is seen from hence.

Monday 5 September 1814 Davis returned to labour; Kendall to cooking. Appledore ill; splinter in the foot. Set the following persons to the pass and bridge:
- 2 carpenters
- 2 sawyers
- 2 quarrymen and blasters
- 2 cutting timber
- 2 labourers.

Blacksmith employed repairing tools and making shoe nails. Shoemaker mending and nailing shoes. The remainder of the men employed in road-making forward under the direction of Mr Hobby and Richard Lewis. John Tye got a week's leave on Friday last to go to Windsor. Sent a soldier on Thursday last to the Governor for blocks, augurs, iron etc. ...

Thursday 8 September 1814 Men at work as yesterday. The wind has been very high and cold from the westward since Sunday last and last night it blew a perfect hurricane. Saw a few flying showers yesterday, but we got scarcely any rain and it appears the wind will carry it away. The country about here very barren. No kangaroo to be seen. Shot one pheasant with tail complete; shot 2 others without tails. It appears to be too early in the season for them, as their tails are some just shooting out and others not at full length. Scarcely any small birds to be seen....

Sunday 11 September 1814 Went 3 miles forward to examine the road with Mr Hobby and Lewis. From the bridge it continues rocky over two or three small passes to Caley's pile; from thence at least two miles further the mountain is nearly a solid rock. At places high broken rocks; at others very hanging or shelving, which makes it impossible to make a level good road. The more the road is used the better it will be.

Monday 12 September 1814 ... Issued a pair of strong shoes to each man. The bridge we have completed is 80 feet long; 15 feet wide at one end and 12 feet at the other. 35 feet of it is planked, the remainder filled up with stone. The fall from the bluff end of the rock was about 20 feet before we began to work. At the left there is a side wall cut from the solid rock. At the right where the ground is lower we have put up a rough stone wall about 100 feet long, which makes the pass to the bridge quite a lane. It is steep from the top of the mountain quite to the lower end of the bridge, a distance altogether of about 400 feet. The bridge and pass has cost me the labour of 12 men for 3 weeks, during which time they worked very hard and cheerful. It is now complete – a most strong, solid bridge, and will I have no doubt be reckoned also a good-looking one by travellers that pass through the mountains.

William's pleasure in the bridge is palpable. He has made a mark on the landscape that will be appreciated by others. What becomes evident, as the project grows more difficult, is how much he enjoys meeting each challenge as it presents itself, and how well he is able to inspire the men to keep at it, month after month:

> *Friday* 16 *September* 1814 Removed forward; found the road completed to 21 miles. At the latter end of this the ground was completely covered with gum roots. Was obliged to turn all hands to grubbing and finishing the road, and with very hard labour nearly completed the 22nd mile by Saturday night.

> *Tuesday* 20 *to Saturday* 24^t ... [arrives at 26th mile] at the foot of a steep mountain. Examined it well and found it too steep to ascend in a straight direction.

> *Sunday* 25 *September* 1814 Went up the mountain; examined it and fixed on the way to make a winding road up. This is the highest mountain in the whole range we cross. From it Windsor stores etc. are distinctly seen as are the wheat fields, farmhouses, etc. There is a river running to the eastward about a mile south of this, the banks of which are so high and steep it is not possible to get down. This river empties itself into the Nepean about 4 or 6 miles higher up than Emu Plains. Went forward to fix on a spot for a second depot. Chose one about 2 miles ahead, close to a small stream of excellent water. We have found water in much greater quantities these last 6 miles than we did before, and all very good.

The work progresses well in this vein, and William is once again able to spend some time at *Clarendon* before facing the most difficult part of the entire project.

Sunday 23 October 1814 ... On Sunday evening Richard Lewis returned from the end of the mountains, about 10 miles forwards, having been with 3 men to examine the mountain that leads down to the forest ground. His report is that the descent is near half a mile down and extremely steep; that it is scarcely possible to make a road down and that we cannot get off the mountain to the northwards to make a road; that it appears to him much more difficult now he has examined the hill, to get down than he was before aware of. ...

Tuesday 25 and Wednesday 26 October 1814 The men continued the same work and getting on extremely well. Wrote to His Excellency the Governor for a further supply of gunpowder to enable us to blow up the rocks in our way; as also rope and blocks to expedite us in building bridges and getting off the mountain.

Monday 31 October 1814 ... Two parties of natives are seen in the low lands to the westward. One within about 2 miles from us; the other about 6 miles.

The original custodians of the land maintained their quiet watchful distance as the road wound its way up and over the mountains.

The descent of the mountain presented an extraordinary challenge. The route marked out by Evans appeared to be impossibly steep. So steep, I discovered, when I went there 200 years later, that it would seem foolhardy to attempt even to walk down it. William tried repeatedly to find another route down—to no avail.

Wednesday 2 November 1814 Fine morning. Thunder with light showers after. Sent 3 men again to examine the descent off the mountains, and ascertained that there is no other way but from the bluff end originally marked. Tomorrow I intend going to survey it as a road must be there made to get off the mountain

Thursday 3 November 1814 At 6 this morning went forward with Lewis, Tye and a soldier to examine the mountain at the end of the ridge 4 miles ahead. Found it much worse than I expected. It commences with going down steep between immense large rocks, when it opens with a very steep gully in front, and round to the left it falls off so steep that it is with much difficulty a person can get down at all. The whole front of the mountain is covered with loose rock, at least two-thirds of the way down;

and on the right and left it is bounded both by steep gullies and rocks, so that we cannot, by winding short to the left, get half length sufficient to gain ground to get down without a number of circular turns both to the right and left, and in that case the hill is so very steep about half a mile down that it is not possible to make a good road to go down and up again without going to a very great expense.

The resources the Governor had made available allowed only for a narrow roadway capable of allowing two carts to pass each other. Macquarie did not want a grand thoroughfare. But the limited resources caused the road descending the mountain to be seriously compromised:

I have therefore made up my mind to make such a road as a cart can go down empty or with a very light load without a possibility of it being able to return with any sort of load whatever; and such a road will also answer to drive stock down to the forest ground. After getting down this said mountain we got into very pretty forest ground and went as far as Blaxland's rivulet, about 2 miles. The grass on it is in general of a good quality; some silky, some hard, intermingled with rib grass, buttercup and thistle. The timber is thin, and kangaroos plenty. In returning back we had to clamber up the mountain and it completely knocked me up. It is a very great drawback to the new country as no produce can be brought from thence to headquarters except [ ] beef and mutton. The sheep will also be able to bring their fleeces up and be shorn on the mountains, or driven to the 2nd depot for this purpose. In either case wagons can fetch the wool. Gorman came forward with a cartload of provisions. From him I learn that Walters has got some fresh Government bullocks at the first depot, but that he could not harness them they were so wild. Sent another man down to assist him. Also sent a man to bring up the remainder of the bullocks that are unable to work from lameness or poverty, to get them down the mountains where there is good food. The Government bullocks have not carried a single load of anything for me since Sunday week last. Made an agreement with Sergeant Minehan and another man for their horse and a cart to remain with us until we have performed the whole of our work, and the sergeant went to the Hawkesbury for them. John Tindall received a hurt in his arm from the fall of a tree. Removed all hands this morning to 45½ miles. Put up the forge for the blacksmith to repair all our tools for the Herculean mountain. Issued to all hands a gill of spirits.

William again looked for an alternative route down. The possibility of violent encounters with the Wiradjuri couldn't be ignored—William and his men were opening a thoroughfare that would change their life and land irrevocably. William did not reflect on the portent of that imminent change in his journal. His attention, as far as he recorded it, was taken up with the task he had undertaken, and with completing it well, despite any difficulties from weather, from the geological features of the mountain, and from the people whose country the road was penetrating.

Friday 4 November 1814 Sent 3 men to examine all the ridges and gullies to the northwards, offering a reward if they found a better way down. All returned unsuccessful. Removed to 47th mile.

Saturday 5 November 1814 Wind to the east, rain and cold. All hands employed on the road. The blacksmith made 8 pikes for self defence against the natives. Lewis and a party took the dogs down to the forest ground. Killed a fine kangaroo, weight about 120 lb. Examined the big Mountain and fixed on the spot where to begin on Monday morning, having given up all thoughts of attempting it elsewhere. John Manning sprained his ankle in bringing up a keg of water from the rocks below. Thomas Raddock ill; believe it arises from the wet weather. There is a timber here which appears to have all the property of the ash. In its young state it is easily transplanted, as the plants are like the white thorn. It grows quickly, tall and straight, bends to anything. When large it splits well and will, I have no doubt, make very good hoops. In its appearance it is like the black butted gum but the leaves are unlike them. The bark ties much better than the stringy bark. In felling the timber trees it cut remarkably free, and in order to try it I cut a small one down and quartered it, which I mean to send to Clarendon and try them for light cart or chaise shafts...

Tuesday 8 November 1814 Employed the same hands in the same manner. Light rain as before. The men very wet and uncomfortable, their clothes and bedding being also wet.

Wednesday 9 November 1814 Removed forward to the extreme end of the mountains as did also the whole of the party. The rocks here are so lofty and undermined that the men will be able to sleep dry and keep their little clothing dry also, which is what they have not been able to do this last fortnight. Left 12 men to finish up the road; all the rest employed with myself. Cold rain set in about noon. Wind S. West.

Two hundred years later I sat under one of those lofty overhangs, imagining how pleasurable it would have been to take shelter underneath them from the cold driving Spring rain. I found a smooth rock to sit on next to what looked like the best spot to light the fire, and imagined warming myself, and drying my clothes, readying myself for the arduous work to come, building the road down that impossibly steep mountainside. Glancing up at the sandstone overhang, I saw with a shock that smoke had blackened the stone immediately above my imaginary fire. Was it the road-builders' fire? Or was this a prized shelter the Wiradjuri people had used for centuries and would have been occupying in this driving cold, if the road builders had not deprived them of it? And after the road was built, and had become a thoroughfare, was this a place where travellers stopped to picnic and boil the billy before tackling the difficult downward journey? I didn't know whose smoke it was above me, but the sight of it linked me, with a vivid intensity, to the history of the place and its contested ownership.

Thursday 10 *November* 1814 Rainy morning. Cleared up at 9 o'clock. Got a good day's work done. Evening fine and starlight.

Friday 11 *November* 1814 Rain commenced before daylight and continued the whole day. Wind south and very cold. Sent Thomas Raddocks to Windsor being very ill. Samuel Freeman the carpenter laid up with a cold and swollen face. James Dwyer ill; pain in the side and breast. Sent 2 carts to the 2nd depot for provisions. Sent the men (3) out with the dogs to catch kangaroos three times this week. Brought home one each day. The bullock driver with 11 bullocks joined me yesterday. All they have done this last fortnight has been to bring me one cargo of biscuits from the 1st depot to this place (43 miles). Turned the bullocks down the mountain to the forest ground where I intend letting them remain to recover themselves until we want to remove forward towards the Fish River. One of them is quite blind. He got into the gully going down, but we got him out to-day quite safe.

Saturday 12 *November* 1814 A very fine day. Wind east and cold. Completed the road to the beginning of the large mountain where we have to descend to the forest ground. Measured it up; it is 48 miles 50 chains. Continued to clear away the timber and rubbish through the large rocks, and to the beginning of the bluff end of the mountains. Two men on the sick list.

Sunday 13 November 1814 Went down to the forest ground, from thence to the rivulet, and traced it to the river about five miles down. Went 1 mile down the river and came back on the high lands, exploring the best ground for a road. The grass on the greater part of the land we went over today is good, the timber thin. The ground is hilly but sound; some parts of it near the rivulet and river is rocky but no iron stone, it being rather of a sandy soil and very good pasture for sheep. The ground on the other side of the rivulet appears also to be equally good for food, thinly timbered and very hilly with good grass clear up to the mountains. The river runs nearly east, and from its course must empty itself into the Nepean River. The horse carts arrived today from the 2nd depot. They brought very small loads indeed. Ordered 2 of the carts to go tomorrow to the 1st depot and to return here again on Sunday next loaded. Saw the working bullocks this morning. They are improving quite fast. Mustered the whole of the tools, harness, etc.; found nearly all right. Ground the axes and put the grub hoes and picks in order to begin tomorrow. Ordered Gorman to issue 4 lbs. biscuits and 8 lbs. of flour to each mess, instead of 6 lbs. each, the biscuits running short and also too bulky to bring so far, being about 90 miles from headquarters.

Monday 14 November 1814 Sick list:
  James Dwyer, cold, pains in limbs
  Samuel Freeman, cold, swelled face
  Samuel Crook, cold, bad eyes
  Patrick Hanrigan, cold, pains in limbs
  Samuel Walters, hurt by a bullock.

The extreme wet weather we had for a fortnight before we arrived here has given most of the men colds, but as they are now dry lodged, and in addition to their own ration have fresh kangaroo at least three times a week, it is to be hoped they will soon recover. So many men sick, and chiefly very useful ones, breaks in on our working party much, and the continuous rain also prevents so much work being done as I could wish. Fine morning, at noon thunder with rain and hail. Wind east, very cold. Steady rain all the evening. Got on erecting the bridge at the beginning of the descent off the mountain, and blowing up the rocks that are in the line of our intended road down to the forest. Find it difficult work, and will cost us much labour ...

Wednesday 16 November 1814 Dwyer and Crook returned to labour. Sullivan laid up sick. Most beautiful morning. Thunder at noon. Thunder in the evening with showers. Got a very good day's work done. The rocks cut extremely hard and cost us much labour. Sent Lewis and Tye back to the 37th mile to see a working bullock left there 3 weeks since. Found it in so bad a state from sore feet and unable to walk to feed that they killed it ...

Monday 21 November 1814 Thick, misty morning. All hands at work on the mountain. At ½ past 10 a.m. it began to thunder and rain. About noon it increased and continued the whole day, at times very heavy. Only four hours' work done this day. Issued to all hands yesterday afternoon a gill of spirits each.

Tuesday 22 November 1814 Thick, moist morning. The sick list reduced to one (Samuel Davis). All hands again on the mountain. Light rains and heavy fogs during the day but the men continued out and did a good day's work. Turned out a great number of very large rocks this day; blew up one. The ground as we dig discovers many more rocks than we expected.

Even as work went ahead on the impossible descent with constant rain, difficulties with food supplies and men sick, William planned ahead to the next stage. He also took time to document the geological and botanical features of the country – country he had not seen before, and that almost no British newcomers had yet seen.

Wednesday 23 November 1814 Cloudy morning with a very cold wind at East-south-east. Cleared up at noon and continued fine the whole day. Thomas Cook and John Ross sick. Sent two carts to Emu Plains with 3 horses and the sergeant and 2 men to bring here a load of flour from Martin's. Sent Gorman with them and he took six weeks' provisions for two of the soldiers that are to be left at the first depot. The other soldier ordered to return here with the carts. Sent John Tye with a soldier and another man to re-mark the trees from the second rivulet to the Fish River, a distance of about 20 miles from hence, and gave him directions to return by a ridge of high land that bears as we suppose from within three miles of the Fish River back to Mount Blaxland, it being my wish to make the road on that line if practicable. They took each half a week's rations with them.

Thursday 24 November 1814 Sick: Thomas Cook, John Ross, John Finch (pains in the back and thighs proceeding from wet and cold). Close morning, but dry weather until 5 p.m. when it misted and continued so all the evening. Wind south-east and quite cold. The men did a very good day's work. Turned out of the road an immense quantity of rock which was handsomely veined, very like marble. The bullocks having been missing since Sunday last sent Lewis to look after them. He returned but could not find them. There is a handsome shrub here very like the laylock. It grows larger but is a pretty flower. The stem of them make good walking sticks.

Friday 25 November 1814 Sick list same as yesterday. Wet drizzly morning. At 10 a.m. it rained so hard as to break off the men from work. Took up a little again at 2 p.m. Turned out the men again and continued to work until sunset. Light rain all the afternoon, harder rain in the evening. Wind south-south-east, quite cold.

Saturday 26 November 1814 Issued to all hands one pair of trousers to each man. The stone on the mountain in general is uncommon hard and flinty. Cuts extremely bad, and some of it will not split. We have been fortunate in turning out very large solid rocks 2 feet thick without breaking them, and we have used but little powder this week. Light rain the whole day. Wind east-south-east blowing quite hard at times and very cold. The men kept out at work the greater part of the day, but so much wet and for so long a period makes them quite cheerless. The working bullocks have not been seen these 10 days, sent Lewis again to look after them and found them up a valley about 3 miles from us east-north-east. Ordered the bullock driver to repair their harness and be prepared to set off with a strong team tomorrow for Emu Plains to bring us a load of provisions. Sick list as yesterday: Cook and Ross getting better, Finch much worse. Carpenter got 100 posts split and 200 rails for fencing the road down the mountain.

Sunday 27 November 1814 [rain and hard work continue.] At 5 p.m. John Tye and his party returned from the Fish River. They brought some fish with them which prove to be the rock cod, weighing about 5 lb. each. They report the waters to be very high and that is has rained constantly from Wednesday evening until a few hours since, in consequence of which they could not examine the ridge which I suppose leads towards the river, but returned the same way they went which is by no means favourable for a road on account of the hills and valleys. During their stay at the river they caught 10 fish and state that had the water not run so strong they could have caught as many as they please. Quite a fine, clear evening.

Monday 28 *November* 1814 A clear beautiful morning. All hands out at work at 5 o'clock. At 5 p.m. turned cloudy and we had a dirty evening but got a good day's work done. At noon the sergeant and Frost returned from Emu ford with their horses and one cart, bringing 2 casks of flour of 336 lbs. each. Allen's horse got stung by something, and was left very ill at Sawyer's Reach. The cart was also left behind. Thomas Adams sick, has a strong fever on him. The stonemason completed the rock a little below the bridge. It has cost us 10 blasts of powder and great labour to get rid of it.

Tuesday 29 *November* 1814 A dirty misty morning. Got a tree 55 ft. long and 9 feet in circumference by the men from the woods into this place as a side piece below the bridge and joining the rock, which is the last we want for this job. Men stuck very hard picking and grubbing the rocks and forming the road. Fine evening.

At the beginning of December a momentous point was reached. The road was well enough completed for William to take his caravan down the mountain— pulled by men, as it was still not level enough for the animals to manage. William gave spirits to the men to celebrate, but he himself was immediately moving forward to the next stage.

Sunday 4 *December* 1814 … At 10 a.m. removed the caravan and cart down to the valley at the foot of the mountain. Took them down by men, the road not being finished sufficient for horses or cattle to draw on it. At 2 p.m. removed 18 chains forward to a valley about 2 miles where there is water. The bullock cart took the provisions etc. forward. At 3 p.m. the horses were brought back by Sullivan and 2 others. They look very well. Gave the promised reward, half a pint of spirits. Mr. Hobby and myself immediately mounted and gave directions where the men are to begin tomorrow under the charge of Watson. He is to put on 6 fellers, 6 fire-makers, and 5 cleaners up of the road. Went on to the river and fixed on the spot to make the first bridge. There is a most beautiful ridge near 3 miles long that leads direct to the spot. Could not see any timber near the place fit for it. Issued to all hands a gill of spirits each. In the evening wind shifted to the westward. At 7 it began to rain. At 8 it came on very heavy and rained nearly all night.

The work continued to be well done and six more men were discharged, with rewards. The summer had arrived, and it was hot and stormy. Work began on new bridges:

Sunday 25 *December Xmas Day* Cloudy morning with light rain until 9 o'clock. The Christmas day continued dull throughout with a southerly wind. At 8a.m., after serving out the rations, went forward to the Fish River and removed our caravan and one cartload there, where I pitched my tent leaving behind 3 bridges to make and 5 miles of road. It being Xmas day issued to the men a gill of spirits and a new shirt each. Examined the river to find the best place to cross it, and fixed on a spot about 10 chains below where Mr Evans crossed...

The work continued on the road and the bridges for the next ten weeks until they reached the site of what is now Bathurst. They saw plentiful kangaroos and emus, ducks and pigeons, and rivers full of fish. William observed the best grass he had seen in the country. His spirits were high and he wrote on December 29: "A fine morning which the birds seem much to enjoy. On the banks of the river the shrubs and flowers also are extremely fragrant." As he set up each working party, he left soldiers to guard them, then took great pleasure in travelling forward to see the country for the first time:

> During three days travelling we passed over a great quantity of most excellent pasturage for sheep. Fine, dry, healthy hills, gravelly soil and good grass, and so thinly timbered that it resembled parks in England rather than a forest. There are few gullies and no swamps, but the hills passed gradually into fine valleys, some of which has fine grass in them. At Sidmouth Valley I never saw finer grass, or more on the same quantity of land in a meadow in England than was here, and just in a fit state for mowing. The whole of a line about 20 miles due west would make most excellent grazing farms, with the river in front and the back on east and west line... Some fish has also been caught this week, and when the men were mustered this morning they were extremely clean and looked cheerful and hearty.

There seems to be an innocence in this account—an innocence that lies at the heart of the newcomers' experience. William and the men were in good spirits as they encountered the beauty and the bounty of the land west of the mountains. He compared it with England, and found it to be better. What was invisible in his account, and perhaps even to his own awareness, was the work the Wiradjuri had done to make the land so bountiful. And there was no question from the newcomers, at least in their formal reports, about what right they had to be there. They had as yet no idea of what the importation of hard hoofed animals would eventually do to compromise the beauty of the land and its bounty. The work the men had engaged in, road and bridge building, felling forests and farming, had been undertaken in England for centuries without the rapid destruction that was to occur in the colony. That would only become evident to the descendants of the newcomers two centuries later...

And so...

William went on to complete many significant public projects for Macquarie. These included the road from Emu Plains to Parramatta Road built in July 1815; the road from Parramatta to Richmond in 1816; the Courthouse in Windsor, designed by Francis Greenway, in 1821–2, and the rectory for the Anglican church. His wife Rebecca, much loved by her family and in the community, died in 1819 after being ill for some months. In 1821 he married Anna Blachford, with whom he started a new family.

Three decades after the journey on the *Minerva,* the *Sydney Gazette* reported William being ill, and the consequent alarm his illness gave rise to in his community:

> The sensation on the public mind, occasioned by the indisposition of Mr Cox, is beyond description, and can be more easily accounted for by bringing to recollection, that very many of the inhabitants of the Hawkesbury enjoy sweet liberty under his auspices, hold land under his recommendation, have reared families in his employ, and, in short, having sat seventeen years on the Windsor Bench, as a guardian to servants in bondage. His humanity has been conspicuous; the dictates of a good heart, have softened the asperity of a harsh master, and subdued the turbulent spirit of an unruly servant; and his judgments have been equally just toward the poorer class of settlers, with all whose necessities brought them under his jurisdiction as a Justice of the Peace. (*Sydney Gazette,* 15 September 1828: 2)

Governor Brisbane was appointed following the Bigge Inquiry. The British Government wanted a penal colony that made transportation an object of real terror. They did not want any weakening of that terror by what it believed to be William's and Macquarie's ill-considered compassion for convicts. Bigge had been appointed to review Macquarie's inappropriate humanitarian policies; his report made it clear Macquarie was no longer their man. Governor Brisbane, who replaced Macquarie, encouraged the taking up of land west of the mountains. The ensuing conflict between the Wiradjuri and the newcomers led, inexorably, to the declaration of martial law. The declaration accused the Wiradjuri of indiscriminate killing and plundering, and it made no mention of their legitimate defence of life and country. The newcomers' attacks had on occasion been just as indiscriminate and brutal, with mass slaughter of men, women and children. The declaration of martial law was in part an attempt to bring military order and rationality to the task of containing the conflict. The declaration does not count the indigenous people as His Majesty's subjects, casting them, instead, as the enemy in their own land.

DECLARATION OF MARTIAL LAW
New South Wales Proclamation

By His Excellency Sir Thomas Brisbane, Knight Commander of the Most Honorable Military Order of the Bath, Captain General and Governor in Chief in and over His Majesty's Territory of New South Wales and its dependencies, etc., etc., etc.

WHEREAS THE ABORIGINAL NATIVES of the Districts near Bathurst have for many Weeks past carried on a Series of indiscriminate Attacks on the Stock Station there, putting some of the Keepers to cruel Deaths, wounding others, and dispersing and plundering the Flocks and Herds; themselves not escaping sanguinary Retaliations.

AND WHEREAS the ordinary Powers of the CIVIL MAGISTRATES (although most anxiously exerted) have failed to protect the Lives of HIS MAJES-TY'S Subjects; and every conciliatory Measure has been pursued in vain; and the Slaughter of Black Women and Children and Unoffending White Men, as well as of the lawless Objects of Terror, continue to threaten the before mentioned Districts;

AND WHEREAS by Experience, it hath been found that mutual Blood-shed may be stopped by the Use of Arms against the Natives beyond the ordinary Rule of Law in Time of Peace, and for this End Resort to sum-mary Justice has become necessary:

NOW THEREFORE, by Virtue of the Authority in me vested by His Maj-esty's Royal Commission, I do declare, in Order to restore Tranquillity, MARTIAL LAW TO BE IN ALL THE COUNTRY WESTWARD OF MOUNT YORK;

And all Soldiers are hereby ordered to assist and obey their lawful Supe-riors in suppressing the Violences aforesaid; and all His Majesty's Sub-jects are also called upon to assist the MAGISTRATES in executing such Measures, as any one or more of the said Magistrates shall direct to be taken for the same purpose, by such Ways and Means as are expedient, so long as Martial Law shall last; being always mindful that the Shedding of Blood is only just, where all other Means of Defence or of Peace are exhausted; that Cruelty is never Lawful; and that, when personal Attacks become necessary, the helpless Women and Children are to be spared.

IN WITNESS whereof I, the Governor aforesaid, have hereunto set my Hand and caused the Seal of my Office, as Governor of the Colony of New South Wales and its Dependencies, to be affixed, this Fourteenth Day of August, in the Year of Our Lord, One Thousand eight hundred and twenty four.

THOMAS BRISBANE

By His Excellency's Command
F. Goulburn, Colonial Secretary

GOD SAVE THE KING!

Indeed. God save the king, and his loyal representatives; the destructive force of their actions reverberates through the centuries to this day.

A Woman's View of the Colony: Christiana Brooks

For much of the first 17 years of their marriage Christiana (1776–1835) and Richard Brooks (1759–1833) lived parallel lives. Christiana and the children lived at 10 The Crescent in Greenwich, near the Naval Hospital, especially memorable, her daughter Jane writes, for its beautiful flower garden (Cox, 1912). In London Christiana had close contact with friends and family with whom she could go to the theatre and concerts, discuss politics, and involve herself in lobbying for improvements in girls' education. Richard was, more often than not, absent at sea, or in the colonies. Christiana had no desire to go to New South Wales, having heard too many stories about the dangers of ocean voyages, from both her seafaring family, and from Richard.

Richard had made four further journeys to New South Wales following his tragic journey on the *Atlas*, in 1801–2. Over the 17 years of their marriage he had continually moved among diverse worlds—at home in London, in the genteel society of Christiana and their children; out on his wild, adventurous ocean voyages, stopping for long periods in exotic locations; and at home in Sydney, more recently, with Ann Jamison, his 15-year-old mistress. After Richard set sail on the *Isabella* in 1812, on his way to London to sell up his property and bring his family to the colony, Ann gave birth to Richard Brooks Jnr.

The journey home to fetch his family had not been without adventure. The drunk and incompetent captain capsized the *Isabella* off the Falkland Islands. He was in no fit state to evacuate the passengers and crew, and so Richard took command. Sir Henry Browne Hayes, his old associate from the journey on the *Atlas*, had absconded with the ship's boat and all the oars, so the rescue had to take place on the longboat, using ornamental paddles that some of the crew had fortuitously acquired in New Zealand. Joseph Holt, too, was on that journey. He played a vital role in setting up the small community on a deserted island so it could survive the long wait for rescue (O'Shaughnessy, 1988).

Once everyone was safely ashore, and had begun to build shelters out of the wreckage, Richard, with a small crew of five men, set out for the mainland in the fourteen and a half foot longboat.[1] He had his charts, sextant and quadrant to navigate with, and they took enough salted pork, ship's biscuit and casks of

---

1   A longboat was an open boat usually to be rowed by eight or ten oarsmen; its rowing benches were designed to accommodate two men each pulling an oar on opposite sides.

© BRONWYN DAVIES, 2021 | DOI:10.1163/9789004446717_018

water, as well as madeira to keep their spirits up, to make it to the South American mainland. It was a precarious journey in which they were confronted with cloudy skies so they could take no directions, with storms and massive waves that swamped the long boat, and a whale that breached close enough to tip the boat. It took 7 weeks to row the 1500 miles to Rio de la Plata, where they were thrown in prison by the local Uruguayan authorities. When they were released they set out for Buenos Aires. There the British consul came to their aid, and eventually to the aid of the ship-wrecked crew and passengers.

Richard was returning to England on this trip after almost four years absence. Governor Macquarie had increasingly pressured him to bring his family to Sydney to settle there. The colony was in need of free settlers who could bring money into the colony and play an active role in managing it. Settlers were being enticed there by promises of land grants equivalent to the resources they brought with them. Richard's resources were substantial:

> Earl Bathurst, secretary of state for war and the colonies, had written to Macquarie recommending that Brooks 'of whose character a favourable report has been received' was eligible to be awarded a grant of land and 'other privileges for free settlers'. He listed as assets his 'considerable herd of breeding cattle which have increased to 200 head'; the fact that his capital exceeded £7000; and that he would take out seeds, plants and instruments of husbandry to cultivate 'some part of the land he became possessed of by purchase and now holds [Denham Court]. (Maher, 2017: 119)

Richard sold his property in London, and Christiana packed up her family's life in Greenwich, and with great misgivings, boarded the *Spring* with her children: Henry aged 15, Christiana Jane 11, Mary Honoria 9, Jane Maria 7, Honoria Rose 6, and Charlotte Sophia Springle, the youngest, aged 3. Christiana's horror of ocean voyages was justified when the *Spring* met with disaster not long after they set sail:

> The *Spring* sailed from London on 14 August 1813. Brooks' entire family was on board—Christiana, their six children, their governess Elizabeth Hall and their housekeeper.... [A] few days out of England off the Portuguese coast, the warship escort HMS *Achae* accidentally collided with the *Spring*, knocking out its main mast. In the confusion to abandon ship, Charlotte was believed lost. She was later reunited with her family when the seamen, noticing the child's face at the porthole pulled her to safety. (Maher, 2016: 118)

They arrived in Sydney on 4 March 1814.[2] His children were amazed at Richard's easy familiarity with the local indigenous people:

> The bumboats came out to meet the ship, along with a number of Aboriginal craft 'all talking to Captain Brooks whom they appeared to know very well', including Cadigal elder and boatswain Maroot and his wife. This impressed the Brooks children, particularly the fact they knew Brooks' name and he in turn was familiar with theirs. Maroot was a local celebrity—the couple was among the few local Aboriginals still surviving after 90 per cent of their people had been wiped out by smallpox. (Maher, 2016: 119, citing Jane Maria Cox's journal)

Richard also had a black servant with him, who travelled with him on all his voyages. Christiana was pregnant with their sixth daughter, Maria, who was born two months after they arrived. On the journey Christiana made friends with Mary Ann, now the young wife of John Piper, the Norfolk Island Commandant who had seduced several young daughters of convicts, including Mary Ann and Margaret Eddington. London had been scandalised by Piper's marriage to Mary Ann, but Christiana was more open-minded, and formed a lifelong friendship with the Pipers:

> Somewhat unconventional in her early years, she remained remarkably free of prejudice and snobbery against the 'convict stain' prevalent in the small society of New South Wales and took people as she found them... Both women were expecting another child during the voyage ... Christiana became godmother to one of Mary Ann's children – Ann Christiana Frances – and later stood by the Pipers in what was to be their spectacular fall. (Maher, 2016: 120–1)

Open-minded as she was in some ways, Christiana would have nothing to do with Richard Brooks Jnr. Whereas Mary Ann, like many wives in the colony at that time, took in her husband's extra-nuptial children, Christiana would neither take young Richard Jnr in, nor even acknowledge his existence.

The colony in that Georgian period was awash with the children of mistresses. Fifty per cent of the children in the colony at the time were born out of wedlock (Maher, 2016). It was generally accepted that men would have extramarital relations. Not only Richard Brooks, John Piper, and David Collins,

---

2 Richard later sold the *Spring* to Edward Lord, the wealthy grandson of a convict who lived in Van Diemen's land, and who married one of David Collins' grandchildren.

but also Governor King, Richard Atkins the drunken Judge Advocate, D'Arcy Wentworth, Charles Throsby, Thomas Jamison, and George Johnston all had children out of wedlock. One mark of a "gentleman" was that he would refrain from impregnating his wife more than once every two years. Mistresses could serve, among other things, as a form of marital birth control. When wives were absent, as Christiana had been, or fragile and unable to bear children, as Maria Collins had been, taking a mistress was the norm. And it is in the nature of norms to be read as "natural". In the absence of a wife, to not have a mistress could be read as going against nature.

It is tempting to read these young mistresses solely as victims of oppressive patriarchal practices. But it's also possible that Ann Jamison saw a relationship with a wealthy, older man as being to her advantage (Alexander, 1999, Maher, 2016). As it turned out, the relationship with Richard was very much to her advantage. Under English law, men were unequivocally responsible for all their children. Because Christiana refused to acknowledge Richard Jnr, Ann was able to keep her child, and Richard settled on her the lucrative lease of a pub on Market Street, *The Rose*, later called *The Rose in June*. It was a profitable business. When Ann died Richard made sure their son was well cared for, placing him with his trusted overseers, the Neales, on one of his properties, and hiring a tutor for him. Richard Brooks Jnr, with his father's support, became a wealthy young man. His father depended on him in the work of expanding his cattle and sheep stations, in a way he could not depend on his son Henry, who had no love of the land and would much rather have devoted his life to composing music.

When the Brooks family first arrived in Sydney, they lived for some time on board the *Spring*, only later moving to a commodious dwelling that Richard owned in Pitt Street. There they were visibly among the elite, riding about in the only privately-owned carriage in the colony, which was big enough to carry the entire family about the town.

To begin with Christiana was horribly homesick. By the time we meet her in her diary and letters, ten years later, she had become deeply immersed in the establishment of the colony. By then they had moved out to their farm, *Denham Court*, near today's Campbelltown.

Christiana's pleasure in being well-to-do, combined with her wit and practicality is visible in these lines to her sister back home in England:

> ... we drive a Carriage and four. Believe me that is not altogether for show, for our family being large, and our new Carriage a very heavy one, and moreover our Horses being young we find it necessary when we are going any longer journey than to Church to put a pair of horses in for headers,

FIGURE 71   Denham Court, Ingleburn, New South Wales, 1916, William Hardy Wilson
             NATIONAL LIBRARY OF AUSTRALIA

> but all four Horses do other work besides taking us about I assure you,
> we keep nothing idle about us. (Letter from Denham Court to her sister,
> August 29 1826)

Soon after arrival in the colony, Christiana became friends with Elizabeth Macquarie, a shy aloof woman, who, like Christiana, was homesick for England.
Elizabeth had had multiple miscarriages, perhaps not unrelated to her husband's syphilis. Like Christiana, she too was pregnant. Elizabeth appreciated
Christiana's witty intellect and her knowledge of child birth and child care.
Christiana "was able to provide her not only with childcare hints but also with
information on the latest London styles in fashion, architecture and theatre, in
which they both had a keen interest as well as a passion for books and music"
(Maher, 2016: 121).

    Christiana was both an avid reader and writer. She wrote voluminous letters,
of which she made copies, and she kept a journal, perhaps with publication in
mind, or perhaps to take the place of the conversations she yearned for. Christiana's love of books was a constant theme in her new life—her letters often
mentioning her longing for them and the difficulty of getting hold of them. She
read good books three times, she wrote, in a long letter to her daughter Mary:

I sent you by Mr. S— Sir Walter Scott's last work. I had just time to *skim* it over but as I always read his books three times with much pleasure you may return it to me after a more leisurely reading on your part. My first perusal is for the *story* which has seldom much merit. My second reading surprises me by the beauties of the sentiments, the correctness of description and the consistency of the characters, and on the third perusal open it at *any* part of *any* volume and some interesting passage presents itself that had before escaped observation, in short you will always find a great deal to admire even in these works of his which upon a first reading you may pronounce "not near as good as the last". (Letter from Denham Court to Mary, July 1826)

I was amused when I read that. A good novel requires, in my own experience, three such readings when I first encounter it.

Another of Christiana's close friends was the young, radical William Wentworth, the son of D'Arcy Wentworth. D'Arcy was a free settler though he had been charged with several counts of highway robbery when still in England. William's mother, Catherine, had been a convict. When William was a schoolboy, Richard Brooks had been given the responsibility of taking him and his younger brother to England on the *Atlas*'s return journey in 1802. There they were educated at the expense of their wealthy relations, at Dr Alexander Crombie's Greenwich School. Young William and his brother were well looked after by Richard on that journey, and Christiana kept a close eye on them while they stayed in England, often having them to stay at 10 The Crescent.

When Wentworth returned to New South Wales he was a journalist, barrister, and politician, working tirelessly, if somewhat erratically, for social and legal reform (Tink 2009). He was also the explorer who, with Blaxland and Lawson, found the route over the Blue Mountains into the interior. Christiana watched William's career with intense interest, and she enjoyed hanging out with him whenever she got the chance. When he was Editor of the *Australian* (not to be confused with the current day *Australian*) she read it assiduously, but when he left it, she was irritated by its lack of style and balance. She wrote to Christiana Jane "As for the Australian it has evidently lent itself to a Party and can no longer assume to itself the title of *"independent"*. I firmly believe what I told you in my last that William Wentworth has, or will, entirely withdraw himself as Editor of that journal" (Letters, October 16 1825). A month later she added: "William Wentworth lives in good style and entertains elegantly: you who know the intense interest with which I regard all that concerns the rising fortune of this young man. You will I am sure be glad to hear such a

FIGURE 72   Portrait of Christiana Brooks by Augustus Earle, 1825
              NATIONAL GALLERY OF VICTORIA

favourable report of him" (Letter from Denham Court to Christiana Jane, November 1825).[3]

Before bringing his family to settle in New South Wales, Richard had already acquired a great deal of property through lending money to well-to-do citizens, as well as officers of the regiment, who needed funds to pay their gambling debts: "With the craze for gambling, Brooks was soon in possession of several horses offered as security by the officers. These were still a luxury item in the colony" (Maher, 2016: 101–2). He also owned Denham Court, the surrounding acres being some of the richest pastoral land in the colony. He had got both his city house and Denham Court from the drunken Judge Advocate Richard Atkins in settlement of a debt.

Richard was appalled on arrival in Sydney to find that the lease he had pegged out in Farm Cove as the base for his trading business, had been taken by

___

3   In the copies she made of her letter Christiana used initials instead of full names. Where I know the names of those she addresses or writes about I have inserted the full name.

Macquarie to form part of the Domain parkland, parkland I now walk through every day. Macquarie granted him in its place an equivalent piece of land at Cockle Bay.[4] From there he set up his business ferrying food from Parramatta, Liverpool and the Hunter to city markets, as well as cedar from the Illawarra. Macquarie had earlier appointed Richard to the court of civil jurisdiction, as one of two men to support and advise the judge advocate, and had further approved him travelling to India to buy further cattle for his expanding herds. Richard also had the task of setting up better trading terms in India than had previously applied.

During the first decade of the family's life in Sydney, Richard had the house at Denham Court built, and the family moved there. It was, and still is, an elegant dwelling, fit to be a destination for the colony's elite—for parties and for staying over to recuperate from the demands of colonial life in the city. The letters and journals that survive were mostly written at Denham Court from 1825 to 1827. By then the Macquaries had long since left as a result of the Bigge Inquiry, which had found Governor Macquarie guilty of too much benevolence toward the ex-convicts and their children. In his place Thomas Brisbane had been appointed, a man not so much interested in governing the colony as studying the southern skies.

Macquarie and Richard Brooks did not always see eye-to-eye, since Richard was anxious not to take sides between the Exclusives and the Emancipists. The Exclusives, the self-appointed aristocrats of the colony, wanted no rights given to ex-convicts or their children. The Emancipists, supporters of the ex-convicts and their children, wanted them to have the right to full citizenship. Like William Wentworth, Christiana was an ardent supporter of Emancipists.

Christiana had her portrait painted by Augustus Earle in 1825. Earle had been shipwrecked off the north coast of the Australian continent and was raising money for his return home through his portrait painting. Christiana was 50 at the time and was rather proud of her lack of wrinkles. She was pleased with her cap, which she thought becoming. Such caps were worn by conservative older or married women and were made of fine linen with a pleated or gathered caul at the back to cover the hair, and a narrow brim at the front that widened to cover the ears and to tie under the chin.

When others commented she should not have worn her glasses for the portrait, she explained that she wanted to be recognised as "Old Mrs Brooks", the title she acquired when her son's first son was born.

> Mr. Earle has been at the portraits for the last week and has succeeded in making a very excellent likeness of Mr. Piper, but Mrs. Piper's I am

---

4   Now known as Darling Harbour

told is quite a youthful picture, without a cap, and in full dress. I own I prefer my homely attire with "Spectacles on nose" etc. more in character as the Mother, Grandmother and old Mrs. B., the two last titles Mrs. Piper cannot boast, altho I suppose she is not very many years younger than myself. (Letter Denham Court to Miss M.S., 27 September 1825)

Her description of herself as the homely grandmother with cap and glasses belies her active engagement in political affairs. She was a critical commentator as well as a dynamic mother, grandmother and friend. Her closest friends were not in any way ordinary people—William Wentworth, the Pipers, and later Mrs Abell, are quite extraordinary people. She was scathing about women who suffered from nerves or hysteria of any kind. As she wrote to her daughters, in relation to Christiana Jane's forthcoming lying in:

> Your Account of H.W. as a Midwife pleases me. I have a great prejudice against women functioning in that profession because I think they are always Rash and easily frightened when there is any degree of danger but as it has pleased God to place my Dear Child in a situation where she can be content with such attendance as the Settlement affords, I think she is fortunate in meeting with a Woman so skillful as H.W. (letter to daughters, 8 July 1826)

That appeal to God's providence was integral to the philosophy of the times. Just as the men appealed to providence to keep them safe on their dangerous ocean voyages, or at war, Christiana appealed to providence at times of childbirth when both mothers and their babies faced the possibility of death. At the same time, the fashionable life she had left behind in London, and its reproduction in the colony, was of intense interest to her.

A newspaper report of a party, hosted by Sir John Jamison, son of the detested surgeon, Thomas Jamison, who had caused Richard so much grief on the *Atlas* journey, gives a vivid glimpse of the fashionable elite of Sydney in 1824. The Cox family and the Brooks family were there, as was John Piper Jnr, most likely the son of Margaret Eddington, and the Miss MacKenzies, one of whom was to become Christiana's daughter-in-law:

The Fashionable World

The Ball and Supper, given by Sir John Jamison on the evening of Thursday last, was of the most fascinating and splendid description. The ballroom was fancifully fitted-up for the occasion. The Company flocked in from 8 to 9: the carriages were rolling rapidly down our streets between those hours. Captain Piper, with his usual zeal in these cases, had his own Band in attendance upon the noble Host. Dancing, consisting of country dances, quadrilles, and Spanish waltzes, presently commenced, and was maintained with the utmost animation till midnight, when the Guests were ushered in to the supper-room, which was entitled to the palm for superior taste in the disposition of the various arrangements that were most happily executed. All the rare and choice delicacies that Australia possesses, whether natural or imported, decorated the festive board, which groaned beneath the weight of excessive luxuriance: upwards of 170 sat down to supper. The rooms were elegantly festooned, and exhibited one refulgent blaze. About one in the morning, the ball-room was re-invested by this concentration of beauty, rank, and fashion; from whence a final retreat did not take place till Sol began to eclipse the twinkling orbs of night, and thus remind the gallant remnant it was time to retire in quest of that transient repose which the imposing scene was calculated to obstruct. Among the personages present, were distinguished His Honor the Chief Justice, and Lady; Captain Coe, H.M.S. Tees, and Lady; His Honor the late Judge Advocate, Lady, and two Miss Wyldes; the Attorney General; the Surveyor General; the Colonial Treasurer, and Lady, and the interesting Mrs. Abell; the Naval Officer, Lady, and Mr Piper, Jun.; A.K. McKenzie, Esq. Lady, and two Miss McKenzies; the Commissioner of Requests, and Family; the Commissariat Officers and their Ladies; John Blaxland, Esq. Lady, and Family; William Cox, Esq. and Lady, of Clarendon; William Cox, Jun. Esq. and Lady, of Hornbill; Capt. and Miss Brabyn; Richard Brooks, Esq. and the two Miss Brooks, of Denham Court; A. Bell, Esq. Lady, and two Miss Bells, of Richmond; James Norton, Esq. and Lady; &c. &c. &c. The whole of the Officers of the three Regiments, now doing duty in Garrison; Major Bates, Royal Artillery; as well as the Officers of H.M. ship Tees, were among the happy group of fashionables that were invited from all parts of the country to this elegant banquet. (*The Sydney Gazette and New South Wales Advertiser,* Thursday 1 July 1824: 2)

A notable presence, even to the journalist, was the "interesting Mrs Abell". She was the daughter of the new Colonial Treasurer, William Balcombe, who had come to the colony earlier that year. Mrs Abell was born Betsy Balcombe. She grew up on the island of St Helena, where Napoleon was confined in the guest quarters of her family's house. Betsy, as a precocious little girl, became, in the two years of his residence with her family, Napoleon's primary annoyer and intimate friend. Napoleon won the affection not only of Betsy; the whole family grew to love him, and they supported him in ways that brought about their undoing. They were banished to England when it was found they had posted letters for him, in order to help him organise his finances.

In England the Balcombes had no source of income (Abell, 1844; Keneally, 2015). Things grew worse for Betsy when she married the scoundrel, Mr Abell, who vanished soon after their child was born, leaving her penniless. Her journal about the years with Napoleon, written some years later, was her only source of independent income (Abell, 1844). When her father was offered a post in New South Wales as Colonial Treasurer, she decided to accompany him. Like other treasurers before him, including William Cox, William Balcombe did not manage the finances well, having no training and no clear instructions from government.

Soon after they arrived in the colony Betsy was appointed to the Committee under the auspices of Governor Brisbane's wife, which was responsible for training young orphan girls to become servants. Christiana too was on that committee. She was delighted by Mrs Abell though she knew there were many, including her daughter Christiana Jane, who disapproved of her. The young Edward Eyre, who was later to become a well-known explorer, wrote of her in 1833: "Mrs Abell was in the prime of life, regular and pretty in features, commanding in form a good figure – stylish in her dress and having a strange mixture of high polish and dash in her manner which was very captivating. She had beautiful hair, a rich nut brown shot with gold in unusual fashion and of an extraordinary length" (cited in Hackett 2006: 8). Christiana was equally captivated even though Mrs Abell was careless of some of the social morés that Christiana and her daughters felt bound by.

Christiana observed that her daughters would fail miserably if they tried to imitate her, yet she could not resist her. She wrote to a friend:

Altho I do not deny that there might be great truth in what you have heard of her, we are expecting Mrs Abell to pay Denham Court a visit. She has been very unwell lately and a change of air is thought advisable. I fear she will find a Country Life a very dull one after the first week. I have written to her to say I am under an engagement to go to I— upon the birth of my Grandson but as I shall be absent only a few days and as the Girls will take every care of her during my short absence I beg she will come and try the effects of a change of air as soon as she is allowed to travel. I expect to find in her a very cheerful companion for she reads and recites beautifully, can tell you the contents of any books she has read, acts scenes in any play she has seen performed, sings sweetly, plays on the Piano, Flute and Flugelet prettily and says and does everything in good taste, yet with

FIGURE 73   Betsy Abell, 1826
             DRAWING BY JODY THOMSON, 2017

all this she is not exactly such a companion as I would choose to have my family long with, for she can and does *swear*, is a free thinker and a free speaker and in short uses more freedom on many points that I can't wish my daughters to Copy. (Letter from Denham Court to Mrs C., July 1826)

Christiana yearned for good conversations, and she experienced a kind of horrified amusement at the flamboyance that she found in Mrs Abell, as well as in William Wentworth and in John Piper. She was later full of praise for Governor Darling's wife when she found her to be a good conversationalist:

I see by your letter that you heard of our dashing entry into Parramatta last week. Our visit to Government House was very satisfactory, we were very politely received by Mrs Darling who is a *sensible*, well bred woman, and very accomplished. Her conversation is easy and pleasant, her subjects well chosen and her manner animated, in short she has what I so much admire and what is so seldom to be met with because so little attended to in the education of Girls "*a talent for conversation*", but you will wonder how I could find this out in a *morning visit*. You must know the length of it. I dare say I sat an hour, but really one topic glided on after another so easily I could find no time to rise and make my parting compliments and yet we did not touch upon the weather, scandal or fashion and I left her considerably better than I found her for she is not *quite free* of the fine lady like complaint of the *Nerves*, for which as everybody knows a little cheerful company is the best remedy for want of which she does not like Parramatta and has changed her intentions of being confined there. She goes to Sydney next week. I am happy to tell you she intends patronizing the Concerts next season, and she says we, *the Ladies*, should make a point of forming a strong party and encouraging such a rational entertainment. You know this has always been my opinion. Another topic on which we touched was the School of Industry. I was tolerably free in my opinion of this institution. Mrs Darling admits she had no idea of the sort of people she would have to come in contact with. I suggested that idea I had formed of adding the present subscription towards forming an auxiliary branch of the Orphan institutions and she seemed to think my idea worthy of consideration. (Letter from Denham Court to Miss McKenzie c. Sept/Oct 1826)

Political Commentary

In her journal Christiana documented the decisions being made under Governor Brisbane (governor 1821–1825) and then under Governor Darling (1825–1831). Some excerpts from her journal offer a vivid insight into the social concerns of the growing colony:

1825 *June* 29 An investigation into the State of the Sydney Gaol has lately been called for at the instance of the Grand Jury and it is to be hoped that some prompt measures will be adopted for the relief of those confined in this dirty, crowded, illconducted Prison – a vessel was some time ago bought by Government to be fitted as a Hulk in which it was projected that those under sentence from any of the Penal Settlements should be confined, but this project like all others of the present *penurious* administration is so slow in its operation that many are fallen for actual want of air, proper food, cloathing and bedding – great blame seems to

rest in the medical attendant, and much of the neglect and want of necessary comfort is attributed to him – but the eyes of the Public are beginning to be opened, and much credit is due to the representation of the
Grand Jury of Sydney for having brought this subject to an investigation.

July 2 1825 The new Superintendent of Police seems a most unbiased
character: Pity that such should ever be corrupted: His justice is dealt
to free and bond with an evenhandedness that is very admirable. – The
Military Officers who have generally considered themselves as privileged
persons do not like being *seriously* reprimanded in the morning by the
Police Magistrate for every trifling breach of the peace which *Gentlemen
of their profession* may commit in a frolic overnight.

July 22 1825 ... for upwards of twenty years the Sydney Gazette was the
only publication of N. S. Wales. In the month of August last the Australian
was first published – In May the Express made its appearance: – and in a
few months we are led to believe that a new paper entitled the Monitor
will make its appearance – Nor should I forget the Stage Coaches which
multiply even more rapidly. Two years ago it was believed that *one* coach
to Parramatta each day could not succeed but the proof how erroneous
was that belief will be found decisive, when it is added that four stage
coaches now run between Parramatta and Sydney daily and one from
Sydney to Liverpool every other morning which returns on the intermediate day. –

We feel the want of an Inland Post which could not be established
without the assistance of Government, but if a Mounted Patrol is established the postage paid for letters would in a certain degree assist in
paying the expense as a Letter Bag could by that means be easily and
expeditiously forwarded from one station to the other. –

Aug 4 1825 The accounts from Norfolk Island are of the most favourable nature – the Island is overspread with fine grass there is a great
abundance of (all) kinds of fruit trees:– the coffee plant flourishes in
luxuriance some of them bearing four or five bushels of coffee – The
various animals left in the Island when it was evacuated in 1810 have
increased to a wonderful extent and Pigs, Goats and Pigeons are very
numerous. – Captain Turton of the Regt. appears to be well chosen as
Commandant for this renovated Penal Settlement, at which as I understand no free settlers are to be allowed to fix their habitation; nor is any
Boat to be permitted to land anything; but if communication must of

necessity be held with ships in distress for water etc. it is to be carried in by the boats of the Commandant, thus it will be really a *place of punishment*, and if the plan is followed with that liberality which is requisite as to the number of military etc. I have no doubt it will answer the desired effect.

Aug 18 1825 I am happy to see from this day's paper that the Hulk or floating prison is fitted for the reception of Prisoners and those destined for Penal Settlements of Port Macquarie, Morten Bay or Norfolk Island, all to be removed forthwith on board the said Hulk—

Aug 20 1825 We have thank heaven no longer cause to dread the iniquitous Decisions of a petulant *school boy* Judge – those days are gone by, and a new and enlightened era commenced, when the Chief Justice Stephen took his seat on the Bench of the Courts in this Colony. He is a man possessed of all the energies of a powerful mind, together with an upright unbiased judgment, and the Colonists seem fully sensible of the blessing which they enjoy in having such a man for their judge.–

Aug 22 1825 It is reported from good authority that the sum of *fifty thousand pounds* in Colonial silver coinage, of sterling value is in the passage to these Colonies for circulation – this is to do away the Dollar system, but it is something like "shutting the stable door when the steed is stolen" the evil of the system has ruined the merchant and another change will only perhaps crush a second who have risen upon the ruins of the first.

Sept 5 1825 It would be as well perhaps if a certain Revd. Divine would not meddle in things out of *time* and *place*

Sept 10 1825 The Bush Rangers at Hunters River are still continuing their depredations: the Constabulary in that part of the territory are even more defective than in the other settlements – query (!) would it not be more advisable to expend some further of the Colonial Revenue in an effective Police rather than squandering it away on Officers (of eight) and twelve hundred and two thousand a year – Let the Council merit the blessing of the Colonists by turning their attention to this subject.

Sept 30 1825 Jury Question:– What all the friends of the Emancipists have vainly endeavoured to bring about is likely to be established by the folly of their enemies – a late Presentment [ ] a Grand Jury fully confirms that

honour and honesty does not always inhabit the breast of the *rich* and
free: that it is not exclusively confined to one class of persons: there is a
strong rumour that there is an intent on the part of the Council to pass
an Act which will put emancipists in possession of all the rights and privileges of full Citizens.

The Exclusives, who Christiana observed were not reliably honest or honourable, had a lot of influence in British Government circles, and had engineered
both Macquarie's and Brisbane's demise, with the accusation that they were
too generous to the emancipated convicts. The conflict between the Exclusives
and the Emancipists came to a head over the arrangements for Governor Brisbane's departure. The Exclusives took control of the events to mark his departure, insisting that only Exclusives could participate, or be involved in deciding
the words spoken to mark his departure. Christiana wrote:

> *Oct* 13 1825 A meeting is called for on the 27th inst. For the purpose of
> taking into consideration the propriety of addressing His Excellency Sir
> Thos. Brisbane on his approaching departure – he may safely be compli-
> mented on his gentlemanly conduct, and on his impartial performance
> of an arduous duty in doing strict justice to every individual, and in keep-
> ing himself unbiased by party principles. I was therefore astonished to
> find any opposition should have been made, to an almost necessary com-
> pliment in the removal of a Governor. Sir Thos. it is true has evinced him-
> self more a man of *science* than a man of business but that was known
> when he was appointed, and therefore, if any blame is due, it is due to
> those who appointed him to a Government never yet filled to content the
> subject or to yield satisfaction to the Administrator ...

Christiana was scathing about the Exclusives and about the grief they gave to
both Macquarie and Brisbane:

> *Oct* 13 1825 A Governor when he comes here should make up his mind
> to bear every degree of contumacy[5] and his Majesty's Ministers at Home
> should grant all due allowance for the misrepresentation of a people
> composed of an incongruous mixture of bond and free, *the latter* by
> far the most discontented troublesome and factious a class very justly
> defined by Governor Macquarie "as possessing base and restless spirits,
> who have ever eaten the bread of unthankfulness and who having found

---

5   Obstinate and wilful rebelliousness or resistance to authority; insubordination; disobedience.

themselves unfit subjects for his Majesty's Navy and Army, or who from their embarrassed circumstances, have taken an asylum here to avoid their creditors"...(*emphasis added*)

The dinners and speeches to mark his departure multiplied, as the Exclusives and the Emancipists vied to outdo each other and to exclude each other. Christiana sarcastically remarked in her journal "If good dinners have a tendency to make people grow *fat* and *strong* the inhabitants of Sydney should become *giants*" (Journal November 20 1825). Eventually it was all over and Christiana recorded in her journal "His Excellency Thos. Brisbane and family sailed in the morning of the first inst., exactly on the very day four years on which Sir Thos. assumed the reins of Government General Macquarie having formally retired from the duties of this Government Dec 1st 1821" (6 December 1825).

Christiana was enthusiastic if wary about the new Governor, and optimistic about what he might bring to the colony:

> *Dec 6* 1825 ... On the 14th inst. I visited Sydney and did not return till the 21 – as this was in itself a great event so great events might be expected, and General Darling's arrival on the 17th may be recorded as an era of some importance to the Colony of N. S. Wales. His Excellency was sworn in on 19th, and on the 20th he landed publicly, and was attended with all due honours. – We hope great things from the administration of General Darling who is represented as being firm and impartial, just and determined; a character which *if he merits it* is just what we need in a Governor. (*emphasis added*)
>
> There are many changes about to take place not only in this Colony, but in our sister settlement of Van Diemen's Land. This is very encouraging to us as it shows we are increasing in importance as "a promising appendage to the British Territories in the East" ...

Christiana shared the longing people had for the colony to be regarded as a legitimate and valued part of the British Empire. Her desire of the Governor was that he would further their development in such a way that they could claim that legitimacy:

> *Jany* 20 1826 Nothing can promise more favourably than the energy with which General Darling has commenced his Government — that he is a man of *business* we have every reason to believe, and that he will cause "everyman to do his duty" we may be allowed to anticipate from the prompt government orders for the re-organisation of the several Public Departments.

Jan 12 1826 There is to be a Public meeting of the inhabitants of N. S. Wales in Sydney this day convened for the purpose of congratulating His Excellency General Darling on his safe arrival on these shores, and upon his assuming the Government etc. etc. We may congratulate the Colonists generally on improvements likely to arise from the subdivision of Govt. labour [ ] The life of poor Major Goulburn was the sacrifice to an accumulation of duties, altogether inconsistent one with the other, and while his life was endangered, it was impossible that with all his exertion of body and mind he could give satisfaction. A Civil Engineer now succeeds to some of his employments and when it is considered that the Public Works – Prisoners – the Roadmaking and Clearing gangs – the Dockyard – and Telegraph are all in this Department, enough employment will be found to occupy the time of two officers instead of one.

Very soon, some unhappiness with Darling began to emerge, though Christiana maintained her support for him in his struggle to bring social order and stability to the colony, in what she saw as a thankless job:

Jan 26 1826 I don't know how some of our great men will relish the late General Orders, but I imagine many of them will be quite unprepared to comply with them. [he is to sign off on everything and not leave it to his heads of departments] I confess for my own part I would prefer one Tyrant if needs must, to half a score petty usurpers.

March 1826 The Governor's orders appear to be issued without respect to persons, the highest in office, or the meanest subordinate appear to be equally called upon, equally required to do their duty. I for my part admire the prompt measures of General Darling, he requires of every man to do his duty as it is pointed out to him: *he* does not *need* any person to tell him what is necessary but appears to be a man of business equally forward in arranging and carrying into execution —

The Darlings were hospitable, and Christiana enjoyed the Balls they held. She wrote to a friend, an account of one such Ball, at which William Wentworth was her companion. She also touches on her grief at the fact that the Pipers were being forced to sell the beautiful Piper Pavillion at Point Piper, and to move inland to Bathurst to a much more frugal existence. Piper had fallen out of favour, and many of her friends from earlier years were gone:

Tis not to be told what gaity and splendour have dazzled my eyes during the last five days that I have been an *absentee* from Denham Court – but I shall endeavour to give you some description.

We set off on Monday morning for the metropolis in a little *Chink* of sunshine which lasted us about seven miles when we were again over-taken by torrents of rain, through which, and some of the worst road I ever travelled, we got in safety to our journeys end by 3 o'clock in the after-noon, and were as kindly received by our esteemed friends at Piper Pavil-lion as ever. On Tuesday altho a very wet morning we paid all our *grand* visits in Sydney and found all the ladies at home. I was much pleased with many of the newcomers and think the society of Sydney very much improved: We could do no shopping on such a wet day and very fortu-nately Jessie and I had our ball dresses all in preparation, I only wanted a small cap and very fortunately succeeded in getting a very becoming one.

On Wednesday we staid at home all the morning. Dined at the B—dressed also there, and went from thence to Government house at nine o'clock. Much company were assembled when we arrived, and in an hour the rooms were crowded, about *ten* dancing commenced and was kept up with great spirit until about two o'clock, and as we did not *sit down* to supper it may be said to have continued without intermission. To say all the *beauty* and *fashion* of the colony was there would be only *common-place* language, so much of the latter was never seen in N.S. Wales before, but I have seen prettier, *many* prettier faces in that room before, and could not but regret that so many of them were absent: in short I seem a stranger among the throng of new faces altho as I had my *dear friend* for a companion the whole evening I was highly amused by his eccentricities.

I was much pleased with the Governor, and Mrs. Darling. They were extremely attentive to the whole company and I do not believe there was a person present who did not in some way receive some marks of their attention. The D—s, both brothers, seemed to be present everywhere, and everything was arranged to give universal satisfaction. The dancing room was fitted up with great taste and it is certainly the *only* room in the colony in which a large party can dance with comfort. I was told by Mrs. Darling that she had the estimate of the company made out by the A.D.C. and that there were present 26 unmarried ladies and sixty unmarried gentlemen but the proportion of married ladies were nearly two to one and they were by the bye by far the handsomest portion and I did not see a prettier woman than Mrs. N. Mrs. A— was not there. Some of the ladies were splendidly attired and all of them well dressed. I do not think I ever took so much notice of dress before, but my beau was a great *quiz* and called my attention to what would perhaps have escaped my observation, but he acknowledged, and I heard it observed in other quarters, that the Miss G—s wore the most becoming Ball dresses sported on this occasion. The bride had also white satin with gauze and flower trimming and is a pretty interesting looking young woman.

The supper tables were laid out with great taste but as I told you before we did not sit down, to the great discomfiture of N.G. and N.C. and some others, who did not admire giving up *hip hip pip* and three times three, the abolition of which custom is one improvement of these enlightened days. Early hours is also another and I heard Mrs. Darling tell Capt. Piper that altho she has given an hour or two latitude on the auspicious occasion, yet they were not to presume on it at a future time… From all that I have said my dear girls you may believe we were much pleased with our entertainment, and I was happy to see so many country folks in town, altho *none* of our neighbours were at the party.

Carriages and four were rattling about in all directions and notwithstanding the unfavourable state of the weather I am persuaded more money has been spent in Sydney during the last ten days than takes place in three months at any other season. For my own part altho I had only Friday to do my shopping, I returned home minus a considerable sum. I hope all the commissions I have executed *for you*, and which will go down by the Packett this week, will please you as well as the last: Mrs. M— had made a purchase of the shirts for you before I arrived or I believe I should not have given 12/– for such coarse ones. They are however strong and well made.

We had two rather gay party's at the Piper Pavillion but I could not enjoy them. On the evening of my leaving the Pavillion I walked out to indulge a melancholy regret like parting from a dear friend with little hope of ever seeing them again.

I found however that indulgence, as it always does, only fostered *weakness* and that I should make a fool of myself, so I determined not to enter the house again as I intended and take leave of each room, but stay on the outside and busy myself in giving directions how to place the load of baggage we had accumulated in a few days sojourn: thus by making myself *busy* I had when Mrs. Piper joined me on the steps at the door, become tolerably composed and as she was much taken up about a little fracas that had taken place among the servants that morning I believe my dejection passed unnoticed and by the time we got to town I was quite myself again.

> We got home by dark last evening: Papa left town on Thursday and I
> am happy to say seems quite well again: I wish I could say the same of
> Honoria but I assure you that she is very far from well. (Letter from Den-
> ham Court to Mrs B.N., 1 May 1826)

Christiana retained her support for Governor Darling, and refused to pass
judgement when others were outraged at his actions in the Sudds affair—in
which his excessively cruel punishment of a soldier led to his death. She was
nevertheless quick to disagree with him when he restricted freedom of the
press by taxing newspapers—a decision he reversed a month later, in the face
of public outrage. Of his lack of popularity, she wrote:

> That Governor Darling is unpopular as a Governor is very true, but it is
> equally true that all the Governors who have gone before were as unpop-
> ular, and with less reason, for although Governor Darling has neither the
> follies of Governor Macquarie or of Sir Thomas Brisbane, he is as obsti-
> nate as the former, and not so easy and mild as the latter, and moreover
> he *makes every man do his duty* and I should not hesitate to take a wager
> that Governor Darling will remain as Governor for the next *Eleven Years.*
> (Journal, 26 December 1826)

Christiana was also actively supportive of William Wentworth's attempts to
establish trial by jury and self-government for the colony:

> *Jan* 26 1827 On the 39th anniversary of the foundation of the Colony a
> Public Meeting of all the free inhabitants of N.S. Wales was convened by
> the Sheriff for the purpose of petitioning the King and both Houses of
> Parliament, that Trial by Jury, and a House of Assembly be allowed in
> the Colony; the meeting was numerously and respectably attended, "The
> Hero of Australia" (one of her sons) spoke at great length, and as a test
> that this speech was the voice of the popular feeling, the "loud cheers"
> and "great applause" which it excited bears ample testimony, as well as
> that those who are opposed to an application for those indulgencies,
> were universally *absentees*: fully aware, I imagine, that all they could
> advance would not gain one proselyte in that Assembly – I believe that
> nothing is more likely to promote Emigration to this Colony than being
> in possession of all the *rights* of *British Subjects.*

She documented the changes she observed in Sydney over the decade since
their arrival, seeing it turn into a thriving metropolis:

March 3 1827 [the bank is redeeming itself] This place which 10 or 12 years ago was a quiet country looking, thoroughly English looking Town, is now a crowded bustling *business like* City – the shops are well supplied generally speaking, and tho the price of Leghorn Bonnets are very high nothing wearable at less than *six guineas*! The price of Tea is very low – good black Tea being only about *one shilling* per pound by the chest.

Family and Friends

A major aspect of Christiana's life that is largely omitted from her journals, concerns her children, their marriages and the birth of her grandchildren. On 3 August 1820, at St Phillips Church, Christiana Jane married Thomas Valentine Blomfield. Christiana Jane and Thomas Valentine spent their honeymoon at Denham Court, before moving to their farm, Dagworth, near Newcastle, then a long way from Denham Court—a day's coach journey followed by an ocean voyage up the east coast, and then inland by river.

In September 1825, Christiana's son Henry married Margaret McKenzie at St James Church in Sydney. After spending their honeymoon at Denham Court, they moved to Littleham farm, which Richard had given to Henry. Christiana had long been impatient with Henry, who lacked energy and drive and showed little interest in his father's business. She had great hopes that his marriage would be good for him. During the honeymoon she wrote to her dear friend Mary Ann Piper at Point Piper. Mary Ann often hosted Brooks family members on their visits to the city:

> My dear Mrs. Piper
> I desire to return you my very best acknowledgments for all the kind attentions you and Capt Piper have shown to my daughters during their protracted visit at Piper Pavillion. They returned home quite enraptured with the gaity and kindness they had partaken in, and the *French paroxysm* seems as strong now as the *Russian Mania* a few months ago. It is lucky these fascinating foreigners do not make longer sojourns among our *Australian fair*, or we should not have a *sound heart* or a *steady head* left among us ...
>
> Henry and his wife left us this morning, they pay a short visit to C— and then you will have a visit from them in Sydney. We have had several of our country neighbours to see us and we have made some calls, but we spent our time so happily during the last fortnight that it has seemed like a *Honey Moon* to us all.

... I think I see a great change in Henry already he is quite a new creature: figure him sitting for hours writing Music: a great improvement on the old custom of lolling on the sofa yawning his jaws asunder. He says of himself he is grown so steady he shall begin soon to talk of Baby and other small matters. (Letter from Denham Court to Mrs. Piper, 20 September 1825)

During Margaret's pregnancy, Margaret and Henry experienced an attack by bushrangers. Christiana wrote to Christiana Jane:

My dearest Christiana

Fearing you may hear an exaggerated account of Henry's Robbery which God knows is bad enough in all the circumstances I write you a few hasty lines to say the Australian and Gazette of this week contains all the particulars, and although *Howe* may have stretched a few points yet he has not violated the truth in any material circumstance – some of the events you are however yet unacquainted with, in which your Sister Charlotte figured I assure you as a perfect *heroine*, and she now says she would sooner see six bushrangers in a house than one snake. Poor child she knows that *death* may be the consequence of the one but she is not aware that *worse than death* might be the event of the former. We cannot be too thankful that no violence was offered to either of the females, but I shall not easily forget the alarm I felt when they came over from Littleham the following morning, and the looks of *hopeless despair* which Henry's visage had assumed. I do not think we can estimate his loss as less than 300 pounds for every drawer and box was broken open, and anything of any value pillaged by those miscreants. Can you conceive anything more horrific than his agony when hustled by four or five armed ruffians into an inner room, and hearing his wife jump screaming out of the window. You know Henry would never keep firearms in his house: and it is greatly to be feared some of his own servants are concerned in it who have represented that being a newly married couple much booty was to be expected of Plate, Linen, wearing apparel &c &c. I have time my dearest for no more at present but will write you a longer letter next week. Farewell. (Letter Denham Court to Christiana Jane, 7 January 1826)

The New Year celebrations that had been held at Denham Court were the topic of Christiana's subsequent letter to Christiana Jane written on the same day. The fascinating Mrs Abell was present at the celebrations:

My Dear Christiana

Many happy new years to you and yours my dearest and may you and your kind Mr Blomfield live to be old Mr. & Mrs. Blomfield for many years.

Our festivities commenced on the 2nd inst. and a party of sixteen from Sydney were joined here by our Country Neighbours, and we sat down to dinner forty in number, besides about fifteen servants in the kitchen. On Tuesday nearly the same party assembled at G— where we also stayed all night: on Wednesday about two and twenty were entertained by Mr. R— of S.V. and on Thursday we had a picnic on Mount Brooks: from which place we returned here to a Rural Syllabub on the lawn: and notwithstanding all previous fatigue a quadrille of sixteen was supported with great glee until midnight. On Friday our kind friends left us for Sydney, and today we are to endeavour to settle ourselves to our usual orderly habits.

I must not forget to tell you that the Piper band were in attendance at all these gay parties, and much enlivened our festivities.

You will perhaps be surprised to hear that Mrs. Abell was of our party and I can assure you tended not a little to grace our rural Balls. I quite agree with you in thinking she is a dangerous companion for young girls. Her manner is too free and *fascinating* for *imitation* – What is delightful in her would disgust in an awkward copy – but she is so good tempered, so accommodating, and so frank that you cannot resist the fascination of her manner ... Altho I do not deny that there may be great truth in what you have heard of her. For the names of the rest of our party I shall refer you to your sisters' letters. They all write to you by this opportunity, and will give you more fully all particulars of our *Rout*. Believe that I am ever my dearest Christiana, Yours affectionately (Letter from Denham court to Christiana Jane, 7 January 1826)

Some weeks later she wrote again of the details of Margaret's pregnancy and its management, and of the fact that her father and sister were on their way to visit her:

Your father and Maria set off tomorrow my dearest for H— R— and I therefore write you only a few lines as Maria can so much better tell you all that has occurred with us since I wrote you last. I am most amused at Maria who says she is sure a sea voyage will do her good but that she "will not be seasick".

I envy the meeting between you and your sister, but I can assure you my dear Christiana we make a great sacrifice in sparing her to you, for she leaves poor Jane and I in very low spirits. We expect Margaret will return with the carriage and it is now settled that she is to divide her time between her two fathers' houses until her confinement which Mr. McKenzie insists shall take place at the B— and as I am a great advocate for young women with their first child having the best advice and attendance I perfectly accord in wishing – it is said her mother expects to be confined with Mr. McKenzie's child in about a month and therefore the same nurse and the same preparations will in a great measure serve both. (Letter from Denham Court to Christiana Jane, 30 January 1826)

Christiana became emotionally involved in Margaret's pregnancy and in her hope for a Brooks heir. She chides herself for thinking that having a male heir matters:

I have given up all idea of going to Town again untill I hear of Margaret's confinement, when I certainly shall go to see the *Heir of Brooks* and what if after all it should not be an *Heir*: I shall be horridly provoked I can tell you for I have set my mind on it. Yet of all people in the world I have least reason to care about such things for I would not exchange my *six* daughters for *six* sons, neither do I ever wish I had one less daughter altho I may have wished for another son. Papa has grown horribly *stingy* lately, this purchase of land takes all the ready money as he assures me but I can tell him he must draw his Purse string soon and it will be something extraordinary if I do not see a little more of Sydney ere it be long. (Letter from Denham Court to daughters, 26 July 1826)

Margaret's son was born after a very difficult delivery. Christiana was by her side and wrote home to the family:

After a week of the most anxious alarm I am, I think, enabled to say today that dear Margaret is decidedly better, she slept three hours from 12 till 2 o'clock this morning, *and again from five till 7, and although she does not know any of us, she* appears more calm *and* composed this morning. On Saturday all day we expected every hour to be her last, for altho the Convulsions were not more violent than upon former days they were of longer continuance and she is daily weaker and less able to bear them. We are all nearly worn out with fatigue; poor Henry is the most attentive and the most anxious Nurse. Margaret is absolutely kept alive by nourishment which is administered every ten minutes and Henry does not leave the bedside for half an hour together and looks wretchedly. We have got a very good wet Nurse for the Child, a Soldiers wife in the 57th, a healthy, strong woman. Mrs B— who I saw this morning assures me she enjoyed herself very much at D.C. last week. I shall be disappointed if you do not prevail on Mrs Abell to stay with you till I come home, and if all goes on well I hope to see you about this day week. Make my Love acceptable to all at D.C. and believe me my Dears. Yours Afftly (Letter from McKenzie household to family at Denham Court, 14 August 1826)

Shortly after Margaret's difficult delivery Mrs Piper's toddler died. Christiana had stayed with the Pipers to assist in Mary Ann's recovery from that birth. In her letter to Captain Piper she offered condolences and the advice that one must accept such loss as God's Will. More helpfully, she offered the Pipers the prospect of a holiday at Denham Court:

My Dear Sir,
You will not I am sure doubt the sympathy of myself and family for your and Dear Mrs Piper's Distress in the late melancholy loss of your dear little infant. I assure you I not only grieve with you on the loss you have sustained but I feel great sorrow for the death of *such a sweet promising Child – I trust this will find you both more reconciled to* the *Will* of *Him who* knoweth what *is* best for us, and as I am convinced change of scene will be of the utmost benefit to Mrs. Piper let me persuade you to bring her up here for a week or ten days, and Mr Brooks and the girls desire to assure Dear Mrs Piper they will do all in their power to amuse her mind. We have a spare room with two beds therefore bring as many of your children as maybe agreeable to you, as soon as you occupy it the better we shall be pleased, and with kind regards from all at Denham Court to Piper Pavillion, I beg you to believe that I am, my Dear Sir, ever Your Sincere Friend (Letter from Denham Court to Capt. Piper, 17 September 1826)

Her letter to Miss McKenzie, her daughter-in-law's sister, continues these reflections on death, and includes the fears for her daughter Mary who has been in poor health for some time:

Would you believe that under any circumstances I could be glad to hear of the death of a Child belonging to Capt. Piper *and* yet so great was my alarm yesterday upon receiving his letter with a *Black Seal* that it was a real relief to me when the letter was opened, to *find* it was *his Child* instead of my *Daughter for I had been impressed ever since your letter of the sixth with the* dread that all my fears for dear Mary were not at an end, and not hearing from Sydney for ten days my anxiety had arisen to a great height and I was quite incapable of opening the ominous Black Seal. Thank God however your intelligence of the dear invalid is much more favourable than it has been of late and I trust she will now continue to mend rapidly. If her recovery is only progressive, a few weeks must make a visible change, and when she is able to ride out, change of air and scene will benefit her more than Medicine. I feel truly sorry however for poor Mrs Piper's distress.

To have such a fine promising Child so suddenly taken off is a great affliction, tho God knows when I have been walking up and down your drawing room with your father on a later melancholy occasion I often thought how much less sorrow dear Mary's death would have occasioned if she had died in her infancy, than if now a disconsolate Husband, surviving friends and a helpless infant were left to bewail her loss – in fact I think we should never grieve at the death of an infant, if we consider from how much sorrow it is probably removed – a mother's feelings at the time may be *great* but they cannot be so *lasting* for an infant as for a Child that *for years* you have had pride and pleasure in...

I am glad to hear such a favourable account of the Baby's Nurse. I thought her a fine stout young woman but was not much prepossessed with her countenance. Is it not time something *should* be thought about giving him a name.

I think of sending Charlotte to Sydney with Capt. Piper if he brings Mrs Piper and the Children up to stay a week or ten days with us. She has so long promised to pay Mrs Abell a visit that the sooner it is over the better. I shall be obliged to you for any attentions you may be inclined to bestow on her and I hope Honoria will continue to see her daily while in Town. (Letter from Denham Court to Miss McKenzie *c.* Sept/Oct 1826)

Margaret's baby did not survive. Christiana wrote to Margaret's mother, Mrs McKenzie:

My Dear Mrs McKenzie,
We were much concerned this morning to hear of the death of your poor little Grandson. We are quite ignorant of the cause and of the duration of his illness, but if he has, as I suspect, died in convulsions I shall be satisfied that God has in his Mercy removed the dear Infant to save his Parents and friends much anxiety and sorrow. I, you know, have always been fearful that the dreadful alarm dear Margaret experienced in the early state of her pregnancy would fall upon the Infant, and that it might be subject to fits or wanting in some of its facultys. I trust his poor Mother will bear this affliction with fortitude and that her health may not be affected, I hope

she will now very soon be able to bear a journey hither, change of air and scene will have a tendency to strengthen both body and mind. Mrs Piper is so much better for her weeks sojourn at D.C. that I hope Capt. Piper will be in no haste to fetch her away. The children are delighted with their holiday and say if Papa and John and William and Alexander were here they would never wish to leave this place. As Mr. Brooks is going to attend the Quarter Sessions at Parramatta tomorrow he will probably have an opportunity of forwarding this to Sydney, With kindest love to dear Margaret and my poor Henry *"whose sorrows seem to have no end"* and with best regards to Mr McKenzie, in which all this family join, believe me my Dear Mrs McKenzie, Yours Very Sincerely

I feel such satisfaction that our dear little boy had been Christened, but we will have no more Richards or Henrys in the Brooks family. (Letter from Denham Court to Mrs McKenzie, 2 October 1826)

This postscript to the letter to Mrs McKenzie hints at a multitude of complex emotions. Christiana had been deeply sympathetic with Henry, yet it is around this time that she and Richard turned away from him. He did go on to produce more Richards and Henrys, but Christiana seemed little interested in them. Her emotional connection was with the children of her daughter Christiana Jane. The rural properties that Richard was going on acquiring were no longer automatically to go to Henry, but to each of the daughters.

Before I leave the topic of births deaths and marriages I should mention that her daughter Jane married into the Cox family:

April 18 1827 Married this day at Campbell Town by the Revd. Mr Raddall Edward Cox Esq. of Mulgoa, son of William Cox Esq. of Clarendon, to Jane Maria third daughter of Richd. Brooks Esq. of Denham Court.

And in 1828 Mary Honoria married a friend of Thomas Valentine's:

Married on 29 Jany. Lieut. W. Wilson of his Majesty's 4th Regt. to Mary Honoria Brooks daughter of R. Brooks Esq of Denham Court and on 8th Feby. embarked on board the Sovereign ... for Madras.

Race War

Finally, I want to turn to Christiana's observations of the race war that erupted during this period. Richard's cordial relations with the local people, observed on his arrival with his family, were continued into the subsequent years. Every year he held a celebratory feast for the local indigenous people around Denham Court. His overseers, the Neales, were respectful of the indigenous people, and spoke several of their languages. But the fact remained, Richard was one of the first, with the help of John and William Neale, and of his son Richard Brooks Jnr, to expand into indigenous land that had not previously been occupied by the newcomers.

Some of the men who were employed in the work in the outmost areas of the colony had no respect for the people whose land they had been moved on to. They stole women from them, for example, and claimed them as mistresses and servants, and had no hesitation in defending what they took to be their own rights. The local custodians of the land took up arms, no longer able to engage in the friendly hospitality they had been wont to offer. They fought fiercely for their land, their livelihood and the dignity that was increasingly being stolen from them. Just as in Tasmania, this led to a declaration by the Governor, of martial law. Indigenous people could now be shot or captured with impunity.

While Christiana partially understood and sympathised with the plight of the original custodians, she also had blind spots that were endemic to the *placetime* she was living in. She had come to love the land and had no concept of it as having been stolen. She wrote of the land in terms drought and rain and productivity, and also in terms of "improvement", that is of its transformation into the land she still missed:

> *July* 1 1825 There has never been a finer season than the present – our grain has all been in the ground a fortnight ago and the seasonable showers (not too heavy) which have fallen all during this month have been of infinite service to the Grass etc.—

> *July* 20 1825 The days of rain of Sunday will forward the Spring which is approaching – I think this winter has been colder than any we have had for the last three or four years but in another month the blossom will be out in the Peach and Almond trees and everything will appear gay and blooming. Pity it is that such a charming season of the year should give anything but pleasure, yet I grieve as the days grow longer and would willingly delay the return of Spring, for *warm* weather so soon follows, and warm weather deprives me of my faculties...

> *Sept 1825* I have been much pleased with the appearance of the country and my late visit to the Hawkesbury although I think there is less

alteration effected by the clearing parties in the vicinity of Richmond and Windsor than in other parts of the country during the last five years – at the period of my last excursion to that neighbourhood it was the most cleared and best cultivated part of the country – now almost all parts within forty miles of the capital are equally improved and you can scarcely travel in any direction five miles without being presented with a fine farm or a clear cultivated Estate —

April 26 1826 Ask them what they think of this weather, for during the last week it has been the most delightfully seasonable weather it is possible to conceive, not a cloud in the sky, and just cold enough to make walking pleasant, and a fire in the evening desirable ... some persons however I know will still find grievances – bad potatoes, bad milk, bad coals – and above all, bad servants; the latter *is an evil* – a tax on our enjoyment which we all feel. In short it takes time to reconcile us to many deprivations which we are obliged to submit to, and also to the bitter thought that we are separated by so many thousand miles, from friends very dear to us: some of us feel that it is *for ever!*

She was impatient for the original custodians of the land to similarly transform themselves into some semblance of Englishness, appealing to conservative notions of decency:

July 1825 I am happy to see our new Superintendent of Police at Sydney has adopted a measure which I have often wondered was not long ago, for decencys sake, found expedient – It is now ordered that the Constables take into custody any of the Black Natives who may be found in the Public Streets not *decently* cloathed – it is disgraceful to a town such as Sydney to meet the Natives of both sexes intirely naked which is frequently the case alth. the inhabitants are very liberal in giving them articles of apparel; which they sell upon the first opportunity for *Bull* or *Tobacco* – but if they are not allowed to appear in the town, but in some sort of Decent dress they will carefully treasure the bounty of the charitable, and no longer put modesty to the blush.

In 1826 the local custodians took up arms against the settlers at Lake George where Richard had substantial property. She explained their hostility, not in terms of the land being stolen, or even invaded, but as a response to bad behaviour of isolated individual convicts. This seemingly liberal idea blinded her to the truth of the situation—that the occupation of their land was depriving the people of life and livelihood:

May 12 1826 The Aboriginal Natives having assembled in unusual numbers in the County of Argyle in the neighbourhood of Lake George, and having evinced some hostility to the stock keepers of particular stations, the Govr. in his usual prompt manner has despatched a Detachment of the 40th and 57th Regts., with instructions to the Officers in Command to put themselves in communication with the Magistrates of that district. This hostility on the part of the Natives will I have no doubt be found, as it ever has been, to originate in outrages committed on them by the stock keepers, an ignorant and brutal race, who by their interference with the females of the aborigines provoke them to revenge. The Governor's Order upon this occasion is humane and liberal, promising equal justice to all. I doubt not the sight of soldiers will strike a panic into these poor simple creatures, and the Officer in Command is a man of experience, who will fully investigate the cause of their present hostility, and should he find that the stockmen and shepherds have committed any violence, or ill treated any of these inoffensive creatures, he will I earnestly hope, bring them forward that they may receive the punishment due to their cruelty.

Her sympathy for the original custodians was also mediated by her perception of them as not fully human; rather, they were poor, simple, inoffensive creatures. What she went on to say reveals a breathtaking blindness that goes hand in hand with the newcomers' claim to ownership:

May 17 1826 By advices from the *Seat of Warfare* we learn that the Natives have for the present quietly dispersed, the *sight of the Red Coats* having had all the effect that could be desired, but a month's sojourn in the neighbourhood of Lake George will tend to insure safety to our Flocks and Herds in that part of the Country – and as the Army have very good Headquarters at T Park and as Kangaroo Hunting, and Parrot shooting are pleasant amusements in that *cold* country, we may expect to see our friends return clad in kangaroo skins – it may be called "Cold Country" when it is added that snow was two feet deep at Lake George on the 9th inst.

It seems the food and clothing of the "poor simple creatures" could be taken for the sake of light-hearted sport of an English kind. And so the war continued, and the attacks by the rightful owners were no longer understandable, other than as evil:

Sept 18 1826 The Aboriginal Natives at both Hunters River and in the New Country (Argyle) are still very hostile: Several murders have been of late

committed by them in the former District, and although the Mounted
Police have been actively engaged in pursuit of them, and have in those
affrays shot two or three, yet they seem so far from being intimidated
that they become daily more and more daring ... things indeed have now
gone so far that something decisive must be done to stop the progress of
this evil, or the Stockmen and Shepherds will not readily be persuaded
to remain at the distant settlements while exposed to the animosity of a
set of untutored savages. As these Natives have never before been known
to proceed to such extremities, there is reason to think some MOTIVE
must exist for their present warfare, which if possible should be ascertained, and if six or eight of them could be brought in as prisoners, it is
likely we should become acquainted with the cause of their animosity,
and probably find it easy of remedy: perhaps our people have been the
first aggressors, or possibly a want of food may drive them to desperate
measures, for it is a fact well known that wherever our stockmen abide,
the Kangaroos and Opossums disappear, our dogs destroying them; and
thus being driven from the coast, and their usual sustenance destroyed,
it is no small evil to these poor simple creatures to be deprived by the
invasion of strangers, of both food and raiment.

She cast them in her journal as "untutored savages", yet there was still hope
in what she wrote that capture might lead to negotiations and to understanding—the germ of an idea that might have led to establishing a treaty. But in a
letter that followed soon after, to Christiana Jane, she had changed her mind,
and the poor creatures for whom she felt sympathy were cast as ferocious animals to be put down in an act of legitimate warfare:

> My dear Christiana
> ... Among our numerous visitors of this week were the *Hero's* from the
> *War*. They arrived here on Tuesday and have brought one Native Chief a
> prisoner. He is a most ferocious looking *animal* and I am sorry to add I no
> longer doubt that *some* of the native tribes are cannibals, for it appears
> that they did actually eat the poor man they murdered at — Farm, but
> from some circumstances it seems evident they were impelled by hunger.
> I hope the execution of the culprit now in custody and that on the spot
> where the deed was committed will strike terror into these savages and
> prevent future outrage and murder. I have time only to assure you of the
> united and affectionate regards of all at Denham Court to all at Dagworth
> (Letter from Denham Court to Christiana Jane, April/May, 1826)

I have dreaded, throughout this project, finding evidence that my ancestors were involved in the slaughter of indigenous people. But here it is stark and unequivocal. Not only were acts of violence committed, but the men who committed them were Heroes of war...

Christiana loved books and interesting conversations, and she was interested in progressive thought that might lift her out of the more conservative views of the place and time she lived in. But she was unable to think her way beyond the declaration of war against the original custodians. She had no doubt about the superiority and desirability of Western civilisation, and no doubt that it was God's providential will that brought British civilisation to the colony.

CHAPTER 18

From Soldier to Farmer: Thomas Valentine Blomfield and Christiana Jane Brooks

Thomas Valentine Blomfield (1793–1857) and Christiana Jane Brooks (1802–1852) were married on 3 August 1820 at St Philip's Anglican church in Sydney. Christiana was 18 and Thomas Valentine 27. Christiana Jane was the beloved daughter to whom her mother wrote many of her letters from Denham Court. Thomas Valentine, who we met in Spain and Portugal as a young man fighting in the Peninsular wars, was still in the army, now posted to the colony. He was a handsome redcoat, and a desirable match for the Brooks' eldest daughter, even though he brought with him no fortune.

The colony was a place where fortunes could be made, and this chapter enters into the space of the first decade of Thomas and Christiana's struggle to make their own fortune. The letters that have survived were written 'home' to Thomas Valentine's family – to his father Thomas Blomfield, his brother Edwin, and his sisters Louisa and Matilda, and also to his young niece Louisa. Their letters offer a vivid portrait of young people making a life for themselves in the colony; it is an endearing and intimate portrait—and at the same time it is harrowing in its apparent lack of care for those who have been displaced, both the original custodians and the convicts, both pushed out of their home-lands, in order to make this fortunate life possible. The United Kingdom had failed all of them, yet its values and practices reigned supreme.

In the earliest letters Thomas asked for help from Edwin and from his father to secure him a land grant, which they succeeded in doing, and then, later, to help with the sale of his commission in the army. At the time of their marriage Macquarie was Governor, and despite his strong support for Thomas Valentine and despite strong support from Colonel Erskine, and even from Commissioner Bigge, the new rules had precluded him from getting a land grant. Officers had not tended to make good farmers, and, further, grants were no longer being given to women.

Richard Brooks, his father-in-law, gave Thomas 60 cattle on their marriage. At the time he had no land or money to give with his daughter. He was building up his own holdings in order to leave each of his five daughters a farm of her own. He had already given a farm to each of his two sons, Henry and Richard Brooks Jnr. In 1820 all the land around Sydney had been taken up. Thomas did not want to follow the surge of settlers over the Blue Mountains, which

© BRONWYN DAVIES, 2021 | DOI:10.1163/9789004446717_019

had been taking place since William Cox built the road over them in 1814. He thought the Bathurst district was too isolated from the city, and too vulnerable to bushrangers. He was interested, rather, in getting a grant of land near the mining town of Newcastle, which was only 10–12 hours by ocean from Sydney; and moreover, his friend Close, from the 48th regiment, was also settling there.

Thomas Valentine began a letter to his father in 1820, apologising for his long silence, and for having married without his consent. He set out to reassure him with a detailed account of Richard Brooks' place in the colony:

> My dear Father,
>
> It is now a long time since I wrote to you or to my brother or sisters. I have, I am sorry to say, put it off from time to time until I must have worn the patience of you all quite out. I have no excuse to offer, and a sufficient apology I cannot frame. I therefore rely on your paternal fondness to forgive me, as also for a step I have taken of the greatest consequence to me in this world, and that without your knowledge or consent.
>
> Therefore, to keep you no longer in suspense – I am married. Now, I think you are astonished, and well you may be. Yes, my dear father, I was married on the 3rd of August (last month) to Christiana Jane, eldest daughter of Richard Brooks, Esq., a respectable settler and a magistrate of the Territory. He was, before he became a settler, a sea-faring man and formerly in his Majesty's navy. He made two or three voyages to this colony, and having realised a considerable sum of money, he brought out his family on the last trip, and sold his vessel and became a settler. He is now a landowner to the amount of 6000 acres and upwards. ...
>
> On my proposing to marry his daughter I told him how I was situated, that I had nothing but my pay. He told me he could give me very little money with her, but he could give me cattle, that he had expended all his money in improvements, etc; that his property should devolve on his daughters, his son being already provided for.[1] I have got 60 head of cattle. I have applied to the Governor for a grant of land for either me or my wife ...

Richard Brooks had not actually been in his Majesty's Navy; but since being in the Navy was much more respectable than being a trader, the Navy had somehow slipped into family mythology. Thomas's letter gives the information that is needed to help him secure his land grant, and he expresses his hope "that if Edwin will take this trouble, that it will succeed". He closes with a description

---

1   Richard had two sons, not one. Since neither Christiana Brooks nor her daughters acknowledged Richard Brooks Jnr's existence, Thomas has it seems no knowledge of him.

FIGURE 74   Portrait of Thomas Valentine Blomfield by Augustus Earle, 1825
             NATIONAL GALLERY OF VICTORIA

of Christiana Jane in the same ironic, humorous voice he used when he wrote
to Louisa ten years earlier:

> Give my love to my sisters. I don't know what sort of an apology to make to
> them for not writing to them. Louisa will want to know what sort of a look-
> ing woman her new sister is. She is of a fair complexion, about 5ft. 5 inches
> in height, fair hair and dark brown eyes and, of course, in my opinion, not
> ugly. Her mother is an elegant and genteel woman. She is an English woman,
> but most of her relations live in Edinburgh. Mr. Brooks is from Devon-
> shire. (Letter from T.V. Blomfield to his father, Captain Thomas Blomfield,
> Rickinghall, near Bury St Edmonds, Suffolk, 4 September 1820)

FIGURE 75   Portrait of Christiana Jane Blomfield
DRAWING BY JODY THOMSON, 2018

Photos were not yet invented, and portrait artists like Augustus Earle had not yet come to the colony. A portrait based on later sketches of Christiana Jane (*above*) shows her to have been a striking young woman.

When Augustus Earle did come to the colony, he did not produce a satisfactory painting of Christiana Jane. The more successful portraits of her parents and of Thomas Valentine are in the Victorian National Art Gallery. Of Thomas Valentine's portrait Christiana Jane was quite critical, though it is a beautiful work of art: "I cannot say the picture pleased me much. There is a likeness, but there is a want of the good humoured and cheerful expression of countenance that he has."

Christian Jane described him to his niece Louisa as having "very dark hair, a high forehead, dark blue eyes, rather a short nose, a small mouth with a fine set of very white teeth, which shows very much when he laughs; a very black beard, and nice black whiskers. Altogether he has a round face, a cheerful, good-tempered countenance habitually when he laughs, which he does often and most heartily. In height is five feet seven, and in my opinion a very good figure, and I know several young ladies who used to think so, too, when he was a bachelor."

A year after the letter to his father, Thomas Valentine wrote to Edwin with news of their first baby, and with the ongoing concern at the prospect of the 48th being sent to India:

> Another piece of news I have to tell you is that I have got a little son. He was born on the 26th May. He was christened in June, and named Thomas Edwin, after my father and you. He is a very pretty little fellow, and begins to be very interesting. They say he is very like me (of course), but I think he is more like my wife's family. His hand, I think, is very like our father's. His grandmother has made him a present of a female calf; if he has luck he will have a good herd by the time he is in his teens. If I cannot get a grant for my wife I shall try one for him, as I intend leaving him behind, when we go to India, with his grandfather, who is very fond of him...
>
> ...[But] I have not the least wish to leave the colony; I now consider it as my home. Mrs. Blomfield and self have been staying up the country at one of Mr. Brooks' farms, a very pretty place about 27 miles west from Sydney and seven from Liverpool, through which place we pass. It lies in the district of Lower Minto. At this farm he has his cultivation and a very nice house. It is the prettiest place I have seen in the colony. From thence I went with Mr. Brooks to another farm of his, in the district of Appin, on the Nepean, or Cow-pasture River, about 30 miles S.W. from whence we started. This is a very nice tract of ground, containing about two thousand acres. This farm, as also two others in the district of Illawarra, on fine islands, he uses as grazing tracts; consequently, there are but huts for the overseers and stockmen, with as much cultivation as provides for their annual subsistence. This district lies on the coast to the southward of this part about 60 miles, but overland it is about 70 miles, and as there is a great tract of country ungranted, he has a good run for his cattle. He has about three thousand acres there.
>
> My cattle are over the Blue Mountains, at Bathurst Plains. The gentleman that has them in charge is just returned from thence. He says they are the fattest cattle on the plains, and when he left thirty had calves. They are kept by themselves, and as they are but a small herd, it accounts for their being fatter than those that are herded in large numbers, the feed not being so eaten up. The harvest will commence the latter end of this or the beginning of next month. The crops look remarkably well. I was quite surprised to see so much cultivation as there is in the districts

of Airds and Appin; I did not suppose there had been so much in all this part of the colony. I think we shall have no need of wheat from Van Dieman's Land this year. If the rain does not set in as it did last harvest the crops will be much more than the consumption.

It was 33 years since the first fleet's arrival, and their very real fear of starvation. And it was only ten years since David Collins' death, and the struggle on the small island colony for survival. Now, in 1821, as Thomas writes, Van Diemen's Land was producing abundant supplies of food for the whole colony. The farmers around Sydney, too, were learning how to survive there, and sometimes to flourish. But their agricultural strategies together with an English imaginary and imported English flora and fauna, had taken better in the cold climate of Van Diemen's Land. But in both places, the newcomers' encounters with the colonised land were a haphazard mix of trial and error as they attempted to reproduce the familiar landscapes of home:

> The rain has set in today, and it looks like wet weather for some time; but at present it will do good, particularly to the maize, which is young, and some settlers are still planting it. The maize harvest is generally in March, very seldom before. Barley and oats are very little grown. I have never seen the latter, neither are beans or peas. Clover and English grasses will soon be plentiful, I mean in a few years. The natural grasses make tolerably good hay, from the land whence the timber has been fallen and burned off. All kinds of vegetables grow in all parts of the colony to great perfection except potatoes, which are, generally speaking, in this part of the colony wet and very bad, but in Van Dieman's Land, they are as good as English or Irish. Fruit is also very plentiful; the strawberries are now in perfection and very plentiful; gooseberries and currants will only grow on some farms and then not very well. But to the southward, I am told, they are in abundance.
>
> A great many settlers have come out and are still arriving in every ship. Those ships which touch at Van Dieman's Land, the settlers liking the appearance of the country, generally remain there, with some exceptions. The great objection to being in that part of the colony is the want of decent society and a criminal and civil court...
>
> There has been but one [rural] criminal court [here]since we have been in the colony, and that was held last year. ... It will be well for the people if the Government continues this practice. The robberies had got to such an extent that three and four hundred sheep were frequently driven off at a time, and if the unhappy settler could find

out the robbers, and had witnesses to prove it, the expense was so
great of coming to Sydney that they preferred putting up with the loss
and remaining at home to keep a sharp look-out after what was left
him... (letter from T.V. Blomfield, Sydney, to Captain Edwin Blomfield,
Framlingham, Suffolk, 20 November 1821)

Many of the convicts had escaped to the bush and became bushrangers, as had
George Watts in Van Diemen's Land. The bushrangers had become, in effect, a
third force, at war with the soldiers-turned-policemen, and sometimes at war
with the original custodians, though sometimes, too, in cahoots with them.
The settlers were a fourth force, taking up land in outlying areas and convert-
ing it into English-style agricultural land.

Thomas was weary of war and conflict. He wanted a simple life with his wife
and children. He yearned for a life like the one he remembered from his rural
English childhood. Six months after the last letter, he wrote again to Edwin
from Sydney:

... You will be surprised when I tell you I have made up my mind to avail
myself of the late order, that captains who have served 12 years, whether
they have purchased or not, will be allowed to sell out, but this indulgence is only to have effect during this last reduction, and when that is
completed the old order to be reverted to, viz, 20 years' servitude. Now I
have made up my mind when our reduction takes place to [apply to] the
Duke of York to sell out, which will be £700 and I shall set myself down
on the banks of the Hunter River, near Newcastle, about 60 miles to the
northward of this port. I shall take my cattle and a flock of sheep from Mr.
Brooks (which he has promised to me), wash my hands of the army, of
which I am heartily tired, and do the best I can with a good grant of land.

I dislike the idea of going to India, where I am sure to lose my health
and that of my wife. Close, of our regiment, has lately got married, and
has sent home to get on half pay. He has got his land down there, and is
already appointed a magistrate, and has commenced building his house.
I wish to place myself down beside him. He is from Suffolk. His mother
is coming out to him. He is a very old friend of mine, and I think in a few
years we shall make ourselves very comfortable...

My dear wife continues in good health, as also little Thomas Edwin.
He was weaned last month, but does not yet run alone. He will be eleven
months old on the 26th of this month.

When are you going to get married? Has Miss Kerr yet changed her
name? Give my love to Mrs. Ray. Tell Miss Ray I don't forget when she, and

her sister Jane, and her cousins from the parsonage house held me down in the garden and rub my face over with gooseberries and currants. Give my love to them all, also to Wingfield, particular remembrance to Mr. Stanford, to Mr. and Mrs. Brown and all old friends and acquaintances. I suppose I shall never see old Suffolk again, unless the soil on Hunter River produces more lining for my pocket than the army. My boy shall be a bullock driver rather than go into the army, if I can avoid it. Christiana joins with me in best love to my dear sisters, yourself, and little Louisa...

... adieu, and believe me, your affectionate brother,

T.V. Blomfield. (Letter from TV Blomfield dated from Main Guard, Sydney (per favour of Captain Sampson, ship Southworth) to Captain Edwin Blomfield, Framlingham, Suffolk, 7 April 1822)

In 1824 the land grant at last came through. It was 2,000 acres, and just where Thomas Valentine wanted it, in the Hunter Valley near the tiny township of Maitland, and near his friend Close. They couldn't build their house until the sale of Thomas's commission came through. There was no financial help available from Thomas's father who had married a third time and had a young family to support.

Christiana Jane wrote to Louisa from Denham Court, sketching out their life in the colony. Although the letters from his sisters have not survived, it is evident from Christiana's response that they were filled with advice for living good Christian lives. Christiana was eager to assure them that their advice was taken, as she took up the wifely duty of threading the two families together:

My dear Sister,

I have often had a great inclination to write to you, and as your brother is absent I cannot write at a better time. He is at present at our own land at Hunter River, a settlement about 150 miles from this part of the colony. The Governor has given us 2000 acres of land, and Thomas writes home to say he is very much pleased with his grant, as it is fine grazing ground and also good for cultivation. He took down our cattle, which are now a nice herd of 160 head. We now only want our money from England arising from the sale of your brother's commission, to enable us to buy sheep, build a small cottage, and purchase agricultural implements. Then I hope, with being prudent and economical, we shall in a few years be very comfortable.

Thomas is rather uneasy at not hearing from either his brother or the agents. He wrote to them both about the sale of his commission more than twelve months ago, and we begin to be anxious, as we cannot commence doing anything to our farm without our money, and as we have been living in a state of uncertainty for the last 15 months (not knowing whether we should be obliged to go on with the regiment or not [to India]) we wish to get settled with our little ones on a farm of our own ...

We received a letter from your droll husband [*John Edwards*] just before Thomas left me in January. It was dated eleven months back, but notwithstanding gave us great pleasure, and caused us both to laugh heartily. I think Thomas must be very like Mr. Edwards; just as merry. I wish you could see him. I am sure you would be pleased to know what a good husband and father he is; so good tempered and cheerful, and at the same time so prudent and thoughtful, and with such a proper sense of religion that you would be thankful. All the good advice contained in the letters of yourself and our elder sister Matilda were not thrown away on him. He often reads all your letters to me and talks so much of you all that I am sure I should know you all from his description...

I am quite delighted with all your accounts of our brother Edwin, and I hope to hear he is happily married and that the lady of his choice is worthy so good a husband as so good a brother must make. You must tell him we laugh at his methodical way of making love. Thomas and I did not take quite so long to think about it, but perhaps we were younger and not so wise, but I can safely say I have never for one moment regretted my choice, and I hope my Thomas can say the same. Thomas describes his sister Matilda as being like my own dear mother. If that is the case I am sure I should like her. Your father, he says, is like a gentleman of our acquaintance here, and he thinks little Thomas Edwin like his father and you. He is a very little fellow, but such a little chatterbox you would be quite pleased with him. Our other little pet, Richard, is a very stout baby and is near walking alone. He is tall for his age, and I think like my family. Their young aunts spoil them terribly.

I am staying at my father's during Thomas' absence, but will soon be obliged to part from all my dear family. I ought to be thankful that I am not going to any great distance or to such an unhealthy climate as India. Besides, I have an opportunity of hearing from them every week, as there is a regular packet, and I can always have the pleasure of one of my sister's company, as mama has promised to spare them now and then, when Thomas will fetch them.

... I beg to join with my dear Thomas in best love to all his family, and if my dear sisters and brothers will write to me I shall always feel pleased in answering their letters, and be assured that I am their affectionate sister, CHRISTIANA JANE BLOMFIELD (Letter from Christiana Jane Blomfield dated from Denham Court, 16 April, 1824)

Three months later Thomas wrote to Edwin about the deep anxiety he had experienced at not hearing from him, and his subsequent relief at the good news. He could, at last, with the sale of his commission and his release from the regiment, begin his new life as a farmer in earnest:

> My dear Edwin,
> Your long-looked-for and most anxiously awaited letter I received the 15th inst., dated Rathkeal, 28th Nov...
>
> My wife and children have been living at her father's. I have been since the beginning of February down at my farm, clearing land and getting in wheat, fencing etc. My cattle are also on my own estate, in very thriving condition. I have not commenced a cottage, as I have not had the means. I returned to Sydney a short time since, determined to raise money somehow, in order that I might take my family down. I was heartily tired of being absent from them. I have within three miles of my farm a cottage belonging to the Government which is lent me until I erect something of my own.
>
> I am now collecting my dairy things, furniture and farming requisites to go down again as soon as possible. I expect to have an addition to my family in about three months. I have, my dear brother, been most fortunate in the choice of a wife. There is not on this earth a better creature, and I love her, if possible, better every day. We enjoy very good health. Our little son (the youngest), has grown a very fine boy. He has run alone these two months and begins to talk. He is nearly as tall as his brother. Tom was always a small child, but he is growing, and is a very funny fellow.
>
> ...We have had a most terribly dry season. Numbers of cattle have died in this part of the colony for want of food and water. I fortunately moved my cattle from Bathurst in time, and they have been on excellent pasturage the whole season. I expect to have upwards of seventy calves shortly.
>
> The natives to the westward of the Blue Mountains have commenced a warfare with the settlers, and have killed a good many of their stockmen that are far in the interior. Many stockmen have left their herds, and hundreds of cattle are scattered about the country, as also thousands of sheep are at the mercy of the natives and wild dogs. The latter are very destructive amongst the sheep. Soldiers have been sent and the settlers have armed many of their men and have killed some of the natives, and I am in hopes that they will be brought to order very soon. I hope the natives in my part of the country will not get troublesome; they are very numerous, and very useful and quiet... (Letter from T.V. Blomfield dated from Sydney to Edwin Blomfield, 30 July, 1824)

While all continued well with his little family, and while he was deeply involved with making a new life on his farm, there were intimations of harder times, of droughts and floods and war.

Thomas reports the war with the original custodians, west of the Blue Mountains, as having been commenced by them. As an ex-soldier he surely knew that they had invaded land belonging to them, and that protecting one's own land against invaders could not be regarded as initiating war. He had so far found the original custodians in the Hunter region to be quiet, and useful to him, though he does not say what use he puts them to. Was it their knowledge that was useful? Did they tell him, for example, that the lake his house looked over was only a temporary lagoon and in the dry would become a meadow? Or how high the flood waters would come when they did come? Or where natural springs could be found in the drought? Presumably not, not just because the imposition on the land of the English imaginary was destroying their own farming practices, but simply because the newcomers could not have comprehended those practices as viable and valuable. It is deeply ironic that one of the main reasons for colonial expansion was that the known agricultural methods had failed England, and particularly failed the poor. It was a country that could not feed its own people. There is little evidence of the settlers realizing that there was much they might have learned about the land they were busy conquering; it was generally only the explorers, and the surveyors who came to appreciate, in small part, their superior knowledge, though the police, too, soon discovered their superior tracking skills in chasing down outlaws. A report in *The Sydney Gazette*, 7 April 1825, elaborated that kind of usefulness:

ABORIGINAL TRACKERS

Several instances have occurred, during the present sittings of the Court, as on innumerable former occasions since the founding of the colony, of the advantages which the Police may draw from these poor people; in the neighbourhood of Newcastle particularly they have rendered the most important benefits to the Crown, and to Society. In the present state of the law they cannot, indeed, be admitted as witnesses in Court; but they are excellent instruments out of Court, for the detection of offenders....

With regard to the aborigines, they have always been more or less useful to the Police; although, in some instances, their services have been miserably ill requited ...

When war did break out in the Hunter region, between the original custodians and the newly arrived farmers, the attacks were at first on those settlers who were known for harsh treatment. At Mt Arthur 300 of the original custodians, the Wonnarua, were killed. There was no mention of that warfare in any of the letters written by Christiana Jane and Thomas from that period, and I have found no record of Thomas having been involved. Of course I hope he was not actively involved—though he was, whichever way one looks at it, inextricably involved insofar as he was taking up their land and overriding their farming practices that had survived for thousands of years.

Christiana wrote to Louisa in June 1825 of her pleasure at moving into the government cottage and being back together with Thomas, busy with the details of establishing their farm, which they had named 'Dagworth' after the farm where Thomas Valentine had been born:

[The cottage] is only three miles from our farm, and in June last year came up for us. Just about the same time we received Edwin's letter, which enabled us to draw our money, and after making many necessary purchases we left my father's house on the 24th of last August to come down here, but we were unavoidably detained in Sydney a few weeks, very much against our will, for want of a vessel, and I was beginning to be very anxious, when fortunately we got a passage in a very comfortable vessel and were only ten hours at sea. On the 21st of September we were comfortably settled in this cottage. You will not wonder at my being anxious when I tell you that on the 27th of October I was confined, and another little boy made his appearance, and a very fine little fellow he is.

You will, I dare say, like to hear something of our farm, which is called Dagworth. It is a very pretty place. Our house stands on a hill, from which we have a very extensive view. On one side we see through the trees parts of Lake Lachlan, and on all sides we see the mountains, which have a very wild and beautiful appearance.

I must now give you a description of the way in which our house is built. The foundations are large trees of a very hard wood, called iron-bark, and the walls are of the same wood. The logs are cuts into lengths of ten feet and are then split into slabs, which are forced into grooves in the foundation, as also into the wall plates at the top. Over this is nailed weatherboards, and the roof is shingled, which has the appearance of a slated roof. The doors and window frames are made of cedar, and to the windows are fastened Venetian blinds, painted green as are the doors. The house is painted white. The length of the house is sixty feet with a verandah all round eight feet wide, which is a very necessary part of a house in this warm climate. It is also a good [place to] walk in rainy weather, and a nice place for the children to play in out of the sun.

Our rooms are all on the ground floor. We shall have a parlour 14 feet wide and 20 feet long, a bedroom the same size, another bedroom 12 feet wide and 20 long, a storeroom for provisions and farming tools, etc., the same size, a small store room joining our bedroom 10 feet square, and a bedroom for Thomas and Richard the same size opening out of our room, [and another] on the opposite side of the verandah, which we shall make a dairy of at present. I do not know if, after all my description, you will be able to make out what sort of a place it will be, and I think I can fancy my little niece exclaim "Well, that will be a queer house of Uncle Tom's," but it is the style of most country houses here.

"But there is no kitchen!" Louisa will say. The kitchens, on account of the heat, are generally detached buildings, very different to the comfortable ones in England. Indeed, all the houses in this country must strike a stranger as being very meanly furnished. The walls are generally painted, sometimes only bare white-washed, with very little other furniture than a table and chairs, a fireplace with no grate, but wood fires burning on the stone hearth or placed on iron dogs. Window curtains are seldom seen; indeed everything that adds to the heat is taken away in summer time, which is eight months of the year. Indian matting is used instead of carpet. It is made of bamboo, and is very white and cool looking, but I must say I like to see a carpet in the middle of the room in winter time, for although not much colder than your summer we feel very chilly and enjoy sitting round a cheerful wood fire of an evening. Now I've told you what sort of a house we shall have when finished, I will tell you how we employ our time.

In the summer time we rise early, but at this time of the year we get up about 7 o'clock. The children are awake at daylight and are soon dressed and running about. After we are dressed we have family prayers. Thomas reads them to myself, the children, and one or two female servants, and both Thomas and Richard kneel by their father and are quiet all the time. After prayers we get our breakfast. Richard and Thomas sit up with us, Richard by me and Thomas by his papa, and when they have drunk their tea and eaten their bread and butter they are in a hurry to get down, so after "Thank God for my good breakfast," away they skip to play with their wheelbarrows, which is their chief amusement.

After breakfast Thomas's mare is saddled and he goes to the farm, where he remains until 4 o'clock. In the meantime I feed my baby, see the house put to rights, give out what is wanted for dinner, teach little

Tom to read, and Richard comes to say his lesson, which is generally P for papa and M for mama, and C for cow or O for Onginge, as he calls orange. Tom [Thomas Edwin] is much amused and says "Poor little thing, he don't know better; when he is as big as me he will say it right, won't he, ma?" We do not dine till five, as Thomas cannot leave the farm sooner, or there would be little work done.

After dinner the children are washed, have their tea and go to bed, after which Thomas and I walk in the verandah until it is dark, and he tells me what he has been doing at the farm. We get our tea comfortably together and enjoy an hour or two in quiet. I generally work and he reads to me, or we talk of the improvements we intend making when we get to "Dagworth."

At nine or ten o'clock we have evening prayers and go to bed, and, if the children will let us, sleep very soundly. As we are 20 miles from any church we read the church service on Sunday to our servants twice a day and Blan's sermons or some other religious book. I dare say it will not be very long before we have a church and clergyman in the neighborhood, as it is becoming a very populous district, and as I have always been used to attending public worship regularly, I shall be very glad when I can do so again, and take my children.

Poor little Tom is always asking questions. The other day I had been telling him that if he was good and said his prayers that God would love him and give him everything. He said directly, "What, lots of pancakes and sugar?" Poor little innocent fellow, that is his idea of everything that is good, but he will, I hope, soon know better. He was four years old on the 26th of last month, and he fancies himself a very tall fellow. He is just 3ft. 7in; very small for his age. I used to think him very like his papa, but I do not think so now. He has a little round face, very light hair and blue eyes, a small mouth and pretty little teeth, and can put on such a sly look. He is very fond of horses and is always talking of them. I think he will be very clever. He has such a good memory, and is always thinking of what he used to do and say when he was at his grandfather's. He also talks of his England grandfather and aunt, as we teach him to think of you. He is much taken with the name of Aunt Louisa, and never forgets to drink your health. He remembers you all also when he says his prayers on going to bed.[2]

---

2   This clever little fellow, Thomas Edwin (1821–1903), was to become Lieutenant-Colonel Blom-field, contrary to his father's ardent wish that he not go into the army.

Richard also says his prayers prettily. He is a very stout, healthy child, very nearly as tall as Thomas and much stouter. He has the most beautiful large dark blue eyes with the longest black eyelashes I ever saw; rather a broad nose, a beautiful mouth and teeth, with such a sweet smile, and light curly hair. He really is a very handsome boy, and, I think, what is better, a good disposition, although rather cross at present, which I attribute to cutting his back teeth.

My little Johnny is a dear little, good boy; he is just seven months old, and as large as most children at twelve. He is like both the other children. He has such a beautiful thick head of hair; it is dark now, but I dare say will become quite fair, as the others did.

I do not know whether I told you that Mr. Close had settled at Hunter's River. He was amongst the first people who took their land on the river. He was fortunate in getting a fine grant of land from Governor Macquarie, and has now a very comfortable house, a good barn etc. He married a particular friend of mine. It was rather singular that Thomas and he, who were such good friends, should happen to marry us, who were playmates. Mrs. Close is a very amiable young woman, but very delicate. We often meet, and while our two husbands are talking about their olden times in the Peninsula and bragging of the number of sweethearts, and of all victories they have had, we are also talking of some of our romping days when we were wild little girls.

Now, do you not think it is very impudent of these gentlemen talking of their sweethearts before their wives? But between you and I, I think they only want to make us think more of them and I believe it is stories of their own making. Whenever Thomas begins I get quite angry and give him a good talking, which is the only way I have of revenging myself ... C.J.B.

P.S. by T.V.B. – My dear sisters, brother John and niece Louisa, – Many thanks for your kind letters. As usual I must acknowledge myself very much in your debt. My Christiana (I must not say my rib, as she does not like it) is sending you a long scrawl, which I think will puzzle you to decipher, about our mode of living etc. ... I am very tired. Have been hard at work all day in preparing some very foul land for wheat, but am sorry to say it has commenced raining, which will throw me back very much if it continues. It is very rich ground, and has been very thickly timbered, and what with roots, stumps, grass and weeds, I have had hard work to get the plough through it. I am also busy with my house, which I thought to have been in long ago, but have been waiting until the flooring boards etc., are seasoned ... I have several times requested you to send me the dates of all your births, as also my father's and Edwin's, that I might remember you on your birthdays, if it were only in a glass of Adams' ale. I am astonished to find myself so old, my hair getting thin and fast changing hue. This goes enclosed to Mrs. Manning [Matilda] with our last year's Almanac, which I dare say will forward you some amusement. I will now say good night. God bless you all, and still believe me, your most affectionate brother and uncle,

T.V.B. (letter from Christiana Blomfield and Thomas Valentine Blomfield [as a PS] from Newcastle, Hunter's River, 2 June 1825)

There was a long gap in the letters between 1825 and the beginning of 1828. In a letter to her niece, Christiana Jane wrote details of her growing family, and of her sister Jane's marriage to Edward Cox (the younger brother of James Cox):

...You ask me in one of your letters if you have any more little cousins. I believe I have not written to you since the birth of our little girl, which event took place on the 30th of June, 1826. She is now eighteen months old; such a very fine child and beginning to be very interesting. Her name is Christiana Eliza Passmore, after my mother's maiden name. What will you say when I tell you perhaps ere you receive this letter you may have another cousin. If a girl she shall be named Louisa Matilda; if a boy Barrington.

I think your Aunt Matilda will say we stock our house too fast now [with children], but in this colony we are only considered very moderate folks. Most people add one to their family every year, and as there are so few disorders fatal to children in this colony there will in a few years be larger grown-up families in this part of the world than any other.

My brother, who is very funny, tells me to make up my mind to two dozen, for within the last year or two he has married into a family of twenty-two, and the mother of them looks almost as young as some of her daughters. They are not all now alive, but I dare say if they had come out here to settle a few years sooner the most of them would have grown up. Their name is McKenzie. After having one and twenty children in England they came out when their youngest child was four years old, and to the astonishment of everybody, after being here twelve months, the old lady was confined at the same time as her sixth daughter [Henry's wife Margaret].

Our three boys are all well and growing up fast, but they are as wild as young kangaroos and as mischievous as monkeys, but not unlike other children at their age. Thomas is still small for his age, but very sensible, manly, and quick at his lessons; very passionate but very affectionate, so that I do not despair of making him anything I please. Richard is a stout fellow, in my opinion a fine handsome boy, an excellent temper, but more mischievous than any of them. Johnny is a little innocent child, very fond of being made a pet of, rather odd looking with very light blue eyes and light curly hair. He is quick like Thomas.

... I take them myself for school for two hours every day, and Thomas is beginning to read very nicely. They can say the church and their other catechisms, besides several of Watt's hymns very nicely. Richard is rather dull, but I dare say he will improve by and bye. I hope in another year to be able to send Thomas to the clergyman of our district to school, as he proposes taking a few pupils above eight years old...

January 20 In April last I made my first visit to my father's since we came down to settle on our farm. My sister Charlotte, who had been staying with me, returned home with me and baby and Richard, leaving Thomas and Johnny with their papa. My father came to fetch me, and we had a quick passage of twelve hours, and on landing at Sydney we found the carriage waiting for us to take us to Denham Court, which is twenty-seven miles from Sydney, and in four hours from the time we left the latter place I had the happiness of finding my dear mother and sisters quite well. It was a happy meeting after an absence of nearly three years, and, could you have seen us all, I am sure you would have thought so.

I went up rather sooner, than I expected, to be present at the marriage of my second sister Jane, which took place on the 18th of April. She was twenty years old, and her husband one year more, so you will say that they are a young couple; but he is a very steady, prudent young man and has a good farm and a pretty cottage, with everything a young couple could wish for to take his wife to. He is the youngest son of a Mr. Cox, who was paymaster to the first regiment that came to this country, and afterwards settled here. He is now a very rich man and has provided for all his family handsomely. My brother-in-law Edward is the fifth son that the old gentleman has seen married, and all are living within a day's journey of their father.[3] Most of them have now large families, and I suppose Edward and my sister Jane will add to the 36 already bearing the name of Cox before many months pass... (Letter from Christiana J Blomfield from Dagworth to her niece Louisa Edwards, 5 January 1828)

---

3 Except James Cox, who went to live in Van Diemen's Land in 1814.

Later that year, in November, Christiana wrote to her sister-in-law Louisa, with further news of their latest child who had been named after her and her sister:

> ... On the 18th of April I gave birth to another little girl, who has since been baptised Louisa Matilda, and I hope she will grow up a credit to the aunts she is named after. She is now seven months old, very lively, and a healthy child, but not so large an infant as most of the others. People say she is like me. I think her eyes will be dark, which is only right, as all the other pickaninnies (Portuguese for little ones, or what the natives call them, having learned it from white people) are like their father, with blue eyes. My father came to see me just before I was confined, and took our two boys, Tom and Dick, up with him, where they remained for three months, when my brother brought them home. My youngest sister, who is with me, states grandpapa and grandmama were very sorry to part with them, as they were a great amusement now they have so small a family. They went to a little school on my father's farm when they were there, and their grandpapa used to take them to school and fetch them home himself.
>
> Tom liked to be at Denham Court because he had plenty of horses to ride, and he used to frighten my mother out of her senses, lest he should meet with an accident. You would be surprised to see the little fellow riding about. He catches our old mares himself, puts a bridle on, and gallops about everywhere. When my father came to see us he brought us his carpenter to complete our house, and by this means we have been enabled to make many additions which have added considerably to our comfort. Thomas has also been making great improvements on the farm by clearing land and making many enclosures. You who live in England can have no idea the labor it takes to bring land into a state of cultivation here, as also the great expense, but I must leave Thomas to tell you all these sorts of things; he can explain better than I can. (Letter from C.J. Blomfield to Mrs Edwards from Dagworth, November 1828)

Two months later Thomas wrote to Louisa, at Christiana's bidding, to fill in details of the farm:

> My dear Louisa,
> I can make no excuse for my long neglect in not writing and shall therefore not attempt it. My dear Christiana is gone on a visit to her mother's for two months. She has desired me to write something, and forward one to my niece Louisa, that has been in my desk for twelve months. We have

now got a little more comfortable in our house by adding more rooms and a good broad verandah to our house. I have been very busy in the clearing and fencing in more land for cultivation, which I expect to reap great benefit from. Our fences in this country are not like those in Suffolk (hedges and ditches), but are made of strong split wood, very hard and heavy, called ironbark ... Indeed, there is no use attempting to cultivate without [such fences], as the crop is sure to be destroyed by cattle, horses or pigs.

I have also felled and partly burned off 150 acres of timber the last year. The labor and expense of getting land into cultivation is very heavy. First to cut down the trees, then to cut them into pieces that can be moved and put in heaps, with the branches to burn, also to take out the stumps and roots. The land I am at present clearing cost me 3 pounds per acre before a plough can be put into it, but the greater part of the expense is paid by the produce of the farm, viz., wheat and meat issued as provisions to the men. I also supply them with tea, sugar, and tobacco, clothing, etc. For these articles of course a percentage is charged on them, and the expense comes easy.

Some of my own bonded servants, who behave well, I employ as free men, and pay them for their work as above, charging them with their provisions, etc., but as bonded servants I am obliged to furnish them with two duck frocks, 2 pairs trousers, two shirts and 2 pairs of shoes annually, also provisions, etc., weekly – 7lbs. beef or 4lbs. pork, 1 peck of wheat, which they grind themselves at a small steel mill I furnish for that purpose – very like the old pepper mill in the old pantry at Dagworth, which I can remember as if it were yesterday, but a great deal larger – also, if the men behave properly, 1lb. sugar, 2oz. tea, 2oz. tobacco, 2oz. soap weekly.

If any of them behave insolently or do not do their work properly, [it is possible to take] them to the magistrate, get them flogged, sometimes 25 to 75 lashes, according to the degree of their offence. I very seldom resort to that remedy, unless compelled, to keep my authority by doing so. I will now say no more on this head, as it will not be very interesting to you, and perhaps you will not understand what I have said...

And yes, it is highly possible that Louisa, back in England, could not have understood how such brutal punishment had become so normative a practice in the management of convict labourers. His letter continues with stories of bushrangers, and of being prepared to defend himself if he has to, and to the details of the drought, and the daily work on the farm, which is prospering, despite the drought and the extreme weather. He begins, though, with an admission, that his memory of home and family is fading:

> ... On the 14th next month, Valentine's day, and my 36th year will be completed. I begin to fancy there is some mistake. It appears to me like a dream, my past life, my campaigns, etc. It's a long time, too, since 1809. I can't bring to my recollection either your features or Edwin's, or your good man's. I have some idea of my father's, also Mr. Stanford's and Wingfield's. I should like very much to have your miniatures, my dear father's, yours, etc., Matilda's, Louisa's, Edwin's and Edwards'. Now, I beg of you to send me some of them, at all events. My Christiana would be delighted at it. ...

> *January 27th* Since writing the other day I have been called upon to attend my friend Close, who had a fall from his horse (a young one) and broke his right leg above the ankle, both bones, and dislocated the ankle joint. ... he has done uncommonly well, having had no fever, and not much pain...

> The weather has been very warm. Yesterday week I rode over to see my sheep, and some of my dogs went with me. The day turned out very hot. The wind was from the north-west, which in this country is always a hot wind in the summer, as if it came from the mouth of a furnace. ... One of my dogs died from the heat and another very nearly. When these hot winds come on we always shut up our house – windows and blinds and every crevice we can find to keep out of the winds, so that coming in from the air the house feels quite cool. To you it would feel warm (about 84 degrees); the verandah, out of the sun about 96 to 100 degrees, and in the sun 118 to 120 degrees. I have known the thermometer to be as high as 134 degrees in one of these hot winds. The country now is in a dreadfully burnt up state, having had but very little rain for three years. When it does come I expect it will come in earnest, when many of the settlers on the banks of this river will suffer from floods. There has been no considerable flood for many years, and many people have ventured to build on places that are subject to very heavy inundations...

> Tell Edwards I am an ungrateful dog for not writing to him. With love to all my relations and remembrance to all old friends. I am almost afraid to think of my father, as I have not heard so long from anyone, and at his advanced age I shall be afraid of all English letters. Your ungrateful but affectionate brother,

T.V. Blomfield (letter from T.V. Blomfield Dagworth NSW to Louisa, 9 January 1829)

Later that year Christiana wrote to the family of her new daughter, Louisa Matilda, and of the drought and of ongoing life on the farm, and a moment of welcome rain. Their two oldest sons are now boarding with the minister who has become their teacher:

My dear Sisters and Brothers,
It is now nearly three months since we received your last packet containing all your kind letters and presents which, as usual, gave us greater satisfaction and pleasure, and I will now perform my part in answering them ...
Our two eldest boys have gone to school; they went to Newcastle, where the clergyman resides who they are placed with, with their papa. The clergyman is a particular friend of ours, and I feel confident that they will be taken every care of. Mr. Wilkinson takes but six pupils, and our boys make two of that number. Poor Richard was delighted at the idea of going, as they are both very fond of Mr. Wilkinson; but when night came he could not contain his feelings any longer; his little heart was full and he wanted his papa to bring him home again. He was quite reconciled when his papa wrote to him the next day, and Thomas is equally happy. He has more spirit than Richard, and will fight his way in the world better.
It is three years since Thomas left his home before to go to Sydney. He has gone up now to settle a few things that require his presence. Among the things to get is his additional grant of five hundred and sixty acres, which settlers of our class are entitled to. He has no money to spend this year, and it requires great economy to keep our head above water, as the last three years of drought have involved the colony in great difficulty. The almost total failure of the grain crops has taken all the money out of the colony to pay for the wheat imported from India, the Cape, and other places, consequently there has been a great fall in the prices of cattle, sheep and horses, neither of them being worth more than a third of what they were two years ago. There is no more money left in the country, and several farmers and settlers have been ruined, particularly those who came here about three years ago, and who paid great prices for their cattle, etc...
A post has been recently established, which I hope will be a benefit to us. Our military establishment at Maitland consists of a captain of the 57th and twenty soldiers, who are mounted and act as police, so that

there is now no fear of bushrangers. Captain Aubin also does the duty of police magistrate. He is a married man, and his wife is a very religious, amiable woman, and he is considered an upright, just and merciful magistrate. They are a great acquisition to our society. Thomas's old friend and brother officer, Captain Allman, is our nearest neighbour. They have a large family growing up. They are most worthy people, and seldom a day passes without seeing one or other of their family. We have a nice view of each other's houses and can see everything that passes. A lagoon, which is generally a fine sheet of water, is between us, but these dry seasons have converted it into a meadow. Our friend Mr. Close is appointed a member of Council and is now in Sydney helping to make laws. His residence is seven miles from us, that we think but a step in this country, and even twenty miles is considered only a pleasant morning's ride. We are situated twenty miles from Newcastle by land, and have an excellent road all the way, but by water it is nearly sixty, from the winding of the river. I will leave Thomas to finish this letter, and to tell you of his agricultural concerns, as I should most likely makes some mistakes. I must not leave off without telling you I am as happy as the first day of my marriage. I have more reason to be thankful every day with my lot in life, though we have not riches we have contentment, and are happy in the affections of each other, and our good, healthy little children. Accept my affectionate love, my dear sisters and brothers, and believe that I am ever you're affectionate though unseen sister,

Christina Jane Blomfield (Letter from Christiana Jane Blomfield from Dagworth to her brothers and sisters, 4 October 1829)

The final letter I include here, was commenced in 1830 and completed in 1831. Little Louisa, their niece, had died. Christiana Jane and Thomas were sorrowful at the loss of the sweet girl they had come to love through her letters. Louisa and John Edwards had stopped writing to them in this period of their grief. At Dagworth they had been struggling with the long drought followed by devastating floods. Thomas had begun to feel real despair. Christiana Jane, too, had begun to despair at her own inability to be the perfect Christian that Thomas's sisters advised her to be. The letter was addressed to Matilda, the most religious of Thomas Valentine's sisters, who had sent them a Bible with passages marked in it that she thought they should read:

My dear Sister,
We wrote you long letters a short time ago and addressed them to Edwin, but as we have not heard from any of you excepting him since

the melancholy intelligence of the death of our dear niece, I am inclined to write a letter wholly to you, hoping you will answer it, as we are most anxious to hear how our poor sister and Mr. Edwards bear their sad affliction. Most truly do we sympathise in their sorrow, and hope that they will receive that consolation which the Almighty alone can give. To me who only knew her from her letters it seems a great loss, for I had pictured her in my mind as everything that was amiable, and felt a sincere affection for her. Then what must her parents and relations who knew her, and were blessed with her presence and affectionate attention, feel, I can easily imagine. But it is a consolation to know she is gone to a better and happier world, where there is everlasting peace, and where she is saved all the trouble and trials of this. As you were with her during all her suffering, I hope you will tell us every particular of her illness, as the slightest circumstance will be interesting to us. What a delightful character does Edwin describe her to have been.

I show her letters to my sisters and all my young friends, that they may take example by her. I have just been reading them over, and it renews my grief when I think I shall never again behold her dear writing. I have also been reading your last letter over, and you need not fancy that we are tired of your good advice, for I am thankful for the trouble you take for our sake.

I only wish that both ourselves and children were nearer to you, that we might oftener benefit by it. Therefore do not leave off giving us good advice and I will endeavour to profit by it. I think I am sincere in saying I wish earnestly to serve God and bring up my children to do so, yet I constantly find myself thinking of worldly affairs and occupied with selfish feelings. I know you will say, then why do you not pray for God's Holy Spirit to assist you. I do so earnestly at times, but still I find I do not overcome my evil passions as I ought; but I will study the Bible that you marked and pray for assistance from the Almighty to do His will.

Your present of books to the children was an acceptable gift and gave great pleasure to them. Books are things we cannot get here but seldom, and anything from England we think a great deal of. The family whom you introduced to us named Wood we see a great deal of. Mr. Wood is appointed catechist in our neighbourhood and performs the duty of clergyman. He is a very good man, and his wife is a cheerful, pleasant woman. They have lately got a small grant close to us of 40 acres, where they intend to build a small cottage and reside there. We are much pleased at their becoming neighbours of ours, as we like them exceedingly. Your brother Tom will give them any assistance he can in advising for the best and in the erection of their buildings.

Our neighbourhood is becoming very populous. We are within a mile and a half of the town of Maitland, which is increasing in size and importance every day. Our proximity to the town and to water carriage will make our land more valuable. These dry seasons have been very trying to us farmers. For the last three years the crops have failed and all the money has been taken out of the country to purchase the wheat that has been consumed, so that the colony is in a distressing state. Settler's farms and property of all kinds are being sold every day by execution to pay their debts, consequently it does not fetch one-fourth its value. A settler now has nothing that he can make money out of, for when people can at these sales purchase cattle, sheep and horses for little or nothing they will not give a remunerative price to private individuals.

February 5, 1831 You will see, my dear sister, that this letter was begun many months ago, but as I have never met with an opportunity of sending it your brother wishes me to finish it, as he is going to Sydney and will send it by the post. When I commenced writing to you we had the prospect of an abundant harvest, for the seasons of drought were quite changed and the country was looking very beautiful, while our crops were very luxuriant; but just as they were ready to reap a heavy rain came on and lasted for many days (quite unusual at this time of year), which brought on a flood, and almost all of our harvest was completely destroyed. Our wheat, barley and potatoes were so many feet underwater, and several acres of maize which was coming up so well shared the same fate. It has been a considerable loss to us, as we expected to have overcome all of our difficulties from the years of drought, and it has been the means of disheartening us very much.

Your brother is completely tired of a settler's life, for every kind of stock has fallen so considerably in value that it is hardly possible for anyone, with the greatest economy (depending entirely, as we are, on the produce of our cattle, sheep and farm) to pay their way. Our Misfortunes did not come singly, for our breeding flock of sheep got the rot from the wet weather, and we lost old and young, nearly three hundred, at a time when they weren't worth more than they would have been at another time of the year, as they have not been shorn, and the fleece of a sheep at the present time is worth nearly as much as the animal itself. Your brother does not, in general, give way at every annoyance – his disposition is naturally cheerful, and he does not fret commonly at things when they go wrong – but even he could not help giving way at times, although we know it is sinful to repine at the ways of Providence. We must recollect we did not come into this world expecting perfect happiness. We have a great many blessings, more than we deserve, and I hope we are sensible of the mercies of the Almighty, and I am sure your brother has also, but there are times when we cannot think everything is for the best, although afterwards we find it is so...

...I wish we lived near you, that you could often talk to us seriously and also our children, particularly to our eldest boy, who is a very passionate, perverse child, but he is very affectionate, and if I had the patience to correct him as I ought, or a mild manner of talking to him, he would, I have no doubt, make a good child; but I am too hasty and sometimes do more harm than good when I chastise him. He has a temper which will do much with fair means, but nothing when compelled. I think you would be pleased with him. He is generous and sensible, but needs great management.

Our second boy has a mild and amiable temper, but very mischievous and his manners are rather cubbish. He is a handsome boy and tall for his age; not near so high-spirited as Thomas. The third is most affectionate but fretful, and an odd-looking child.[4] Our eldest girl is a nice gentle child, very fair, and Tom thinks like what he remembers Georgiana at her age; she is quite a Blomfield. Our Louisa is a lively little dark eyed girl, very amusing; just at the age to be a pet with papa. She is said to be like me, but I do not see it, but she is like my family. Barrington Wingfield is just twelve months old and a very fine child. He has been very ill lately, which has reduced him considerably, but I hope he will soon recover his looks. I think his will be a passionate temper; he is very lively and will soon run alone. We have our boys at home, as the clergyman whom they were with at Newcastle gives offence to the Government, and his dismissal is a great loss to our boys. We are going to have a tutor at home.

March 15, 1831 Your brother sent me a few days ago your welcome parcels from Suffolk, and I need scarcely say how much I value your pretty presents, particularly from their being the work of my dear friends. I shall have great delight in wearing them for your sakes, and the truly valuable work sent by my dear sister is a treasure indeed. I trust it will make a lasting impression on me. The account you gave of my own sister is indeed

---

4 This odd-looking fretful little boy was to become a minister of the church, with a life that could only have increased his fretfulness, all three of his wives pre-deceasing him.

gratifying.[5] I knew you would all like her, and I think so much of all your kindness to her. She has written a full account of her visit to my mother, and I am quite impatient to get the letter to hear what you are all like, and I know she will give me a minute description. Your brother is to bring me the letter, and I expect him in a day or two.

He has been in Sydney nearly five weeks and has been to see all his friends. He has been staying to see my father's English packages landed, as he was unable to attend to it himself, having been very ill from the effects of an accident occasioned by a wild cow running at him while on horseback and goring him in the calf of the leg, while returning from one of his journeys to his cattle stations in the interior. The confinement necessary from such an accident has injured his health, and he is weak and rather inclined to be hippish.

He is a good father, and has advanced Thomas £300 to enable us to settle our difficulties. He knows we are not extravagant, and has a high opinion of Thomas' prudence; therefore he has helped us, but he would not give us the least assistance did he think we had brought our difficulties by extravagance or bad management. His wool sent to England last year fetched a high price, which has given him the means of helping us. In other respects he is as badly off as his neighbours...

I have got a tutor for my boys, and he goes on well at present. They have their school in a small verandah room, so that I can step in every now and then and see that everything is going on right. The young man has been well brought up, but has unfortunately committed some crime of no very serious kind, which has brought him to the country. He teaches them English, grammar, geography, arithmetic, history and French. He was sent to me by a friend of ours whose children he had been instructing for two years; they are now too old to require his services any longer. His method is good and our children obey him, and at the same time are fond of him. They all take their meals with him, and three boys sleep with him in one of the back rooms which I have roughly fitted up for them, but which is weatherproof and comfortable, though not plastered. Their religious instruction I take upon myself. They come in to me for an hour of a morning, when they read a portion of Scripture, which I explain to the best of my ability, and I encourage them to make remarks on what

---

5 Christiana Jane's sister, Mary, had married William Wilson, a good friend of Thomas's. They were posted to India where William became very ill, whereupon they were posted to England, making it possible for Mary to visit Thomas's family.

they read. This hour is considered quite a recreation, and I endeavour to make it a pleasure to them.

I have been making a few alterations in my house since Tom has been in Sydney, which I think he will approve of. I have taken the boys' room and made it into a room for ourselves. It is the long room at the side of the house with the two small windows, and the prettiest room in the house. The windows face to the east, and the morning sun, rising over Captain Allman's farm, which is just opposite, and shining on the lake, is a lovely sight.

We have climbing roses, which grow over the side of the cottage and peep in at the windows. I assure you when I wake of a morning it looks so cheerful that I fancy it is one of the happiest little cottage rooms in the world. Our own bedroom I have converted into a second parlour. We now have a dining and breakfast room, which opens onto the verandah. I wish you could just take a peep at us sometimes. I think I should like you to see us at tea on the verandah. It is our tea room in the summer months.

The end at which we have our evening meal has the same prospect as our present bedroom. The posts of the verandah are covered with a beautiful creeping vine called "Dolichos," a native of the Cape of Good Hope. Its appearance is something like ivy, and grows just as thick, and there's a beautiful lilac pea blossom. It not only covers the posts, but hangs down between them in festoons and forms a nice shade; and the roof of the verandah is also overgrown with it in many parts, making our cottage appear quite a picture.

In the front of the house is a round grass plot, in the centre of which is a white cedar. The branches are spreading, and it bears a blossom like the English lilac, the scent being the same. Under the tree the children play. I am so contented with my home that I fancy it is everything that is beautiful, but I forget how very little you would think of it after the beautiful places in England; yet I think you would admire our cloudless sky and lovely moonlight nights, and last, though not least, the happiness you would see between my good husband and myself. He thinks as much of his home as I do, and in every letter I get he thinks there is no place like it, though most places that he sees our grander and better in point of buildings. I believe I may say he thinks that there is nothing like his own old wife.

26 *April* 1831 *T.V.B. adds:*

My dear Matilda,

... I am very much gratified at Mrs. Wilson having seen my father. She seems to me the link of the chain that has connected us together, as I have long given up the idea of seeing any of you again. I am so pleased that so near a connection of my wife's family should have seen you all, and that you like her so much. We missed Mr. Edwards' merry letter amongst the last packet, and hope he is now fully recovered, as well as our dear Louisa. How I should like to see you all again to talk over my boyish days and take some of our old walks. I suppose your favourite windmill is still going. I should recollect many objects that I now entirely forget. My memory is not very retentive, nor was it ever so, and I am sorry to say it is getting worse.

T.V.B. (Letter from Christiana Jane Blomfield from Dagworth to Matilda, commenced 18 August 1830, with postscript from Thomas Valentine, April 1831)

Two years after this letter was completed, Richard Brooks died, followed by his wife Christiana in 1835. Denham Court was left to Christiana Jane. And so they left their pretty cottage and their life among friends in the Hunter Valley, along with its trials and tribulations. In addition to the children they tell of in their letters, Thomas Edwin, Richard Henry, John Roe, Christiana Eliza and Louisa Matilda, they had seven more children: Barrington Wingfield, who died

FIGURE 76   St Mary the Virgin Church built by Thomas Valentine and Christiana Jane
             Blomfield in memory of Richard and Christiana Brook
             PHOTO BY ROGER BOYD, 2016

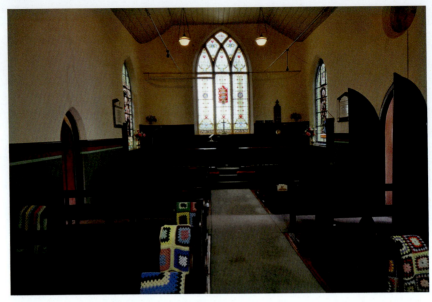

FIGURE 77   St Mary the Virgin Church, interior
              PHOTO BY ROGER BOYD, 2016

FIGURE 78   St Mary the Virgin Church, stained glass window
              PHOTO BY ROGER BOYD, 2016

at the age of five, Arthur, born in 1831, Henry Wilson born in 1833 (my great grandfather who married Margaret Cox), Edwin Cordeaux born in 1835, Euston born in 1837, Frank Allman born in 1840, and Alfred, born in 1842. At the same time they adopted Honoria's three children. She had been devastated at the death of her husband Edward Riley in 1836, and had been unable to care for her children. She died in 1839. Those three adopted children were Alexander, Margaret (who married Thomas Browne alias Rolf Boldrewood), and Christiana.

A task that Richard and Christiana had left them to carry out at Denham Court was the building of a church. The beautiful St Mary the Virgin still survives, and it is where Richard and Christiana Brooks are buried, the main window above being dedicated to their memory. Thomas Valentine and Christiana Jane Blomfield are also buried there.

It is a beautiful little church, and it was perhaps a significant sign for the local squatters and landholders that the land had been successfully anglicised, and the family elevated, unequivocally, to the elite of the colony, and the empire—secure in their privilege, and in their sense of a rightful place in the land both they, and Christiana Jane's father, had appropriated.

In the next chapter I go back to the question of the opening up of the interior that commenced with William Cox's building of the road over the mountains. I will deviate from my practice of building my story of colonisation solely out of the lives of my ancestors. While my great (x3) grandfather Samuel Perry features in this next chapter, I have turned to others, such as Thomas Mitchell and Charles Sturt, to further flesh out the encounter between the British newcomers and the original custodians of the land.

CHAPTER 19

Deputy Surveyor General: Samuel Perry and Surveying and Mapping the Land

At the end of Chapter 16 I left William Cox, caught up in his moment of pleasure in the landscape west of the Blue Mountains. It was an unexpected landscape; not an untended wilderness, but a vast park of open grassland, with some open forest cleared of undergrowth, and patches of more dense forest and scrub (Gammage, 2011). In this chapter I trace the movement into indigenous country that happened in the subsequent decades. I draw on the journals of Samuel Perry (1787–1854), my great (x 3) grandfather, the journals of his boss, the Surveyor General, Thomas Mitchell, and finally the journals of Charles Sturt, one of Australia's best-known explorers.[1]

What we now know is that the original custodians of the land had used fire-stick farming to create those parklands that so surprised the newcomers. They used fire to create fresh pick for kangaroos, to clear the undergrowth, to provide ease of movement for people and animals, as well as shelters for different species. The strategic lighting of fires had prevented trees from becoming too dense in open forested areas, had enabled some plants to grow that could not germinate without fire, and had cleared out unwanted insects. Their mode of hunting was to entice animals to congregate where there was new grass and shelter. Their careful management of rivers and wetlands had ensured clear flowing water and a healthy environment for fish and eels and other water-dwelling creatures. The abundance was managed so that no species took over at the expense of other species. Bridges had been built by teasing soil away from tree roots, causing them to fall over rivers at strategic points; stone walls had been built to create weirs that created breeding grounds and ease of fishing; and wells and dams had been built wherever water was otherwise scarce (Gammage, 2011). The overall effect was open country of rich grasslands with large trees growing at intervals, bordered by forest without dense undergrowth: it was, just as William Cox had found it, like "a wild but beautiful park, which reminded one of the domain of an English noble" (W. H. Leigh cited in Gammage, 2011: 16)

The work of land-care was largely invisible to the British newcomers' eyes. What they imagined they saw was undisturbed Nature, which was beautiful,

---

1 Neither Mitchell nor Sturt are my ancestors.

© BRONWYN DAVIES, 2021 | DOI:10.1163/9789004446717_020

bountiful, and desirable—a land begging to be dominated by Culture. They were there by God's grace, for Whom they brought the ways of the known world to bear on that natural, uncultivated landscape and its people.

The Culture–Nature binary is threaded everywhere through their accounts, inter-linked with a range of other binaries. Binaries are not simply paired opposites, but function in a hierarchy, in which one of each pair is dominant over the other. Binaries take their meaning in relation to each other. Integral to that meaning-making is the implicit relation of dominance and subordination. The nature–culture binary does not function in isolation from other binaries, such as those in the table below, but is entangled with them.

The newcomers approached both the land and its people from the perspective of each of the dominant terms. While they depended on those identified as subordinate—and in some cases loved and admired them, they were rarely in doubt about the superior value of their mode of being and doing.

Dominant term	Subordinate term
Culture	Nature
Civilised man	Savage
Man	Woman
Rational mind	Emotional body
White	Black
Conquest	Defeat
Honour	Ignominy
Christian	Heathen
Hierarchical order	Freedom/chaos
Individual	Collective
Heroism	Obscurity
First	Last
Active	Passive
Light	Dark

That binary logic was not consciously adopted, but was everywhere present in their language, in their actions and in the ethical principles they lived by. Samuel Perry was inevitably entangled in those ways of thinking, being and doing.

Samuel Perry came to the colony 15 years after William Cox opened the way over the Blue Mountains. He worked in the New South Wales Survey Department from 1829 to 1841, first as Deputy Surveyor General and then as acting Surveyor General from 1837. Samuel oversaw the mapping out of numerous towns and cities, including the city of Melbourne, then still part of New South Wales. He managed Mitchell's office when Mitchell was off on his frequent

FIGURE 79   Portrait of Samuel Perry as a young man
             OPPENHEIMER, 2009

journeys or writing his books. Because Mitchell was an impossible boss, and because the Survey Department's funding was siphoned off for Mitchell's expeditions, Samuel had inadequate resources to carry out his own work. His journals sometimes read like a never-ending catalogue of misery and disaster, leavened with self-mocking humour (Oppenheimer, 2009).

Samuel's education had been in the classics and languages, and then in art. He was charming, funny, poetic, whimsical, and long-suffering.

He had been appointed as Military drawing master at the Royal Military College Sandhurst from 1819–20. In New South Wales he sketched and painted scenes with a group of friends, who painted in the style they called "after Captain Perry". Reproductions of many of his exquisite watercolours can be found in Oppenheimer (2009).

When Samuel first came to Sydney, with his wife Caroline, and their children, they lived in George Street in the inner city. They later moved to the top of William Street, which is two minutes from where I live. This particular space, now known as Kings Cross, is a space I have been inexplicably drawn to

FIGURE 80   Sydney Harbour Looking East from Darlinghurst, Samuel Perry
PLATE 26, OPPENHEIMER, 2009

for decades, long before I knew I had any ancestral connection to it. Though this area is now one of the most densely populated places in the country, when Samuel painted the harbour from here, there were only trees and water to be seen, with the Heads of the Harbour in the distance, and a narrow winding dirt road running down to the city.

He was given a land grant of several acres, lying between Darlinghurst Road, Bayswater Road, Roslyn St and Ward Avenue—land that had belonged to the Cadigal and Wangal people.

Samuel's father, Jabez Perry, had been a gold-beater:

> This ancient occupation involved the flattening and hammering of gold nuggets between the membranes of the large intestine from cattle – a process that produced fine and thin papers of gold leaf. These could be used for decorative gilding on carved wood, on paintings and furniture, and on the edges of quality books. A gold beater was also involved in the printing business and would own and run the operation of making vellum for specialist publication. (Oppenheimer, 2009: 1)

Jabez died when Samuel was a child, and Samuel was taken into the care of James Perry, who lived in Tavistock House in London. James Perry was a publisher, and owner and editor of the *Morning Chronicle*. He was a successful writer and a *'bon vivant'*, who "was part of the Coffee House society of Whig Politics in London" (Oppenheimer, 2009: 3). The Perry children, now including Samuel, were tutored by Richard Porson, "a brilliant but eccentric classicist" (Oppenheimer, 2009: 4). At age 15 Samuel was enrolled as a cadet at the Military College of Great Marlowe, where he studied maths, geography and administration, as well as French language, topographical drawing, mapping and draughtsmanship.

Once signed up in the army, Samuel found himself at many of the same battles on the peninsula as Thomas Valentine Blomfield, though I don't know if they ever met. Samuel described the storming of the castle of Badajoz, a turning point in the defeat of Napoleon, and a point of terrible shame for the English, given the pillaging and looting that followed. There is a charcoal sketch of the castle among Samuel's works of art (Oppenheimer, 2009: 15). Like Thomas Valentine, Samuel Perry also had a very sorry nag to ride on. He wrote in his journal:

> I was riding one of the ugliest horses that ever graced the French Cavalry. The sorry brute (part of the booty of Vittoria) had probably been taken from a plough after Napoleon had expended all his best for the Russian campaign, but my orderly servant, a Spaniard named Francisco Bravo, was leading an English horse that I usually kept in reserve for a gallop. On I jogged on my drowsy wartyfaced lopeared roachbacked camel footed brute to Oyarzun ... (Oppenheimer, 2009: 16)

That humorous description of the warty-faced brute led into a story of high adventure, as Samuel delivered vital messages across enemy lines, and feasted with military leaders along the way.

After the war Samuel spent time mapping and building bridges in Belgium, and later he and Caroline lived in the West Indies. He had courted Caroline, the daughter of James Johnson, architect and builder, when he was on leave in London. They were married at Hammersmith in London, on 12 April 1817, when he was 25 and she was 21. Like David Collins, he had courted a woman with a substantial fortune to inherit. That fortune, too, was seriously eroded by complications in a will. Her remaining fortune was nevertheless sufficient that they made a nuptial agreement that she would not forfeit her fortune upon marrying as was then the custom. When they came to New South Wales in 1829, Caroline became joint owner of their various properties (Oppenheimer, 2009).

Not long after completing Buena Vista, the magnificent sandstone house they built on their land grant, they decided to leave it. Although it was a perfect location for Samuel, as it was a pleasant walk into the city to work, and for Caroline, who could have visitors there with ease, his boss, Thomas Mitchell, had become their close neighbour, living in Craigend. Relations with him were so difficult that they sold Buena Vista and moved to the rural location of Long Cove.

Caroline and Samuel were committed to providing their children with an excellent education. Their oldest son, Thomas Augustus (1818–1872), my great (x 2) grandfather, was not of a scholastic turn, leaving school as soon as he could to work for Samuel's friends from Military College, the Dumaresq brothers. They had land grants in the Hunter valley at Muswellbrook and Scone. Thomas was later to marry Selina Rose Marlay, and it was the ninth of their children, Mary Maude, who married James Nivison, my great grandfather.

From the 1830s new towns were being laid out further north and westward from Sydney, and Samuel often found himself travelling in territory still defended by the original custodians. None of those journeys proceeded without military guards, but they also had guides chosen from among the local people. Samuel brought to his account of those journeys some of the same humour and self-mockery of his wartime writing, as he found himself on yet another sorry nag, with his equipment in such a poor state of repair due to the shortage of funds in the Survey Department, that almost everything, at one point, was to fall into the river they were crossing.

Samuel made half-hearted attempts to document the lives of the local people he encountered on his travels, but he found the ceremonies, such as the corroborees, boring and repetitive. His accounts were deeply etched with the inevitable ambivalence embedded in binary thought. He admired the skill of the local people he encountered; he willingly depended on them, and he envied them in their 'State of Nature'. At the same time, he regarded them as people who were there to serve and obey his will, and he defaulted rapidly to threats of violence if they made themselves a nuisance:

> 7 *November* Shortly after daylight an Aborigine appeared with a spear and accompanied by his gin. I gave him tobacco and he was civil... Shortly after we were established a kangaroo hove in sight and was speedily run down by the dogs. Soon after one of the blacks attached to our party brought us a wild duck, and while we were unpacking one of them killed and stuffed for me a flying fox. These natives are extremely inoffensive and their affections easily won by a small present of tobacco...

8 *November* A sound sleep and a breakfast of kangaroos steaks fried with salt pork completely restored me from the fatigue and annoyance of yesterday...

Honey gathering: The agility with which the natives climb the trees is surprising. A liane with a noose at one end is all the assistance they have except a tomahawk with which they cut notches in the bark and by this means – twisting the right leg to one end of the liane and holding the other in the left hand they almost run up the tree.

9 *November* Crossing Kings River 6 Aboriginal natives with their tomahawks and implements of war cut a passage (up the bank) the scene of which in a few months will be lost. The remainder of the baggage was unloaded in the river and carried by hand to a spot fixed on for our encampment. In a few minutes fires were lighted and very shortly after the whole part was housed – the children of the forest under sheets of bark – those of civilisation under canvas brought sixteen thousand miles over sea for that purpose. On examination of our effects it was found we had not suffered so materially as might have been expected [from the river crossing where their baggage fell into the water] and we set to work to cook the kangaroo that one of the blacks had killed during our march.

20 *November* We are obliged to remain on the south bank until some of Mr Ralfe's tribe shall have made some canoes to take our baggage across the River which in moderate seasons is fordable at this place. To construct a canoe is the work of half an hour when there is bark near the spot.

25 *November* Black killed a diamond snake and I was much surprised at the quickness of the eye of the black. While approaching some rocks I heard him call out suddenly "take care there's a snake". Of course I immediately sprang on one side ... Shortly afterwards coming to a stream which we were to cross the black called out "My God master there's a snake" and when he had driven it away he said "bel like that fellow – he murry saucy fellow – that fellow bight he kill". The diamond snake was brought to camp and cooked for Toby's dinner. The flesh appeared beautifully white and had I not felt such a horror of all the snake tribe I might have been tempted to have eaten some. (Oppenheimer, 2009: 61–64)

Two weeks later the clash of views in Samuel's thinking was stark. On 8 December he had had a perfect meal and the weather was glorious. He lapsed into humorously bad French to express his satisfaction with his meal. He imagined his life better than that of kings and referred to his indigenous hunter as his 'gamekeeper'. He quoted from the Bible, describing the local people as having a superior life to that of civilised nations. But shortly after, that same evening, he became bellicose in response to a request made of him. He bemoaned the negative effects of colonisation on those importunate men who made their demands on him. They had, in his eyes, betrayed themselves by coming to want access to the very worst of Western civilisation:

> 8 *December* After Dinner. I never relished Wild Duck so much in my life. It was shot to my *gout,* cooked to my *gout, a la minute* and eaten to my *gout, sans facon,* but with very excellent mustard, pepper and salt, a very excellent appetite and washed down with a pint of *vin delicieux.* King William IV did not dine better. After my dinner my Game Keeper came for instructions – Kangaroo-Duck-Teal or Wonga Wonga. If every day were like this the bush would be a paradise, glorious solitude!!! But when one reflects on the original curse, "In the sweat of thy face thou shalt eat bread". The savages enjoy this solitude. They evade the curse and receive the blessing – "having dominion over the fish of the sea and over the fowl of the air and over every living thing that moveth upon the earth". "Like ravens they neither sow nor reap", "Neither have storehouse nor barn; and God feedeth them". What is the curse? Cain was a tiller of the ground. *"Consider the lilies how they grow and toil not".* It appears that care and anxiety constituted the original curse. Nature has provided for all, but not for the artificial wants created by care and refinement.
>
> 10 *pm* Company betrays the savage. When my people are away he tells me he wants money, first to buy grog, then for some other purpose! Then he wants trousers then a shirt. He then talks of fighting blacks he asks what I have in my pocket and when I tell him a knife, he says the Commandant always gives a knife to those who go out to conduct parties; I tell him we can fight too when necessary. We use no waddies but if a fellow is saucy we blow his brains out. (Oppenheimer, 2009: 64–65)

Samuel saw his own race cursed by the cares and refinements of Culture, and it horrified him that the children of Nature, who lived like Kings, might want access to them. He was aggrieved by their desire for goods the newcomers brought with them, and he called on his lethal powers to fob them off.

The cantankerous Surveyor General, Thomas Mitchell, who caused Samuel so much grief, also had occasional moments of insight into the problem the newcomers were bringing to the land. He outraged successive Governors when he expressed those views. At the same time, his inability to get on either with his workers or the Governors also translated into a total inability to get on with the local people he met during his explorations. He wrote, for example, of the changes he had observed in the waterways between 1835 and 1845:

> ... instead of being limpid and surrounded by verdant grass, as they had been then, they were now trodden by cattle into muddy holes where the poor natives had been endeavouring to protect a small portion from the cattle's feet, and keep it pure, by laying over it trees they had cut down for the purpose. The change produced in the aspect of this formerly secluded valley, by the intrusion of cattle and the white man, was by no means favourable, and I could easily conceive how I, had I been an aboriginal native, should have felt and regretted that change. (Mitchell, cited in Gammage, 2011: 313)

Mitchell was a difficult man, as Samuel Perry discovered to his cost. He was a thorn in the side of successive governors, who were outraged by his failure to obey them and to respect their authority. In 1848, for example, he condemned the imperial order to stop the original custodians from taking care of the land with their complex firing practices:

> The omission of the annual periodical burning by natives, of the grass and young saplings, has already produced in the open forest lands nearest to Sydney, thick forests of young trees, where, formerly, a man might gallop without impediment, and see whole miles before him. Kangaroos are no longer to be seen there; the grass is choked by underwood; neither are there natives to burn the grass ... these consequences, although so little considered by the intruders, must be obvious to the natives, with their usual acuteness, as soon as cattle enter on their territory. (Mitchell cited in Gammage, 2011: 316–7)

He argued, briefly, that it was unreasonable of the newcomers to object to the killing of their cattle or sheep when they had all but exterminated the local fauna, thus depriving the local people of their traditional food sources. Killing kangaroos, he suggested, should be made illegal. He worried, on the other hand, that if the wild cattle multiplied (wild cattle that had escaped from government stock), and were thus plentifully available to the 'natives', the natives would also breed up and become formidable enemies. The only choice, he concluded, was either to civilise them, or obliterate them. It was not reasonable, he thought, for him to be expected to do the arduous work of colonisation, while putting his own life at risk (Mitchell, 1838).

Mitchell constantly fell out with the local custodians of the land on his travels, and did not hesitate to shoot at them if they appeared to be a threat to him. He was contemptuous of them when they showed no sense of obligation toward him when he gave them gifts, and even more contemptuous when they claimed the right to decide who could drink their water (Mitchell, 1838). He was a thoroughly unpleasant man, notwithstanding his occasional moments of insight into the plight of the land and its people.

Charles Sturt, the explorer, in contrast, formed very positive relations with the local people he encountered on his expeditions, though in the end he too was to betray them. He quite clearly loved and admired the 'natives', and he received love and loyalty in return. He wrote in his journal:

> These two natives, Camboli and Nadbuck, were men superior to their fellows, both in intellect and in authority. They were in truth two fine specimens of Australian aborigines, stern, impetuous, and determined, active, muscular, and energetic. Camboli was the younger of the two, and a native of one of the most celebrated localities on the Murray...
>
> Camboli was active, light-hearted, and confiding, and even for the short time he remained with us gained the hearts of all the party.
>
> Nadbuck was a man of different temperament, but with many good qualities, and capable of strong attachments. He was a native of Lake Victoria, and had probably taken an active part in the conflicts between the natives and overlanders in that populous part of the Murray river. He had somewhat sedate habits, was restless, and exceedingly fond of the *fair* sex. He was a perfect politician in his way, and of essential service to us. I am quite sure, that so long as he remained with the party, he would have sacrificed his life rather than an individual should have been injured. I shall frequently have to speak of this our old friend Nadbuck, and will not therefore disturb the thread of my narrative by relating any anecdote of him here. It may be enough to state that he accompanied us to Williorara, even as he had attended Mr. Eyre to the same place only a few weeks before, and that when he left us he had the good wishes of all hands. (Sturt, 1847 vol 1: 43–45)

Whereas Nadbuck would have defended Sturt and his men to the death, Sturt was not so successful in defending Nadbuck and his people:

> Here, or near this spot also, the old white-headed native, who used to attend the overland parties, was shot by Miller, a discharged soldier, I am

sorry to say, of my own regiment. This old man had accompanied me for
several days in my boat, when I went down the Murray to the sea coast in
1830, and I had made him a present, which he had preserved, and shewed
to the first overland party that came down the river, and thenceforward
he became the guide of the parties that followed along that line. He
attended me when I came overland from Sydney, in 1838, on which occasion he recognised me, and would sleep no where but at my tent door.
He was shot by Miller in cold blood, whilst talking to one of the men of
the party of which unfortunately he had the charge; but retribution soon
followed. Miller was shortly afterwards severely wounded by the natives;
and, having aneurism of the heart, was cautioned by his medical attendant never to use violent exercise; but, disregarding this, when he had
nearly recovered, he went one day to visit a friend at the gaol in which
he ought to have been confined, and in springing over a ditch near it,
fell dead on the other side, and wholly unprepared to appear before that
tribunal, to which he will one day or other be summoned, to answer for
this and other similar crimes. (Sturt, 1847 vol 1: 86–87)

Nadbuck, it seems, survived Miller's attack. One of the evils created by the
newcomers, for men like Nadbuck, was a new form of jealousy and rivalry
between tribal groups. The favours of the white men could be exploited, and
they interfered with old, negotiated understandings. Some of the settlers delib-
erately exploited those rivalries, setting different tribal groups against each
other (Watson, 2009). Sturt continues:

On the 5th of January we crossed over from the Darling to its ancient
channel, and on the 6th Mr. Browne left for Adelaide. On the 8th I
reached Lake Victoria, where I learnt that our old friend Nadbuck had
been speared by a native, whose jealousy he had excited, but that his
wound was not mortal. He was somewhere on the Rufus, which I did not
approach, but made a signal fire in the hope that he would have seen
it, and, had they not been spoiled, I should have thrown up a rocket at
night. However Nadbuck heard of our return, and made a successful
effort to get to us, and tears chased each other down the old man's cheeks
when he saw us again. Assuredly these poor people of the desert have the
most kindly feelings; for not only was his reception of us such as I have
described, but the natives one and all exhibited the utmost joy at our
safety, and cheered us on every part of the river. (Sturt, 1847 vol 2: 120)

But the love Sturt felt for Nadbuck and his dependence on him, did not
dismantle the power of binary thought that asserted the superiority of white

men's culture. In reflecting on the significance of his explorations, for example, Sturt wrote:

> Let *any man* lay the map of Australia before him, and regard the blank upon its surface, and then let me ask him if it would not be an *honourable achievement to be the first* to place foot in its centre.
>
> Men of undoubted perseverance and energy in vain had tried to work their way to that distant and *shrouded* spot. A veil hung over Central Australia that could neither be pierced or raised. Girt round about by deserts, it almost appeared as if *Nature* had intentionally closed it upon *civilised man*, that she might have one domain on the earth's wide field over which the *savage* might roam in *freedom*.
>
> *I had traced down* almost every inland river of the continent, and had followed their courses for hundreds of miles, but, they had not led me to its central regions. *I had run* the Castlereagh, the Macquarie, the Lachlan, the Murrumbidgee, the Hume, the Darling, and the Murray down to their respective terminations, but beyond them I had not passed—yet—I looked upon Central Australia as a legitimate field, to explore which *no man* had a greater claim than myself, and the first wish of my heart was to close my services in the cause of Geography by *dispelling the mists* that hung over it. (Sturt, 1847 vol 2: 1–2, emphasis added)

"Any man" in this passage is a white man, who strives to be the first (white) man to tread on, to throw light on, to map, that shrouded (dark) territory which is only known to 'savages'. Sturt wrote himself into existence, here, as a heroic individual—as if he had not depended on the many other men who travelled with him, including the guides from among the custodians of the land. He wrote as if he had not been absolutely dependent for his survival on the hospitality, generosity and knowledge of the guides, and the hospitality of the local inhabitants of the country they passed through. Rather, he believed, it was God who had kept him safe—evidence enough, for him, that he was fulfilling God's providential plan:

> I returned indeed to Sydney, disheartened and dissatisfied at the result of my investigations... for, although at the termination of the Murray, we came upon a country, the aspect of which indicated more than usual richness and fertility, we were unable, from exhausted strength, to examine it as we could have wished, and thus the fruits of our labours appeared to have been taken from us, just as we were about to gather them. But if, amidst difficulties and disappointments of no common description, I was led to doubt the wisdom of Providence, I was wrong. The course of

events has abundantly shewn how presumptuous it is in man to question the arrangements of that Allwise Power whose operations and purposes are equally hidden from us, for in six short years from the time when I crossed Lake Victoria, and landed on its shores, that country formed another link in the chain of settlements around the Australian continent, and in its occupation was found to realize the most sanguine expectations I had formed of it. Its rich and lovely valleys, which in a state of nature were seldom trodden by the foot of the savage, became the happy retreats of an industrious peasantry; its plains were studded over with cottages and cornfields; the very river which had appeared to me to have been so misplaced, was made the high road to connect the eastern and southern shores of a mighty continent; the superfluous stock of an old colony was poured down its banks into the new settlement to save it from the trials and vicissitudes to which colonies, less favourably situated, have been exposed ... Such, there can be no doubt, have been the results of an expedition from which human foresight could have anticipated no practical good. (Sturt, 1847 vol 1: 12–14)

Creating maps of territory previously unknown to white men, and being the owner of the first white foot to plant itself on the terrain of the subordinated other, was to fulfill God's plan, bringing honour to individualised, intrepid explorers.

Map-making had been crucial to the defeat of Napoleon, and to the domination of new territories incorporated into the expanding British Empire. In that sense what Sturt understood himself to be doing was not new. It was very new, however, for the custodians of the antipodean land that they traversed and mapped. They could not have anticipated the destructive force the newcomers would bring with them. Some did see the danger and attacked; others befriended them, open to what they had to offer. The newcomers brought betrayal with them, as Samuel Perry wrote. It was a multi-faceted betrayal that modern day Australians can barely comprehend.

In a final passage of Volume 2 of his journal, Sturt laid out what he believed to be the only possible future for the original custodians. He was distressed at the conflict that had now become rife among them when they visited each other. With deep misgivings, he spelled out in detail the necessity of severing the children forever from their tribal culture if they were to survive. To a present-day Australian this passage can only evince a sense of tragedy and horror, as we know only too well the dreadful aftermath of the policy he recommended. No matter how much respect he had felt for the people he had come to care for, and who had ensured both his survival and his personal glory, there was a social order that must, over time, assert itself in the colony:

> The Murray tribe, as well as the tribes from the south, frequently visit their friends near the capital, and on such occasions some scene of violence or dispute generally ensues. Frequently the abduction of a lubra, or of an unmarried female of another tribe, brings about a quarrel, and on such occasions some angry fighting is sure to follow; and so long as that custom remains, there is little hope of improvement amongst them. The subject of ameliorating their condition is, however, one of great difficulty, because it cannot be done without violating those principles of freedom and independence on which it is so objectionable to infringe; but when a great ultimate good is to be obtained, I cannot myself see any objection to those restraints, and that interference which should bring it about. There is nowhere, not even in Sydney, more attention paid to the native population than in South Australia, and if they stand a chance of improvement it is there. Whilst every kindness is shewn to the adult portion, the children are under the direct care of the Government. There is, as I have elsewhere stated, a school, at which from thirty to forty boys and girls attend. Nothing can be more regular or more comfortable than this institution. The children are kindly treated, and very much encouraged, and really to go into it as a visitor, one would be disposed to encourage the most sanguine expectations of success. As far as the elementary principles of education go, the native children are far from deficient. They read, write, and cipher as well as European children of their own age, and, generally speaking, are quiet and well behaved; but it is to be regretted that, as far as our experience goes, they can advance no farther; when their reason is taxed, they fail, and consequently appear to be destitute of those finer qualifications and principles on which both moral feeling and social order are based. It is however questionable with me whether this is not too severe a construction to put on their intellect, and whether, if the effect of ancient habits were counteracted, we should find the same mental defect.

> At present, the native children have free intercourse with their parents, and with their tribe. The imaginations of the boys are inflamed by seeing all that passes in a native camp, and they long for that moment, when, like their countrymen, they will be free to go where they please, and to join in the hunt or the fray. The girls are told that they are betrothed, and that, at a certain age, they must join their tribe. The voice of Nature

is stronger even than that of Reason. Why therefore should we be surprised at the desertion of the children from the native schools? But it will
be asked—What is to be done? The question, as I have said, is involved
in difficulty, because, in my humble opinion, the only remedy involves a
violation, for a time at all events, of the natural affections, by obliging a
complete separation of the child from its parents; but, I must confess, I
do not think that any good will result from the utmost perseverance of
philanthropy, until such is the case, that is, until the children are kept in
such total ignorance of their forefathers, as to look upon them as Europeans do, with astonishment and sympathy. It may be argued that this
experiment would require too great a sacrifice of feeling, but I doubt this.
Besides which, it is a question whether it is not our duty to do that which
shall conduce most to the benefit of posterity. The injury, admitting it to
be so, can only be inflicted on the present generation, the benefit would
be felt to all futurity. I have not, I hope, a disposition for the character
of an inhuman man, and certainly have not written thus much without
due consideration of the subject, but my own experience tells me we
are often obliged to adopt a line of conduct we would willingly avoid to
ensure a public good. (Sturt, 1847 vol 2: 283–285)

These deep ambiguities and ambivalences were embedded in the *spacetimemattering* of colonisation. Even the most sympathetic of the map-makers and
landholders, who formed good relations with the local men and women they
encountered, nevertheless turned against them when they defended their territory. The natives must take up colonists' beliefs and values, and they must
serve the white men and women who would be their masters and mistresses,
with none of the privileges that were taken for granted by those they served.

It is a sorry story of encounter, of ordinary people entangled in the act of
colonisation. The newcomers' ethics, their language, and their ways of being in
the world, shaped what they saw and heard, the choices they made, the stands
they took, and the bids for survival they participated in, at a terrible cost for the
land and its people.

CHAPTER 20

From Scottish Tenant Farmers to Landed Gentry: Mary Wightman and Abraham Nivison

This chapter brings me full circle to the beginning of this project where I set out with my mother to visit my grandmother, Al, on the New England Table-lands of New South Wales. Al's grandparents, Mary Wightman (1812–1873) and Abraham Nivison (1809–1895), arrived in the colony in 1840. Mary and Abraham were married in 1839, 100 years before Norma married Tom, who married in 1939. Mary and Abraham were the children of tenant farmers, and grew up on the vast estates of the Third Duke of Buccleuch in Dumfrieshire. The Third Duke had taken over the estate from his father in 1810. During their young lives, Mary and Abraham experienced revolutionary changes to their way of living and the forms of agriculture that were practiced on the estate.

As a young man growing up in the 1700s the Third Duke had been tutored by Adam Smith, who had given up his professorship at Edinburgh University to take the young man's education in hand, travelling with him around Europe to meet the men who were developing new ideas about agriculture, housing, economics, philosophy and literature.

The Third Duke brought these ideas, from Adam Smith and from the other philosophers he encountered on his travels in Europe, to the management of the Buccleuch estate. As a result Abraham, at the age of 10, moved from his simple mud house into Bournemouth House, a two-storey stone farmhouse with a slate roof. And he and Mary, along with all the other farm-workers' children, could attend the schools that the Third Duke established on his land. The Third Duke brought new agricultural methods to farming on the estate, trebling its productivity. Along with new knowledge and vastly improved living conditions, his workers were given significant new responsibilities.

Notwithstanding those improvements Abraham's family suffered a number of untimely deaths. His mother, Jean, died in 1827, when Abraham was eighteen years old. His sisters, Isabel and Mary, died in 1813 and 1831. His brother William died in 1836, and his father, James, in 1837. His older sisters Grace and Margaret and his younger sisters, Alison and Jean, had married and left the farm. His brother Alexander had also married and gone elsewhere in pursuit of a profession other than farming. After his father's death, only his sisters, Isabel (named after the little sister who died) and Elizabeth, were left to him to care for.

© BRONWYN DAVIES, 2021 | DOI:10.1163/9789004446717_021

Mary was the daughter of Alexander Wightman and Jean Bell. She was the youngest of the Wightman family until her little brother John was born when she was 11 years old. Like Abraham she benefitted from the introduction of schooling, the improved living conditions and the increased productivity brought to the land by the Third Duke. In 1832, Mary's brother, Adam, migrated to New South Wales with his wife and children, paving the way for Mary and Abraham to follow. Adam was employed managing the land of Col Dumaresq at Muswellbrook, near Singleton. He also leased his own land and built a hotel there. In 1838 Mary's father renegotiated his lease and gave Mary her inheritance. Abraham sold his family's estate, and after providing for each of his two unmarried sisters, he and Mary were free to marry.

The Nivisons and Wightmans were Presbyterian. The Scots had long fought the English over their right to maintain their Presbyterianism, attempting at times to install it as the dominant official religion in Britain. All my English and Welsh forebears were Church of England, and it wasn't until I encountered the Nivisons that I had stopped to think about the significance of religion in all their lives. At first the Presbyterianism of the 1840s seemed very different from the Church of England religion I had grown up with. But as I delved deeper, it was the similarities that became more interesting.

Both the Presbyterian and the Church of England church condoned the act of colonisation. If Almighty God wanted the land to become a Christian land, and if Christians killed the heathen in the act of taking their land and later living on it, then that must be what God wanted. If people inevitably fell into evil, not treating the heathens gently, but with violence, that too must, by definition, be part of God's plan. Those who flourished did so with the aid of Divine Grace. While the action of harming the heathen would require repentance on the one hand, it would require faith in God's plan on the other. Both religions, in the 1800s, were engaged in a complex balancing act between individual free will, and the determinism of God's plan.

Another influential concept at play, for both, which was integral to the voluntary mass migrations taking place, was *messianicity*, or promise:

> Messianicity is the open-ended promissory quality of a claim, image or entity ... things in the world appear to us at all only because they tantalize and hold us in suspense, alluding to a fullness that is elsewhere, to a future that, apparently, is on its way ... To be alive is to be waiting 'for someone or something that, in order to happen ... must exceed and surprise every determinate anticipation'. (Bennett, 2010: 32)

Mary and Abraham's decision to migrate was thus not necessarily based on a careful plan with a desired end which they proceeded to put in place; rather what they moved toward, what *pulled them*, the *messianicity*, was an image of an emergent promise yet to be realised—a transformation that would 'exceed and surprise' their expectations. And the God they trusted in would play a vital role in their success or failure, as they followed the pull toward a new and prosperous life.

Queen Victoria was crowned in 1840, the year after Mary and Abraham left for New South Wales. Bishop Charles Blomfield, a cousin of Thomas Blomfield, gave the sermon at her coronation, justifying colonisation as the spreading of the goodness inherent in the word of God. He desired for the newly crowned monarch that she oversee the peaceful spread of the Gospel throughout the known world: "the pure Gospel preached to all the people of the land; and the consequent growth of every thing that is *lovely and of good report*" (Blomfield, 1838: 5–6).

The Wedding and the Journey: 1839

At the wedding, only days before Mary and Abraham set sail, it is said that Mary wore a veil from the Buccleuch family, which had been gifted her by a friend. That veil was then supposedly passed down in each generation to the oldest daughter. But no-one knows where the veil is. Jillian Oppenheimer (1989a) is inclined to think, in the absence of the veil itself, that the story is a myth; and she doubts that Mary would have had high enough status to be its recipient.

But perhaps the gift of the veil was real. There seems to be so much that was so very sensible about Mary. She waited so long to get married—in order to ensure, perhaps, that they could move without the difficulties her brother Adam and his wife had experienced travelling half way around the globe with small children. She waited until they were in a strong financial position before marrying and setting out. The veil opens up a reading of Mary and Abraham in which they are not only sensible, pragmatic Scots, but also romantically entangled; and perhaps, too, it opens the possibility that the Nivisons and Wightmans were sufficiently well-respected by the Duke's family and their immediate circle to attract such a gift.

According to Jillian, the journey by sea from Scotland to Sydney, and thence Newcastle, then upriver and overland by bullock-drawn dray to join Adam in Muswellbrook, would have been miserable for Mary, given that she was probably both seasick and suffering morning-sickness. When I first read Jillian's account of Mary's misery I imagined she must have further information about Mary's character that supported the view of her as miserable in the face of such an adventure. But there was, she told me, no further evidence. Her reading was based on historical fact—the conditions on the ships at that time were appalling.

It is true that on board there were features of those early ships that were hard to bear, over and above their cramped quarters, and the wild unpredictability of the seas they sailed over. The toilet facilities, for example, were often on the deck, and passengers must relieve themselves over the back of the ship without any screen to make their doings private. Some women are said to have died of constipation, so appalled were they at this lack of privacy (Watson, 1984).

At the same time the seas in 1839 were alive with multiple life forms. There were nautili or 'Portugese men of war' swimming on the surface of the water, glittering pale red and light blue; there were flying fish, and sea-birds, dolphin and whales, and the vivid night-time skies. The oceans were criss-crossed with passenger ships and trading vessels back and forth to the Americas, to the Indies, to India, Africa and Australia; there were pirate ships; and whaling ships—whale oil then being the primary source of light and heat. There were slave ships,[1] and there were convict ships. The ships' captains exchanged messages and letters back and forth as they crossed the oceans. There were days when no wind blew and the seas were flat as glass, the ship becalmed; and yet other days when the seas were crowded with adventure and with horror.

Did Mary and Abraham look out at these new elements of life on the ocean, or was their gaze turned inward, to life on board the ship, to the people they were travelling with, who were setting out on the same adventure? And in their own cabin were there tender scenes of seduction and pleasurable love-making? Perhaps they lay on elegant appliquéd bed linen that Mary had sewn for their marital bed, and soft flowing white nightdresses that Abraham could gently remove as they gave in at long last to the pleasures of the flesh they had for so long denied themselves.

Or perhaps they had not denied themselves. At that time in Scotland there was a startling number of pregnancies out of wedlock, and even more startling, countless pregnant women taking men to court in order to force them into marriage. Mary and Abraham started their family on their honeymoon, which was to last for seven months or more, depending on the winds, the currents, the fog, and whatever else they encountered along the way. If Abraham was reading the Bible to Mary each morning, as Jillian tells us he did throughout his life, perhaps he read from 1 Corinthians 7: 1–40:

---

1 Though slave trading had been partially banned in 1833, the Royal West Africa Squadron captured 1,600 slave ships and freed 150,000 Africans between 1808 and 1860.

The husband should give to his wife her conjugal rights, and likewise the wife to her husband. For the wife does not have authority over her own body, but the husband does. Likewise the husband does not have authority over his own body, but the wife does. Do not deprive one another, except perhaps by agreement for a limited time, that you may devote yourselves to prayer; but then come together again...

Or perhaps from Proverbs 5: 18–19:

Let your fountain be blessed, and rejoice in the wife of your youth, a lovely deer, a graceful doe. Let her breasts fill you at all times with delight; be intoxicated always in her love.

Did they stroll together afterwards on the deck, taking in the steady breeze of the trade winds? Did they look at the glittering stars studding the black canopy of night, looking for the changes in the sky as they plied their way ever southward, through the tropics to South America, to South Africa, across the Indian Ocean and south of the Australian continent, into the Pacific Ocean, and up the east coast to Sydney? Did they learn from the Captain and his mates how to read the sea with all its dangers and beauties? Did they call in at exotic ports and experience new smells and tastes and sounds and sights they could never have dreamed of? Did they find all those new impacts on their senses exciting and invigorating, even though it was sometimes also terrifying?

At the time when Mary and Abraham had been planning their marriage and the long voyage to the colony, the British government was beginning to actively encourage such migration. It was concerned at the negative image the colony had developed, as a place full of rascals. Victor Hugo, with tongue in cheek, wrote of the lives of rascals who escaped their home countries:

It is a curious thing, but it could almost be said that escape from one's country opened up the possibility of new careers, particularly for dishonest characters. The quantity of civilisation that a rascal brought with him from Paris or London was a valuable resource in primitive or barbarous countries; it was a useful qualification and made him an initiator in his new country. It was not by any means impossible for him to exchange the rigours of the law for the priesthood. There is something phantasmagorical in a disappearance, and many an escape has had consequences that could not have been dreamed of. An absconding of this kind could lead to the unknown and the chimerical: thus a bankrupt who had left Europe by

some illicit route might reappear twenty years later as grand vizier to the
Great Mogul or as a king in Tasmania. (Hugo, 2014/1866: 142)

In a reversal of the thinking following the Bigge Inquiry, in which it had been
recommended that the colony should be maintained as a hell-hole to act as a
deterrent to would-be criminals at 'home', the new thinking in 1840 was that
transportation to the colony should cease, and respectable families should be
encouraged to migrate and change the colony's image. New South Wales' life as
a penal colony was coming to an end, and its new, scarcely apprehended identity as a jewel in the British Crown was glimmering in the background. Global
trade had expanded as Adam Smith had predicted, and New South Wales was
valued as a vital trading post. Farmers who might feed the colony and provide food for the transport and trade ships were in demand. Land grants and
assisted passage were being offered to encourage migration. In 1835 a bounty
scheme had been developed for couples and young women (men in the colony
outnumbered women 4:1), with shipping agents receiving a bounty for each
suitably skilled migrant they could secure for the colony's employers.

Abraham and Mary were to transform themselves from tenant farmers to
large landholders, who would found a dynasty on the New England Tablelands.
They were to become the sponsors and employers of Scots families making the
journey after them to New South Wales.

On arriving in Sydney, Mary and Abraham went north by sea to Newcastle,
and then inland by dray, to Muswellbrook where they joined Mary's brother
Adam. There they had the baby conceived during the journey, and they stayed
on until their second child was born. During that period, there was a prolonged
drought from 1841–2, and a severe recession that lasted until 1843. Mary's
brother, along with many another newcomer, was driven to ruin, and forced
to sell up.

When the drought and recession ended, Mary and Abraham bought up the
lease on Ohio station, further north from Muswellbrook on the south-eastern
edge of the New England Tablelands, adjacent to the small village of Walcha.
Walcha began in the 30s and 40s, and in 1842 a wool road was being constructed
between Walcha and Port Macquarie. In 1852 Walcha was gazetted as a village
with a blacksmith, a general store and a flour-mill.

The explorer John Oxley had described this land in 1818 as "the finest open
country, or rather park, imaginable: the general quality of the soil excellent"
(Gammage, 2011:15). It was the land of the Dunggaddi people who had cared
for it for more than 60,000 years. They lived up on the tablelands during the
summer and, in the icy winters, moved down into the gorge country where fish
and other wildlife were plentiful.

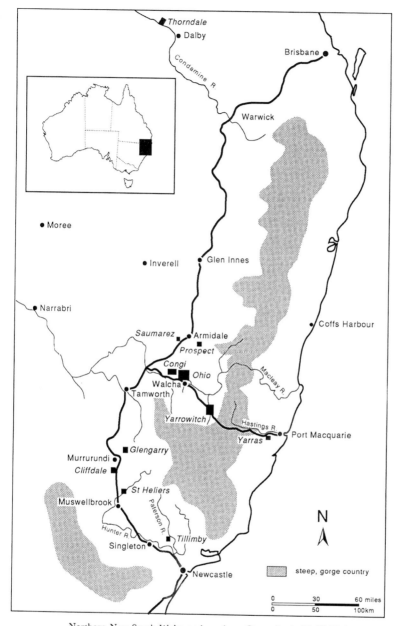

Northern New South Wales and southern Queensland. (D. Hobbs)

MAP 6　Northern New South Wales

OPPENHEIMER AND MITCHELL 1989A: 26

FIGURE 81   View from Ohio gardens of the creek at Ohio
             PHOTO AUTHOR, 2018

The landscape of Ohio looked remarkably like Dumfrieshire.

In the early years they had lived very simply in one of the existing work-ers' cottages on the farm until they built a two-storey stone house. Their life on Ohio station in some ways repeated the changes they had gone through in their young lives. It began in a simple cottage, and after ten years they moved to the beautiful two-storey stone house that my grandmother, Al, grew up in.

Mary Nivison bore seven children, four sons and three daughters, between 1840 and 1854. James Alexander, my great grandfather, was born in 1848.

The vast majority of the labour in New South Wales at that time was carried out by convicts. Landholders could be assigned convicts to work as domestic servants, as shepherds and farm labourers, clearing land, building houses and roads. Mary and Abraham preferred not to use convict labour. Mary's sister-in-law had written in her letters about her distress at the pain of hearing the convicts groan fearfully in the night, their chains clanking. J.D. Laing, the first Presbyterian minister in New South Wales, believed that convict labour was turning New South Wales into a 'dung hill' and that the peasants no longer needed in Scotland should be brought where they were desperately needed in New South Wales. The land itself he observed was glorious, and all that was needed was "some Scots with whom to share it" (Watson, 1984: 89). With the bounty system and government-assisted passage it was possible for Mary and Abraham to bring out Scottish families to work on Ohio. As well, they employed indigenous women in the house and indigenous men about the farm.

All the new ideas the Third Duke had brought, from his travels in Europe with Adam Smith, could be translated into this new environment, enabling Mary and Abraham to flourish. Over their lifetimes they extended their hold-ings so that each of their sons could become wealthy graziers on surrounding

FIGURE 82   Ohio
PHOTO AUTHOR, 2018

New England properties. The change in their status in their new environment was transformational, as Victor Hugo might have predicted. Abraham came to hold new powers he could not have dreamed of when he set out from Scotland. His position in the community now resembled that of the Duke back home. He was instrumental in building the first Presbyterian Church in 1857 and the school in 1859, and he played significant roles such as local magistrate in court hearings in Armidale, where his judgements were considered to be fair and just. Without a British upper class, the large landholders were required to become the new elite, fulfilling many of the functions the Third Duke, back in Dumfrieshire, had fulfilled. Abraham and his fellow landholders became responsible for the creation and maintenance of the local social order. Abraham was inexorably drawn into that position, moving from boy born in a rude mud hut in 1809, to Lord of the Manor in 1860.

Mary developed a thyroid condition that eventually led to her death in 1873 at the age of 59. In the last years of her life she lived in a bed-sitting room on the ground floor, with a nurse who took care of her, living in an adjoining room. The magnificence of her dress in a photo (*overleaf*), taken in the final years of her life, offers a glimpse of their wealth and of the status they now occupied in the New England community.

Was the transformation in their lives, as they understood it, made possible through God's good grace? Or was it through Abraham's practical good judgement on what would make good farmland, and his decision to wait until the severe drought was over before taking up land? Or was it the support and companionship they offered each other? Or did the roots of the transformation lie in the colony being based on a British concept of class, where landed gentry of

FIGURE 83   Abraham and Mary, 1850s

independent means ruled the land; and in the absence of those gentry, a new elite was created from among the landholders? And underlying all of these was the assumption that the land of the 'savages' could be taken.

At the time Jillian was writing her book about the Nivison clan, Patsy Cohen and Margaret Somerville (1990) were researching the lives of the original custodians of the land in the New England region after they had been removed onto a reserve. Their book was *Ingelba and the Five Black Matriarchs*.

'Ingelba' was one of two pieces of crown land reserved for the original people on the Tablelands. It was approximately 30 miles from the Nivisons' Ohio. As a child, Patsy Cohen was one of the stolen generation, a victim of government policies that stemmed directly from the attitude that Charles Sturt set out at the end of his journal in 1847. Patsy and her siblings were taken away from their indigenous mother by government agencies while their father was fighting in the Second World War. They were placed in an orphanage and moved between orphanages and foster homes, always unsuccessfully, until finally the decision was taken to send Patsy back to her grandmother, who lived on Ingelba.

FIGURE 84
Abraham the patriarch
OPPENHEIMGER AND MITCHELL 1989A

The elders remembered living on Ingelba apart from white people. Some of them left the reserve to work for them, and in rare cases they became trusted and even loved friends. One of the five matriarchs remembered by the participants in the Ingelba story, was Granny Wright. She had been born in 1834, around the time when squatters were first taking up land around what would become the town of Walcha. The elders who remembered her and her life on the Ingelba reserve told her story—a story in which many of the newcomers' ways had already become intrinsic to life on the reserve.

> *Annie*: with Granny Wright we had the best, 'cause she could cook. To this
> very day I can remember all 'er cooking. She used to make—she had a
> hamper and big ovens like this she used to cook bread in. Big iron camp
> ovens, she 'ad two, to bake 'er bread in. I used to make the yeast for 'er. We
> used to boil the yeast, the yeast weeds—herbs they used—hops, they call
> them, hops, that's what they called it ... They done all their shoppin' in
> Newcastle and Sydney ... They used to buy tins of jam, all their groceries
> and flour and that sort of thing, until Errits come to Walcha. The bullock
> wagons and coaches used to bring it down. They knew everything what
> to buy. They, the girls was well educated—there was Aunty Bella, Aunty
> Annie and Aunty Jessie. The girls were well educated. They had a good
> teacher at Ingelba in those days ... (Cohen and Somerville, 1990: 125)

Maisie, one of the elders, told the story of when Granny Wright had lived with her family on Ingelba when Maisie herself had been a child. Granny Wright

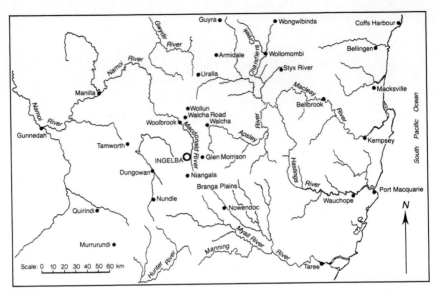

MAP 7   Ingelba and surrounding places
COHEN AND SOMERVILLE 1990 FRONTISPIECE

always wanted to walk up to Ohio, some 30 miles distant, a walk she had done
regularly as a younger woman:

> *Maisie*: I think Mum might've had Granny Wright [to care for when she
> was elderly] more than the other daughters or daughters-in-law. 'Cause I
> can remember Granny Wright, she wasn't a very tall old lady and she 'ad
> a crippled foot, they never used to wear shoes. We used to have to watch
> her in the morning—she 'ad 'er bed there, mother had one of those real
> big tents and she had her bed there... And we used to have to watch her
> and she'd come round and she'd look. She was that type, [she'd] see if
> you're asleep and then she'd sneak off and try and trick you by coverin'
> 'er tracks. She used to say she was going up to Nivison's to work, yeah, you
> see the big station goin' into Walcha? She was always sayin' she was goin'
> up to Nivisons. My Grandmother too, Grandmother Morris, she used to
> work there too. She used to take Mum—there was an old English lady up
> there teachin' Mrs Nivison's children and she took a liking to my mother
> and she taught her. They did domestic work and things. (Cohen and
> Somerville, 1990: 125–6)

Patsy told another story of the affection felt for her grandfather by one of the
graziers known as "old Brazil":

Patsy: Well, when I took Pop back [to Ingelba] just before he died that old Brazil, one of the old cockies from out there, Bim and Ronnie were there this day, and 'e [Brazil] was tryin' to chase the young bullock around and 'e couldn't and 'e come over to the camp, the hut, and 'e said 'Could you boys help me round this bullock up?' And 'e looked over and 'e said, 'That's not bloody old Alf Boney standing over there?' And the boys said, 'Yeah that's 'im,' and 'e just ran over and put 'is arms around Pop and said, 'I thought you died years ago Alf', and hugged and kissed him. (Cohen and Somerville, 1990: 40)

Despite those bonds of affection the system of apartheid remained intact. The original people were confined to life on reserves. They were not allowed to give birth in the hospital, but must pitch a tent in the hospital grounds. The teachers allocated to the reserves were often uneducated.

Granny Wright, while building friendly relations with the local landed gentry, offered hospitality to those who had fallen foul of the British justice system. She took care of a bushranger, most likely Fred Ward, the bushranger who lived in that district. Fred's wife and accomplice was Mary-Ann Bugg, who had a convict father and an indigenous mother.

Annie: Well, it's a funny thing while ever they was down there chasin' the bushrangers, Granny was feedin' one of them back 'ere. Grandfather said, 'If anybody comes here, give 'em a feed, feed them'. And she done that, she fed one of them. And 'e worked for 'er too, done everything 'e could for 'er. I suppose 'e was dark. There must've been some of the black bludgers there (laughs). Well, she's never been frightened 'cause the bushrangers were around that time and she was never frightened.

Lulu: No she was never frightened, they were good to 'er.

Annie: No, she'd give 'em a feed. Or give any old tramp that went past a feed, take 'em in and give 'em a feed... (Cohen and Somerville, 1990: 125)

The custodians of the land had rules of hospitality that might put the newcomers to shame. Fred Ward was eventually hunted down and murdered by a policeman with whom he had gone to school. Once deemed to be outside the law, however unfairly, *for the poor* there was virtually no way to return to a life in which you might be treated with dignity and respect in the New South Wales legal system.

For the landholders, their role was to administer the law rather than to be on the receiving end of it. The function of the magistrates, as it was understood at the time, was to deter, through brutal punishments such as flogging or hanging, the repetition of crimes committed by the lower orders. Those crimes might be no more than associating with proven criminals. And 'associating' could be impossible to avoid if the criminals were members of your family, as in Fred Ward's case, or if they came to you for hospitality in a time of need. Fred Ward escaped from Cockatoo Island, where he had been unjustly incarcerated, and was to become known as Captain Thunderbolt, 'gentleman of the road'. He had a reputation for always being courteous, never robbing those who had been kind to him, being considerate of women, and never shooting to kill. He survived as a bushranger, it is said, for longer than any of the others.

Among the records of members of my New England Tablelands family, I find this in the memoir of my cousin Charles Edwin Blomfield, who was born in 1864:

> The only bushranger that I remember in New England was Thunderbolt, and he was shot when I was very young. My father [Edwin Cordeaux Blomfield] when riding out on the Boorolong Run one day met a man, and after talking to him for a while engaged him to take some horses up to Queensland. After leaving him he came on one of the shepherds who asked father if he had met a man and when my Father said "Yes I've engaged him to take some horses up to Queensland" the shepherd says "That's Thunderbolt; he won't take any horses to Queensland for you". My father met him again on the run after that, and of course remembered him; he asked Thunderbolt why he had never touched any of the Boorolong horses, and Thunderbolt replied "I wouldn't touch any of your horses, Mr Blomfield" and when my father asked why Thunderbolt said "Remember when you were at Lue (that is a station near Mudgee where my Father got his first experience) a little boy called Freddy Ward used to come over for the Doctor's mail. I was that little boy; many a good feed you gave me. I won't touch your horses. (Blomfield, 1945: 10)

Like Edwin Cordeaux Blomfield, James Alexander Nivison, my great grandfather, had a positive encounter with Thunderbolt. Jillian tells the story, which she got from her father, of James sitting down by a creek under the shade of a tree, sharing his lunch with Thunderbolt and whiling away the hours talking about their shared passion for good horses (pers.comm 18-09-16).

Edwin Cordeaux's father-in-law did not fare so well. Charles Marsh, of Salisbury Court, was at the Walcha Race Meeting and Circus when Fred Ward was

FIGURE 85   Entrance to Thunderbolt's cave
PHOTO AUTHOR, 2016

also there among the crowd. Fred had closely observed who made the big wins, and Charles Marsh had won £100. After the races Fred called on him to relieve him of his winnings. Thomas Perry, too, James' Nivison's father-in-law, was no more fortunate in his encounters with Thunderbolt. Jillian writes of Thomas Perry:

> Throughout his life he bred and raced thoroughbred horses. He was among the first of the local families to organize and attend race meetings throughout the north. The Perry's were renowned for their hospitality, love of music and entertainment, and may have used some of their homegrown Lumala wine when friends visited. He, jokingly, became known as the 'King of Bendemeer'. The bushranger Thunderbolt, who recognized Perry's fast and wellbred racehorses, and knew that a good horse could outpace the policemen chasing him, was prone to stealing them. A family story has been told of Thomas Perry chasing Thunderbolt around his stockyard on a moonlight night shouting "Surrender you scoundrel" as, with a laugh, Thunderbolt mounted on a Bendemeer racehorse and station saddle, jumped the yards and raced off into the night. (Oppenheimer, 2009: 148)

As the police continued to fail at capturing the bushrangers, who were at work throughout the colony, the government placed increasingly high rewards on their heads. Those rewards, twenty or thirty times a worker's annual salary, stacked the odds against them. Whereas some had been sympathetic and supportive of them, as Granny Wright had been, and Edwin Cordeaux Blomfield and James Nivison were, it became increasingly dangerous to be seen in their company, and more and more likely that they would be shot with intent to kill, either by the police or by members of the public. As had happened to Johnny O'Mealley in 1863, Fred Ward was shot and killed for a handsome reward.

And there the stories of my forebears end, at least for now.

Epilogue

When I asked my son Paul, as we walked along the street in Copenhagen recently, if he thought he would ever read this book, he said 'maybe, some day'. Tracing ancestors, he observed, is something old people do when they are nearing death, and afraid of being forgotten. He said that kindly. And there is some truth in what he says; it *is* old people's business, and there *is* a fear of being forgotten that drives it—but that is not what this project has become. The threads of my spider's web have taken on their own life, expanding and illuminating—illuminated like a thousand drops of dew in the early morning light.

Finding the entangled lines of force that animated my ancestors' lives has opened up new ways of questioning–being–knowing, far beyond what I imagined at the outset—taking me beyond familial connections, and immersing me in a re–turn to the colonisation of New South Wales, and to what drove that mass migration. I have come to know those acts of migration and colonisation through the specificity of individual ancestral lives. And in that act of coming to know, I have put aside the familiar refrain of guilt and blame and moral judgement, and instead, opened myself up to the question of each ancestor whose life I have written about: 'What was it to be this'?

Such writing asks a great deal. It is not based on a linear conception of time in which the past is past. Each past life is entangled in the present and the future, and entangled in who I have become, and go on becoming, in the act of writing. Such writing, takes up the, sometimes painful, task of coming to know what has been hidden.

All writing, Cixous says, is:

> ... a way of leaving no space for death, of pushing back forgetfulness, of never letting oneself be surprised by the abyss. Of never becoming resigned, consoled; never turning over in bed to face the wall and drift asleep again as if nothing had happened; as if nothing could happen. (Cixous, 1993: 3)

The act of colonisation, the treatment of the 'savages', the taking of their land, the oppression of the poor and of women. All these open up an abyss that one might deny, or turn one's back on, as if they never happened. But how *did* they happen, and what sense can be made of them, through those past ancestral lives?

FIGURE 86   Tangled roots of a Moreton Bay fig tree
            PHOTO AUTHOR, 2018

I lived my younger life as if I were a unique and separate individual who could in large part shrug off the past. But the past, with its plunges into the abyss, its torturous challenges, its passion and its grief and its rage, both my own, and those of my ancestors, has made it clear to me that I am materially, ethically and linguistically *of* the world that I have sought to understand. Not one, or a self, but *of* that world. My own being and becoming, and my ancestors' being and becoming, are entangled in intra–actions with the world and its becoming.

My explorations of the traces that my ancestors have left of their lives have changed my present and my past and my future. I haven't returned to their lives, but rather I have *re–turned*. Intra–acting with them, and with their placetime–matterings, has affected me in surprising and unexpected ways. Approaching them without moral judgement, I have recovered webs of family connections, but much more, in coming to comprehend the transience of life, and its complex and contradictory beauty, I have also discovered its continuity.

At this point, at the ending of this project, I can't pinpoint where it all began. Was it that day when I visited Helsingor (Elsinore) castle and saw, in a magnificent ballroom, a huge globe of the world on which Australia was missing, and in the elegant open fireplace, brass firedogs almost identical to those in the fireplace of my Australian childhood home? Was it that coming together of a concept of the world, in which Australia was missing, with a vivid, material connection between that place in Denmark, and the heart of my childhood home, that set me off? Was it in that moment in Helsingor that the story of the unrecognized, undocumented son of the Danish prince came to matter to me?

Or was it in Dublin, and Maynooth, and Bristol, finding myself enmeshed in intensely pleasurable conversations with Irish colleagues, where our love of story intimately coincided, when I began to wonder how it was that I was so strongly connected to Ireland, when no stories of Irish ancestors had ever been told?

Or was it my puzzlement over knowing nothing of my father's mother, and the questions that the silences about her life raised for me as I grew older? How was it that Jean's life had gone missing from our family stories?

In each generation we leave the home of our parents; we seek new ideas and new knowledge and in doing so we are alive in the world; we evolve, and we make our own lives. But even in the act of leaving, we are *of* our parents' world, materially enfolded in memories of it, and affectively entangled in what we have inherited. Memory, Barad says, is integral to the entangled enlivening of being:

> To address the past (and future), to speak with ghosts, is not to enter-
> tain or reconstruct some narrative of the way it was, but to respond, to
> be responsible, to take responsibility for that which we inherit (from the
> past and the future), for the entangled relationalities of inheritance that
> 'we' *are*..., to put oneself at risk, to risk oneself (which is never one or
> self), to open oneself up to indeterminacy in moving towards what is to–
> come. (Barad, 2014: 182)

We might forget our ancestors and lose any capacity to recognize and respond
to the lives they lived, or the passions that drove them. In such forgetting we
become ignorant of ourselves and of what is to come: but "there is no moving
beyond, no leaving the 'old' behind. There is no absolute boundary between
here–now and there–then" (Barad, 2014: 168).

In re–turning to those past lives, I found myself entangled in them, though
I began knowing almost nothing of them. I was the stranger within, interrupt-
ing the stories that had already been told, and setting out to remember the
unremembered. I have become "the surprise, the interruption ... the stranger
(within) returning unannounced" (Barad, 2014: 178). And with that re–turn I
have taken up a different sense of responsibility from the one I began with.

I was threaded through with those thick tangles of ancestral spacetime–
mattering; I wanted to be able to *respond*, to be of them, among them, to recognize them—and to comprehend the multiple entangled forces that impacted
on them. This book is my response, my response–ability toward my forebears,
a response–ability that is to them and to me—not separate from me. And nor
are the harms they have done separate from me. As we Australians, both those
descended from the original custodians and those descended from the newcomers, move closer to finding some means of reconciliation, it has seemed
vital to me to acknowledge those harms, and also to make sense of the people
and their spacetimemattering. I have benefitted from the history of colonisation, though until I began this project I was largely ignorant of how it had taken
place and of what part my forebears had played in it. My response–ability is
not just to my forebears; it must also be to those whose lives they affected, for
better and for worse.

Each person I have written about here, I have become intrigued by—not
just my forebears but people they encountered, like Bennillong, Cole–by and
Arabanoo, and Joseph Holt, Johnny O'Mealley, and Captain Thunderbolt. The
memories of them are precious to me—and their struggles to survive and to
create life touch me profoundly.

Existence of each individual life is extraordinary—a gift so precious it can barely be comprehended, even though it is at the same time everywhere. The moments when the quality of light is glimpsed, or the soft wind blows across the field of grass, or when a child's face lights up with joy, those moments of existence make it seem impossible that violent wars will break out, and that all, in the end, will turn to dust and be forgotten. In a way this book is an act of remembering that defies that inevitable forgetting; it holds each life and treasures it, in all its complexity and beauty and pain. It reaches, at the same time, toward a recognition that we humans are all *of* the world, and that the end of any one life is not the end of life, or of humanity, or of the world. We are of the world, and the world, for now, will continue.

Appendix 1

George William Hope Davies wrote a newspaper column in which he reflected on the Second World War and its implications for Australia. His *nom de plume* was 'G.W.H.D'.

War Sciomancy

COMMUNISM

FRANCE fell to the German invaders, owing to the dissension amongst political leaders; dissension which had gradually been getting more and more marked for years, until at the actual invasion, politically, she was rotten to the core.

The production of munitions, and all the machinery so vitally necessary in modern warfare, had for years been lamentably curtailed, owing, in the main, to disaffection and disunion, generally, in the ranks of Labour.

France was a capitalistic country. Communism is only another name for anti–capitalism, and France was just riddled with Communism. The French Army was also riddled with Communists. That the Communists were hand in glove with the German propagandists there is ample evidence to show. The French Army was ripe for defeat before a single German soldier set foot on French soil.

It is on record that bodies of French troops broke and fled, shouting, "We have been betrayed! We have no more ammunition!"

Today the once proud and powerful French nation is grovelling at the feet of Nazi Germany.

What is the position in Australia today?

Half the Federal Members of Parliament owe almost abject allegiance to the Official Labour Caucus. The Labour Caucus is dominated by powerful Unions. Those Unions in their turn (in the words of Mr. Hughes), are riddled with, and dominated by, Communists. The Communists themselves are working hand in glove with German and Italian spies and propagandists.

On the face of it, Australia is in the same position France was before she fell.

That ninety per cent of Australians are loyal to the core is beyond all reasonable doubt. The average Unionist has no say at all in the "politics" of his Union; knows little and cares less.

Before it is too late, it is the urgent and paramount duty of the Federal Government of Australia to throw down the gauntlet to the subversive Communistic and deadly menace to Australian national safety that has cork–screwed its way into the vitals of Australian politics, and doing its utmost to delay and strangle our war effort.

Reports are to hand that the British Government is about to take action against subversive Communistic activities in England.

(*By G.W.H.D.*)

War Sciomancy

IRELAND

THE BRITISH COMMONWEALTH OF NATIONS, of which Southern Ireland is an integral part, is at war with Germany and Italy. "Eire," as she has christened herself, enjoys to the full all the privileges of membership of the British Empire. Self–Government, freedom from all foreign aggression, absolutely master of all her internal affairs, and free to trade where and with whom she chooses; an idyllic position for any country to be in. That she has this freedom and protection is unquestionably owing to the fact that she is part of the British Empire.

The Government of Eire has decided to remain neutral in this war. In other words, she has refused to fight on the side of Britain. She has refused to allow Britain the use of three very valuable bases on her western coast. Her brilliantly–lighted cities act as a guide to German invaders. Eire is in fact a grave menace to England's safety.

Taking then into consideration all the facts, the inescapable conclusion in the mind of a disinterested observer is that the "Rulers of Eire" are desirous of coming under the domination of Nazi Germany, and believe that they would be better off than they are at present.

Knowing, as all the world does, what happened to Denmark, Norway, Holland, Belgium, and Poland, under German domination, the attitude of the people of Eire is very difficult to understand; is, in fact, an insoluble mystery. Another mystery, although not altogether insoluble, is why Britain has not taken some steps to free herself from this menace to her safety.

All the far–flung countries, scattered the wide world over, included in the British Commonwealth of Nations, have voluntarily rushed to the assistance of the Mother Country in the hour of her deadly peril.

The one and only lone exception is Eire. The pity of it!

(*By G.W.H.D.*)

War Sciomancy

RUSSIA

POLITICALLY, economically, racially, and geographically Russia is the stumbling block in the path of Hitler's plans for the subjugation of Europe. Eliminate Russia and the position would be that the Balkan States, including Greece and European Turkey would be easy. Likewise Spain and Portugal. She has got the rest. Russia has a powerful army and air fleet, and so far has not been exhausted in any way by the ravages of the Axis Powers. On the contrary, she has benefited by trade with Germany and expansion of her territories. Russia has categorically stated on more than one occasion that she will not tolerate the occupation by either Germany or Italy of the Balkan States. The German interference in Roumania obviously is in conflict with Russian interests, and has caused considerable friction between the two countries. The ancient prophesy of the monk, Johannes, in 1600, fortells the entry of Russia into the war. The trend of events so far certainly points to that happening. It may not be for some time yet. But when the opportune moment arrives there is no doubt that she will enter the war on Britain's side. A victorious Germany, supreme in Europe, would be a deadly menace to Russia. Germany's only way into Russia is over the Polish or Roumanian borders, and she is the only country that could do so with any chance of success. Fearing such an invasion Russia has massed huge armies on both these fronts. Racially the two nations are as far apart as the Poles and hate one another like poison. Russia has everything to gain and nothing to lose by the downfall of Germany. The recent meeting between Molotoff and Hitler was apparently abortive. The Russian was evidently instructed to give away nothing; not to enter into any agreement or pact that would have the effect of retarding or limiting in any way his country's freedom of action. Hitler is painfully aware that with his dwindling resources to have to resist an attack by a powerful enemy on his eastern front would be little short of calamitous. If pressure in the Mediterranean should cause Germany to invade Bulgaria, such action might well be the signal for both Russia and Turkey to declare war on the side of the British Empire, America, and gallant little Greece.

(By G.W.H.D.)

THE WAR

THE MONK JOHANNES in 1870 prophesied that this war would take place, that it would be started by Germany, and waged by her with terrific violence, that France would be partly overrun, that Britain would be fighting against the aggressor—also Russia, that France would ultimately come back into the fray, and that Germany would be utterly defeated, after which Europe would be divided into 22 free States, and a long period of peace and prosperity would follow.

Look at the position in Europe today—what has happened and what is likely to happen? The fact that Russia is massing troops on the German frontier ostensibly against German aggression—but probably only awaiting a favourable opportunity to attack a powerful and potential invader, would make it appear that there is a quite reasonable prospect of this ancient prophecy coming true.

Should Russia decide that the time is ripe, with her powerful air fleet and huge mechanized army on one flank, and Britain with her Navy and air fleet on the other, plus a re–vitalised France, Germany with her shortage of war supplies, would inevitably be overwhelmed.

Though deprecating the placing of any reliance on these ancient prophetic utterances, it must be admitted that some of them have had an uncanny knack of proving true.

Let us hope that this one will enhance the reputation of the ancient prophet.

(By G.W.H.D.)

Appendix 2

George William Hope Davies published this short story under his *nom de plume* '*G.W.H.D.*'.

Never Argue with a Woman

Billy McGee got up out of bed, stretched himself luxuriously, did a few calisthenic exercises by way of loosening up his muscles, grabbed a towel and made a beeline for the bathroom.

As the breakfast bell had gone, being Irish and impatient, he knocked loudly on the door, and called out, "Hurry up, it's nearly eight o'clock." Almost immediately the door was flung open, and Billy got a large wet soapy sponge bang in the face, a voice remarking, "Don't you tell me to hurry up; that's some hurry up for you."

Before he could get the soap out of his eyes his assailant had disappeared around the corner. He yelled out, "I'll get even with you; you hit and run scaly banshee." Getting no response, he proceeded to the shower and shave, and in due course sat down to breakfast.

Being a seaside pub and only having arrived the night before, he saw no one he knew, so settled down to enjoy his bacon and eggs. He had just got to the second egg when a slim well–dressed damsel, about eighteen he judged, sat down right opposite to him. It was one of those round tables that hold four, and not too big at that.

She smiled and said, "Nice morning."

"Er, yes," said Billy.

Then followed a deep silence, punctured with crockery rattles until in desperation Billy remarked, "Er! Staying long."

"Er, yes."

Another long silence. Then:

"Excuse me rubbing my eye, it's a bit sore; some cow smacked a soapy wet sponge on me; sort of thing you would expect in a place like this; did you ever get smacked in the eye with a soapy sponge?"

No, not yet.

What would you do if you got smacked in the eye with a wet sponge?

Well, it would all depend.

Depend on what?

The wet sponge.

I don't quite get you.

Well, if the sponge is properly wet and soapy and it is properly propelled, and it lands good and hard.

I see. Then you reckon it's all right if the cove that slings the sponge can get away with it, and it's right to splather a cove in the eye with a soapy sponge.

No, I don't, but you said what would I do if I got smacked in the eye with a wet sponge. I said it depends on the sponge.

Aw, cripes; but you never said what you would do if you got hit in the eye with a wet sponge.

But I didn't get smacked; it was you that got smacked, and now you want to make out that I got smacked in the eye.

I never even thought of such a thing.

Well, you said that if I'd got smacked in the eye with a wet sponge, what would I do? Well, I didn't, it was you that smacked me.

I did no such thing. How could I smack you, when I was the one that got smacked.

It's all the same; you would have smacked me if I hadn't smacked you first.

Oh! So it was you that smacked me in the eye with a wet sponge!

Who said that? I said you said I smacked you and I said it all depends. So if I smacked you you must have smacked me first, and that's about what you would do.

Holy smoke; I ... I ...

Don't swear at me because you got smacked; you want to smack everyone about the place. For two pins I'd smack you in the eye with this sausage.

Great Scott!

Huh! Scott, a decent Scotchman wouldn't waste soap and water, let alone a sponge on an Irish mug like you, you start talking to some other people and leave me alone, or I'll call the waiter.

Oh! So you will call the waiter, and I'm Irish. Well, just to show you that you're right for once, next time I see you near the bathroom I'll smack you in the eye with a wet soapy sponge, and wot's more I'll wash your dirty face with it.

No, you won't, because you have not got a sponge, and there's only one in this house, and that's the one I smacked you with, And I've still got it. So smarty, you call the waiter like you said you would. Just what I would expect a crank would do; hit a woman in the eye with a wet soapy sponge and then call the waiter.

For once Billy did the right thing; he rose up, bowed politely and said, "You win, I smacked myself in the eye with a wet soapy sponge."

Ha! Ha! Ha! Then that settles it; you admit that you hit me in the eye, and that you haven't got a sponge, or soap either, and you can't take a joke. Good morning.

As he walked towards the door she called after him with an idyllic, dainty, disarming smile, "Might see you in the surf later."

Billy grinned.

What happened in the surf I might tell you later.

References

Abell, B. 1844 Recollections of the Emperor Napoleon during the first three years of his captivity on the Island of St Helena: Including the time of his residence at her father's house, "The Briars". [Second edition 1845 with appendix; third edition 1873, revised and added to by her daughter Mrs Charles Johnstone].

Achilles, S. 2012 *Literature, ethics, and aesthetics. Applied Deleuze and Guattari.* New York, NY: Palgrave Macmillan.

Ahearn, B. 2013 *Beyond the Sea: the life and times of Murtagh Ahern a convict transported for life from Ireland to the colony of New South Wales: 1802. vols 1 & 2.* Dural: Rosenberg.

Alexander, A. 1999 *Tasmania's Convicts. How Felons Built a Free Society.* Sydney: Allen and Unwin.

Austen, J. 1968 *Pride and Prejudice.* London: Heron Books.

Austen, J. 2012 *Persuasion.* Amersham, Bucks: TransAtlantic Press.

Baird, J. 2017 *Victoria. The Queen.* Sydney: HarperCollins *Publishers* Australia Pty Limited.

Banham, W. G. 1994 *Eugowra. Its History and Development.* Orange: Eugowra History Group.

Barad, K. 2007 *Meeting the Universe Halfway.* Durham & London: Duke University Press.

Barad, K. 2008 Posthumanist performativity: Toward an understanding of how matter comes to matter. In S. Alaimo, & S. Hekman (Eds.), *Material feminisms.* Bloomington: Indiana University Press, 120–154.

Barad, K. 2010 Quantum entanglements and hauntological relations of inheritance: Dis/continuities, spacetime enfoldings, and justice–to–come. *Derrida Today* 3.2, 240–268.

Barad, K. 2012 Nature's queer performativity. *Kvinner Køn Forskning.* 1.2, 25–53.

Barad, K. 2014 Diffracting diffraction: cutting together–apart. *Parallax* 20.3, 168–187.

Barthes R. 1993 *Mythologies.* London: Vintage.

Bateson, C. 1974. *The Convict Ships 1787–1868.* Sydney: Library of Australian History.

Bennett, J. 2010 *Vibrant Matter. A Political Ecology of Things.* Durham: Duke University Press

Blomfield, C. 2016/1838 *A sermon preached at the coronation of her most excellent majesty Queen Victoria in the Abbey Church of Westminster June 28, 1838.* Delhi: Facsimile Publisher.

Blomfield, C. E. 1945 *Reminiscences of Early New England by Charles Edwin Blomfield in 1945, supplemented and criticised by Sir Hugh Croft, W. G. Blomfield, Rev. E. Norman*

McLie, T. A. Everett, and C.L. Smith (The initials of ECB refer to my father). Viewed at the Heritage Centre, University of New England and Regional archives 5–1–2016.

Blomfield, T., Blomfield T.V. and Blomfield C. 1926 *Memoirs of the Blomfield Family. Being Letters Written by the Late Captain T.V. Blomfield and his Wife to Relatives in England*. Printed at the Armidale Express Office.

Blomfield, E. V. 1950 *An account of Blomfield families*. 30 copies issued privately.

Blomfield, G. 1981 *Baal Belbora. The end of the dancing*. Chippendale: Apcol.

Boldrewood, R. 1990/1888 *Robbery Under Arms*. Australia: Angus and Robertson.

Bronte, C. 2014/1847 *Jane Eyre*. London: TransAtlantic Press.

Campbell, A. 2017 *Of sheep and other things. A farming odyssey of the Campbells in Australia*. Perth: Alex Campbell.

Chen, M.Y. 2012 *Animacies. Biopolitics, Racial Mattering and Queer Affect*. Durham: Duke University Press.

Cheney, E. 2013 Goimbla Station attack. *Eugowra News*. Sept, vol. 17, 18.

Cixous, H. 1993 *Coming to Writing and Other Essays*. Cambridge: Harvard University Press.

Clune, F. 1947 *Ben Hall*. Sydney: Angus and Robertson.

Cohen, P. and Somerville, M. 1990 *Ingelba and the Five Black Matriarchs*. Sydney: Allen and Unwin.

Collins, D. 1798 *An Account of the English Colony in New South Wales*. Vols. 1 & 2. London: T. Cadell Jun. and W. Davies. Re–issued 1975 Fletcher , B. H. (Ed). Sydney: A.H. & A.W. Reed Pty. Ltd.

Cox, C. and Cox, R. 1988 *Life at Clarendon. The reminiscences of Cornelia and Rosa Cox*. Launceston: National Trust of Australia (Tasmania).

Cox, J. M. (Brooks) c 1912 (Transcribed Houison) *Jane Maria Cox (Brooks) Journal*. State Library of NSW B391.

Cox, R. 2012 *William Cox. Blue Mountains Road Builder and Pastoralist*. Dural: Rosenberg.

Currey, J. 2000 *David Collins. A Colonial Life*. Melbourne: The Miegunyah Press.

Davies, B. 1989 *Frogs and Snails and Feminist Tales. Preschool Children and Gender*. Sydney: Allen and Unwin.

Davies, B. 2008 Re–thinking 'behaviour' in terms of positioning and the ethics of responsibility. In A. M. Phelan & J. Sumsion (Eds.), *Critical readings in teacher education. Provoking absences*. Netherlands: Sense Publishers, 173–186.

Davies, B. 2017 Animating ancestors: from representation to diffraction. *Qualitative Inquiry* 23–4, 267–275.

Davies, B., Gannon, S., McCann, H., De Carteret, P., Stewart, D., & Watson, B. 2006 Reading fiction and the formation of feminine character. In Davies, B. & Gannon, S. *Doing Collective Biography*. Maidenhead: Open University Press, 35–60.

Dawes, F. V. 1989 *Not in Front of the Servants*. London: Random Century Ltd.

Deleuze, G. 1991 *Bergsonism* (Trans. H. Tomlinson & B. Habberjam). New York: Zone Books.

Deleuze, G., 1995 Breaking things open. In G. Deleuze. *Negotiations* 1972–1990 (Trans. M. Joughin) New York: Columbia University Press. 83–93

Deleuze, G. & Guattari, F. 1994 *What is Philosophy?* Columbia University Press, New York.

De St Hilaire Simmonds, D. 1999 *Cobb & Co Heritage Trail Bathurst to Bourke.*Mudgee: Cobb and Co Heritage Trail.

Dixon, T. 2015 *Weeping Britannia. Portrait of a nation in tears.* Oxford, U.K.: Oxford University Press.

Elberling, E. unpublished. *Memoir.* Trans. C. Kallenbach.

Ellis, R. 2006 *The life and times of Frank Gardiner.* Eugowra: Eugowra Historical Museum and Bushranger Centre.

Fellows, R. A. 1985 *Sir Reginald Blomfield: An Edwardian Architect.* London: A. Zwemmer.

Fitzpatrick, J. C. L. 1923 *Those were the days.* Sydney: NSW Bookstall Company.

Fletcher, B. H. 1975 Editor's Introduction. Collins, D. *An Account of the English Colony in New South Wales. Vols* 1 & 2. A.H. & A.W. Reed Pty. Ltd. Sydney, xiii–xxxi.

Forests NSW. September 2011 *Working Plan for Boshes Creek Flora Reserve Macquarie Region. Version* 1. TRIM File F20 11/01307

Gammage, B. 2011 *The Biggest Estate on Earth. How Aborigines made Australia.* Sydney: Allen and Unwin.

Golder, H. 1991 *A History of the New South Wales Magistracy.* Sydney: Sydney University Press.

Gordon, S. 2017 Indigenous Recognition: Turnbull Government's Rejection of Uluru Statement from the Heart Indefensible. *ABC news* 27 Oct 2017, www.abc.net.au/news/2017–10–27/decision–to–reject–uluru–statement–is–indefensible/9093408

Grahame, K. 2016/1908 *Wind in the Willows.* London: The Folio Society.

Grenville, K. 2008 *The Lieutenant.* Edinburgh: Cannongate.

Guilford, P. O. 2007 *Grace Virginia.* Tenterfield, NSW: Patricia Guilford.

Hackett, I. 2006. *Balcombe Family and "The Briars" Park.* Mt Martha, Victoria. Mornington Peninsula Shire.

Hardy, T. 2012/1886 *The Mayor of Casterbridge.* Amersham UK: Transalantic Press.

Hickson, E. 1966 Cox, William (1764–1837) *Australian Dictionary of Biography,* Vol. 1, Melbourne: Melbourne University Press.

Hoffman, B. T. 2006 *Art and cultural heritage: law, policy, and practice.* Cambridge U.K. Cambridge University Press.

Hugo, V. 2014/1866 *The Toilers of the Sea.* (Trans. J. Hogarth). London: The Folio Society.

Irish Identity http://www.irishidentity.com/extras/places/stories/cavantowns.htm viewed 18–10–17.

Johnson, S. Dr. 1750 *Rambler* Saturday 17 November 70.

Kass, T. 2009 *A Thematic History of Harden Shire. Final Report,* June 2009.

Keneally, T. 2015 *Napoleon's Last Island.* Sydney: Vintage Books.

Luxon, N. 2016 Editor's introduction. Farge, E. & Foucault, M. *Disorderly Families. Infamous letters from the Bastille Archives.* (Trans. T. S. Railton). Minneapolis: University of Minnesota Press.

Maher, C. 2016 *Richard Brooks. From Convict Ship Captain to Pillar of Early Colonial Society.* Dural: Rosenberg.

Malins, P. 2007 'City folds: injecting drug use and urban space'. In A. Hickey–Moody and P. Malins (eds.) *Deleuzian Encounters. Studies in Contemporary Social Issues.* Houndmills: Palgrave Macmillan, 151–168.

Maxwell–Stewart, H. & Kippen, R. 2014 Sickness and death on male and female convict voyages to Australia. In P. Baskerville & K. Inwood (Eds.) *Lives in Transition: Longitudinal Research from Historical Sources.* Montreal: McGill University Press.

Mitchell, T. 1838 *Three Expeditions into the Interior of Eastern Australia.* London: T. & W. Boone, Bond Street.

National Trust n.d. *Entally House. Historic Site.*

Officer, L.H. & Williamson, S. H., 2017 "Five Ways to Compute the Relative Value of a UK Pound Amount, 1270 to Present," Measuring Worth. https://www.measuringworth.com/ukcompare/relativevalue.php. Viewed 18 01 2017.)

Oppenheimer, J. 2009 *Perry. Soldier and Surveyor. Samuel Augustus Perry, 1791–1854 Deputy Surveyor General, New South Wales.* Armidale: Ohio Productions.

Oppenheimer, J. & Mitchell, B. 1989a *An Australian Clan. The Nivisons of New England.* Kenthurst NSW: Kangaroo Press.

Oppenheimer, J. & Mitchell, B. 1989b *Abraham's Tribe. The Descendants of Abraham and Mary Nivison.* Walcha: Ohio Productions.

O'Shaughnessy, P. (Ed.) 1988 *A Rum Story. The Adventures of Joseph Holt. Thirteen Years in New South Wales 1800–1812.* Kenthurst NSW: Kangaroo Press.

Paterson, A. B. 1983 *Illalong Children. The story of Banjo Patterson's Childhood.* Sydney: Weldon Publishing.

Philip, I. P. 2016 A voice through lips of marble. *Look* 0216, 22–5.

Readings, B. 1996 *The University in Ruins.* Cambridge MA: Harvard University Press.

Referendumcouncil.org.au/.../Uluru_Statement_From_The_Heart_0.pdf.

Reynolds, H. 2012 *A History of Tasmania.* Port Melbourne: Cambridge University Press.

Ryan, L. 2012 *Tasmanian Aborigines. A History since 1803.* Sydney: Allen and Unwin.

Ryan, L. 2013 The black line in Van Diemen's Land: success or failure? *Journal of Australian Studies.* http://dx.doi.org/10.1080/14443058.2012.755744

Selth, P. A. 1974 Pottinger, Sir Frederick William (1831–1865) *Australian Dictionary of Biography vol.* 5. Melbourne: Melbourne University Press.

Sturt, C. 1965/1847 & 1849 *Narrative of an expedition into Central Australia vols* 1 & 2, Adelaide

Tink, A. 2009 *William Charles Wentworth. Australia's Greatest Native Son.* Crows Nest: Allen and Unwin.

Turner, E. 1894 *Seven Little Australians.* Melbourne: Ward, Lock and Co. Ltd.

Walsham, A. 1999 *Providence in Early Modern England.* Oxford: Oxford University Press.

Watson, D. 1984/2009 *Caledonia Australis. Scottish Highlanders on the Frontier of Australia.* Milson's Point: Random House Australia and Vintage Classics Australia.

Watson, D. 2016 *A Single Tree. Voices from the Bush.* Melbourne: Hamish Hamilton.

Watson, J. 2009 *Blood language.* Carlton: The Miegunyah Press.

Whitaker, A–M. 1998 *Distracted Settlement. New South Wales after Bligh. From the Journal of Lieutenant James Finucane* 1808–1810. Carlton: Melbourne University Press.

Whitaker, A–M. 2014 *William Cox and Cox's Road. A Bicentenary Souvenir.* Sydney: Printed by sos Print and Media Group.

Williams, N. 2018 *Colony: Australia* 1770–1861 *and Frontier Wars.* Melbourne: National Gallery Victoria.

Wright, F. 2015 *Small Acts of Disappearance. Essays on Hunger.* Sydney: Giramondo Publishing Company.

Index of Authors

Index of Subjects

Printed in the United States
by Baker & Taylor Publisher Services